PRIDE OF OUR ALLEY

The Life of Dame Gracie Fields

Volume I: 1898 - 1939

BY SEBASTIAN LASSANDRO

Pride of Our Alley: The Life of Dame Gracie Fields
Volume I; 1898-1939
© 2019. Sebastian Lassandro. All rights reserved.

Published in the USA by:
BearManor Media
P O Box 71426
Albany, Georgia 31708
www.bearmanormedia.com

Printed in the United States of America
ISBN   978-1-62933-420-2 (paperback)
        978-1-62933-421-9 (hardcover)

Book and cover design by Dan and Darlene Swanson • www.van-garde.com

Table of Contents

'Our' Gracie.

Acknowledgements

With my thanks to:

Ben Ohmart, Daniel and Darlene Swanson, Brian Tedesco, Hazel Provost, Sarah Hodgkinson, Julian Jefferson, Janet Emsley, Richard Farnell, Roy Hudd, Dame Vera Lynn, Barbara Dickson, Tommy Steele, David Steadman, Sue Devaney, the Aza family, Janice and Gary Steel, Carrie Christie, Marianne Mullen, Mervyn Rossini, Laurence Rossini, Steve Hull, Becky Woolstencroft for her photo assistance and support, The Basil Dean Archive at the University of Manchester, Rochdale Link4Life, Dave Haddock, Beryl Down, Dave Jessop, Guy Stansfield, Marisa Macdonald, David Timmins, Melanie Stansfield, Edward Beckerleg, Raymond Dolling, Scott Wallace Baker, Janice and Gary Steele, Keith Stansfield, Astrid Hoole, Chris Grant, Sarah-Jayne Yallop, David Hornby, Barry Britten, Graham Turner, Tony Lee, Theo Morgan, Adam Endacott, David Hornby, Maurice Warburton, Jim Craig, Michael J Burn, Ben Stock, Jean Chadwick, Karen Lynne, Graham Howes, Lorraine Brook, Alan Duckett, Mark Fox, the British Music Hall Society, the Lady Ratlings, Jackie Settle, David Reed, Adam Borzone, Serena Daroubakhsh and the Jess Yates Estate, the Rochdale Observer, the Manchester Evening News, Cherry Red Media, BBC Radio Manchester, BBC Radio Lancashire, Movietone News, Pathe.

With extra-special thanks to Chris Webster, Shaun Hewitt, and especially, John Taylor.

Without their support, knowledge, and, most importantly, friendship, this book would certainly not have been possible.

For Nan,
who saw Gracie Fields.

'Sally in Our Alley' (1931).

Foreword

"They keep asking me to write my life stories,
but everybody knows enough about me."

Gracie Fields, 1979

Gracie Fields was a great artiste. She could have been a classical singer, but fate made her into one on the most enduring figures of popular culture in the twentieth century.

She made people feel happier and more positive and made working-class women into strong role models, although she had aspirations to be something else.

She was loved by millions, and that's a marvellous legacy.

Kind regards,
Barbara Dickson

Although I appeared in charity shows with Gracie Fields on a number of occasions, I only spent time properly with her once. All I can remember of her is that she was a great performer and had a most interesting range and tone to her voice.

I have always considered her to be one of the greats in our profession. She had a style of her own and could always be recognised by her voice.

Yours,
Dame Vera Lynn

Even in old age, the voice of Dame Gracie Fields never lost its focus, its "buzz." Here was an instrument that, by default, found its way into the mask of the face and high into the cavities of the head. This ensured that "Our Gracie" would always make herself heard. Her voice never collapsed into the back of the throat, leaving her to battle with a husky and woolly tone.

In her prime she always had the most enviable vocal evenness throughout her extensive range with no sign of the dreaded "break" so often evident in light music today. We know that she had vocal talent as a child, and that early start and the time spent in the mills of Lancashire must surely have helped her achieve her vocal free spirit. Singing for her own pleasure over the decibels of the machinery, she would have to resolutely put her voice into the head to enjoy the sensation of vocalizing and avoid going home each night with a sore throat!

The "default" mechanism was thereby secured in a totally natural way, unhindered by any preoccupation, with textbook technique and singing coaches! Her natural exuberance and joy of living coupled with a grim determination to make the most of factory life seemingly freed her from any concerns about the altitude to which she could take her voice.

The dictionary definition of coloratura is "the extemporary or written decoration of a vocal melody in the shape of runs, roulades, and cadenzas of all kinds." A coloratura soprano: "one with a light, flexible voice equal to the demands of coloratura." The famous Act Two Queen of the Night aria from Mozart's "The Magic Flute" takes the singer up to F, above Top C whilst in light opera. Sullivan's "Poor Wand'ring One" with its famous vocal gymnastics has a potential top Eb in the cadenza. Both illustrate the top end of Gracie's comfort zone!

Perhaps she would describe this as "going oop!" I wonder how many of her fans realised that they were being indoctrinated in the wonders of operatic technique each time they bought one of her records? Her brilliance further enabled her to use such elasticity to wonderful comic effect by sending herself up and making us laugh. *Because I Love You* would have to be one of my "Desert Island Discs." Here she switches effortlessly from coloratura to nasal comedy miaow; the first explosive "B" on the word "because" is totally surprising—and hilarious for that reason! The best comedy is so often the simplest, and it's joyful when a truly excellent vocalist can also make us laugh.

Little wonder that her sensational West End debut led to opera, theatre, and variety stars paying tribute to her. So, whether we listen to "Mrs Binns' Twins," the vocal agility of "Sing As We Go," or the achingly gorgeous "Danny Boy," we can salute a unique and special voice. A natural God-given sound—one of the first singers I grew to love and appreciate as a child—along with Dame Vera Lynn and Joan Hammond. All possessed that priceless gift of vocal warmth and smooth tone. Moreover, like any vocal star, they sang for you, not at you. In more recent times, Barbara Dickson and Nancy Lamott have continued this compelling style of vocal art and performance. When Gracie sang at the Lewisholm Stadium, Manhattan, with the Metropolitan Opera Orchestra, it was at the personal request of the Met's renowned and powerful General Manager, Rudolf Bing. (How many opera stars would have wished for the same?) Of the performance of Britain's "Queen of Hearts," *The New York Times* simply wrote, "No other monarch could have done it more stylishly."

David Steadman

A 1938 publicity photo.

Introduction

Home, home, there's nowt
like my Lancashire home,

I long for the place of my birth, take me
back to my heaven on earth.

- *"In a Little Lancashire Town"* (1936), recorded by Gracie Fields.

THE NORTHERN MILL TOWN of Rochdale derives its name from the River Roch, which flows directly through the centre of town. A settlement has been recorded in the area since Roman times. Lying in the foothills of the Pennines, and less than ten miles away from Manchester, the Industrial Revolution of the 1800s brought great socioeconomic changes to the town and Rochdale quickly became one of the world's largest cotton producers, home to over a hundred and fifteen mills. Prior to this the area had a long and varied history, including a mention in the *Domesday Book*, a residence of Lord Byron, and the "birthplace of co-operation," when in 1844 the Rochdale Equitable Pioneers Society formed the world's first consumer co-operative movement, which is still widely acknowledged today.

Highly typified by the "clogs and shawl" imagery of the northern working classes, the cotton and flax mills which dominated Lancashire's skyline were the beating heart of Rochdale, and one of the town's daughters was to become the voice of a nation. Although Gracie Fields lived away from Rochdale her entire adult life, the town had a strong impact on her and remained firmly close to her heart. Her songs often conveyed a sense of nostalgia for the industrial environment in which she grew up, and she often performed her comedy songs with a Rochdalian dialect, giving direct allusions to the place of her birth. Many of her songs feature direct references to the town, such as the famous "The Rochdale Hounds," which describes a comedic hunting outing based on the real Rochdale Hunt (disbanded 1965), and the parodic line in "There's A Lovely Lake in London, there's a lovely lake in Rochdale, they call it Hollingworth," which, according to the song, was a "gradeley place for courtin'!" Many of Gracie's Rochdalian friends were not happy, however, when in 1931's "Pass! Shoot! Goal!" Gracie sings as a supporter of Rochdale's opponent football team, Oldham Athletic, and not of her own town's Rochdale Hornets!

Nevertheless, in interviews and in private, Gracie fondly remembered the "quietness of the cobbled streets" as a wonderful memory of her childhood, and not the "huddled, damp, hard little town" it has so often been personified as.

When *Lancashire Life* asked Gracie in 1956 what Rochdale means to her, she replied, "Rochdale means 'first.' In Rochdale I first opened my eyes. In Rochdale I first cried, first laughed, heard birds sing for the first time. I sang, too, for the first time in my life. I was even spanked for the first time in Rochdale. And in Rochdale I wore my first pair of clogs. My first, and almost only, schooling took place in Rochdale at the Parish Church School. My first tram ride around the town, my first swimming lesson in the baths, and, when very young, slipping into the ship canal along with the other children for an extra swim during the hot summer days. My first job was an errand girl for a confectioner's shop [...] my first song on a stage was sung at the Old Circus, where now stands the Hippodrome.

"My work since then has meant travelling the world over to great places and small, but 'home' to me always means Rochdale and its gradely folk. My memories are ever sweet and homely. I see all Rochdale's lovely parks and gardens, the beautiful walks all so near—Healey Dell, Hollingworth Lake, and all the rest. On my travels, too, I am reminded so often all over the world of home whenever I see the machinery and products of Rochdale proudly stamped with the names of her great manufacturers."

For Gracie, the town really was home. She felt she belonged there and often joked she would move back to the town "if only it was by the seaside!" On more than one return visit to the town Gracie exclaimed that although she didn't have a house in Rochdale she could go to any front door and be offered a cup of tea or a bed for the night, which she knew was absolutely true. Whenever she visited the town crowds of thousands turned up to cheer their favourite daughter and to offer a civic welcome to the freeman of the borough. Her humble beginnings instilled in Gracie a sense of nostalgia for her hometown, which she was to keep for the remainder of her life in creating and maintaining the persona of a Lancashire mill girl, unchanged by fame and fortune. She was one of the people, summed up by the intensely personal pronoun which was afforded to her, by which she was recognised all over the world: simply "Our Gracie."

Rich people sent Gracie roses, poor people knitted her tea-cosies. She was able to rub shoulders with the rich at palaces and hotels, going "proper posh," but equally at home singing in a tea room or up a set of ladders on a building site. In an article in 1939, the film critic C. A. Lejeune described Gracie, "As much a part of English life as tea and football pools, our green hedged fields, and the Nelson Column." This is something which Gracie remains today.

Gracie's story has never been told in its entirety. Written in 2019, the fortieth anniversary since her death, this book aims to be the most complete and accurate biography of Britain's first superstar. Charting Gracie's humble beginnings to the dizzying heights of her success before the outbreak of the Second World War, this is Gracie Fields' story, told for the first time in its entirety.

My thanks to everyone who has assisted and supported me in the writing of this book, especially my long-suffering family and friends who I have bored senseless for years with talk of 'that there woman Gracie Fields.' Special thanks to my Dad, Joe, for driving me to countless museums up and down the country when I was growing up –and taking me to Rochdale for the first time! Most importantly, thanks to my Mum, Christine, for allowing me to fill the house with Gracie treasures; for continually despairing at the postman's deliveries and for assisting me ably on our many trips to the Isle of Capri.

Sebastian Lassandro

-January 2019

The author at the grave of Gracie Fields in Capri.

CHAPTER ONE

1898–c.1910

I once made up my mind to
delve into my family tree,

To find from which particular branch
I claimed my ancestry.

—"The Family Tree" (1938), recorded by Gracie Fields

BRITAIN'S GREATEST EVER FEMALE variety artist was born to well-documented humble beginnings on a snowy January morning in 1898 in the Lancashire mill town of Rochdale. In later life, Gracie recalled how she was born "half and half," half out of one day and half in the next, but the date on her registered birth certificate is January ninth. The strong and hardy daughter of the North was born above her paternal grandmother Sarah's fish and chip shop at 9 Molesworth Street, and was the first of four children born to Fred Stansfield and Sarah Jane Stansfield (nee Bamford). As Fred's mother and wife were both Sarahs, his wife was known to the family as Jenny (Janey to some friends) as a derivative of her middle name. From this point in the narrative we shall only refer to Fred's mother as Sarah.

The couple's first child was born whilst they were living in the two-room house above the fish and chip shop owned by Sarah, who shared the property with them. She was christened Grace on February 2, 1898 at Saint Chad's Church, the same church where her parents were married less than five months previously. Gracie told *Home Chat* magazine in 1928 that this is where her musical career began, "with a good smart top C from my cradle. They tell me it was a striking note, a compelling note that brought me what I wanted." The young Grace was joined by siblings Elizabeth (Betty) on March 31, 1901; Edith (Edie) on June 26, 1903; and Thomas (Tommy) on June 28, 1908.

Gracie's paternal grandmother, affectionately known as "Chip Sarah," was a dominating yet matriarchal figure who often supplied Gracie and her sisters with a spare halfpenny if they'd all been well behaved. With a fondness for bright and garish colours, which rubbed off on Gracie, the "gaudy Queen Victoria" (as Gracie later described her) was often fondly remembered by Gracie when she affectionately looked back at her childhood.

Sarah's father, Gracie's paternal great-grandfather, William Stansfield, married Elizabeth Shutt of Harrogate at Leeds Parish Church in January 1834. By the time their first child, Thomas, was born in 1834 the couple had moved to Hebden Bridge, where William was employed as a book-keeper. Thomas was baptised at Heptonstall Church on November 9, 1834, but died in infancy. Their next child, Mary Ann, was born in 1836. Sometime after this William and Elizabeth took their young family to live on Oldham Road, Castleton, Rochdale. Four further children were born over the next ten years: William (junior) in 1839, John in 1841, Elizabeth in 1844, and Sarah, Gracie's grandmother, on May 15, 1848. By this point the family was now living in Wood St., where Sarah was born.

The Stansfields moved several times but stayed in Castleton. After Oldham Road, by the 1851 census they had moved to Milkstone Road, where William's wife, Elizabeth, died. In the 1861 census William is shown as a widower living in Myrtle Place with his young family.

William junior married Emma Hey on June 6, 1867 and is believed to have moved to Ireland by the time of the 1871 census. The other children were living in Bilberry Street in the 1871 census, but William senior had died shortly before this. William junior and Emma's first child was named Elizabeth, possibly after her grandmother, and was born on December 30, 1869 in Rochdale. The next child, Herbert, was born in Dublin in 1873 and, the last of Emma's children, Joseph, was born in Thornton, Bradford in 1874. Emma died in 1877 in Rochdale, and William junior then married Elizabeth Anne Wild in 1881 in Rochdale and went on to have seven more children, most of whom didn't survive childhood. William junior ended up living at 14 Ventnor Street from at least the time of the 1901 census until his death in 1922. His youngest son, Leonard, was still living at this address well into the 1930s.

The three children born to William and Emma married and later emigrated to Canada either before or very early in the First World War. Elizabeth married Harry Taylor during the time she was living in Low Moor, North Bierley, Yorkshire. Herbert, who had joined the First Battalion of the Durham Light Infantry and was stationed at Bradford Barracks at the time of the 1891 census, married Agnes Oates, the daughter of a soldier. It's believed he fought in South Africa in the Boer War, but at the time of the 1901 census he was a police constable in Rochdale. He possibly went back into the military as he served six years with the Fifth Battalion of the Lancashire Fusiliers according to his attestation papers when joining up in Canada. Joseph Stansfield married Laura Bentley and lived at 7 Partington Street, Milnrow at the time of the 1901 census. He was a joiner by trade and emigrated to Canada in 1910, with his family following him the next year.

Harry and Elizabeth Taylor started their family in Yorkshire, where

Isabella and Herbert were born and had two more children, William and Arthur, after they moved to Rochdale. The family emigrated to Canada in 1913. Herbert and Agnes Stansfield had ten children, the youngest James and John C Stansfield being born in Canada in 1916, possibly twins. It's not clear when Herbert emigrated, but his wife and family, except for Walter, who had died in 1913, crossed the Atlantic in 1915. Joseph and Laura Stansfield had four children born in England: Carrie, born 1901; Edna, born 1904; Frank Hall Stansfield, born 1907; and Ernest Hall Stansfield, born 1908. All the emigrations were to Edmonton in Alberta, which is where Gracie Fields met some of these families in 1940 and why it is important at the outset to provide a chronology of this complicated family tree.

In *Sing As We Go*, Gracie's 1960 autobiography, she indicates that her grandmother, Sarah, had worked in a coal mine as a trapper when she was six, this job being to close heavy iron doors which stopped fire-damp explosions from spreading, enabling the ponies and coal buckets to pass safely through the pits. However, it is doubtful that Sarah worked in a mine as a youngster, as The Mines Act (1842) prohibited all children under the age of ten from working underground in coal mines. Sarah was born in 1848, and this act would have been in force for twelve years when she was six in 1854. It is possible that an earlier, different family member worked in the mines as a child as legislation would seem to prove that it could not have been Sarah.

Further to this, Sarah's father, William, must have been reasonably well-to-do, and it is unlikely that he would have sent to her out to work. He was a bookkeeper at the time of his marriage in 1834, and in the 1851 census he is described as "Commission Agent for a Carrier," with one of his sons, William junior, being "Railway Goods Agent & Clerk in Charge" on the railway south of Bradford in West Yorkshire. It is hardly likely a family such as this would send a little girl down the mine. Maybe by the time Gracie was writing her autobiography some of the family stories had become a little distorted. Or did Gracie perhaps wish to exaggerate her humble beginnings?

Sarah, who is listed variously as "Cotton Weaver" and "Cotton Operative" from the 1861 to the 1891 censuses, met the son of a wealthy Rochdale mill owner in early 1871, and after a brief courtship was left pregnant as his parents forbade the association. The illegitimate child was Gracie's father, Fred, born August 24, 1872, who never knew his own father and who reportedly died young due to complications of alcoholism. (Does this mean Fred didn't know who he was or just that he had died or moved before Fred was old enough to know him?) Not much is known about Fred's childhood except that he used to visit the Rochdale Circus to see the various touring shows. The circus used to have open fireplaces in the house to keep audiences warm, and Fred took along large potatoes which he placed in the fire to be ready when the show had finished. Fred and his mother lived on Bilberry Sreet with Sarah's sister, Mary Ann Stansfield, and husband, Robert Wolfenden, as well as Sarah and Mary Ann's brother, John. Barring John, the family had moved to 1 Brook Street by the 1881 Census. (Interestingly, Fred and Sarah are listed as Wolfenden and not Stansfield.) Ten years later, Fred and Sarah—alone—(now Stansfield again) were living at 14 Vavasour Street.

After their mother, Elizabeth, died, Sarah and John had initially lived with their father, William, until his early death in 1871. By the 1871 census they had moved in with their older, married sister, Mary Ann Wolfenden. At this time John was described as suffering from "fits," and he became an inmate at Dearnley Union Workhouse, where he was diagnosed as a lunatic.

Sarah married James (Jim) Leighton from Liverpool on November 25, 1891 (he outlived her by 13 years, Sarah dying on January 30, 1917, by which time they were living at 4 Back Oldham Road, and Jim in March 1930), listing her age as ten years younger than she actually was on the marriage certificate. Fred began his training in the local mill and soon became one of the area's most skilled engineers. In the early 1890s the twenty-year-old Fred began working on cargo ships carrying freight and goods from Manchester and Liverpool across the Atlantic, stopping for a brief period with a distant relative in Massachusetts. On one particular journey he travelled to New York on the Etruria, leaving from Liverpool on November 2, 1895. In the ship's register he is shown as "Mechanic" on the outward journey, and "Fitter" on arrival. Travelling on the same boat, in the saloon, was twenty-year-old Winston S. Churchill, a second lieutenant in the Fourth Hussars. Churchill was on his way to Cuba to report for the *Daily Graphic*. Whilst there he acquired a taste for Havana cigars, which was to become his trademark in later years. Over a period of seven years Fred carved out a meagre existence on the transatlantic crossings, and on his return home to Rochdale he acquired somewhat of a celebrity status himself. Having bought a brown Stetson hat and a pair of pointed cowboy boots from California, Fred was known colloquially in the pubs as "The Rochdale Cowboy." Fred continued to work on the ships as a mechanic, with a trip on February 19, 1910 aboard the Laurentic to Boston; the Arabic on May 20, 1913 to Boston; and also the Saxonia on November 11, 1914 to Boston.

Gracie's maternal grandparents, Sarah Elizabeth Holt (a third Sarah!) and Charles Bamford, born 1853, married on December 9, 1876. Gracie's mother, Sarah Jane Bamford (Jenny), was born to them on September 19, 1877 at No.1 Uncle Sam's Place on Richmond Street in Rochdale, but it had been said by Gracie in her autobiography that Jenny had been orphaned by the age of ten, which isn't true, and this belief may have stemmed from the unfortunate term of phrase Gracie used when she described Jenny as having been "the orphan of a couple flighty parents."

Her father Charles is given as being a labourer on Jenny's wedding certificate, as opposed to being given as deceased, which is how Fred's father was given. In actuality, Charles lived until 1911, and maternal grandmother Sarah, also had not died when Jenny was young, as has been stated in other publications. By the 1911 census this Sarah, long separated and soon to be widowed, was living with Jenny and Fred (now moved on from Chip Sarah's home) at 45 Kenion Street, and is registered as lodger as opposed to Sarah's mother.

In the 1911 census Jenny and Fred have three borders living with them, Sarah Elizabeth Bamford, aged 57 (Jenny's mother), and Joseph Bamford, aged 16 (who was born Joseph Lawton Bamford at 20 Gladstone Street, Oldham on October 20, 1894 and was Jenny's younger stepbrother, and thus uncle to Gracie Fields), and Sarah Elizabeth's second husband. On Joseph's birth certificate his father's name is missing, which suggests that he was illegitimate, but the Lawton name could indicate who his father was.

At the 1901 census Joseph is shown as the stepson to Thomas Walton, aged 61, a tripe dealer from Oldham who had married Sarah Elizabeth Bamford in 1899 in Oldham, where she was living with her daughter, Sarah Jane, and youngest daughter, Amy, born 1887, and so Gracie Fields' maternal aunt, at Court 1, Garside Street, Oldham. This was Sarah Elizabeth's third marriage (who was now just using the name Elizabeth). It is possible that after Thomas Walton's early death in 1910 Sarah Elizabeth reverted her name to Bamford and then took her son to live with the Stansfield clan at 45 Kenion Street in Rochdale.

Gracie remembered that Joseph Lawton Bamford had fallen off a tram and had hit his head on one side and his nose was flattened, but he had a good voice and used to sing in Rochdale pubs and sell newspapers. My mother couldn't bear anything ugly and she arranged for him to go into hospital to have his head put straight. When he came home with that done she looked at him and said "Oh, dear! I forgot about your blasted nose!" He didn't, and to the family he was always known as Flat-Nose Joe.

For reasons previously unknown, but it seems likely to do with Thomas Walton (her stepfather) as a youngster, Jenny (Sarah Jane) had lived with one of her mother's sisters, the piously religious Aunt Margaret, on the outskirts of Rochdale at 80 Sparth Bottoms Road, Castleton, until she took up lodgings with fellow mill girls closer to the factory, as opposed to living in Oldham with her stepbrother, sister, and stepfather.

Sarah Elizabeth married for a fourth time on October 2, 1915, when she married collier Frank McLoughlin at Rochdale Parish Church, and died in the influenza epidemic of 1918. Gracie recalled she couldn't say her last husband's name properly, and just for devilment we'd ask, "What's your name now, Grannie?" In later life Gracie remembered her maternal grandfather was "a bit barmy. My mother would tell stories about how he would work very hard, make a lot of money, and then get a cab and stay in it until the money was all gone, going round singing at the top of his voice."

Margaret Livesey (nee Holdsworth), Gracie's maternal aunt, was the eldest of three daughters of local pub landlords John and Margaret Holdsworth (nee Sibbald). John was born in Halifax, Margaret in Scotland, so from both her maternal and paternal sides of the family Gracie had Yorkshire blood. Margaret was born in 1847, with Jenny following in 1854, and Charlotte Otley in 1859. Charlotte died at the age of four in 1863. Margaret's daughter, born May 9, 1887, was also called Margaret—following the family tradition. This youngest Margaret,

Jenny's cousin (and therefore Gracie's first cousin once removed), was to later play an important part in Gracie's life as her dresser and aide during the 1930s.

Gracie's mother, Jenny, attended church weekly and went to Sunday School in both the morning and evening. Her aunt told her that she should go to further Bible study classes, and so mid-week Jenny went off to the Band of Hope class in Rochdale, but more often than not she missed the class as the call of the local theatres and music halls was too great and she found herself sneaking in to watch the houses. In later life Gracie recalled, "Mother had an extraordinary beautiful voice, and if you have a beautiful voice and you go into the mill, you dreamed of the theatre. Mother took herself very seriously, and she wanted to be an opera singer." Becoming a regular face at the front of the Rochdale Hippodrome, the kindly theatre manager allowed Gracie to sit in a free seat, known as Poet's Corner, while her aunt thought she was studying the Bible at the Band of Hope.

A keen and gifted singer at church and at school, Gracie often cited that her musical ability came from her mother, and certainly her drive and determination came from her. Gracie's sister, Betty, in her unpublished memoirs, recalled, "Had I been the first born instead of the second I would have been a great disappointment to my mother, who had a very good singing voice, and I knew I hadn't . . . Grace was an extension of herself. I strove to sing and get more attention, but in vain." Jenny's youngest child, Tommy, remembered, "Nobody could scrap with Mother. It was the intense pressure of stage-struck Mother." It's a well-documented fact of Gracie's childhood that Jenny was the driving force of ambition behind her children, who she wanted more than anything for them to go on to a career on the stage and make a living in front of the footlights. Having failed to do so herself, as she had given birth to Gracie when she was twenty-one, when she saw talent in Gracie she banked on it. "She felt that she could get one daughter out of this rut and poverty if she pressed hard enough," Tommy recalled.

It is rumoured that it was whilst walking down Rochdale's Drake Street, dressed in his favoured cowboy attire, that Fred first met Jenny. He was walking home from one of the many local pubs, pausing to look in shop windows, and she was tailing him with keen interest in the "theatrical" personality who had become the talk of the borough. Every few feet Sarah stopped to inspect a "fault" with her clog as she shadowed Fred looking in the shop windows. After a few minutes of this Fred approached Sarah, saying, "Tha's havin' some trouble with yon clog, miss. Let me fix it for thee," recalled Gracie. An astounded Sarah accused him of being false and a fake, not being a theatrical at all but, in fact, a native Rochdalian. However, in 1938, when Jenny and Fred visited America together for the first time, Gracie remembered, "Father went to Massachoosits [sic] as a mechanic. It was just after that he met Momma in a Rochdale dance hall." Nevertheless, whichever story is true, if either, the pair courted each other at the local dance hall, fell for each other, and were married in Rochdale Parish Church on September 1, 1897—with Jenny already five months pregnant with Gracie.

At the wedding Fred turned up in his cowboy hat and boots brandishing an expensive Havana cigar which he had been saving for such an occasion as this. The verger asked Fred to remove his hat and put out his cigar and took them to the vestry for safe keeping during the service. Fred, feigning dismay at this, shouted down the church to him, "Tha's best bring me 'em back when tha's done wi' 'em!"

"Mama could've sloshed him for doing that!" told Gracie. "It was just his sense of humour." As previously mentioned, Fred is not believed to have known his father. On his marriage certificate his father is given as being "John Stansfield/Deceased"—his lunatic uncle on his mother's side.

Newly married, the couple moved in with Fred's mother at 9 Molesworth Street. Formerly a barber's shop, Sarah Stansfield had spent her life savings to buy the property—contents and all—and held her own auction in Rochdale to sell off the barber's contents. As there wasn't a great call for barbers, with boys/men usually having their hair cut at home by their mothers/wives, Sarah managed to sell all the stock and gain a profit from her sales. With this she redecorated the upstairs of the house and installed fish and chip fryers in the downstairs room. Gracie recalled this as being the "tiniest, smelliest, dingiest little fish shop in the North of England." With three customers inside, the rest had to wind their way along the pavement and wait their turn to enter Chip Sarah's domain. During the revamping Sarah took in up to four lodgers at a time to help pay for the redecoration and conversion. With fish and chips being a stock meal of the Northern working classes, which had developed in the neighbouring town of Mossley over thirty years earlier, Chip Sarah opened Rochdale's first fish and chip.

When Grace was born in January 1898 Fred was working as an engineer for Robinson's Engineering Works and Jenny was helping Sarah out in the fish and chip shop. A typically Northern tradition was established in the shop as Sarah and Jenny gave many of their customers depreciating nicknames, some of which Gracie recalled in later life as "Cold Again Joe," "Sloppy Clogs Tuppence," "Ma Big Ears," and "Packet o'Cigs."

Fred and Jenny shared one of the two upstairs bedrooms and Sarah and Jim shared the other, but when Gracie came along—and subsequently her two sisters and brother—Fred and Jenny had to move out. Ever frugal, Jenny always saved a cut of her husband's money in the teapot above the fireplace so that the family could "move oop in t'world," having aspirations for much bigger and better things.

"Movin' oop" was a common theme of Gracie's childhood. It was said that whenever Fred got a sixpence or a shilling rise at work Jenny declared it was time to move house. On a wage of twenty-seven shillings a week from Robinson's, Fred sometimes returned home to find that Jenny had packed everything up on a handcart and was in the process of moving on to the next street. Gracie recalled this comic scene many years later in a television interview with Michael Parkinson, as she explained that she might one day be carrying all the pots and pans and the next the family aspidistra to the next house. Without at the time knowing the significance this potted house plant would have in later life, Gracie also stated, "Everyone up North, everyone has an aspidistra plant. My grandmother used to put paper flowers between the leaves of hers."

However, in her unpublished memoirs, sister Betty disagreed with the reasoning for the constant moves, stating, "The real reason for the moves was that Mother outplayed herself and the neighbours wanted to get back to their privacy." Brother Tommy, in an interview in later life, gave yet another less sentimental reason. "We moved house every time we couldn't afford to pay the rent, and we had to do a sort of moonlight flit. My mother was so bad she used to forget to tell my father where she'd gone. He'd arrive home and find nobody there—everybody else had moved!"

The Stansfields, during their years of "movin' oop," are known to have lived at 45 Kenion Street, as listed in the 1911 census (now with Jenny's mother, Sarah, and two lodgers, one being "Old Fred," who we shall come to later) as well as having addresses at 10 Baron Street, which was the property they lived at the longest, circa 1902 to 1910; 16 Watmough Street by 1914; and they are also known to have spent time on Hughtrede Street and Lyland Street, off Milnrow Road in the time between censuses.

Admitting that she was a tomboy when she was younger, "I was always going climbing up on the slates," Gracie learned to swim in the Rochdale shipping canal and used to dangerously play on the tramways which connected the town to neighbouring districts. Gracie's mother used to practice her top notes by calling her daughter down from the rooftops, which she had to do on one such occasion to find Gracie as she had arranged a small audition with a vocal coach named Marie Santoi (whose real name was Mary Fuller). Coaxing her daughter down off a high ledge, Gracie cried all the way to the audition—not because she was scared or because Jenny had reprimanded her, but because she had to come in from playing out!

As a child, one of Gracie's favourite Rochdale shops was Samuel Smith's Greengrocers on Drake Street. Sometimes Gracie would sing Mr. Smith a song and he would give her cut slices of fruit which she would take back home to share with her sisters. Another favourite amongst her and her school friends was Chadwick's Wet Rake. "We would stop for a ha'porth of chips here and for a ha'pporth o'toffee on Maclure Road," remembered Frances Ellis, an old school companion of Gracie's, in the 1970s. Gracie quickly found she could often sing to get what she wanted, and this included singing and performing acrobatic tricks for Bob Brieley, who mended the Stansfields' clog irons next door to the fish and chip shop on Molesworth Street.

Wanting to be an acrobat when she was old enough instead of the theatrical performance career her mother had in mind for her, Fred installed a small gymnasium in their current home's coal cellar, including trapeze bars from which Gracie delighted in hanging from upside down. Harbouring her talents in the cellar, and later performing daring tricks in front of friends and neighbours, Gracie became adept at spinning a cartwheel—something which she later incorporated into her stage act. Well into her 50s, Gracie was cartwheeling across the stage of the London Palladium, something she earnestly rehearsed on her terrace at Capri, along with serving tea to guests by high-kicking her way from the house to where they were sitting, overlooking the Bay of Naples.

Gracie's acrobatics in the cellar in Rochdale were soon stopped one day when Jenny ordered Fred to install two rings and rope between the bars, on which she hung some left-over material. "You can now play theatres," she told Gracie, and so Gracie and Betty obliged as they came up with little routines and songs to rehearse for the neighbours instead of her favoured acrobatic antics. Whilst baby Edith guarded the admission fees—pins and buttons collected in a tin—Gracie performed musical routines and Betty performed comedy for the neighbourhood children who used an upturned set of ladders as theatre seating. This probably came from copying her mother who, as Betty remembered, used to give "Lavatory Concerts" in the six lavatories at the back of Molesworth Street. Often Fred and Jenny would disagree over this and Jenny would exclaim to the children, "I don't know who's coming with me, but I'm leaving." Gracie recalled, "I always wanted to go with my dad. He had a sense of humour and lots of character. He would come back from the pub stinking drunk and I'd try to sneak him upstairs quietly."

Weekly, Jenny would go to the local theatre and return to Molesworth Street, remembering the songs and the jokes she had heard. She would go around to her neighbours announcing it was showtime, and they would all take a seat with an open door in the lavatories as Jenny would perform her routines for them. Gracie eventually became part of this act, but Betty was always too shy to perform in front of the adults. For their performances with the other children, however, Gracie and Betty rehearsed fervently for the shows in preparation for what Gracie later described as "the big earner"—the Rochdale May Day celebrations.

As the factories closed their gates and took the day off to celebrate May Day, Gracie and her friends often went to one of the town's large installed May Poles to dance around and entwine themselves in the ribbons with their friends. On one particular year Jenny had other ideas and provided Gracie and her friends with an old broom handle and some leftover pieces of material. These were cut up and used for ribbons for their own May Pole, which Gracie, Betty, and her friend with the impressive jubilee name, Ruby May Diamond Victoria Rylands, carried around town. One person short to have an effective May Pole dance, Gracie called on one of her school friends who was well off and coaxed her to put on her best white silk dress, offering the chance to walk with their May Pole as their May Queen. Visiting all the pubs frequented by Fred, her father's friends spotted Gracie, and as both the celebrations and the drinking went on Fred's friends became more generous with their donations to the May Queen and her little singing friends—by the end of the day the girls had earned 530 pence!

Gracie cites this as the first time she ever sang to earn money, with the song an old music hall number entitled "When the Sunset Turns the Ocean Blue to Gold." The feeling she described was of electricity. Gracie felt different and enchanted that people were actually paying to listen to her. On another occasion with Ruby, the two girls were being teased by some of the older girls in the area. "We've got new clogs, Gracie!" and "We've got new ribbons, Gracie!" they shouted. Quick as a flash, Gracie retorted, "Well bugger yer, we've got nits!" The two girls did go and get some new ribbons though, but this was an event which, quite literally, haunted Gracie.

Watching a funeral procession heading to Rochdale Cemetery, Gracie noted how the wreaths and flowers were tied up with pretty ribbons, much nicer than the ones Gracie and her friend had in their hair. The pair went to the newly placed flowers in the churchyard and carefully unpicked the ribbons from the offerings, replacing them with their old and worn ribbons from their hair. With cunning, Gracie told her friend she must tell her mother that Gracie's mother had given them the ribbons, and vice versa, and the plan seemed settled. The next morning, however, the girls rushed to each other saying they both had nightmares of the man in the grave chasing them, accusing, "You stole my ribbons!" Too frightened to return to the cemetery, they threw them away in fear of eternal torment.

Another holiday incident occurred at Whitsuntide. In the North of England, Wakes Weeks were when all the local factories, collieries, and other industries closed down for the week and took a week of unpaid holiday. The local areas all collaborated so that a town and its neighbours wouldn't all be off during the same week, mainly so that the local holiday resorts wouldn't be inundated with tourists in one week. To dress her daughters up for the celebrations Jenny had gone to Polly Pickles, the local dressmaker who lived three doors away, and ordered three pretty, matching deep purple outfits to wear to the festivities in town. As she was admiring her girls and tidying their hair before they went out she saw the daughters of their neighbour across the road, Mrs. Colclough, wearing the exact same outfits. Realising she had told her neighbour, who had taken keenly to the idea, she got her daughters the exact same outfits from Polly, Jenny tore the outfits off her own children, saying, "You'll use those for school and to play in the dirt instead."

Gracie and her two sisters all shared one big bed, and each night before they retired Jenny tightly wound strips of rags in their hair to make it curl. Betty's hair was a brilliant fiery red, "which matched her temperament sometimes!" recalled Gracie, whereas Gracie's was naturally blonde-tinged with red. As Gracie slept the mischievous Betty often undid her hair curlers so in the morning Jenny had to redo the children's hair, making them late for school. Not that this was any major problem in her eyes however, as Gracie later remarked, "Mother didn't think school was necessary as far as I was concerned. 'You'll find out when you grow up, it'll all happen.'" When she was younger Jenny had to pay tuppence a week to go to school, and therefore it was a necessity for her to go, but she thought it much more beneficial for her daughter to stay home with her, especially as she already had a career marked out for them. Betty, however, loved going to school and was devastated when her mother sent her to the stage following her elder sister in later years.

Although not a regular at school, Gracie said that when she did actually attend Rochdale Parish Church School she enjoyed learning, and throughout her life remained a great lover of books. Jenny had given up working in the mills and was taking on as many odd jobs as she could to "earn some brass." These included cleaning and domestic work at some of the big, posh houses in Rochdale, where Gracie sometimes went along to help her with work—and to help her finish off the leftover rice pudding or roast beef. Gracie later resented Jenny, referring to her work as "skivvying," as she considered her well above that. Fred was still working in the factories, and as a sideline he ran an illegal betting shop from his chicken shed on the local allotment. From here, Betty remembered he also ran games of "rat worrying" and "throw the penknife at the chicken," which a six-year-old Tommy thoroughly enjoyed.

At the age of seven Gracie suffered a rupture. "I don't know what really caused it, but all I remember is that she had to be taken to a hospital in Manchester and was away for three weeks," Betty wrote. Jenny took Gracie on the train to Manchester, and as opposed to getting a horse-drawn cab from the station to the hospital, carried her daughter all the way in her arms. Betty, too, suffered during childhood—a bout of scarlet fever saw her sent to a recuperation centre four miles outside of Rochdale. "I don't remember much about it except that I remember my father carrying me in a taxi with blued-out windows that was used for lunatics." Their younger sister, Edith, suffered from adenoids, which were removed one afternoon by the family doctor who called around whilst the family were all having tea and promptly scraped them out in their living room!

Gracie returned from hospital with the top of her legs strapped together with leather and splints, although these didn't last very long as Gracie was too busy being a child and having fun with her friends, playing games such as hopscotch and jacks and dobbers. In an interview with Iona Opie, Gracie recalled some of her childhood games. "We hadn't enough money for the fancy plastic jacks, but we just used to use four stones and a marble." A wooden hoop was also used for enjoyment. "I ran around miles with that." Playing hopscotch was a favourite game of the young Gracie's even though the streets were covered in chalk. When no chalk was available games of hide and seek and skipping were played, with Gracie's favourite comic rhyme being: "Hickerdy-pickerdy-eye-salickerdy-pumpalery-jig. Every man that has no hair generally wears a wig! Out goes she, out goes she!"

The summer following Gracie's illness, 1906, the Stansfield family took a trip to Blackpool together for the first time. Many years later when playing the town during a concert tour Gracie remembered her first association with the seaside resort. "They were giving free tickets to poor children. Dad was a fitter, earning about 28 bob a week, so we didn't quite qualify. We were supposed to be in bed by seven in them days, but I was so brokenhearted about the Blackpool I wandered about the streets till all hours. When I got home I got a good clouting! But Ma, bless her, finally forked out the two and six or three and six necessary, and we all came to Blackpool. I remember Ma baked a cherry cake for the occasion and forgot to take the stones out of the cherries. There was such a performance getting the stones out, she vowed never to look at a cherry cake ever again! I remember going on the sands and getting lost under the pier and getting another clout for that!"

On another occasion in the 1930s Gracie remembered, "I had some good holidays when I was a little girl with my two baby sisters. We filled a big old kitchen bucket with water and put a bit of salt in. Then we paddled, and that magical old iron bucket was Blackpool or Brighton or any place we saw on a postcard! And wherever it was, the tide was always in. Sometimes in summer Dad took us on a penny tram ride from Rochdale to Hollingsworth Lake. He lifted us on a high wall to sit and eat our sandwiches and share a bottle of lemonade. I've seen a bit of the world since those days, but I've never tasted champagne better than lukewarm fizzy lemonade that we passed from hand to hand, with sticky little earnest fingers marking the next share."

Another one of these holidays was on Rochdale's Yelloway coaches to Devon, as Gracie's father was then working as an engineer for Yelloway bosses Robert and Ernest Holt. The trip had been organised by Edward Bryning's printing firm, who took their staff to see the Torquay Regatta every year by train. However, due to a train strike Yelloway coaches were persuaded to provide a charabanc instead, and Gracie was among the 26 people and one dog who went along on the trip to Paignton, where Gracie won ten shillings, a pair of roller skates, and a purse in a singing competition on the sea front.

Enquiring at the local theatre, the Circus of Varieties at Newgate, with Mr. Grindrod as to whether there was any work going (not that Mr. Grindrod would've been the best person to ask as he was only the commissionaire and the doorman), Jenny eventually got a job cleaning the stage of the theatre. Her own aspirations of going on the stage had, in one way come true, as she used her operatic voice as she was cleaning the boards going about her work. As she started to earn a bit of money herself the family bought a twenty-pound piano on which Gracie taught herself by ear to play, and Betty took weekly piano lessons from a friend of her father's.

On one move, to 10 Baron Street, the family almost directly faced a theatrical boarding house, and whenever big touring companies came into town Jenny squeezed her family into one room and let out the remaining rooms, mainly just to establish contact with "the theatricals."

This developed into taking in theatrical washing and drying it in her kitchen on washing lines which Fred installed. Gracie recalled, "Mother wanted this to be kept a big secret, and we carried the washing to and from the theatre wrapped in newspaper." This was so that the neighbours wouldn't realise what they were doing. With the house looking like a Chinese laundry, Gracie decided she could earn a few pennies herself and took to cleaning the six outside lavatories which belonged to Baron Street. With the neighbours paying a halfpenny each, Gracie got on with the work and often copied what she had seen her mother doing by singing loudly as she busied herself with the task at hand.

Rose Bush, a singer from the Midlands whose real name was Rose Lilian Turner and who had originally been one of Montague Robey's Famous Midget Minstrels, was a friend of George Formby (senior), heard Gracie singing and exclaimed she had a lovely voice. Lily, as she was known to friends, was lodging at the boarding house on Baron Street opposite Gracie's home whilst performing at Rochdale's Old Circus as a male impersonator and descriptive vocalist, and was aware that Newgate and Evelyn Taylor were running a competition at the circus on Evelyn's song, "What Makes Me Love You as I Do?" Lily suggested to Jenny that Gracie, who she had heard singing in the street, should enter to compete for the prize of ten shillings and sixpence. This encouragement opposed the opinion of Gracie's voice held by Mr. White, her school headmaster, who made her mime to the hymns in assembly, telling her that her voice was too loud and raucous and put the other girls off! The admissions register of Rochdale Parish School, Coventry Street, for February 11, 1910, reads: "Grace Stansfield: left to go on the stage."

On returning to Rochdale in 1933, Gracie went back to her old school and performed on the stage there. She told the children gathered, "This is one of the proudest moments of my life. I always watched sister Betty and sister Edith singing in concerts and shows on here, and

Mr. White would never let me sing because I was too loud." Jenny had instilled in Gracie that the louder you sing the better you are—and the young Gracie could sing very loud.

A little shy, and a little worried about talking to strangers with non-Rochdalian accents, the story goes that Gracie took Lily home to her mother, who was instantly awed that a theatrical had taken an interest in her daughter. Fred tried to scare Jenny by telling her "kids under the age of ten can't enter competitions, someone in't'pub said it," but this didn't deter her. Jenny had sung loudly outside theatrical boarding houses herself in the hope that she would get noticed, and now that her daughter had, she felt she had made the big time already.

Offering singing lessons for free, Lily trained Gracie to sing "What Makes Me Love You as I Do?" but early on in rehearsals Lily realised that Gracie couldn't sound her aspirant itches properly, and "What" was coming out as "Wot." Try as she might to teach her otherwise, Gracie ended up singing the song with its many "whats" as "qwot," which clearly sounded well enough over the footlights, because dressed in a white cotton dress, costing one shilling eleven pence, with material bought from Whiteley and Taylors, Gracie came joint first with her "qwots." Whilst she enjoyed telling this story in interviews with musical examples, there is only one known instance of Gracie performing the song in its serious entirety other than her debut of it, and this was in a live theatre recording made at the Stoll Theatre, London, in 1938 for one of her Fairy Soap sponsored commercial radio shows.

Following on from her success in the competition, Fred's boss at the local factory paid Gracie ten bob as part of a smoking concert, and also at Rochdale Provident Hall singing the religious "And the Little Child Shall Lead You" in a Grand Complimentary Benefit Concert on September 28, 1910. Hereafter, Grace Stansfield, "Rochdale's Clever Little Girl Vocalist," began appearing in charity concerts around the borough and performing for tuppenny pork pies, which she carried back home in an umbrella to share as supper with her family. Later in life Gracie comically remembered participating in concerts in Rochdale, Oldham, Castleton, and Norden, winning so many tuppeny pork pies her sisters dubbed her "The Pork Pie Queen" and her mother and Gracie suffered constant indigestion. "We used to stuff ourselves like little pigs with those pork pies!"

When Lily Turner next had work Gracie went along with her and made her debut at W.C. Horner's Empire Music Hall in Cow Lane, Burnley. Although Fred refused to sign a note telling the school she was sick, Gracie went along to the afternoon concert anyway. Recalling the act, Gracie remembered, "Lily wore short velvet pants with a manly coat. It was a funny sort of dress. She used to sing the songs with such feeling." Gracie stood in the gallery of the theatre singing the chorus back to Lily. During one performance an old lady sitting next to Gracie thought she was a heckler trying to disrupt Lily's performance so she "gave [Gracie] a good sloshing" with her umbrella. A very upset Gracie returned home to her mother, who chastised Lily for not letting her go on the stage with her. From then on Gracie went on stage with Lily in one of Lily's old dresses altered to fit her, in garish brown and pink. Lily later remembered, "It was a sort of novelty and I paid her seven shillings a week and kept her. At the time I was singing a song, 'A Time Will Surely Come a Day,' written for me by George Foster. It was the chorus of this song she sang." During the three months Gracie was with Lily, Lily arranged it that Gracie had a trial run at the Stalybridge Hippodrome singing one of her songs, "No One Like Mother, No Place Like Home," written especially for Lily by Pat Duddy of Liverpool.

When Lily announced to Jenny she was retiring from the stage to marry Charles Langton, a Rochdale stockbroker, Jenny quickly dissuaded her, as she intended to keep her only link to the world of show business close. Lily took Jenny's advice and remained on the stage another year until she finally decided she did indeed want to retire, as travelling back home to her family at 51 Molesworth Street in Rochdale was proving too strenuous, especially after the untimely death of her husband. By then, however, Gracie had already moved on to bigger and better things. Jenny and Lily eventually fell out, as Jenny wanted to keep Gracie's professional stage debut dress, but Lily also wanted to keep it, as it was, after all, her own costume. The stubborn pair argued over the dress' ownership, but Lily would not relent, and in doing so sacrificed her own wedding dress, which Jenny still had in her possession after cleaning it for her. Lily died aged 55 of a heart attack in August 1939, and Gracie (who sent £2 for flowers) is remembered on Lily's headstone with "In Memory of Rose Langton, from Gracie Fields."

By 1910 Grace Stansfield was being billed as Gracie Stansfield for local charity concert performances. This included a charity concert at the Rochdale Hippodrome on Saturday, August 20, on a bill with Arthur Weber, Arthur Sharp, and Rochdale's Professional Military Band, and at Pringle's Picture Palace in Rochdale for a week from June 25 with Bertini and Happy Atwood as lantern warmers for the silent films being shown.

Through a contact of Lily's, Gracie auditioned for Clara Coverdale's Boys and Girls, a touring troupe of children who were support acts on variety bills around the country. Mrs. Coverdale was in the process of setting up a new touring troupe, to be known as the Nine Dainty Dots, and Gracie was given a place with the tour even though she was up to six years younger than her colleagues. On the first night of the tour, in Hull, the other boys and girls found out Gracie's age and made her learn vigorous dance routines, ensuring that she would be too tired and strained to work the next day, in an attempt to jeopardise her place with the company. The girls put Gracie through her paces and, in throbbing agony, she cried all night whilst the three other girls in the troupe shared a bed. Betty was also given a place with this touring troupe but was sent home early due to the fact she didn't have enough talent.

After a week of not performing Gracie went home agonised with strained ligaments and a twisted neck, and her father suggested she should go back to work in the factory and "forget all this stage lark." When she'd recovered, Gracie returned to the troupe, determined as ever, where she learned to sing and dance, but she was still treated badly by the other girls, who made her run all the errands in town. This near-bullying seemed to be a common theme with the various troupes that Gracie performed with, but it did not put her off from achieving her mother's dreams.

Whilst in Newcastle with the Nine Dainty Dots, Gracie approached Madame Priscilla Haley, the manager of Haley's Garden of Girls, who gave her a place with the touring company of up to fifty girls. After working her short contract with the Dainty Dots, Gracie joined Madame Haley on tour seven weeks later. It was during her time here that Gracie caught the landlady's son in bed with one of the girls whilst Gracie was taking around hot water so the girls could wash before bed. Horrified at what she had seen, Gracie turned and ran whilst the girl shouted for the man to "catch her and do the same to Grace!" Conflicting reports exist of what actually happened, as to whether or not Gracie was caught by the boy or if she managed to throw the jug of hot water over him, but it is known that Gracie managed to barricade herself in her bedroom with a chest of drawers and the door had to be broken down the next morning. Gracie only ever spoke about this publicly once in later life, and said, "I remember I was carrying up some hot water, that I was so petrified with nerves. I got into the room and remember pushing furniture and blocking up this door. I got home a few weeks after, and the girl was nasty to me and was always terrified that I'd tell the boss." Gracie was so worried that she was sent home, where she developed St. Vitus Dance and was sent to Rochdale Children's Convalescent Home at St Anne'son-Sea for six weeks. After this incident Fred demanded that there was to be no more theatrical talk, and Jenny sent Gracie to school for a year.

It was during this time that Gracie became a "half timer," spending half of the day at school and half of the day in the factory. Getting up with the "knocker upper" at five in the morning, Gracie was at the factory by six with "a tin of tea in one hand, a tin of sandwiches in the other" to earn her 23 shillings a week. At J and J Walker's mill factory on Woodbine Street, Gracie's job was a cotton winder, but she spent more time singing and dancing for her fellow mill workers instead of winding the cotton. Prior to this she had taken a job in a local paper mill and had also run errands for a confectioner and bakery, Burrow's Cake Shop, but was dismissed from both positions for "singing and dawdling on the job too much." It is also claimed that Gracie worked in Wellfield Mill on Woodbine Street, Pouches Mill, and also Brierley's Mill on Holland Street, although the authenticity of these accounts is unverified.

Around this time, Jenny and Fred's neighbour, Fred Ogden, affectionately known as "Old Fred," came to stay with the family, initially for a short while. Ill in health and unable to run a whole household on his own, Fred moved in with the Stansfields for a couple of days whilst he sorted his home out, but he didn't leave and became part of the family himself. Gracie remembered, "The first time I came home and found him at tea I lost my appetite. He looked creased and gnarled, his chin shone with spilled juices. I grew to realise that Old Fred was not repulsive, it was merely that the crowded years had made his face well-thumbed, like a Bible."

It was through Old Fred Gracie learned an act at the Rochdale New Hippodrome, Jessie Merrylees, had taken ill and the theatre manager was desperate for a replacement. Almost instantly Jenny rushed Gracie to the theatre and secured her a booking of 35 shillings. (The 1908 brick-built Hippodrome had replaced the wooden 1882 Old Circus.) Impressed with Gracie's rendition of "The Dear Little Shamrock," management kept her another week, and Jenny decided she would go back into the mill herself, aged thirty-two, in place of Gracie, as another chance like this may never arise. Jenny went to work at John Pilling's mill on Norwich Street as a weaver. "She did the noisy work, whereas I did the posh work." After the years of drudgery Jenny saw a chance and wouldn't let it get away from her clearly talented daughter, even at her own sacrifice.

Staying at home whilst Jenny went to the mill, Gracie, now aged fourteen, was taken on by another touring troupe, Charburn's Young Stars, who were based in Blackpool. The troupe was in Rochdale for the May Day celebrations of 1912 and, at Jenny's insistence, Gracie sang outside the window of their lodging house, which caught the attention of the troupe's manager, and it was arranged that Gracie was to join them the following week. In the 1970s, Mrs. Emily Brooks recalled, "Mr. Charburn was looking for more children for his tour, and myself and a girl I worked with in the mill called Elsie Howorth went to audition." But Mr. Charburn, who had originated the troupe, had actually passed the touring company over to Richard Llewellyn Griffiths by this time. Whilst on this tour, Griffith's wife, Daisy, gave birth to their daughter, Violet Gwendoline, in London in 1910. Being the "baby" of the company, Gracie often looked after her, and nicknamed Violet "Babs." "This stuck for life, and everyone, family and friends, referred to Violet as Babs," recalled her son, Mervyn Rossini. For the tour Elsie was taken on, both she and Gracie were given consent forms which their parents needed to sign before they could join the troupe in Blackpool. A row ensued between Fred and Jenny, who both had different opinions on the matter, especially the four and a penny train fair to get to Manchester. Old Fred came up with the answer: a singing competition that night in Middleton with a cash prize of five shillings.

Knowing that Mother and Father wouldn't even discuss the tram fare to Oldham, a neighbour agreed and took Gracie along to the competition. "I wanted to cry going out in front of all those Middleton foreigners," explained Gracie in later life. But she won the first prize. When it was revealed she was from Rochdale and not Middleton, the shouts from the audience caused her to be disqualified from the competition. Believing Gracie to be the best act regardless, the kindly judge of the competition slipped Gracie the five-shilling prize from his own pocket as he saw star potential in the little girl.

With enough money to take the train to Blackpool the next week, the little with the big voice was all set for her big break.

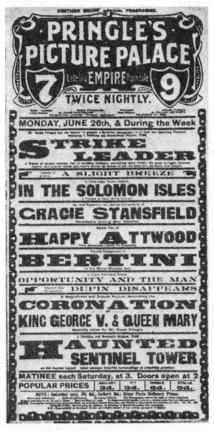

Two early posters featuring a young Gracie Fields

A publicity photo. (1928).

CHAPTER TWO
c.1911-1918

What makes me love you as I do?
What makes me think you're so divine?

- "What Makes Me Love You?" (c1900),
performed by Gracie Fields.

WITH A SIGNED CONSENT form and the necessary four shillings in her pocket, Grace Stansfield was ready to go to Blackpool and try her luck with a new touring company. The other members of the group were again older than Gracie, all being aged between fourteen and sixteen, but Richard Griffiths had seen potential in the little Rochdale girl and decided to give her a chance. Before she left, however, her mother, at the suggestion of the local theatre manager, decided Gracie should have a stage name. Gracie remembered, "Mother was the only pro in the family. She was theatre mad. I couldn't be away for a week's holiday, she'd send me a telegram: 'Your public's fickle.'" Her Father didn't have a say in it, and her mother's auntie relentlessly told Jenny she was sending her daughter to the devil.

Mervyn Rossini, the grandson of Richard Griffiths, remembered, "During the time she was away with Charburn's Young Stars she became a friend of the family, and being the most maternal of the troupe she tended to look after my mother when necessary. Richard encouraged her to sing the comedy songs with which we are all so familiar, but initially she did not like that because she would say, after the show (sometimes in tears), 'They're all laffin at me.' Richard persuaded her to continue and explained about laughing 'with' and not 'at.'" Of her time with the troupe, Gracie remembered, "The first time I swam in the sea was at Redcar with Charburn's Young Stars. There were six boys and six girls, and a boatman wanted to adopt me. I wrote and told my mother, she wrote back and told me to get on with my job."

For a while she had been touring as "Gracie Stansfield," but deciding that the name would be too long on a theatre bill and that she would "never be a star wi' a name that long!' Jenny and Grace tried to come up with an alternative, one of which, Stanna Field, Gracie instantly dismissed. "How many folk are called Stanna?" (But she used this pseudonym in later life on sheet music covers as she translated Italian lyrics into English.) The stagename chosen was simply Gracie Fields. At the time of the 1901 census, boarding with Robert and Mary Ann Wolfenden (Fred's aunt) was an assistant sanitary inspector named James Fields. There was possibly close contact between the Stansfields and the Woolfendens, and it is possibly from here that Jenny just had the "spark" to shorten Gracie's name to Fields because of James. Jenny had "Gracie Fields" printed onto business cards by Bryning's Printing Works, with "Versatile Comedian" underneath her name. These cards were promptly thrown into the fire when the local theatre manager asked, "How long has she been a man?"

Many have claimed ownership over the changing of Gracie's name—almost as many as those who claimed that she worked with them in the mill or went to school with her. The most pertinent, although not definite, claim to the changing of Gracie's name came from Alderman Charles Bryning of Rochdale, who worked in the family business, Edwards and Bryning's Printing Works, on Baron Street. He claimed it

was he who came up with the name change so that they would fit easily onto business cards, and he charged her 7 shillings 6 pence for 200
letterheads. In later years Lillian Aza, Gracie's manager, often quipped,
"So many people have laid claim to 'discovering' Gracie Fields that I'm
thinking of hiring out the Albert Hall and taking them all out to tea."

When Gracie arrived in Blackpool she began her training in earnest
with the girls and immediately realised she would have a better time
with this particular group than the others she had worked with. Gracie
had to sing every kind and type of song imaginable, which she explained
was wonderful training. "We didn't have microphones in those days, and
yet if you knew your job you could get over the footlights alright."

Although performing from town to town, wearing an apple-green
silk dress with handkerchief points around the hem, the youngest member of the troupe still had to go to school, as Mr. Charburn tried to ensure the girls still got an education. Whichever town the troupe were
performing in that current week the girls were sent to school. Due to the
group never staying in one town more than a week, this would clearly
have been disruptive to a child's education, and Gracie remembered she
used to be sat at the side of a classroom "with a book I couldn't read until
it was time to break loose to go back to the digs and have some fun."

Jenny Stansfield wrote to her daughter frequently, telling her of all
the things which were happening in Rochdale, but more importantly,
who she would be on the bill with the next week. She took in *The
Performer* and *The Stage* newspapers and wrote to Gracie, "Next week
you're on stage with Gertie Gitana, don't forget to learn all the songs."

Developing as a mimic, Gracie tried to make friends with the stage
manager of each theatre she worked in so that he would allow her to stand
at the side of the stage to watch the performance. As other girls cottoned
on to this idea Gracie changed tact and went up into the fly-loft instead to
watch the performance from above. When the stage crew refused admit-

tance, as they believed it was too dangerous, Gracie went to sit in the or-chestra pit with the conductor or bargained with him to keep the pit door open so she could hear the performance in the dressing-room corridor.

Maidie Scott, Gertie Gitana, Victoria Monks, and George Formby Senior are the four artists Gracie thought were "the most marvellous in the world," and who she claimed she took the greatest inspiration from. In the 1930s Gracie recalled, "There can only be one reason why I chose four out of the hundreds of other stars I might have mimicked. I had those four personalities inside me before I'd ever met or heard them. They're inside me still. And do you know, I feel certain that just as you put sand and water and stone and suchlike into a cement-mixing machine and it comes out cement, so God put a bit of Monks, a bit of Formby, a bit of Gertie Gitana, and a bit of Maidie Scott into me—and they came out Gracie!"

Whilst Gracie was with Charburn's Young Stars she took to mimick-ing the likes of her favourite artists to entertain her fellow troupe mem-bers, as well as her family when she returned home on leave from the tour. The touring juvenile performance lasted half an hour, and Gracie had to sing around twenty minutes per performance to earn her four shillings a week. This earned her great attention with the audiences, and eventually her pay was increased from four to eight shillings, as Mr. Charburn realised audiences were taking to his youngest troupe mem-ber very quickly. Along with the pay rise came her own solo song, the sentimental "Coax Me," which sister Betty later recorded. As she often imitated George Formby on stage, "Who can put a Lancashire song across like him?" Gracie burlesqued the song, and the audience roared with laughter at Gracie's accurate interpretation.

Now earning an extra four shillings, Gracie saved up and treated her-self to a "proper theatrical's wicker basket" to carry her belongings around, which she proudly had engraved with her initials. On a train station plat-form during one trip with the juveniles, Gracie's wicker basket was misplaced in the confusion and was sent to the local theatre, as the basket was clearly a theatrical's type. Gracie went to retrieve the basket and realised why the stationmaster had thought to send it on, as topping the bill at the theatre was someone with the same initials stencilled onto the wicker case, George Formby. Starstruck at meeting her idol, Gracie was handed the case back and forgot to ask for his autograph. "I was happy, though, that our initials were the same. That were [sic] good enough for me."

Away with Charburn's for over two years, Gracie was a very home-sick little girl as she lived her mother's dream. Over Christmas 1912, Jenny sent Gracie's sister, Betty, to be with her so she could have some company away from home. With no money for anything special, Gracie decided to treat her younger sister to an orange—of which she bought the two biggest she could find at a very cheap price. Getting back to her lodgings and carefully unpeeling them, the two sisters greedily bit down onto their Christmas treat only to find they were in fact grapefruits. It was during her time with the troupe that Gracie saw London for the first time. Whilst there her mother wrote to her to go to see Shirley Kellog at one of the music halls, which Gracie promptly did, paying for a seat in the Gods, and had her first experience of a West End stage. One of the girls in the troupe adored singing "The Bonnie Banks of Loch Lomond" in a little Scotch costume, and Mr. Charburn decided Gracie should try the song out to see what interpretation she could give to it. Gracie, how-ever, wanted to feel what the leading ladies were doing and then sit back and watch what everyone else was doing.

When the troupe were visiting Ashton-under-Lyne, one of Rochdale's neighbouring towns, one of Gracie's friends in the company asked her to take her to Rochdale so that she could meet "Chip Sarah," known far and wide across the provinces thanks to Gracie. Her friend wanted to see all the places Gracie spoke about while she was away. As Gracie had been away from Rochdale for over two years, only a childish memory survived of the area. Her memory was of a restaurant deluxe with the affluent Sarah in charge of the magnificent fish and chip domain—a tale which she had extolled the magnificence of to all her friends. Not knowing what queer tricks the memory could perform, and how deceptive it could be, Gracie proudly and eagerly marched her friend away in search of Molesworth Street.

Without trouble the old street was found, but what had happened to the fish and chip shop? The two girls walked past it once without noticing it, but on their return Gracie spotted the dilapidated and ramshackle little place. Horrified and aghast with dismay that the shop was not the one from her memory, Gracie ushered her friend along to hopefully try and find a "posher" shop on the next street, doubtful very little had changed since the day she last saw it, but when the girlfriend asked, "Is that the place?" Gracie rose to the height of her five-foot, and in a haughty tone asked, "What do you dare insinuate? Don't be daft, we're in the wrong street." With eyes working overtime in search of a fish and chip palace, Gracie's prayers were answered, as the poshest chip shop in Rochdale just happened to be on the next street. In an exhibition of the same family pride which Jenny was renowned for, Gracie passed this chip shop off as her own and quickly ushered her friend away, back to the Ashton tram before she could ask to go inside.

In later life, Lillian Aza commented that Gracie was "the finest houseguest you can possibly have. When she was young and first went on the stage her mother told her that even if she is in digs she'd always got to give a helping hand and make the beds, wash up, help in any way you can." This stayed with Gracie throughout the rest of her life. The Stansfields, Gracie remembered, were very untidy. My mother was very untidy, but my father had the feeling of being tidy. We didn't have any nails on the walls, and I can always see him putting his coat carefully on a chair. My mother would go up to the door with her shawl as if she was going to hang up her shawl on the door, and dropped it on the floor." Gracie cried, "Mumma, you know very well there wasn't a nail there! I've just watched you drop it on the floor!" and Jenny replied, "I know, but there should be a nail there!" Unlike her parents, Gracie had a tidy feeling, which came from a Scripture lesson when she was younger. As the disciples went to see the resurrected Jesus' tomb his robes were neatly stacked, and Gracie took something from this. Before bed she always neatly arranged her sister's and her own clothes, which she continued to do whilst she was touring with the juveniles.

Another religiously-related story occurred one afternoon when the young Gracie went to see *The Sign of the Cross*, which was playing at Leeds' Theatre Royal, while the juveniles were playing at the famous City Varieties. In the evening, while making up in the dressing room, Gracie entertained the other girls in the troupe with a rendition of the "Daniel and the Lion" scene from the play she had watched that afternoon. When Gracie came to the shrieking business, her scream was so realistic and plainly heard by the audience that attendants, members of the public, and even a policeman at the back of the circle, thinking there had been a murder, dashed around to the back of the scenery to see what the matter was.

Bored of reading the same positive reviews every week, "I was just never interested," Gracie sent the clippings back home to Jenny with a portion of her eight shillings. When Jenny realised Gracie was receiving the best notices in the show, she ordered her to come home and try her luck at going out on her own. Sending out her only professional photograph, wearing a silver dress with stars and moons from Polly Pickles' shop, to agent J. Bannister Howard in Newcastle (and not Hamilton Dean of Nottingham, as cited elsewhere), Gracie was heartbroken at the reply. Scrawled across the photograph, folded in half, was "Hardly suitable." This was upsetting for Gracie and fuel for Fred to send her back to the mill. Gracie remembered this incident over thirty-five years later when she wrote to J. Bannister Howard. "In all my career, right up to the present day, that was the biggest blow I ever had. It knocked all the conceit out of me, and I went back to my juvenile troupe cured."

Under the management of Ernest Dottridge, Gracie secured a week at the Oldham Palace, which lead to a summer season in August with Cousin Freddy's Pierrot Show at the Cosy-Corner in St. Anne's. The stage was a little beach hut with rows of deckchairs as seating, and Gracie was to earn £3 a week from Fred Hutchins. Initially, Gracie later recalled, she "resented doing that sort of work because I'd been on the bill with all the top stars." Taking up lodgings at the Jubilee Cottage for the season, Gracie's work on the pier show consisted of a few serious songs and playing the stooge during Cousin Freddy's magic act. In a scene set in a laundrette, called "Transfixed," a false argument was meant to ensue over Freddy not having paid his washing money, at which he was to tap Gracie with his magic wand, where she would promptly stop her broad Lancashire accent and turn to stone, with him stealing away with the unpaid washing.

Full of nervous energy, Gracie gave the Pierrot everything she had, and as the comic argument escalated to the roars of the audience's laughter Freddy forgot to "turn Gracie to stone" as the pair continued to ad-lib with each other. "I learned a lot from Freddie. Comic timing, not minding to be laughed at, and how to be a generous performer. I went on and people started laughing, and from then on I've enjoyed creating laughter." Initially, Gracie didn't want to perform the sketch in a broad Lancashire accent, but Freddy insisted on it if she wanted to "go off to London and get her name in lights." In 1936, whilst filming *The Show Goes On*, Gracie suggested him for a comic cameo role in the film, and the pair again worked together on a BBC programme in 1939 when they recreated their original act from St. Anne's, both dressed as Pierrots. (Another little interesting fact is that Freddie also launched the career of bandleader, Jack Hylton, who Gracie starred alongside in France during her war tour of 1939.)

Taking a few week's work from Manchester agents Bradford and Pierce around the Lancashire area, Gracie appeared in a week's stint at a cinema in West Houghton as a lantern cooler. Sandy Powell, who was also on the bill with his mother, described, "As the films went so long, the projectionist needed time to cool them down." In an interview with Sandy in 1978, Gracie remembered their first time working together was in "some very horrible little town, with an angry mother and a little lad. I think I was about fifteen, and I don't think anybody came in the audience!" During the run, Percy Hall, from Manchester's Percy Hall's Variety Agency, visited the theatre. Pleased with the talent he saw, he immediately booked Gracie for an audition in Manchester. Another turn as a lantern cooler saw Gracie playing the Todmorden Hippodrome singing "coon songs" from December 1, 1913, in a capital bill starring Virgil Ashworth, Hyam Long, and the films being *Bloodhounds of the Law* and *A Knife of Fire*.

Buying her daughter a new over-sized hat, Gracie and Jenny headed to Hall's at 180a Oxford Road, and returned back to Rochdale with a contract for a Christmas Pantomime from Ernest Dottridge and Charles H. Longden. The contract was signed by Gracie's mother, as Gracie was too young to sign, and was completed on March 25, 1914. The document stipulated Gracie was to provide her own tights, shorts, and stockings, and appear in the show for £4 a week. Before the Pantomime other local engagements came up, which Gracie took.

Gracie received her first newspaper review at the Empire Music Hall in Burnley from July 20, 1914, with Isobel Carrol, The Joannys, The Two Fords, Florence Smithers, and "Gracie Fields the double voiced girl" before the Empire Theatrescope film. At the Empire Music Hall in Burnley on July 18, 1914, as a lantern-warmer with The Two Fords and Will and Nell, Gracie's bill matter was described simply as: "The girl with the elastic voice," and "The girl with the double voice." The following week at the Accrington Grand, Gracie was described as a pleasing comedienne in a bill which starred Dezso Kordy, Rich Taylor, and Stanley Whorne.

By Christmas that year Gracie was starring in the pantomime *Dick Whittington and His Cat*, playing the Princess of Morocco at the Oldham Palace, and had to "be painted from head to foot in a light brown paint." She received the best revues, much to the chagrin of the principal boy, who told the director to cut Gracie's solo number, "Are We Downhearted? No!" As Gracie's lyrics echoed the sentiments of those left at home by the soldiers going to war, Gracie's rally cry to keep the home fires burning was well received by the audience, and they responded best to her. With professional jealousy this was cut, and instead she was given a sentimental ballad, "There's Someone Who Wants You," which Gracie burlesqued, again mimicking George Formby Senior.

After Gracie had been entertaining at a wartime charity concert a few weeks before her contract with Hall was signed, she met a gentleman who was to be her first sweetheart. A Rochdale man, twelve years Gracie's senior, who Gracie recalled, "I don't remember ever being in love with him, and it didn't amount to anything serious." Still only sweet sixteen, the man's mother and father were very keen that they should make a match of it and were hoping he would be able to drop his girl, whom he had been courting for the past eight years and who they did not like. A committee meeting was held at the Stansfield's house, and Jenny and her friends agreed it would be very unfair for Gracie to go out with this man, who already had a girlfriend. Supposing that Gracie gave the man the best eight years of her life, and then along came another girl much younger to steal him away—much as Gracie was doing—the possibility didn't hold well for the committee table. Gracie called it all off, never giving a proper explanation for it, although in later life admitted, "I'm sure I didn't care one way or another, it was mainly Mama worrying over the romance. He was a rather good-looking chap, but a bit snobbish, and I used to get awfully irritated with his strong, slow, Lancashire accent." In another interview about relationships Gracie recalled, "Mother used to ask about boyfriends, and I never fitted into the category that I could go out and flirt."

Another booking came the week beginning February 23, 1915 at the Derbyshire Hippodrome with Tim Carlisle and the Three Iklmctas in "a classic cycle act introducing novelty" with Doris, the child wonder. Gracie was again listed as a "versatile comedienne and mimic." Whilst in Rochdale, Gracie was engaged to perform at a social event at Beaconsfield Conservative Club on Baron Street in aid of the Poor Children's Trust, with fellow Rochdalians, Mr. JJ Howarth and Miss Bradley, Miss Humphries, and the Misses Asquith. It was Grace Stansfield who achieved attention in the *Rochdale Observer* as offering a "wonderful rendering of songs" to Ashworth's Band on March 12, 1915. It was during this March 1915 performance that Old Fred Ogden took ill with fever and passed away in a state of delirium at the age of seventy one. As the nurses were going through his possessions an envelope containing £100 was handed to Jenny with a note telling her to use it as she thought best. After paying off a few family debts, Gracie was sent to six half-hour tap dancing lessons in Manchester with professional clog dancer Mr. Corlett.

Percy Hall, after seeing Gracie in pantomime and realising she could now dance, agreed to see her at his offices again, and signed her for a touring revue called *Yes, I Think So*, agreeing to solely represent her for two years, beginning April 3, 1915. The engagement contract, again signed by Jenny on April 16, 1915, really meant that her daughter had "made it," as she was exclusively under contract to the review manager, Louis J. Seymour. At five pounds a week, with half of any money earned on top of that going back to Hall, Gracie was finally on the road to becoming a theatrical. Gracie sang one song to open the revue and another nearing the end of Act Two, and the production was produced and premiered at the Hulme Hippodrome in Manchester on April 19, 1915, and which Gracie stayed with until February 1916.

Yes, I Think So promised to be a "topical, musical, and whimsical revue" with book by Louis J. Seymour and Charles B. Baker and music composed and arranged by Cecil Howarth. "Gorgeous Scenery, Elaborate Costumes, Delightful Music, Striking Effects, Artistic Dancing, Continuous Laughter from Beginning to End." The show, which was more of a framework for a series of songs and dances, starred Louis J. Seymour in the leading role alongside Goldie Collins, Banjahara the Indian Vocalist, May Harper, Brook Kimberley, William Melbourne, Pat Aza, Frank Hartley, Fred Wright, John Wilton, Annette Cambrai, Archie Pitt, and "a mammoth beauty chorus." When the show played the Empire Hippodrome in Ashton-under-Lyne on June 14, 1915, the bill was shared with May Sherrard (The Female Dan Leno), the Hovis Brothers, and Le More with his thought-reading dog, with orchestra conducted by Cecil Howarth.

The story concerned a man about town, Harry Gordon, who found he had overrun his bank account and decides to flee to Egypt. Confiding his story to the secretary of the Walpole Nightclub, a solicitor's clerk tries to help Harry, having good news of a fortune, but the secretary of the club takes him for a writ-server and is thrown out of the club. This clerk tries various subterfuges to get at Harry, and follows him to Egypt, where he received an unhappy announcement that his Uncle in Australia had left him £100,000 providing that he marry a girl with golden hair and blue eyes—of which Harry's lady matched the description.

The opening scene of the show was set at the Walpole Night Club before a love scene played out between characters John Wilton and Flora Rey at Charing Cross Station as the company departs to Egypt, of which followed an Egyptian ballet sequence with all of three ballet dancers, set at the Gizch Gardens.

Louis Seymour sang the title song of the revue as a duet with Goldie Collins, as well as "Where the Boys Are," a touching and inspiring military melody. Gracie played Grace Darling and received good acclaim with the number "Mississippi Lu" and her impersonation of Gertie Gitana with "Wonderful Baby." Other good songs are given, including a new tongue twister by Wilton, which included "My Idea of Paradise," "Where are the Brave Old Boys?" "Keep on Shining Moon" and "What Have We to Worry About?" Archie Pitt and Eric Melbourne were a source of great fun in their Charlie Haplin routine, which was described by one reviewer as "one of the best imitations of the one and only Charlie Chaplin we have seen on film or in the flesh," and Archie offered the patter-song "Pretty Patty's Proud of Her Pink Petticoat."

Another review stated, "The humour is of an acceptable kind and is provided in plenty, the efforts of Archie Pitt, a genuinely amusing comedian, being ably supplemented by Jack Hartley and Reg Maovers. Miss Mona Frewer is excellent as Marie St. Clair, the pet of the nightclub. As Wilton, the club secretary, Mr. Archie Pitt keeps the audience in roars of laughter by his dry humour and his patter, which is gay as well as amusing. Archie Pitt, who, as Hilton, the secretary of the Walpole Club, is a never-failing source of merriment with his whimsical humour."

Starring alongside Gracie in this revue, and evidently achieving good billing, was a thirty-year-old Jewish comedian named Archie Pitt. Archie's grandfather, leather merchant Abraham Selinger, and second wife, Gale, moved to London's East End from Bavaria in 1870 with their children, Sigfried, Helena, Morris, Cornelia, Flora, Sydney, and Oska, and lived on Nottingham Place in the Mile End Old Town area. It is likely that some of their children, who were all born whilst still in Germany, died before the family emigrated to England. In December 1881 Morris married Elizabeth Asch, and by the 1891 census they had completed their family of five children: Clothilda Ash, born in St. Giles in 1879; Archibald Abraham, born in Dulwich in June 1882; Berthold Gabriel, born in King's Cross in 1883; Edgar Henry, born in Stratford, London in 1885; and Percy Samuel, born in Mile End in 1888. The 1901 census has the family living at Nicholas Street in the Mile End Old Town, with Morris listed as a manufacturer of lamp shades, Archie as a commercial traveller, and Bert and Edgar as commercial clerks. The family were quite well off, as there is mention in the census of them having at least one servant per household.

The 1911 census records the children living in Liverpool at 15 Baker Street, at the boarding house of Harriet Rudler. Archie is listed as a "Music Hall Comedian," with his brothers as "Music Hall Dancers." Archie's first appearance on the variety stage was in 1900 as a comedian and singer, and was in the process of planning his own touring revue. When Archie's father died in 1920 his mother moved with Hilda to a home in Brighton, where Hilda married Isaac Finberg in 1929, shortly after her mother's death that year. Hilda died in 1958, Edgar in 1967, Bert in 1953, and Percy in 1985. (To complete the picture, Edgar married Esther M. Hall in 1920 and Berthold married Lillian Stracey, the daughter of an upholsterer, born in 1902, at a marriage ceremony in Lambeth in 1923.)

Although Gracie stated she didn't particularly rate Archie Pitt as a comic and was surprised when the audience actually laughed at his jokes and not at him, she writes bluntly in her 1960 autobiography, "His act was rubbish." With Gracie favouring the Lancashire George Formby over the Cockney Archie Pitt, her standards were set high, and the "pale-faced Cockney" who paid more attention to her act than the tour owner did unnerved the young girl and she tried not to pay him too much attention. This even led to Gracie dining away from other members of the troupe, taking her meals upstairs in her lodgings whilst the rest remained at the dinner table. At other times Gracie even stayed in lodgings miles away from the theatre and the rest of the company, as Jenny had recommendations from the theatricals, so Gracie had to walk miles to the theatre—before Archie put a stop to this.

With the First World War underway, the touring company often visited hospitals and recuperation centres to entertain injured soldiers back from the Front and to hand out signed postcards to boost morale. Although Gracie was too young to sign a contract, it was at this time that she developed her signature, as the earliest documented autographed photograph of Gracie was signed on December 29, 1916. Gracie returned home with the show to Rochdale, making her professional debut in her hometown at the Hippodrome the week beginning November 30, 1915.

On Gracie's eighteenth birthday, in January 1916, the cast were playing at the Hamilton Hippodrome and Archie brought a bottle of champagne back to celebrate. As in Noel Gay's song, which Gracie was later to have success with, "Only a Glass of Champagne" changed her thoughts for Archie. The company had travelled to Preston from Hulme on the train the Sunday before, and Archie had enquired whether Gracie wanted to share his two-bed room at the lodgings. Having procured no other sleeping arrangement, Gracie agreed to this. One day she was visited by a young girl from Manchester who told her that Archie was married and had a child, and that he was suing for a divorce to be married to this young girl. A shocked Gracie realised how it looked that she was sleeping in the same room as a married man "who wasn't acting very much like a good father, brother, or husband," so she decided to lodge elsewhere following this. Gracie often said in later life that Archie signed her autograph book on her sixteenth birthday, when in actuality he signed it on October 29, 1915. In his flamboyant script he wrote: *My*

love to little Gracie. It is possible you will be a "big" artiste one of these days.
"Yes I Think So" Revue, Archie Pitt.

Professional jealousy seemed to take the better of the revue's owner, Louis J. Seymour, who frequently gave Gracie—the third leading lady— a new song to perform, subsequently taking it away from her when she had made it a success, and performing it on stage himself. As he was top of the bill, Gracie claims she didn't mind this happening to her and didn't see it as any personal snub against her. Either way, it provided her with an invaluable lesson of how to craft a song and make it her own.

Yes I Think So toured the provinces for eighteen months, and during its run made an appearance at the famous Collins Music Hall on Upper Street, Islington for the week commencing June 25, 1915, and also the Old Middlesex Music Hall on July fifth of the same year. During its runs in London, Gracie told the Cockney, Archie, how she much preferred food "oop North," and that a bowl of tater ash couldn't be beaten. Trying to persuade her otherwise, he gave her a bowl of London's finest delicacy, jellied eels. Thinking they were pieces of diced snake, Gracie threw them on the floor and promptly ran away screaming, much to the company's amusement. Although her first instincts of Archie warned her against him, the pair got to know each other during the year and half on tour and Gracie admitted, "During that time whenever anything went wrong for me, Archie insisted on putting it right."

When the show reached Motherwell on January 7, 1916, Percy Hall wrote to Gracie asking her to sign on for his next revue, *Splash Me*, at a salary increase of one pound. The *Yes I Think So* company had met the *Splash Me* company whilst playing one of the bigger towns, and the other show was a fast-paced racy revue which Gracie didn't feel comfortable with. She also wasn't happy with the fact that one of the members, on being introduced to her, "slapped my bottom heartily and asked if I ever got cold at night." As *Yes I Think So* ended Gracie received her first bouquet from the other girls in the chorus—a basket of fruit which she was thrilled to receive and carried all the way down from Scotland on the train back to her mother, who more or less dismissed it in anticipation of all of her stories from being on the road.

Archie had been in the process of writing his own revue and insisted that instead of joining *Splash Me*, Gracie should come and work with him on his new show. Gracie was reluctant to sacrifice a contract at six pounds a week until Archie promised to match it and also to buy her out of her current ten-year contract. Percy Hall got word that Gracie was planning to leave, and that she had apparently been causing dissent in the ranks of the company, and wrote:

> We have heard of the sarcastic remarks you have passed, and we wish it to be clearly understood that whilst we hold your mother's signature as your exclusive agents, and until such a time the agreement may expire, that you have nothing to say in this matter.
>
> It is quite evident that you have forgotten to realise that it was us in the first place who booked you in Revue, and instead of getting a word from you, it seems we are getting nothing but abuse. However, this has got to stop. You will understand that we are quite firm on this, that you leave irrespective to the advice you receive from other people or your own opinion. We only want to point this out to save unnecessary arguments.

On the same day, December 24, 1915, Percy Hall also wrote to Gracie's mother:

> You say in your letter that "you have finished with Gracie's business." We have two proposals to make:
>
> 1st: If you want our agreement to be cancelled, that you pay us from the very beginning of Gracie starting with the show 10%

commission for all the work she has had—which we are legally entitled to according to the office copy you signed.

2nd: That the agreement still holds good, which you must adhere to as your child is under age, and her word is not worth anything in a court of law.

You must understand that we cannot work for nothing, which we have done since we had Gracie. It is about time we started to make something, and don't forget that it was us who booked her with Seymour, and we cannot afford to let everybody try and do it on us. We are quite prepared to fight this in a court of law, and will do so if necessary.

Archie agreed to smooth things over and bought Gracie out of her contract with Percy Hall for £12, which was paid weekly until June 6, 1916, when he had completely bought out her contract—although there were several reminder letters from Hall, as Archie was "not keeping to [his] arrangement." Lillian Aza, Archie's sister-in-law and later Gracie's manager, remembered that Archie paid ten pounds to buy out Gracie's contract, but Gracie remembered this in later life as twenty-five pounds, which possibly took into account the £10 Archie gave Jenny Stansfield for the opportunity of sole representation. After using the company's first week's salary on properties and scenery, Archie successfully managed to arrange his first touring revue, which Gracie helped him name *It's a Bargain!* ("A revue in an Office" including the droll comedian Archie Pitt. Silvern, Talkative Conjuror, and Ivor Vinter) and which opened on the "Number Two" circuit on February 7, 1916 at the Manchester Tivoli Theatre. (Gracie, Archie, and Mona had left *Yes I Think So* early, and the show continued to run without them until March 1916.)

Gracie's contract with the newly established Archie Pitt Agency was signed by both Jenny and Gracie on July 15, 1916. Lasting for five years, the contract stipulated Gracie could not accept any other engagement unless it was first cleared by Archie, and she would pay him 10% commission on any engagement entered from the signing date. The contracted also states, "Archie Pitt will at all times use his best endeavours for the betterment of my position." Archie had taken up a set of offices at 149 Balham High Road in London, which he was using as his theatrical base. His three brothers, Pat, Edgar, and Bert, were going to be on the tour with the show, with Gracie playing the second leading lady to Mona Frewer's top billing—who Archie had also purloined from Percy Hall.

It's a Bargain promised to be "musical, topical, and brim-full of comedy" with 24 artistes in a 75-minute show, featuring elaborate scenery and elaborate dresses (if necessary)." The script, a scrappy jotter book consisting of 20 handwritten pages by Archie and Mona Frewer and notes of where to include songs and dances, was passed by the Lord Chamberlain's Office on February 4, 1916.

The show was produced at the Tivoli Theatre in Manchester on March 18, stage-managed by Jack Thuro with musical direction by H. G. Grimshaw and wardrobe by J. Hubbell. The twenty-four members of the company were able to choose if they wanted to take a salary or shares within the company, although salaries were not available until the show was actually making profit. Presented by Messrs. Royle and Ryde, the tour tentatively set out in April 1916, already in debt. With shaky finances from the very start, Mona Frewer had to pawn her jewellery for the show and Gracie and Archie arranged with fifteen landladies to let them owe their rents. Often playing to half-empty theatres, the ambitious revue heralded "Some scenery! Some dresses! and Some girls!" During the dress rehearsal of the show Royle and Ryde both agreed Gracie was not on stage enough during the show, which was eventually extended to one hundred and ten minutes. By the end of the tour Gracie was on stage for over eighty-five of those minutes.

Described as the greatest epidemic of laughter, the peculiar mannerisms of the leading aristes helped make *It's a Bargain* a success. The plot revolved around a manager trying to obtain an increase in salary from Mr. Hook, the principal of a large commercial concern. Archie played Mr. Hook, the charming lover of Peggy O'Dair, played by Mona Frewer, whose winesome rendition of "The Harvest Song" was billed to be exceptionally pretty. In the review, Gracie played Sally Perkins, the first of many Sallys that she would play in her career, and her ludicrous ways added all to the fun. Other Pitt/Frewer songs included "Who The? What The? How The?" "Pick of the Family," with Gracie singing "Alabamy Jubilee" and Gertie Gitana's "Iola."

Eric Thornaby and Sally McGreggor completed the original cast of five, but as the production toured more acts were added. Dancit gave several displays of dancing, but the actor who most amused the audience was Jimmy Clarke, the page, whose quiet humour and solid expressions made up a good deal of the comedy of the play. The tour also starred Jack Leighton, Beatrice Chalmers, Miss Hope Brown (the French Victoria Cross heroine with her comic monologue, "The Women Who Wait") a dancing sextet, a "bunch of beauties," supporting soprano, Irene Majorbanks, and speciality artist, Mimie also appeared throughout the tour, which ran until August 1918, when it closed at the Long Eaton Coliseum after a successful final week at the Middlesbrough Empire.

Starting up in business, Archie enlisted the assistance of his three brothers in getting him on the road with the review. Archie's brothers, Bert, Percy (known professionally as Pat), and Edgar Selinger, had been performing on the stage as The Three Aza Brothers or the Aza Trio since 1911, a comedy musical act who adopted their name as an advertisement for a brand of cloth in return for free stage costumes.

Their grandparents had emigrated to London in 1870 and started a lampshade-making business, whose products apparently made their way into the homes of royalty. Whilst Archie tried for a career on his own, his brothers worked up an act which was a mixture of singing, dancing, and comedy with an Oriental flavour. Seeking a name for themselves, and perhaps even sponsorship, they approached cloth manufacturers Viyella, thinking they might call themselves the Viyella Boys. Whilst not keen on the idea, the company was launching a new type of fabric, Aza, from the Egyptian word for petal. As it happens, the new cloth, which the Aza Boys took their name from, was not a success, but their act was. Bert could play the violin, Pat the piano, and all three could dance—to a degree.

The trio had travelled overseas with their act and enjoyed mild success as far as Berlin, Budapest, and Paris. When Archie began to set up his revue Bert was running a blouse factory. His later wife, Lillian, later commented, "He was friendly with the manageress. The problem was, so where his brothers, and so he left the business to work for Archie partway through the run." At the outset of World War One all four brothers were called up for National Service, but Archie was determined that they would not be sent out to fight. On the day war was announced the trio were actually in Belgium and found time to fit a fortnight's engagement in Ostend before returning after the outbreak. Bert slashed his arm, Pat joined the Army but became a chronic neurotic and was discharged, and Archie sat for hours with tobacco bags under his arms to excite his heart, although Gracie wrote to the office stating he had duodenal ulcers and was excused for this reason. Edgar accepted his role and became a tailor for the Army.

Although not the greatest comedy act to ever grace the variety stage, their reviews were positive—that is, except from Jenny Stansfield, who thought they were terrible and should be told so! Bert soon realised this and had a change of role within Aza Agencies as, at the suggestion of scrap-metal dealer Jimmy Brennan, he took over as tour manager of the revue after they had appeared in Darlington three months into the tour. Bert joined the company initially as orchestra conductor but was soon replaced when it was realised that he wasn't proficient at reading music. Instead, he took over the business and management side of the review.

Bert recalled years later, "It was in the early stages of the First World War when I received a telegramme asking me to join [the show]. I borrowed the fair, and arriving just before the evening performance, paid my 9d for a seat in the circle and thoroughly enjoyed the show. I thought the two principal girls, one a comedian, the other a straight soubrette, were quite outstanding. I went backstage to meet the manager and warmly congratulated him on his two leading ladies." It turned out that Bert had that evening seen Gracie perform in both roles, as the other leading lady was off ill, and he "met for the first time the straight, cool, merry glance of Gracie Stansfield of Rochdale. That moment had remained vivdly in my mind until today, for though I would have been a bold man to foresee the scope of her future triumphs, yet I knew quite clearly that I was talking to the girl with the seed of fame and possibly genius within her."

During the two and a half years *It's a Bargain* toured the company often played to empty houses and often had weeks when the booking ledger read "VACANT," as they couldn't find a venue to fit them in or they couldn't afford to move to the next town. Charging 2d for seats in the pit and 6d in the stalls, the audiences just weren't coming, and at some theatres even if the company were playing to full houses they would still be in debt at the end of the week. The tour was booked in for a week's run at a theatre in Aberystwyth during its eleven-week run in Wales over summer 1917, and as the company arrived they had difficulty finding the theatre. That was because it wasn't really a theatre, but more of a hall above a shop—and with no piano. With no room for any scenery, a heavily abridged version of the show was presented. The company only made 11 shillings that week, of which Gracie's share amounted to a total of 4d. This story was still being told by Bert Aza over fifty years later, who recalled, "Even some of those small audiences were a blessing in disguise, for, with only a handful of people in front, we often ragged our own show, gagging and fooling to an extent. We would never have dared with a full house. Gracie was superb in these romps and her natural flair for burlesque had plenty of scope."

More often than not Bert travelled on to the next town to beg the booking theatre to pay for the cast's train or bus fare so that they could meet their engagement. On one occasion, where the company was booked to play West Stanley in April 1917, Bert travelled to Liverpool to try to borrow the fare needed plus an extra £40 for scenery and props from Arthur Williams, theatre manager of the Garston Empire. The manager didn't agree to this, only offering to pay the fare, not the necessary extra.

But luck was smiling. Just when Bert's telegram arrived saying he had secured train fare but nothing else, a wealthy young local tradesman was sitting next to Archie in the tearoom where he and Gracie were, and overheard the conversation. He had seen the barebones of the show that week and told Archie it would eventually turn out be a fine one. Horrified at Bert's telegram, the young businessman offered to loan Archie as much as he wanted, forty pounds, with the proviso that he paid it back when he could. As the tour grew and began to earn money Archie kept his word and paid him back in regular installments. During the run of Archie's next show the same man returned to him and asked if he could borrow £5, as he had lost his job and was down on his luck. Archie refused this, and instead gave him £40 and told him he need not worry about paying it back.

Although the show was relatively well-booked during its two and a half year run, there were times when the booking's log was "VACANT," and Bert wrote to *The Stage Newspaper* asking for theatres to book the show, exclaiming, "Is any more recommendation necessary?" after printing the names of theatre managers from their previous visits. Return visits were common with this show in 1917, with the company playing

Rotherham twice in four months, Barnsley twice in five weeks, and Leeds and Chatham three times in three months. To *The Stage*, Bert put a spin on this as "audiences love this show as we break theatre records!" as opposed to the fact it was cheaper to book the show than keep the theatres dark for a week. In 1916 Archie had to cancel nine weeks of tours around South of England "owing to the fact of the refusal of some members of my company refusing to go near London due to German air raids."

Archie's leading lady, Mona Frewer, took ill during the tour and often had to miss performances, at which Gracie would go on in her place. In doing this, Gracie clowned her first song on the professional stage, having already attempted to burlesque songs in the juvenile shows and having been adept at impersonating songs such as "My Sweet Iola" and "Lily of Laguna" at home to her family. This came about because Gracie was fed up of seeing her conductor taking a severe lack of interest in her performance, so she decided to make her sit up straight and send her off-key, rushing through the bars of music in double time. The conductor was a young Jewish singer from Leeds named Annie Lipman, who had been turned down for a job by Archie but had been accepted by Bert. Annie had started as a chorus girl before becoming the company's conductor after an impromptu performance in the digs one evening, when Annie decided to conduct the rowdy chorus with a poker from the fireplace. Annie would go on to play a very important role in Archie and Gracie's future life.

Annie was born Annie Rachel Lipman to Hyman and Phoebe Lipman, Polish/Russian Jews who arrived in Leeds sometime after 1881 as a result of persecution of Jews in their home countries. Most Jews settling in Leeds did so in the central area called Leylands, a Jewish conclave similar to Whitechapel in London, with most working in sweatshops creating finished textile goods. Through the early 20th-century most of Leylands was demolished for city-center development and major road building.

At the time of the 1891 census, Hyman, a tailor, and Phoebe were living at 34 Cobourg Street, and by 1901 the family had moved to 69 Bridge Street with Hyman now describing himself as «Beadle of Synagogue."

Phoebe died in 1909 and Hyman took up with Sarrah Cohen, although there is no record existing of their marriage. The 1911 household census return was signed by Annie Lipman and shows Sarah brought two sons with her: Harry and David Cohen. Annie, born in Leeds in 1891, is shown as a tailoress and had a younger sister, Dora, born 1894. At this time they were living at 10 Lovell Street, off North Street, which is when she first went to one of the many local theatres to see Archie Pitt about perhaps procuring a job with the company.

Gracie was achieving great reviews with her regular impersonations of George Formby and Gertie Gitana, but especially with a new impersonation of Charlie Chaplin's character, The Little Tramp, which he premiered in *Kid Auto Races at Venice* (1914), which was one of the first films Gracie saw at the cinema. Archie specifically sent Gracie to "the pictures" to work on her routine, and after watching the film twice back-to-back, Gracie stated she was "walking down the high street as though I was Chaplin himself!" As the character gained worldwide fame Gracie nearly broke her neck trying to get the impersonation correct, and after she had worked on it the impersonation was excellent. Mona Frewer, not liking the attention that Gracie was getting, waited in the wings one evening as Gracie came off stage, in a scene which called for impressions of Gertie Gitana, George Formby, and Charlie Chaplin, and exclaimed "Imitations! That's not a performance! Any monkey can do imitations. You're no good. You've got no personality of your own. You just live on other people's personalities, on other people's brains, and pick at them!" From there on in Gracie dropped the sketch and never did an impersonation on the stage again, replacing it instead with a sketch in which she dressed up in her pyjamas and took a teddy bear on stage with her to sing to.

When Mona Frewer eventually decided to retire from the stage to convalesce, Archie offered Gracie a pay rise and the role of leading lady in the show. In later interviews when Gracie had "made it" as a star, Archie described how he gave her carte blanche to do whatever she wanted to do in the review as he soon realised that it was Gracie Fields the audiences were coming to see, and not *It's a Bargain*.

Filling in the gaps in the cast after a reshuffle, which included the additions of Linda Thornhill, Maya Wynn, Hilda Harrison, Maureen Cavanagh, Dolly Mountford, and the Star Sextette of Dancers, Jenny sent both Betty and Edith to work with her sister to begin their education on the stage. Betty joined the review first in Lancaster in the third week of January 1917. Bert was sent to meet her at Lancaster Station and was told to look for "a leggy girl with golden curls." He saw her and said, "You're little Betty, aren't you?" Betty mistook Bert for his brother and threw her arms around his neck in greeting. Suddenly realising that she had hugged a stranger, she gave a started cry and ran down the platform, hotly pursued by Bert! Betty also remembered that during this tour some doctors came from the local asylum to the theatre and Betty got her first grown-up kiss from one of them, although she thought it "was a mucky business and he a dirty fellow for sticking his tongue in my mouth." Betty also recalled the awful conditions which the tour played in, and that the male juvenile lead was travelling with his baby son, who got sick and died whilst on the tour. The devastated cast all filed into the child's bedroom at the boarding house to pay their respects, and the young Betty placed a few flowers in the child's hand.

In the daytime the cast members visited hospitals and Army camps in the aid of boosting morale, and it looked likely for a brief period that Archie and Bert would be conscripted into the Army, but they both got exemptions. Whilst the review was in Salisbury the company performed for Australian and New Zealand soldiers who were camped near

Salisbury Plain. Fearing any unsolicited advances toward his girls who had been performing for them in the daytime, Archie ensured that the cast members walked around the town in twos just in case of any trouble. Gracie was on tour when Grandma "Chip Sarah" Leighton died of heart disease at her home, 4 Back Oldham Road, Castleton on January 30, 1917 at the age of 68. Gracie was unable to return to Rochdale for the funeral, held at Rochdale Cemetery on February second.

Further gaps in the cast were filled by Bert, who held auditions for the new girls when the show was playing in Leeds. Sensing talent in the young Betty, Archie began to train her professionally—much as he did with Gracie—and to shape her in mind for her own possible revue in the future. Betty said Archie was relentless and cruel at bringing talent out. After shouting at her one evening for nearly falling asleep on stage in front of the London audience in Poplar, and for not coming up with anything original, Betty had a turnaround and stopped the show the next evening with a comic dress she had dug from the bottom of the theatre's costume trunk. As the youngest member of the company, and a reluctant member at that, Betty had received no theatrical training and claimed, "Gracie was constantly ashamed of me, for I was always in trouble for my dumbness."

In 1918 with the show still on the road, Fred Stansfield accepted a job in the London-based Gillette's Engineering Firm, and apprehensively the Stansfields moved to 25 Myddleton Square, Islington. A far cry from "going oop" in Rochdale, the family rented two bedrooms and a living room in the four-story building overlooking the peaceful park of Myddleton Square, which served as the family base from 1918 until 1923. Archie paid for all the relocation expenses from Rochdale. When not on tour, Gracie and her sisters used to stay here with her mother, father, and Tommy, whilst Archie either stayed with his mother or in his offices in Balham, which doubled as a living space. Although Fred was reluctant to move to

London, Jenny saw this as the final rung in the ladder of "going oop" and told him firmly that she would never live in Rochdale again. Gracie frequently turned down offers from other touring reviews, claiming solidarity with her fellow Pitt Productions members, including refusing a lucrative contract of fifty pounds per week from an Australian tour manager.

Although Gracie said she would never mimic another artist on stage, Archie was impressed with her retentive memory and how she could impersonate artists after only hearing them once. He looked into getting permission to use other artist's songs during his review, but when he found he could not do this he came up with an alternative plan. Knowing how adept Gracie was at taking to new songs, he continually ensured Gracie got new songs and performed them in the style of other popular artists, endeavouring to keep the review fresh and up to date whilst not incurring legal proceedings. All the while, he was working on his second independent show, which he hoped to premiere in 1918.

The review was titled *Mr. Tower of London,* and was set to make Gracie Fields a star.

The 'Mr Tower of London' company. (1922).

CHAPTER THREE

1918 - 1927

Today I'm in the shadows, tomorrow maybe,
The clouds will lift and let the sun shift over to me.

- "Looking on the Bright Side" (1932),
recorded by Gracie Fields.

ARCHIE STARTED CREATING MR. *Tower of London* whilst the company was still on the road with *It's a Bargain,* and it was primarily written so the successful group of theatricals would be kept together. Gracie admitted, "It was perhaps the worst show ever written, and Archie knew it." Undeterred, Archie, who everyone in the company called Daddy Pitt, encouraged the cast to work on the show as they toured. The original script, handwritten by Archie in an oversized exercise book, was submitted to the Lord Chamberlain's Office for review, and was passed by Ernest Bendall to open on October 28, 1918, who judged it to be, "A revue of the scrappy order, with no attempt to link together its series of episodes of farcical burlesque. Starting with a sketch of the blundering management of a butcher who takes over a drapery store, it proceeds to some cross talk between the leading comedians about the wedding of a stingy man's daughter, and thence to the conversational humours of the passengers in an old horse omnibus. There follows a comic concert party leading up to the broad fun of a police court presided over by a wag suggestively named My Justice Startling. Then there is trouble with a lodger over his demand for an early cup of tea and over an allotment conducted after the manner of a pantomime rally. The jokes are, most of them, distinctly common, while the 'business' is of a very hackneyed kind. But there is no impropriety, if very little taste, in either."

Mr. Tower of London opened at the Long Eaton Coliseum, Nottinghamshire on October 28, 1918—the very same theatre where *It's a Bargain* had closed two weeks previously. Having finished at the town with a perfect review which audiences loved, the company was unsurprised when the Nottinghamshire audiences didn't take to Archie's new show. Selling all the scenery from *It's a Bargain* to fund the new show, after three months of touring, whilst still constantly working on it, the cast began to enjoy it as they altered scenes and routines to suit their particular talents. Eventually rehearsal rooms were hired in the New Brighton Tower in Liverpool, where the show was intensively honed and perfected on Sundays when not travelling to the next theatre, and where Gracie would always ensure when she was teaching the girls the dances she would always join in the line with them, "so they couldn't say I wasn't part of the family and was Mrs. High-and-Mighty not joining in."

With dresses by Madame Roberts (actually, the girls of the company were led by Gracie in sewing their own dresses) and initial scenery by Royle and Ryde, the company set off on tour not knowing how much of a success they had on their hands. Throughout slumps, strikes, and hot weather the review toured the provinces and played to as many small theatres, halls, and rooms as would book it. In a series of clever burlesques interspersed with tuneful singing and bright dancing, the review featured a larger cast than *It's a Bargain*. Alongside Archie at the helm of the show was a comedian named Joel Mitchell, who provided most of the comedic diversion. Over the seven years *Mr. Tower of London* toured, the accounts book shows it made profits of over £400,000 and was seen by over seven million people in every major town and city in the United Kingdom.

Along with Archie and Joel, when the tour first opened Gracie provided a quaint style and vocal eccentricities, whilst Harry Dean, Hilda Farrand, Sybil Hudson, and Ernest Maybury all contributed to their own scenes, assisted by a well-trained chorus in support. Every artist was well paid when the company was making money, and every chorus girl was paid sufficient to keep herself well and to put something by. In interviews Archie expressed, "Everybody is pleased to see everybody else doing well." Two other members of the chorus were Betty Stansfield and Edith Fieldstan, who themselves were receiving positive notices. Whilst Betty chose to use her real name for the stage (later in the run she changed it to Fields, in line with Gracie), Edith chose the pseudonym Fieldstan, although it doesn't take a cryptologist to realise how she came about choosing this name, and soon enough she too followed suit and changed to Fields.

Split over five scenes, which actually constituted as one small episode with different actors doubling up for different parts in the show from a drapery store to a cottage to the top deck of an omnibus and an allotment garden, Archie played the titular Mr. Tower, as well as a courtroom judge and a sailor, with a comedic number "Oh! Those Waterbabies." Betty Fields was given two solo routines in the show, "Ragatime Ragamuffin," sung to a group of unruly newsboys, and a sentimental "In Grandma's Day." With the chorus dressed as rouge et noir pierrots, Gracie took to the stage in a striking folly dress to sing "Dad and Mammy's Golden Wedding Jubilee," "I'd Like to Marry, but I Couldn't Leave the Boys," and "She Lives Down the Alley." In later years it would be a different song about an alley which would become Gracie's signature song. Two songs were written especially for the production, the opening number,

"We Have a Motto," telling the audience to pay attention to them, and also "Special Constable's Glide."

On the opening night at the Long Eaton Coliseum the curtain rose on Gracie dressed as a housemaid plucking a chicken. The whole point of the scene was that every time a chicken feather fell on the floor a feather duster sprang up from where it landed. In total, there were about a dozen feather dusters being operated by a complicated series of ropes and pulleys as if they were dancing. On the first night not a single rope worked, so the sketch was immediately dropped. Another scene which was cut took place in a vegetable garden containing an enormous cucumber. The whole point of the sketch was that when the cucumber came finally to be plucked it was to be revealed as Gracie. Instead, the person meant to "pluck" Gracie missed his cue and the vegetable lay deserted on the stage in silence. Having to do something, Gracie got up, bowed to the audience, and exclaimed, "I'm a cucumber." This made the actors laugh more than the bewildered audience as the curtain fell to silence.

One of Gracie's greatest and much heralded comedy scenes in the review was her appearance in the courtroom scene, where instead of defending herself her character of Sally Perkins strayed away from her defence and went into a comedy monologue on "how to aspirate the H." The scene was based around a divorce proceeding of a downtrodden husband and his Lancashire mill-girl wife with a strong right arm. In another episode, Archie played Sailor Jack Tar, who returned from the sea to find his wife had run away. He set out to the country to find her and came upon a cottage with two Tommies in the garden who he befriends and agrees to stay the night. The truth of the scene was revealed, however, when Tar discovered the owner of the cottage was actually his wife, who was doing more than her bit to support the war effort . . . Another scene abundant in broad farce took place on the top of an omnibus and showed Mr. Tower's attempt at driving as Arthur Stott attempted to take fares off passengers, eventually throwing Joel Mitchell from the top of the bus for lack of payment. (When Tommy Fields later joined the touring company he took the place of the fare collector and was well remembered for years after by audiences in this hilarious scene.)

During the 1919 railway strike, and one of the worst fogs London had seen in many years, the company had to hire a lorry to get from Selby in Yorkshire to the Queen's Theatre in Poplar. Packing the props, scenery, costume, and chorus into the back of a van, the driver lost his way more than once, with Gracie exaggerating, "We nearly ended up in the Thames!" Finally arriving at the theatre at five o'clock in the evening, leaving one hour to unload the props and scenery and get on stage for the first house, the company found a replacement review had already arrived as the manager feared that Archie's show would not make it. It later transpired that four rival reviews had jumped in Mr. Tower's place and were ready to go on if the company failed to show. Instead, the review broke box office records in Poplar, and whilst playing in Poplar the entire company had to be vaccinated against smallpox, as an outbreak had occurred in the area shortly before they arrived.

When the company were in Llaneli they put on an extra show a day at nine in the morning so those coming out of the coalpits from the night shift would be able to see the review which everyone was raving about. Coming on stage, the tired and ridiculous Gracie addressed the audience, "Eeh Arch! Where'd we get all these chimney sweeps from at this time o'morning?" Remembering her stay in Llaneli on her return visit to the area in 1937, Gracie recalled, "One evening in the audience we had two opposing football teams of miners. We got one half to sing against the other." Each team roared louder to drown out their rivals, egged on by the company on stage, and in the end it turned out more as a communal sing-along rather than a performance in a theatre. This continued into the next morning and only ended when the angry theatre manager turned the house lights on and locked the front doors."

As the tour progressed through the years extra scenes were added and songs were replaced to keep the show fresh and up-to-date, including the colourful scene of "Mr. Tower's Cabaret." When the review visited the Elephant and Castle Theatre in December 1919, not only had it expanded to six scenes, but it was billed as "dressed above anything that has visited these parts for a very long time" with the guarantee that "you will never have laughed as hard before in your life." By the time the show had reached the Stockport Theatre Royal it had been on the road for eighteen months and 900 performances and was described as without doubt the most comical show before the public. Playing a return run in Grimsby in November 1922, the press reported the company was playing to packed houses reminiscent of pre-war theatre, even though there were attractive bills at other theatres in the town. Gracie would do the shopping for the company in each town until Wednesday, and by then she would be recognised by shopkeepers and people in the town and would refuse to do the shopping after Thursday, where she would "much prefer to be in bed resting than rehearsing all the girls."

Not all the reviews were positive. When the show was presented in Euston, one reviewer wrote, "Described as a 'musical comedy review,' there was no plot, and save for a stray little gag here and there, no comedy of a topical nature." Whilst praising both Archie's comic ability and Gracie's singing, overall the Euston audiences seemed unimpressed with the show. By this time Archie was advertising in newspapers for new reviews, large or small, which he could manage and send out on tour, which would become the start of his touring review empire. Gracie was still receiving favourable reports, whilst the show itself suffered some criticism as it was suggested the condensing, or the complete removal, of certain scenes. Many were surprised, however, that in three years of touring the show had not come to the attention of any West End producers, with the closest they got to Leicester Square being the badly critiqued week in Euston in June 1920 and shows at the Shoreditch Olympia and the Ilford Hippodrome. Although the show had played for a total of seventeen weeks in London's provincial theatres, it had not yet made it anywhere near the larger houses of the West End.

In one of the many out-of-the-way towns which the show played, at which Gracie comically quipped, "They were behind the times. So much so that they were still taking bets on who would win Waterloo," the company were not receiving laughs at all. Playing until Wednesday, the audiences were flat, and on Wednesday afternoon the theatre manager explained it was "this business about an omnibus. The town has never seen one, and they don't understand what one is!" Throughout the tour, whilst playing almost every town in the country, many of the "flea-pit theatres, where a fireplace was a luxury," the cast cut their teeth on the stage and gradually made a name for themselves. They always travelled to the next town on Sunday mornings by train in the early days, often begging their fare from the next theatre's manager, and eventually they afforded their own transport lorry.

In the fourth year of its tour, after 2,056 performances, the show was rescened and redressed as bigger theatres finally started to book. One of the new cast members, Roy Parry, had recently returned from the war and had been with the company for six months when it was decided to upgrade the production. Born Anthony Royston Parry in Wigan on July 14, 1894, Roy designed the sets, scenery, and electrics, which were built by himself and George Jewitt—as were many of Archie's subsequent shows. Betty Stansfield and Roy were married on April 8, 1922 at St. Mark's Church in Myddleton Square, near where her parents were living, and their first child, Archie Anthony Parry, was born on January 13,

1923 after apparently being conceived during Betty and Roy's "unhappy honeymoon."

In later years, Betty wrote, "Sex was horrible, we were both too shy. I got in the family way during my honeymoon, but I'll never know how." The pair had hardly spoken to each other before their marriage (in her biographical notes Betty refers to Roy as her boyfriend, but it was only whilst working a week in Wigan when the cast went to tea at the Parry family home that Roy's sister took Betty aside and told her that he loved her. The following day, in Betty's words, "Roy said 'Will you marry me?' I said, 'Yes.' I don't think either of us knew what we were doing. We just didn't know how to communicate."

They were married two weeks later, never having been alone other than for the proposal. They were still virtual strangers as the weeks went by, struggling on with the unhappy routine of Roy coming home at 2.00pm when the pubs closed after the show, going to bed to sleep off the beer, whilst Betty would sit and knit or go to her sister's until it was time for the theatre. When little Archie Anthony (known to the family as Tony) was born, Betty reluctantly sent him to live with Jenny and Fred in London, and later their home in Peacehaven, whilst his parents were both relentlessly on tour in a Pitt production.

This caused an element of resentment with her mother for Betty, who later wrote, "My mother didn't give him up until he was fourteen," in a controlling and domineering relationship, which involved Jenny dragging the child around to theatres regularly at all hours of the day, often to three houses per day, which his mother did not agree with.

Around this time, Archie Pitt also moved his premises, taking over an address at 84 Charing Cross Road before moving eventually to offices at Princes Chambers above the Prince of Wales Theatre. Bert Aza, who had established his own theatrical agency in 1926, took up rooms at 22 Charing Cross Road, which would remain in the family as the agency headquarters until after Lillian Aza's death in 1984. Bert's wife, Lillian, was a bright young secretary who worked for Michael Lyon, one of the top agents of the day, and suggested to Bert that he should open his own agency, showing him how to run a successful theatrical business.

By its third year the show was being billed as "undisputedly the biggest revue success ever" with "the great comedienne Gracie Fields in a £200 talk to transfer to a London show." This would not happen, however, as Gracie had renewed her contract with Archie on May 1, 1919. Her new contract stated that she was to appear as the principal artist in any of the said management's productions, but that she would find her own wardrobe for the tour. Gracie's four-year contract saw a gradual pay increase the longer she stayed with the company, starting her first year at £20 a week, which doubled by her fourth year. By the time the company was earning big money Archie doubled Gracie's contract to £100, and she suggested that her father retire from work, "where instead he took up boozing and gloating about his daughters," remembered Betty.

Provincial towns clamoured for *Mr. Tower*, and owing to so many requests, theatre managers continually rebooked the show as often as they could. Return trips were a regular thing over the seven years, with the Queen's Theatre in Poplar having the most returns with six visits, and all the major cities and towns having frequent return trips. In an interview given by Gracie in September 1920 whilst she was performing at Newcastle's Palace Theatre, the interviewer reported how Archie was the most genial of managers and offered the interviewer most of the particulars relating to Gracie's stage career: Gracie being the least inclined to talk about her career to reporter. rchie was trying to coax her out of her unassuming disposition as he realised what star potential he actually had on his hands—and just how many thousands of interviewers would flock to her. As it transpired, by 1935 Gracie Fields was heralded as the most interviewed woman in the world.

From 1918 until 1923 *Mr. Tower* ran continuously with only a two-week break during Christmas 1922, and was even offered an American tour in its entirety, which did not materialise. In her autobiography, Gracie wrote, "I am easily dominated, and Archie dominated me." This extended well beyond the footlights, when on Saturday, April 21 1923, the forty-one-year-old Archie and the twenty-five-year-old Gracie were married at Wandsworth Register Office. Rather than a conventional romantic proposal, Archie merely suggested to Gracie that it would be in her interest to marry and life would be just the same if she agreed. The marriage certificate was signed by Fred Stansfield and Bert Aza as witnesses, and bizarrely both Archie and Gracie change their ages on the certificate, with Gracie listing her age as twenty-four and Archie listing himself as thirty-eight.

After the ceremony, a party of fifty, including all the members of the cast, retired to the Crichton Hotel Restaurant in Clapham Junction, next door to the Grand Theatre where the show was playing. From there they all piled back to the theatre and a newsreel was filmed of all fifty of them comically piling out of one car and into the theatre—an effect achieved by a black piece of cloth and a queue of fifty theatricals waiting their turn. No announcement was made to the theatre, but the audience was tipped off during the interval and cheers of congratulations were shouted at the final curtain.

In a retrospective newspaper article about her wedding, Gracie recalled Edith and Betty forced her awake that morning and she had completely forgotten what was going to happen that day. "Of course something was going to happen, but what? What on earth could it be?" Gracie's dress of emerald green was banned on the morning by her mother as a sign of bad luck, so Gracie went shopping in Islington on the morning of her wedding, finding a dress of Crepe Romaine in soft beige and a hat to match. The chorus girls sent dozens of flowers, and Betty, Edith, and Annie Lipman sat frantically trying to sew new dresses to match Gracie's new outfit. Although tremendously happy but tremendously nervous, Gracie married Archie in a service whose very simplicity lent it a dignity which is often lacking in the sumptuous proceedings in a church. Gracie was given away by her father, Fred, and Archie by his brother, Bert. What is interesting is that both Gracie and Archie lie about their ages on their marriage certificate, with the pair both listing themselves younger than they actually were!   *Why repeat this?*

Gracie described Archie as a "passable imitation of Svengali" in later life (in reference to Daphne Du Maurier's character). He took over where Jenny left off in looking after Gracie. After an unhappy couple of days' honeymoon in Paris, the pair returned home to continue the tour of *Mr. Tower* and to finally get a cup of tea, which was an impossibility in Paris. "A black picture" is how Gracie described this period in her life, although she did appreciate the good work Archie did for her in helping her to become a star. "It wasn't happy. I couldn't tell you what it was, it was a black, black existence for me." She implausibly said in later years that she had only agreed to marry Archie after turning him down many times, as she feared he would fire her if she continued to refuse.

By May 1923 the company had grown and now included Gracie's younger brother, Tommy, who had just left school. Tommy had no desire at all to go on to the stage and had wanted to go to sea. Jenny insisted, however, that he must follow in his three sisters' footsteps, as at sea "you won't earn a lot of money. If you do well on stage you'll be able to see all the places you want to see even if you went to sea." The reviews heralded, "Master Fields has the potential to grow into a promising comedian," but his main role in the early days with the company was to sell postcards with Gracie's photo in the interval of the show. This was Tommy's apprenticeship in show business, in a career which would see him achieve success in his own right as a variety comedian and pantomime star well into the 1960s.

When the company played the Preston Hippodrome in 1923 Gracie took Tommy out to get him fitted for his first pair of full-length trousers, in which she said he "looked like Fred Astaire!" As his performance skills developed he was given the part of the bus conductor in the well-remembered sketch. He recalled one hilarious episode in later life. "At the end of the scene Gracie pulled her skirt off to change for the next number. One night she was at the side of the stage in her blue knickers, and the stage hands were too afraid to tell her that she'd forgotten to put her skirt on. As she was going on stage I said to her, 'Where's your skirt?' Roaring with laughter, she walked on her hands and knees so the audience wouldn't see her."

At one theatre during the tour—Tommy misremembered this as Belfast, but *Mr. Tower* did not play any Irish dates)—Tommy was astounded to see the crowds chanting Gracie's name outside the theatre. The roaring crowd broke the theatre doors down as the demand for tickets was so high. To stop a stampede Gracie popped her head out of the dressing room window and shouted that she'd put a matinee on Saturday so that they could all see her. Tommy reminisced, "Certain people are blessed with magnetism: Winston Churchill, Maurice Chevalier, Grace, Edith Piaf, and even Hitler must have had magnetism. It's almost a form of hypnotism, and you can hear a pin drop. Gracie certainly had magnetism."

As Gracie's popularity increased and rival companies were trying to book her to go on tour with them, Archie and Bert put out a press advertisement "owing to a malicious rumour." The advertisement stated: "We find it necessary to announce that Miss Gracie Fields is still with Mr. Archie Pitt's *Mr. Tower of London* review."

As the times and tastes rapidly changed, Gracie introduced new numbers to the show. Over the years that *Mr. Tower of London* toured Gracie is known to have performed many numbers. The following, although not exhaustive, is the most extensive list of her *Mr. Tower* songs that has been collected: "The Jungle Band," "What do You Mean by Loving Somebody Else?" "The Garden Suburb," "I Know Her and She Knows Me," "You Didn't Want Me When You Had Me," "You Taught Me How To Love," "The Sheik of Araby," "Lovin' Sam' (The Sheik of Alabam)," "Deedle Dum," "Wanna," "Me No Speak-a Good English," "I'm Gonna Charleston back to Charleston," "Somebody's Wrong," "As Long as He Loves Me," "Bye 'n' Bye," "All that You Can Hear is Yum-Yum-Yum-Yum-Yum!" Music was also performed in the interval of the show, including the "King Tut Foxtrot," which was composed by Archie.

Mr. Tower of London played its 3,000th unbroken performance in Leeds on August 13, 1923. Whilst playing in the town, Gracie and her irresistible mannerisms took a busman's holiday and visited the Leeds City Varieties, which she last played whilst in the juvenile troupes. Another visit to Rawtenstall's Palace Theatre saw the audiences literally laughing in the aisles at the bus sketch. By this point Archie engaged a new scene-shifter by letter, who the cast referred to as "Good old George." George had a wooden leg, and this was realised when the company all noticed that their wicker clothing baskets all had a hole punched in the top of them. It transpired that George had been walking on top of them in the moving van and his leg had gone through the lid of each one. During the run he was made a stage carpenter, a job he seemed to know very little about. Having set up the bus scene in one town, it all began to wobble and shake. On the verge of collapse, the cast made it off the bus safely to discover that the frugal George had held it together with just one nail. As much as they liked him, he was promptly dismissed from the company for nearly accidentally killing them.

A hectic tour schedule meant playing in theatres up and down the country each week, and Gracie would often spend the matinee-free afternoons taking a tram or bus as far as they could take her into the countryside, away from the town and the theatre, riding out to get the air. Whilst the company were in Barnsley, Archie received a letter from legendary West End booker, Sir Oswald Stoll. He requested the show fill in for a cancellation at the London Alhambra the following week. One of the leading theatres in London, the company didn't know if it was Christmas or Easter! Instantly, Gracie began organising things for the next week, including hiring two extra chorus girls to fill out the stage, one of who, Lilly Birchall, came from Rochdale. Urging any girl who knew how to use a needle did so, Gracie bought a mass of black silk material and ran up bloomers and costumes for all the girls in the company to dress the show for the West End audiences and to fill out the stage in colours!

By opening night the girls had made five sets of dresses for the twelve girls on stage, and Gracie was more interested in their dresses and how they performed than taking to the stage herself. "I earned about twenty-eight pounds, and spent it all on those dresses," Gracie remembered in later life. She was more than pleased when the reviews after the opening night gave special mention to the dresses and with the "Good Luck" telegram which had arrived for her from Evelyn Laye. Betty, however, remarked in later life, rather bitterly it seems, "Gracie's dresses were a disaster." Archie made Gracie promise not to tell anyone the dresses were made by herself and the other girls, as he feared that people would think the tour too poor to afford a wardrobe mistress, when in reality there had never been the necessity for one before. The best reviews, however, were saved for "Miss Gracie Fields [...] a young artist who is going to make a big stir in the world of entertainment. She has talent and personality in abundance, and an inexhaustible reserve of that mysterious quality that the Americans ex-pressively describe as 'pep'. Her versatility, moreover, is exceptional."

The company opened at the Alhambra Theatre in Leicester Square on July 30 1924 and knowing this would be big business, Archie had postcards of Gracie specially printed with a reverse which read, "Miss Fields will make her West End debut. Booking open now." He had also written a *Rules of Behaviour* manifesto which he pinned to the dressing room doors, as he believed the West End to be a "den of vice" and he didn't want any of his chorus girls falling into sin, and to be wary of the "stage door pansies that are after more than an autograph." Following the opening, critics said of Gracie, "She has been left to squander her talents on the more or less arid wastes of the provinces and suburbs." Archie's naive script of comedy, simple affairs, and back-chat received mild reviews, but it was Gracie who the press appreciated most.

During the "Mr. Tower's Cabaret" scene Gracie came down a large set of stairs concealed behind a large white fan, wearing her one-model frock of silver tissue, off the shoulders, with a crinoline skirt. She hit the audience with her new interpretation of "You Didn't Want Me When You Had Me," ending abruptly and leaving the stage quickly. In the hands of Gracie the old song was given a rebirth, and the West End audiences went wild for it, being recalled four times to the stage on the Tuesday evening's performance. Gracie had even rehearsed a proper genteel bow for the London audiences instead of her usual errand-boy whistle, but as she took her bows she totally forgot and whistled anyway.

Part of Archie's manifesto warned the girls about any gentlemen hanging around the stage door with flowers and invitations to dinner. This prospect excited the chorus girls, who were disappointed to only find "a bunch of pansies waiting for us instead!" as Gracie recalled on the BBC years later. Fearing the two men waiting for her were actually there to harm her rather than get an autograph, Gracie splashed ink everywhere as she signed her name in a hurry and rushed into the waiting car!

When the company got home to Myddleton Square, Jenny Stansfield wasn't there. Gracie had told Jenny she would secure her the best seats in the house during the week as long as she didn't come to the opening night—Gracie feared she would mess up in front of her mother. Jenny eventually came in, having been to the theatre on the bus and sitting in the gallery on her own. There was no way after twenty-five years of trying to make Gracie a star she was going to miss her daughter's opening night on a West End stage, even if Gracie didn't want her there. Rather than read the reviews the following morning, Gracie took an early bus to the Tower of London to visit the real place for herself. Never dreaming that the quaint mill girl from Rochdale with the elastic voice would make it in London, Gracie was photographed with a Beefeater inside the Tower gates, smiling proudly.

Part of the West End's fascination with Gracie was that the audience never knew what she was going to do next. Whilst there was a script to be mostly adhered to, accepted by the Lord Chamberlain's Office, Gracie had been playing the same part for over five years and this gave her a little bit of leeway with her interpretations and ad-libbing, and Archie practically gave her carte blanche to do so. Herbert Farjeon of the *Daily Express* called for the West End managers C. B. Cochran and Andre Charlot to return immediately from their summer holidays to see the extraordinarily versatile Gracie Fields to acquire her for the London stage.

In his glowing review, Farjeon hyperbolically wrote, "If, before she makes her final appearance tonight, some West End manager does not see Gracie and give her a fat contract and the best dressing room for her next review, Gracie Fields will return to the provinces, and I, a Londoner, will be deprived of the enjoyment of a first-class comedienne." Two unnamed West End theatre managers were also quoted in the papers expressing they had both tried to secure Gracie for London, but that would not leave *Mr. Tower of London* unless there was a guarantee for the rest of the company, as the show was a family affair.

Following their West End success the company went immediately back on tour and next played a week at the Manchester Hippodrome. Whilst here, Bert Aza began talking to West End managers and showing them the figures of how busy the houses were whilst they played there, in an attempt to secure a booking for the London Coliseum. This did not come to fruition, however, but the tour returned to the Alhambra the following October for a two-week run, and Gracie accepted a £100 solo cabaret spot at the London Coliseum. "This was a place that I'd always dreamed about playing," wrote Gracie in her unpublished memoirs. "I used to tell Mother that I'd earn £100 at the London Coliseum when I was younger, and now was my chance!" Appearing alongside Gracie in her West End solo debut, which opened on September 29, was Madame Lillebil, Clarice Mayne, Stanislaw Idzikowski, Ivor Vintor, the Forde Sisters, and Harry Tate. The following week starred Clarice Mayne, Jack Edge, the Cycling Bruntettes, Madame Lillebil, and Jackie Coogan— the child star of Charlie Chaplin's *The Kid*. When Sir Oswald Stoll paid Gracie her first £100 cheque she later said, "I didn't know whether to cash it or to frame it!" Having previously turned down many lucrative offers, this was the first £100 which Gracie had solely earned herself, and she regretted for years she didn't ask for a copy of the cheque which she could indeed frame.

Wanting to see how she would fare away from the review, Sir Oswald Stoll booked Gracie for a week at the Coliseum (with the intention of her understudy going on stage in *Mr. Tower*). But realising she had a twenty-five-minute break in the business at the Alhambra, Gracie worked out that this gave her time to dash up Cranbourn Street, down Monmouth Street, and arrive in time for her opening number at the Coliseum. With no time to get nervous for her Coliseum audience, Gracie performed her numbers, took her bows, and rushed back again to the Alhambra in time to go on for the next sketch in *Mr. Tower*. This "rushing around the West End," as Gracie later described it, was a precursor to 1928, when Gracie would be playing up to four separate engagements in one night. Gracie recalled in later life, "I remember when the revue was at the Alhambra I appeared at the Coliseum at the same time. I was very worried. The first time I appeared alone on the huge Coliseum stage I felt like a fly, and the main reason I did it was because with having to dash from one hall to the other I had no time to wonder whether I should do well or not! For a week I did five shows a day."

During the week's run at the Hackney Empire, on November 15, 1923, Gracie made a visit to the HMV studios at Hayes in Middlesex. It was later claimed by Archie Parnell, theatre impresario Val Parnell's brother, that it was his idea to get Gracie into a recording studio. Here, she acoustically recorded two of the current numbers she was performing in the show, "Romany Love" and "Deedle Deedle Dum." For one reason or another these recordings were never issued, and when Columbia was looking to issue her first recordings on an LP in the 1960s it was discovered that the original masters no longer existed, most likely disappearing in a purging of their archives. Gracie joked to the press, "Boris sat on them by accident!" or, in another interview, "a clumsy studio engineer" did.

Gracie next went into the recording studio in April 1928 to record her two most recent review hits, "As Long as He Loves Me" and "My Blue Heaven." Again, these recordings were never issued and the master recordings have never been found. Gracie recalled, "It happened I was doing 'My Blue Heaven' and 'As Long as He Loves Me' and I was probably overacting it as I had no idea of recording methods. You don't learn how to clown, it happens when you get fed up of singing the same song straight over and over. With my acting the goat, anything to take the monotony off made them comedy."

Over the seven years that *Mr. Tower of London* toured, Gracie is reported not to have missed a performance, and played the part of Sally Perkins at over 5,824 performances, 4,000 of which were unbroken by holidays. During one Christmas in an out-of-the-way market town, Archie insisted his leading lady must stay in a hotel, so he booked Gracie a room at a local establishment. When they opened the door of their room they were both stopped dead in their tracks by the bare floors, mismatched wooden chair, an orange box for a table, and iron bedstead with a homemade patchwork quilt. "The only source of light in the dingy garret was a candlestick stuck in a ginger-beer bottle." Not quite the luxurious Christmas Eve which he and Gracie were expecting—more like Christmas in the workhouse.

But this was not the worst lodgings which Gracie and the company stayed in. During one stop-over the company was dining with the owner of a particular hotel when a fat, brown rat ran from out of the skirting boards. Gracie screamed, "and poor Jimmy the Rat ran away," quickly followed by Gracie, who flung her clothes back into her suitcase and bolted for the door. Other landladies remained friendly with Gracie for many years after she had stayed with them, as they looked after the young girl in a matronly sort of way.

By the end of 1924 Gracie and Archie had their first home together, with Gracie's family, on Upper Street. Although Jenny and Fred started in London, living at 25 Myddleton Square, a ground-floor apartment with two bedrooms and a sitting room, where Gracie and the family stayed when on a break from touring, they had moved and taken up lodgings in a little maisonette at 72A Upper Street, Islington, above a sweet shop. Gracie and Archie both appear on the electoral register between 1926 and 1929 living at the Upper Street address, and it is likely they lodged with Gracie's parents in Upper Street whilst they were playing their London show, as Archie's premises on Charing Cross Road only consisted of offices. Archie paid all the bills for the Upper Street address even though Fred was earning well at the industrial firm he had moved to London to be with. The pair hired a Lancashire housekeeper, Mrs. Nuttall, whilst her daughter Edith did the cleaning of the apartment.

As demand became higher and theatres became larger, Gracie's Auntie Margaret Livesey came to join her on tour as her own personal dresser and assistant. Auntie Margaret was really Gracie's mother's cousin, but was closer in age to Gracie than she was to Jenny. In later life Gracie said, "There has never been a time before a show when I've not been a bundle of nerves and butterflies." Mainly because she was nervous of doing the wrong thing, and having been with Archie for over twelve years now she knew what a hard taskmaster he could be. As her fame increased Archie ordered Gracie a chauffeur-driven car as he lapped up the fame his review and his wife were both achieving. The great difference between Archie and Gracie, however, was that Archie was at home with the celebrity status, Gracie was not. She much preferred Bert and Archie do all the business deals and the press reports, eagerly assisted by Annie Lipman, who had become sort of Archie's secretary and number one.

After the untimely death of Richard Griffiths, the manager of Charburn's Young Stars, in 1924, Gracie wrote to his Daisy to ask if her daughter, Babs, would like to join her in London and be trained as a dancer. Mervyn Rossini remembered, "My Grandmother wanted my mother to complete her education, but my mother was very keen to join the show. Grace took her under her wing and had her trained as a dancer and looked after her." After training, Babs joined Archie Pitt's dancing chorus, The Pitt Girls.

As *Mr. Tower* inevitably drew to a close Archie continued to expand his empire and look for new talent to add to his agency. One such talent was Bertram Gutsell, professionally known as Bertini, who joined Archie's agency in 1925 when Archie had spotted his musical ability whilst the show was rehearsing at Bognor's Theatre Royal. Coincidentally, Bertini had starred with Gracie in one of her first appearances at the Rochdale Hippodrome in 1910. It was around this time Archie secured other reviews and was sending other tours out on the road, as he would continue to do so until the mid-1930s, establishing himself as one of Britain's foremost theatrical producers. (A full list of Archie Pitt's reviews can be found in the Appendices of this book.)

On the last night of *Mr. Tower of London*, December 13, 1924, on a return booking to the Leeds Empire, Gracie forgot her lines. After 5,824 performances, emotions got the better of her, and the rest of the company, as they all broke down in tears that it had come to an end. Full up with trouble at the pending separation from the company, and with the sympathetic audience watching the final night of a now very famous company, Gracie broke down the one and only time.

Mr. Tower had ended its successful run, so 1925 and 1926 were mainly spent for Archie and Gracie in planning his next success, time which Gracie would later regret taking away from the musical stage. The first of Archie's plans to reach fruition was the creation of a junior pit orchestra, Archie Pitt's Busby Band of 13, also known Archie Pitt's Busby Boys, which included Bertini, Nat and Bruts Gonella, Freddie Wood, Max Abrams, and George Latimer. A second group of instrumentalists, known as Archie Pitt's False Romantics, were a playing sextet who achieved success on board the S.S. Laurentic.

His first review after *Mr. Tower*, *A Week's Pleasure*, opened at the Burnley Palace and Hippodrome on January 5, 1925, and Betty Fields headlined the show alongside Walter Amner, Harry Gould, Tom Fancourt, Harry Daniels, Gerald Burrows, Claire Ruane, Regina and Frinton, June Stirling, Pat Aza, and featured the Tower Dancing Girls and the Famous Busby Band of Thirteen. The Busby Band were a group of orphans from the local Salvation Army who Archie had selected, sponsored, and paid for musical instrument tuition. *A Week's Pleasure* was presented in nine scenes, "with the greatest railway setting ever seen on the stage and a fully working revolving door which needs to be seen to be believed!" At the beginning of the run Betty was joined by Edith and Tommy, but they had left by September to rehearse for their own next show. The story concerned Myrtle Muggins (Betty), the maid of the Littlewit family from Slowborough who were going away to Blackpool on holiday with their maid (Betty) and her boyfriend, Sydney Wattle (Walter Amner), to assist their idiosyncrasies on the trip.

Betty's premier number was "I'm Scared to Death of Holding My Breath Under the Water," which was picked out especially by Gracie for her, although Betty particularly disliked the song. They were also joined later on in the run in 1926 by a seventeen-year-old comedian, Tommy Trinder, who acted the male comic lead to Betty in replacement of Amner. Gracie had no stage part in this show, and described it later as the brightest and the best that the provinces ever saw, but holidaying from the stage meant working on the costumes and the hats for the company. Betty had been hailed an out-and-out success and made a name for herself apart from Gracie, but during the run in Portsmouth in April 1925 Betty took ill and Archie asked Gracie to step into the breach and save the show at the last minute. Gracie took over Friday, April 15 1925 at the King's Theatre Southsea, and the following week in Sheffield, where there was no getting in at the theatre. Betty's illness came in the form of a breakdown, accumulated following the birth of her son, and kept her away from the stage for two years. *A Week's Pleasure* ran for six months longer than that. Whilst a replacement for Betty was looked for Gracie reluctantly took her sister's role in the show for a fortnight, to rave reviews, but causing discord within her own family.

Having been away from the theatre herself for a number of months after the hectic years touring with *Mr. Tower*, Gracie felt she was out of touch with audiences and feared she would be a big flop in comparison to her sister, who was achieving glowing reviews, which Gracie gladly rejoiced in. The revue was tremendously popular and broke box-office records set even by *Mr. Tower*. When the show was presented in Lancashire and Yorkshire, extra matinees had to be added to accommodate the people that wanted to see the show, and both Betty and Gracie felt if Gracie had not already faded into her sister's limelight she was well on the way to doing so. After a couple of weeks with the show Betty took back her place, and continued to do so until the show closed on January 22, 1927, at the same theatre which it opened two years previously.

Following her breakdown, Archie sent Betty to recuperate with his parents in Brighton and arranged for her baby to be brought down to her from Jenny's clutches in London. Betty spent days riding out on the bus along the South East coast and found a little development called Peacehaven, which was just being established along the Telescombe Cliffs. She decided this would be a good base for her mother and father, and told Gracie about the area, who immediately went out to visit with Archie.

Being close to London, she and her sisters could come down on the weekends, catching the last Brighton train after a show, and then taking a bus to Peacehaven and walking the mile or so to the house she had in mind for them. Archie bought Gracie's parents a house there as a gift, which Tony Parry later suggested was because of the conflict of control over his child bride. The house was named Telford and stood at number 12 Dorothy Avenue. Delighted with their little house, Jenny and Fred moved to Peacehaven with the young Tony, with, for the first time, a maid of their own.

Due to the lack of planning and regulation authorities, Peacehaven was perhaps one of the only places in England where a tidy villa could be found next to a wheel-less tram. Peacehaven, not actually having a harbour as its name might suggest, but jutting along the South East coast, close to the cliffs and eight miles from Brighton, the Stansfields set up home in the rural area. The cliffs were a popular suicide spot and disposal area for stolen cars, which the one local policeman, Mr. Hutchins, couldn't keep up with, so part of the beach in the late 1920s looked like a scrap-metal yard. During the twelve years Tony Parry lived with Jenny and Fred, he remembers Fred took up daily attendance at the local pub, the Dew Drop Inn, and frequent rows occurred between the adults as

Jenny rationed his spending money for ale, calculating to within half a pint how much he would be able to drink with his rations.

Setting off on his bicycle on an unmarked pathway across the fields, diagonally connecting Telford with the pub, Fred would leave at precisely eleven o'clock each morning and return at two in the afternoon, after a sufficient drinking session. Tony remembered Jenny would often stand at the back window of the house, exasperated, and exclaim, "Yer bike looks boozed!" Having successfully managed to drunkenly ride the bike the one and a half miles from the pub, he often fell at the last hurdle, hurtling through the rhubarb patch and into the back door, where he would snooze in front of the fire for the rest of the afternoon. When at home Fred tended to his chickens, which he kept in a coop in the back garden, and he allowed the milkman to graze his carthorse in the long grass at the bottom of their estate.

1925 saw a new revue for Archie Pitt's Busby Boys, *Way Out West,* which included a "safety first" sketch, a very similar one to which Gracie would record in later years on an HMV disc. The show featured a young comedian, Duggie Wakefield, who came to the production after touring with *On the Dole* with Thomas F Convery. Duggie would eventually gain popularity on his own merit, and also go on to marry Edith Stansfield at Telescombe Church in June 1930. Through the stress of *A Week's Pleasure* Archie himself became ill, which affected everyone in the company as they rehearsed for Gracie's return-to-the-stage revue, *By Request.* Rehearsals began at the New Brighton Tower Theatre in August 1925 and were acknowledged generally to be a struggle, especially with Archie having five different tours on the road by this point. In the early rehearsal days it looked likely the show would be cancelled before it even reached the stage, for Archie to focus on his other tours.

However, as the old theatrical adage goes, the show did go on, and ran for over two years. In the draft notes of her unpublished memoirs,

Betty details how she remembered, "The show struggled for nine weeks touring the North of England," and when it reached Oldham Betty came along to see it, where backstage Gracie told her sister of her personal failure. Even though her voice was better than ever, Gracie felt the people weren't reacting to her as well as they did during *Mr. Tower*, and she felt she had lost the theatrical spark along with her confidence. Betty tried to convince Gracie she was wrong and perhaps it was simply audiences that didn't appreciate her style, but as the tour dragged on for Gracie she came to realise the problem was that she had sat idle for too long since the end of *Mr. Tower*, and to keep audiences interested she had to keep herself constantly in the public eye. Regardless of her personality and individuality built up during her touring years, Gracie's eighteen months away from the stage simply made her one of the crowd.

In early September 1925 rehearsals began on Archie's next review, *By Request,* at the New Brighton Tower, promising beauty, grandeur, originality, talent, and comedy. A film experiment was choreographed by Gracie and Archie as the chorus was filmed on September fourth in the grounds of the Tower. On Monday, September 15, 1925, Archie's *A Week's Pleasure* with Betty in the lead closed at the Tower, and *By Request* opened the following week on the 21st, with the script having been passed by the Lord Chamberlain only two days before.

By Request was presented originally in eight scenes, which later expanded to eighteen scenes and later back down to sixteen, with script by Archie, costumes by Nellie Newton, and scenery again by Roy Parry and George Jewitt, built at Ernest Howard's yard in Northampton. The company was managed by W. H. Eveleigh, and the opening night reviews detailed how "no stone has been left unturned to make this new revue a masterpiece of beauty." The Mayor and Mayoress of Wallasey, Mr. and Mrs. Rawlinson, attended the opening night's performance, which packed the Tower theatre to capacity, and following a standing ovation

Archie took to the stage to thank everyone involved at the start of this new run.

Alongside Gracie in the starring roles of the revue were Tommy and Edith, with Frederick Derby, Ted Cowan, Doris Curzon, Victor Herman, Dorothy Tristran, Albert and May Hallett, and the Sixteen Pitt Girls—who were reportedly trained by Gracie—with orchestra conducted by W. H. Everleigh. Early on in the run in Wigan in October 1925, Frederick Derby was unable to appear so Archie travelled from London to take his place in the revue, and stayed for a number of weeks. Annie Lipman also had a stint as conductor in January 1927 after W. H. Everleigh left, until Philip Vierke took over full time. Later in the run, as members of the company left, the names to have appeared as turns in *By Request* were: Cedric Miller, W. E. Stephens, John Sinclair, Arlette Ravenna, Rose Murray, Josephine Ellis, Lily Birchall, Una Grenoff, Duncan Sims, Amy Brownson, Doris Barbero, Margaret Evelyn, Ernest Hire, Walter Cross, Iris and Ethel Smallman, Bert Brownhill, Fred Willet, John Dunkley, and accordion player Fusco.

On January 11, 1927 in Oldham, Fusco was replaced by another accordionist, Nino Rossini. His opening reviews told how he was especially clever playing popular dance tunes on the accordion with Italian bravado, and had the house singing choruses and stamping their feet in great bravado. Playing the piano accordion with tremendous dexterity, Nino played all the season's popular songs, including "Because I Love You," which Gracie would later go on to record. During the run Nino was given his own scene, playing Charleston medleys for Edith and Tommy to dance eccentrically to. He and Tommy struck up a lifelong friendship. Tommy and Nino would eventually go on to establish the double act, Fields and Rossini, in early 1928, with Rossini playing the accordion and Tommy performing the violin and eccentric dancing.

By Request opened with the artistic scene of a group of autograph hunters waiting to get the autograph of the stars, inspired by Gracie's experience of the pansies at the stage doors in London. The next scene, "New Friends," featured a comedic conversation between new neighbours, with Gracie playing Mrs. Cargo, an erring wife telling her neighbour of her various tactics to ensnare travelling salesmen and to get "one oop" on her husband. The musical numbers "Oh Flo!" and "You Can't Make Love While Dancing" featured large company routines, and Gracie achieved great success with the number "You Ought to see the Old Folks Now!"

The highlight of the show for many critics was the scene "At the Waxworks," set in the dungeons of Madame Tussauds after hours. As Gracie and Tommy, dressed in sailor suits, pester Cedric Miller as the attendant, a whole manner of statesmen and murderers come to life, tormenting Miller, who finished the scene crying on Dr. Crippen's shoulder, and Tommy becoming so frightened by a ghost that he swaps clothes with a nun to hide. Act One concluded in a lavish Persian garden scene. In Act Two, "A Guilty Conscience" and "True Love" reportedly provided good entertainment as Gracie played a loquacious servant to Edith and Tommy Fields' Lord and Lady. The sketch "In Hospital" also achieved good notices, where a little girl, Gracie, takes her father to hospital after he receives a blow to the head from his wife. Whilst in the waiting room they overhear the conversation between two workmen who have come to repair a damaged skeleton in an adjoining room, with a whole farce routine following about misheard ailments of various patients and the fainting song, "Going, Going, Gone!" In this scene, Gracie's eccentric ankle movement and her tomboyish whistle give added piquancy to her performance. The only complaint, from a Nottingham reviewer, that the eventual death of Gracie's father in this scene "left a nasty taste in our mouth."

To one journalist Gracie remarked, "I only know that I feel all the parts I take. For example, as soon as I get into a little girl's clothes in the hospital scene I feel I am just a kiddie, and my voice naturally goes like a girl's. It just happens, that's all. Our revue is largely a family affair, and I prefer that to London for the present. Beside, *Mr. Tower* was averaging more than £200 a week profit. I may have a season in London some time, but I am not worried about it. Frankly, I prefer the very small towns where one can be more free and easy. I love to make little alterations in my exits and entrances. I can never understand artists who do the same turn in exactly the same way night after night, with every movement precisely the same."

One of the most remembered scenes of the show was "Designing in Crinoline Days," in which eight of the chorus girls dressed as Dutch artists, painting the crinoline white dresses of the remaining eight whilst on stage—which was repeated years later in *The Show's the Thing*. Whilst the scenery and costumes were heralded overall, the same Nottingham reviewer from June 1926 complained, "We wish Gracie Fields would drop the ugly dresses and make-up of *True Love* and *In Hospital*. Our cup would then be full." The same pedantic reviewer furthered, "The waxworks scene is incomparably the feeblest of the many feeble waxwork scenes we have suffered, and the figures are quite revolting."

As usual with touring revues, Gracie often changed her repertoire as new songs were released. She and the company are known to have performed during the run: "You Ought to See the Old Folks Now," "You Used to Say 'Aha!'" "Away From You," "Mary's Mouth," "Cheating on Me," "Could Lloyd George do It?" "To Me," "Jacko," "In Sunny Italy," "That Means Nothing to Me," "You Forgot to Remember," "Only a Faded Rose," "Tonight Belongs to Me," "After Tonight We say Goodbye," "I Do, You Know I Do," "Mr. Waterhouse's House," "The Devil is Afraid of Music," and for the first time in her career Gracie performed "Our Avenue," a lockjawed number which she would still be performing over forty years later.

Following its success in *Mr. Tower of London*, "As Long as He Loves Me" was also added into this show. Nino Rossini was achieving success with a popular number, "Because I Love You," and Gracie liked this tune, so she added it into her repertoire of the show during September 1927. Other artists in the revue performed "Could Lloyd George do It?" "Crinoline Days," "My Girl's Mother," "Save Your — for Tomorrow," and "Maire, My Girl." Edith scored a great solo success with "When a Blonde Makes Up Her Mind," and in duets with Tommy in "Sweet Child" and "I'm Wild About You."

Whilst Gracie was described in early reviews for the show as "better than ever" and "a vivacious little lady with a style all of her own," it was Edith who was attaining the best write-ups. One Wigan reviewer described her as "a completely different artist. She has a fascinating manner, and in both singing and dancing she does everything in an accomplished style." For the first time, Tommy was attracting attention as a mirth provoker, an able lieutenant in playing a screamingly funny soft schoolboy, over six feet tall, who bleats like a nanny-goat. His solo song and comedy dance item was frequently well reviewed, with the picky Nottingham reviewer remarking, "What a terrific straight kicker he is!"

When the show played Sheffield, who had last seen Gracie step into Betty's place in *A Week's Pleasure*, the reviewers were particularly harsh, stating, "She does little that has not been done by her previously. That once funny burlesque of 'What'll I Do' ought never to have been thrown at us again." These sentiments were echoed by the *Liverpool Echo*, whose reviewer believed, "These twice nightly shows do not bring out her best qualities." On June 2, 1926, Archie's next revue, *False Alarms*, opened at the New Brighton Tower. Still on tour, Gracie's doctor advised her to pull out of *By Request* on September 22, owing to throat trouble, but Gracie would hear none of it after having completed 4,000 unbroken performances in her previous show.

Whenever there was a weekend out in the show the press reported Gracie and Edith went over to Paris to catch up on the latest fashion trends, including Astrakhan coats and cloche hats. Gracie told the papers, "Last week we wore Russians. Nobody seems to wear Russians in Paris, but there were some small ones with fur around the top which took our eye." Gracie was often accompanied by Archie's daughter, Irene. In the same interview Gracie laughed how the reviewer thought Edith's accent was American, condemning, "Nay, lad, she's from Lancashire and pretending to be from London!" On July 11, 1926 Gracie attended the Covent Garden Variety Artists' annual ball—the first of many such events she would attend throughout her life.

Whilst *By Request* toured the countries, the Northern rail services agreed if the company bought at least twenty-eight tickets per journey the scenery would be able to travel for free. Often cheaper than having to pay to move the scenery themselves, more often than not the company paid for the twenty-eight seats and donated the spare tickets to anyone who was at the train station queuing up to buy tickets for the same journey. When the company played Rochdale in April 1927, whilst all the members lodged at Harefield Hotel, Gracie stayed with her old family friend, Bertha Schofield, still running an off-license at 2 Milkstone Road.

Starring in the show with Gracie was Lily Birchall, who had joined *Mr. Tower of London* in 1923 and was also in this review. In later years her brother, Harry, remembered sitting in the wings watching *By Request* one evening. As Gracie made her exit from the stage into the darkened wings she tripped over Harry's legs and fell flat on her face. She got up, dusted herself off, and told the young lad, "Yer'd best watch where you puts them legs next time!" Gracie returned to London for a charity matinee concert on February 27 in aid of the Talmud Torah buildings at the London Pavillion, alongside the Two Bobs, Percy Home, Flotsam and Jestom, Noni, Fred Barnes, and Gracie's childhood idol, Maidie Scott. In Rotherham on April 5, 1927, Gracie and the company appeared in a concert at the Royal Theatre promoting local professional charities, and on April 28 Gracie appeared in another charity matinee at Daily's with Harry Green, Debroy Somers, Fred Barnes, and Chris Chatton. In July of 1927 Gracie and some members of the company were photographed at Torquay's lido pool, with Gracie donning a swimming cap and chequered bathing suit.

After an absence in the West End of three years Gracie returned to the Alhambra stage in a variety performance on November 21, 1927, described, "Wearing a silver crinoline dress and golden syrup hair, Miss Fields looks demure and exquisite." Alongside Gracie was Tommy Fields and Nino Rossini, Val and Ernest Stanton, the Jovers, Joe Termini, Con Kenna, the Three Eddies, the St. Vincent Sisters, and the Hong Kong Troupe. During this performance Gracie premiered her rendition of "Charmaine," which would become a favourite in her repertoire for the rest of her career. In her set, Gracie also performed "Because I Love You," "Our Avenue," "But I Do, I Know You Do," and "I Wonder what Became of Joe," in which she demonstrated she is quite skilled at footwork as well as vocal acrobatics. On her opening night the audience's applause called Gracie back for an encore in front of tabs, and she performed "As Long as He Loves Me" again. The next week, whilst Fields and Rossini moved across to the Coliseum, Gracie was retained at the Alhambra in a new bill comprising of Joe Termini, Albert Whelan, Horace Kenney, Archie Glenn, the Three Eddies, and Daphne.

Following this London engagement the show travelled back north to Blackpool, where Gracie told, "There's nowt like coming home to Lancashire and your own folk. I like Lancashire audiences, and I like this Blackpool audience, but by gum, they make you work!" Whilst here, Gracie and the company all went out for a day on Pleasure Beach and spent as much time as they could on the sands, where Gracie was photographed by Nino Rossini riding a shire horse. Around this time, in late November, rumours began circulating in the papers that Gerald du Maurier wanted

Gracie for the serious stage the following year.

Whilst playing Walsall in September Gracie caught an infection in her eye from a dirty towel and decided rather than find a replacement for a few weeks she would leave the company altogether. A replacement was sought, and this came in the form of Betty, who came out of theatrical retirement to save the company as she joined Edith and Tommy on tour. In her unpublished memoirs she remembered, "I was amazed to find that Edie had taken over half of Gracie's work, and she wouldn't let me do anything worthwhile." This was the first time Betty had experienced professional jealousy, which was especially shocking, as it was from her younger sister, who she had helped to train years before. Betty gradually worked her way into the show whilst Gracie was away, with a few comedy scenes in which she could outshine Edith. Her last performance as a stand-in was in Aldershot, where the Duke of Gloucester sent her a note to say although he was disappointed not to have seen Gracie in the show, he was pleased to have seen Betty. When Gracie returned that same week a military band met the company on the last night as they exited the theatre, playing Gracie's and Betty's songs. When Gracie eventually left the show she bought each member of the cast a gold watch with their name and the title of the show engraved on its reverse.

Presented in thirteen scenes, *False Alarms*, written by Archie, opened in May 1927 with Joe O'Wray in the leading role, supported by Betty Fields accompanying Joe Baker, Constance Neville, Bryn Gwynn, Freddie Hackin, Edward Hooper, Billie Barclay and Gracie Egbert, Xenia and Aston, the Famous Pitt Girls, and the Jazz Revellers. The story concerned fireman Jimmy Flames (O'Wray) who comes into fortune—and blows it all on nightclubs and a trip to Spain. Betty achieved success with "I'm Tired of Waiting for You" and "I Love My Old-Fashioned Man," which she performed on BBC Radio on August 28, 1928, shortly after *False Alarms* had finished its run.

Whilst *By Request* was on tour, Nino Rossini met his future wife, Babs Griffiths, and the pair were married in September 1928. Their son, Mervyn, remembered, "Their comedy act was, apparently, a great success. From what I remember of my parents talking, they would start with the comedy and then Dad would astound the audience with his music, and then Tommy was a very good dancer and also played the violin."

Nino had started playing the piano accordion from a young age, and was one of eight children born to Italian immigrants in Clerkenwell, the Italian quarter of London. He worked as an asphalter and saved enough money to stop work for a few weeks so that he could concentrate on his music. Mervyn recalled, "After about six weeks or so he would run out of money and would have to start work again, which would stiffen up his hands. He repeated this process many times until he gave up asphalting completely and earned a living in nightclubs and in theatres. He would practice up to eight hours a day." After the war, Nino gave up playing the accordion due to the death of variety and started a company of specialist contractors in the construction industry, which traded successfully until 1994, twenty-nine years after Nino's death.

Fields and Rossini joined Betty Fields on her six-month tour of South Africa in 1928, which began on March 16 as they set off aboard the Armadale. Betty had written a comedy duologue which had achieved some success on the British circuits between herself and her "rather attractive partner" after *By Request* had finished. Betty described this as "the first love affair of my own choice," but she tried to cancel the South African dates when she realised "I wasn't his type." His "type" being men. Embarrassed, Betty tried to pull the South African tour, but Bert Aza insisted she honor her contract, which she did, and the group returned to England via Madeira aboard the Walmer Castle in June that year. After their return, Betty and her theatrical partner split, much to the annoyance of Bert Aza, who had arranged a contract tour for them, and Tommy and Nino arranged to go into Archie's next big production, which was to be presented in 1928.

A publicity photo of Gracie. (1928).

CHAPTER FOUR

1928

And though you left a tear as a souvenir,

I'll always remember my dear, because I love you.

- "Because I Love You" (1928), recorded by Gracie Fields.

1928 WAS A VERY busy year for Gracie, and the year which solidified her name in the national conscious and in which she truly became a superstar.

In the early months of 1928 Gracie turned down the offer of a trip to Broadway to perform, the second such refusal of a trip across the Atlantic in a few years. Broadway was currently dominated by Al Jolson and the arrival of the talkies, with Warner Brothers' *The Jazz Singer* (1927) breaking every box-office record ever known. The prospect of talking pictures coming across the Atlantic was becoming a worry, as many variety artists thought the introduction of talking films would lead to mass unemployment in the music halls. To combat this, the Variety Artist's Federation began appealing to audiences to boycott cinemas and visit the theatre, creating their own manifesto against the talking pictures. Gracie was against this lambasting, however, and told the *Daily Record*, "You might as well stop the sun from shining as stop the talkies. The public will naturally want to see them. Why would they not?" This pragmatic attitude clashed with the views of the likes of Harry Tate and Harry Lauder, but Gracie saw a future in the films, even though many of her peers did not.

Following the closure of *By Request* at the Birmingham Grand on December 17, 1927, Tommy Fields and Nino Rossini started their own act as Fields and Rossini, and shared a bill with Gracie at the London Alhambra in November 1927. Rather than be managed by Archie Pitt, they signed with Julius Darewski and successfully worked together until 1938. Conn Kenna, Joe Termini, Val and Ernie Stanton, the Jovers, and the Vinton Sisters shared the bill with them at the Alhambra in 1927, and whilst there Gracie received a calling card bearing the name "Sir Gerald du Maurier," on which he had scribbled underneath, "I would like to see you." At the time du Maurier was London's greatest theatrical talent and held the affection of hundreds of society girls and admiring audiences. His plays at the St. James Theatre attracted royalty, and he was well known as an actor of great reserve and distinction. When Auntie Margaret let him into Gracie's dressing room at the Alhambra he announced he wanted her to be his next leading lady in his forthcoming play. The play was Walter Ellis's *S.O.S., Secrets of Society* (retitled to *Suspected of Sin* for the novel publication), and was to open in February 1928 at the St. James Theatre. Promising to send Gracie the script so she could "measure the part" (and also assess whether she thought she could maintain a non-Lancastrian accent for long enough), du Maurier agreed to let Gracie think about the role, which consisted of 25 pages, and decide whether or not she felt comfortable enough to take part in the serious production.

Two days later Edith helped Gracie dress her for a meeting with du Maurier in a new society outfit, but at the last moment Gracie changed her mind and rushed upstairs to change into "everything Edie told me I shouldn't wear to meet him." This included her favourite emerald and scarlet tartan kilt, purple Hungarian blouse, fur coat, and Scots' Tammy. Archie was taken aback by her attire, realising the importance of the meeting, but not bothered by his opinion, Gracie entered du Maurier's dressing room in the striking outfit. "I could walk down Regent's Street in Joseph's coat and not feel a bit abashed," Gracie later told the papers. The actor need not have worried about Gracie taking the part, however, as Gracie soon made him laugh by announcing in broadest Lancastrian that she'd "measured oop the part, lad." After measuring it she had concluded that the she could do the play, as the "speeches were long enough for me not to slip," and that she would be at rehearsals the following week. As she was booked for a brief holiday in Paris, Gracie took the play's script with her to France and rehearsed late at night in her hotel room with Edie and Irene Pitt, transforming from Gracie Fields to Lady Kate Weir, a "hard and scheming woman of the world."

Gracie recalled of her first rehearsal, "The first thing Sir Gerald had to do in the play was to lead me to a chair and ask, 'Are you all right, darling?' He did that, then he bent down and gave me a long, sloppy kiss." The kiss wasn't in the script, and Gracie didn't know what to do. So, in typical comic fashion she fished for her handkerchief concealed in the arm of her blouse and blew her nose heartily to cover her embarrassment and to wipe away du Maurier's kiss. There was a rustle of amusement from the watching actresses, who thought it comical but not at all properly theatrical. A few nights later Gracie visited Gerald's home, where she dined with his wife and three daughters with the intention of going over their scenes in rehearsal after the meal. A little tipsy, Gerald began to tell Gracie how he wanted her and went in for a kiss."Eeh, get away! Yer old enough to be my father!" she told him, standing up and leaving in embarrassment. The next day at rehearsal Gerald called Gracie to his dressing room and attempted to kiss her again. This time she slapped him across the face and he promptly began to cry at what a fool he had been. Nevertheless, this sorted his senses out and he never attempted to make a move on her again. Gracie remembered, "Gerald fell in love with all of his leading ladies—and they all fell for him—but I wasn't standing for any of that. I had a job to do."

Many of the West End's leading ladies came to the early rehearsals to try to tell Gracie how to perform the lines properly, but she soundly ignored them and continued to rehearse the way she would have done for any of Archie's revues. One morning, Gracie strolled into the rehearsal studios—packed with the West End's leading ladies—and promptly cartwheeled around the room. When upright, she stood in the centre of the room and said, "Right. Can any of you buggers do that? No? I thought not. Now let's get on with the knittin'!"

Du Maurier arranged for Gracie to visit a society duchess from Mayfair who was running a dress shop in the West End so that she could put her imitation skills to use and perhaps pick up traits for her own character of Lady Weir. The shop owner had a heart problem, like Gracie's character, and Gracie carefully observed the woman, taking elements of her character to incorporate them into her own performance. When Gracie arrived back home she told Archie that if she accurately copied any of the lady's mannerisms she'd be laughed off the "serious stage" as if she was back in *Mr. Tower of London*, as she was so ridiculous.

Becoming firm friends during the production after his initial advances, Gracie and du Maurier went out to lunch together every Wednesday afternoon, and there was always a token or trinket "From Gerald to Gracie" next to her place setting. On one occasion he presented Gracie with an expensive velvet ring box, which he nonchalantly tossed across the table to her, and inside was a diamond engagement ring. Gracie slapped him yet again and walked out of the restaurant, only to find out that it was part of Gerald's sense of humour, and in reality it was a Woolworths' ring placed in an expensive box. du Maurier often asked Gracie to perform comedy dialect songs backstage to entertain himself and the fellow cast members, which she delighted in doing.

"We were ordinary people in heart, the same," she remarked years later.

The play opened with Gracie receiving great press support in her first "straight" role, on February 11, 1928, and ran "six exceedingly happy and thrilling months" which Gracie remembered in *Sing as We Go*, closing on July 28 after 192 performances. Described in the script as "slim, erect, fascinating, and talkative," Lady Weir's costume was of beige crêpe de Chine with touches of brown with a matching scarf and beige and gold kasha coat. The opening night was the source of great worry for du Maurier, as many of his friends told him Gracie would undoubtedly slip back into her "broadest Lancasheer." Throughout Act One, du Maurier remained uncertain as to whether or not Gracie would slip up. Gracie recalled, however, that the great actor himself was the one who forgot his lines, missing a few of her cues, and so she had to cover for him, reeling off the lines she had memorised verbatim, knowing she could never move from the script like she could in review. From her opening lines, "Oh, what a dinky little place. I like this immensely," Gracie won the audience and reviewers over.

In the following morning's newspapers the press gave the production a not entirely favourable reception, because of the "laboured, improbable story," but one reviewer wrote, "Gracie Fields looks attractive, but she really is a most unpleasant lady." She had succeeded in her part.

Owen Heriot and Lady Weir arrived late one night at the Swan Inn, Uppington, the lady being under the impression it was to be a love episode. Not so the gentleman. Years ago, his dead wife had been accused of stealing some famous pearls and his career at the bar had been ruined. The real thief was an adventuress, who subsequently became the wife of a well-known politician, Sir Julian Weir. Heriot had inveigled Lady Weir to the country in order to extort from her a confession that would clear the reputation of his dead wife. There is an acrimonious discussion and the lady retires to her room. In the morning the maids find her dead in bed, but she had left a letter, clearing the name of Heriot's wife from the stigma that had rested on it.

When King George V came to visit the play he asked du Maurier why he had chosen Gracie for the part, to which he answered, "There is something refreshing and sincere about her. This play's a tragedy, but it takes a great comedienne to play great tragedy." Tommy Fields admitted later he was sceptical of Gracie playing the part of a Lady, as she was a "completely Lancashire girl." Fearing she would not be able to pull the part off, Tommy was astounded when he saw his sister's performance. Speaking to Tommy after the show, du Maurier said Gracie was "absolutely phenomenal, but I lose a quarter of the audience when she dies, as they dash over to the Alhambra or the Coliseum to see the contrast to what they've already seen. I only wish that I could do it."

Gracie's character first appears on page eight of the script and leaves in a hysterical fit of maniacal laughter on page 33, never to return and dying of a heart problem. The audience find, through discussion in Act Two, that Lady Weir has been murdered, so Gracie was able to return to the Coliseum to perform in the second house vaudeville show, which also featured Anton Dolin, who became a lifelong friend of Gracie's, and return back to the St. James to take her curtain calls at the end of Act Three. This began on March 12, 1928, and factoring in matinees and weekend performances, Gracie was doing twenty-six performances per week. This increased later on March 16, 1928 as Gracie took up a latenight cabaret spot at the Cafe de Paris, and the start of her run at the Coliseum for a week from March 12. In total, Gracie was earning £600 from her three shows, excluding recording contracts and royalties from Gramophone releases. Gracie's 32 performances a week is a feat still unrivalled in West End history. It is not known how Gracie missed taking a curtain call in *S.O.S.* to appear in her other engagements, but it is more than likely that she had to do so.

At the Café de Paris, Gracie's personal musical director was William Pethers, and so friendly she became with William (and his wife Meta) that Gracie agreed to be the godmother to their son, Ronald. During one performance at the Café de Paris, and the mad rushing from theatre to theatre,

Gracie had forgotten her change of stage clothing, and so a pregnant Meta had to swap outfits with Gracie while she performed her cabaret spot.

Gracie and Gerald du Maurier again teamed up in September 1929 for a celebrity charity cricket match at the actor's orphanage in Langley, Buckinghamshire, of which he was one of the founding patrons. The match was between the boys of the school and a celebrity team captained by du Maurier, also featuring Henry Ainley. It was a great press opportunity to photograph Gracie larking around with the famous actor with whom she had performed the year before. It is through taking inspiration from du Maurier, and his support of this charity, that Gracie eventually went on to open her own orphanage in Peacehaven. During a recording session on March 25, 1930, Gracie recorded "Douglas Gordon," which was never issued commercially, but presented to Gerald as a special gift.

Away from legitimate theatre, Gracie made her first ever radio broadcast in vaudeville on January 10, 1928, the day after her 30th birthday, starring alongside Art Fowler with his ukulele, Rex Evans, Ciceley Debenham, and Neil Kenyon. Throughout the year, Gracie made a steady stream of broadcast for the BBC, her next being with brother Tommy and Nino Rossini three days later; in vaudeville with Wish Wynne in *Sukie's Silk Scarf Sketch*, Arthur Chesney and Eric Cowley, Leslie Weston, the Emile Grimshaw Quartet on February third; a programme of her own sketches and songs on February 13.

A few weeks after the king had been to visit the show, Gracie received the first of ten invitations to take part in a Royal Variety Performance at the London Coliseum, which was to be Gracie's first performance in front of the Royal Family. Held on March first, the king remarked, "I think it is the best programme of the series of Royal shows which I have seen," with the show running without a hitch from the first curtain until the final strains of "God Save the King." Long before the Royal Family were encouraged to "shake your jewellery," the king sang along to Lilian Burgis' rendition of "Loch Lomond," and the queen offered Noni the Clown a flower from her bouquet after his touching act, "Nobody Ever Sends Me Flowers," affected her deeply. With the papers heralding, "Variety should feel proud that the king and queen honour their shows," Gracie was just pleased she had managed to go on stage and take part, despite her nerves. She cited this performance as the only time in her career when she was truly scared, and after receiving hearty applause from both the king and queen, Gracie became a firm favourite of the Royal Family.

Describing her feelings about the show, all Gracie had to say was, "How dizzy I felt through the whole thing." She played her part in *S.O.S.* at the St. James, died as usual, then headed to the Coliseum where she had to wait. "Oh, it was a dreadful wait before I went on the stage for my ten minutes." Wearing a white ring velvet dress in a Grecian style and trimmed with pearls, which she had designed herself, Gracie performed "Our Avenue," "Because I Love You," and "Charmaine." Trying not to look at the Royal Box, as she had been instructed, Gracie's section preceded the raising of the theatre's great purple and gold curtain to show the audience the marvel of the new revolving stage and the newly painted St. Michael's setting.

Following this, at the specific request of Sir Oswald Stoll, Gracie started a season at the Coliseum, "in new and old favourites," which ran from March 12, where she took to the stage at 9pm. During the run she sang "As Long as He Loves Me," "We're All Living at the Cloisters," "Did You Mean It?" "So Tired," "Because I Love You," and "Tonight You Belong to Me." Alongside her on the bill was Mr. and Mrs. Graham, Power and Bendon, Keane and Whitney, Keller and Lynhc, the Four Fellers, Moffat, Lillian Burgiss, and Vera Nemchinova with Anton Dolin. From May 28, Gracie was appearing before packed houses at the Alhambra, achieving great reviews singing "Diane" and "Charmaine," in a variety show which also starred Sophie Tucker, Will Hay, and Lilly Morris, and on May seventh she began another week at the London Coliseum in a show featuring Herman Darewski, Iris Hoey, Norman Long, the English Ballet, Fred Duprez, and Jack De Lair.

From the first week of June Gracie was appearing in variety at the Victoria Palace, where it was cited, "Miss Gracie Fields' methods of unexpectedly burlesquing her own ballad singing is a fruitful cause for laughter. But though she is a natural comedienne who seems happiest when causing fun, she can sing a straight ballad with the best of vocalists, and it is really surprising how much she can put into a number."

A second attempt in the recording studio occurred on April third, when Gracie went into H.M.V.'s studios to record her by-request hit, "As Long as He Loves Me," and Irving Berlin's "My Blue Heaven," which was popular at the time. Gracie stated, "I was probably overacting it, as I had no idea of recording methods. You don't learn how to clown, it happens when you get fed up of singing the same song straight over and over." Her voice came across perfectly well over the gramophones, but her comedy didn't hit the mark.

Gracie was back at the Coliseum for a week from April 16, alongside Will Hay, Cedric Hardwicke, Bert Whelan, Christiane and Duroy, Vittorio Orsini, Renee and Godfrey, Evelyn Braine, and Stetson. She returned to the recording studio exactly a month after her first trip on May third, again with Berlin's "My Blue Heaven," but this time backed with "Because I Love You," which Gracie was burlesquing in her cabaret act. Never burlesquing a song until "It has had a Good Hiding," Gracie put a few good notes into her recording session, which Archie had told her she wasn't to do. Coming out of the Hayes studio, Gracie had infinitely less hope for this record than her previous attempts, but the engineers were happy with it and agreed it was to be issued.

A few days later one of the managers of H.M.V. came to Gracie's hotel in Southampton with the first copy of her disc. When it was played, Gracie failed to believe that it was her voice she was hearing, as she didn't think she could sing as high as the recorded voice. The record producer reassured her it was indeed her voice, and when the record was released it was an instant success. Although there was some disapproval from music publishers, as this was the first time "Because I Love You" had been comically burlesqued, the sales shone through, and thousands of copies of Gracie's first published recording were sold. Many years later, Gracie's third husband, Boris, was rerecording some of her old 78rpm recordings and transferring them to cassette. Gracie, in later life, recalled, "Because I was working so hard years ago, I never listened to a record, only when I passed it when I'd made it. Recently I was listening to some with my husband, and I was a bit extraordinary. I'd never heard a voice like that! I thought, *Is that mine?*"

When the record was released on June 24, the reviews were very positive for Gracie. One contemporary review read:

"Gracie Fields's first record of a series she is to make for H.M.V. is so attractive that one can anticipate a run of success for her ... The singing is lifelike and real so that only a little imagination is needed to feel the presence of the popular comedienne ... She is, of course, supreme in her art of burlesque, and her new record is a ting of joy and refreshment which will bring her a new host of admirers. There is no denying her artistry or the perfection of her diction. She sings the two songs with deft little touches of humour, introducing a whimsical pizzicato effect which will provoke a smile even from the most obdurate highbrow. "

On June 25, Gracie made her debut at the Café Royal, Regent Street, in a midnight performance. With reviewers writing, "I believe that Gracie Fields could sing in a thunderstorm and still pull it off," her repertoire of simple songs, dramatic ballads, and comedy numbers were enthusiastically received. Accompanied by Miss Ruby Stewart with Hal Swain's orchestra, Gracie beat every American at their own game and was presented with a basket of flowers so large it took two commissionaires to carry it off.

Although a newcomer to cabaret, Gracie seemed to take to it very quickly and became at home in her new surroundings, even in the 140-degree heatwave that London was currently experiencing. One reviewer suggested she was too good for cabaret while he choked on his stick of asparagus as she burlesqued "My Blue Heaven." She was so successful that the Café booked her to appear in the Louis XVI suite for a further month, where her spot increased, allowing her to wear a bewildering succession of dainty frocks as she performed as freshly as if she had not already appeared up to three times before that day. This was extended even further on the July 19 when Gracie went to the Bohemian Cafe to give the clients a surprise song or two. When her cabaret season ended, Captain Nigols-Pigache eagerly told the press Gracie was to return for another stint in October, which was set to be a more ambitious affair with a far larger production, but this engagement was never fulfilled.

Returning to variety in mid-1928 saw Gracie in a brief run at the Victoria Palace from July ninth, also starring Will Hay, Harry Weldon, Les Fluher, Syd Moorehouse, the Brennans, and Iris Carr. Gracie's vast proliferation in the West End caught the attention of BBC producers, who wanted Gracie to appear on one of their shows. More radio appearances followed, including on July 18 a show also starring Billy Mayerl, Gene Gerrard, Gwen Farrar, and Ella Retford, where she performed two numbers, one comedy and one sentimental song. As a contrast, *Hamlet* was being broadcast on the other station. Later that same evening, called back by popular demand, Gracie reappeared as a surprise guest in a show with Bransby Williams, the Three New Yorkers, Harold Scott, and Elsa Lanchester.

Her next broadcasting foray came a few days later, as the demand to hear more of Gracie was so high, on July 21, where she again performed from London and Daventry, before performing at the Folkestone Pleasure Gardens with Richard Neller and Fred Wynne on August 19. More radio appearances followed, with a solo stint on September 11 and in the *Vaudeville* programme on September 24. Assisted by Lady Tree and Charles Laughton, Gracie broadcast an appeal for the League of Mercy on October third and was back on the air in *Vaudeville* programme on October 8.

Following the success of her cabaret engagements and her previous performances throughout that year, Gracie was asked to take part in a bill which sought to bring variety back to the Palladium in September and make it the number one variety theatre in the world. Recently taken over by George Black, the Palladium was going through a terribly bad patch as the modern audience had become relatively apathetic to the old music hall, but Black posted black and yellow posters around London advertising, "Variety is coming back to the Palladium."

People began to queue up for the first evening's 6:10 performance as early as ten o'clock in the morning, and when the second house audience was about to enter, Argyll Street was almost impassable as people who had tickets for the performances fought through the congested mass of those who did not. Set amidst gay curtains and bright hangings with modern cut-out scenery, the crude scenery of the old music hall was nowhere in sight, as under the control of George Black and Rhodes-Parry, they determined the return of variety to the Palladium. During the second house, Sophie Tucker made an unexpected appearance on stage, singing two of her numbers, and finally gave a speech amidst enormous enthusiasm, saying she was shortly leaving London and heading home to the United States.

Gracie and Sophie Tucker had previously worked together during a week at the Alhambra, and Sophie had offered to finance a trip to America for Gracie, where she believed Gracie would tear the roof off in cabaret. Sadly, this did not come to fruition, mainly due to Gracie's already full schedule of concert engagements and upcoming revues. When Gracie eventually did make it to America in 1931, Sophie told her she needed to add jewellery to her neck and arms and to wear bright and glittery rings. Gracie said, "I felt like a Christmas tree when I went on. I felt uncomfortable and I wasn't me." However, the pair remained firm friends throughout their lives, and were photographed together as Sophie holidayed with Gracie in Capri in 1951, each with a handsome young man on their arm as they went out for a night on the town.

Debuting for the first of many performances at the Palladium for the revival of variety on September third, in a bill also starring the Seven Hindustanis, Dick Henderson, Ann Codee, Ivor Novello and Phyllis Monkman in *The Gate Crasher*, Madameoiselle Tamara, Billy Bennett, and a whirl of dance from various troupes. Gracie was overawed as she came onto the stage in a brilliant outfit of mauve chiffon. She took her green scarf from around her neck, threw it onto the piano, and announced, "Ee, it's all a bit grand for me!" Even so, Gracie told the papers the morning after the Palladium's reopening, "Variety is going to be a big thing once more, and there are splendid chances for artists at the moment." Putting it down to pep and spirit, Gracie near-dismissed the accolades of her success at the opening night's performance, at which she sang five of her popular numbers and introduced the new "Without You, Sweetheart."

Although some critics suggested the reopening night's bill was ill-arranged and each turn had too generous an allowance of stage time, Gracie's appearance was well received by the packed house, who applauded her coy wheedling and mock-comedy, enjoying her so much that Billy Bennett could not start his act until Gracie had returned to the stage to take a second bow. Noticing Gracie had stopped the show, Val Parnell went straight to her dressing room and immediately booked her for a second appearance the very next week, continuing Black's determination to attain high variety standards at the Palladium in the future. George Black paid over £1800 to attain stellar artists for his opening fortnight's separate bills, of which Ivor Novello and Phyllis Monkman attained a fee of

£550 for the fortnight. During the second week, Gracie was moved from Act One to almost the top of Act Two, alongside Achilles and Newman, Clarkson Rose, Kathleen O'Hanlon and Theo Zambini, Richard Crean playing highlights from *The Mikado*, and the same group of dancers from the preceding week.

Another BBC radio broadcast followed on October 12, with Gracie headlining the show with Elsie Carlisle, the BBC Dance Orchestra, the Balalaika Seven, and Tommy Fields. Following on from her success in the English Cabaret, the opportunity arose for Gracie to perform at the Theatre de l'Appollo in Paris from October 15 to 18. She accepted the engagement not only to gain experience, but also "so I could have a short holiday." In her first overseas show, Gracie starred alongside over-sized xylophonist Teddy Brown and was billed as the "Great English Comedienne." Her first appearance completely captured the French audience, which for the most part scarcely understood her songs and couldn't particularly appreciate her comic methods. Yet everything the comedienne did during her set of six songs got over in her unmistakable way. Her inexhaustible fund of spontaneous humor of the communicative brand ensured she was a hit. Gracie performed her latest record release, "Our Avenue," with the play on words harking back to her "What Makes Me Love You" days, but this time purposely failing to pronounce her H's. (Interestingly, in the recorded version issued by H.M.V., Annie Lipman's voice can be heard on the recording as she chastises Gracie for not pronouncing any, "not even a young 'un'!") In Paris, Gracie also sallied into sentimental rhapsodies of "Ramona," which she later bur-lesqued, along with the comedic "Laugh, Clown, Laugh!"

Perhaps most daringly, Gracie performed in another language for the first time. Picking up the song "Reviens" whilst in France, Gracie came on for her sixth encore and announced she was to sing a song in French. "It may be more Lancashire French, but we'll give it a go." The song, which she had learned phonetically, was excellently received by the audience and was later recorded in England for H.M.V. Halfway through the French lyric on the recorded version Gracie pauses for breath and announces, "By gum! It took me a long time to learn that line!" Some enthusiasts have commented this spoils an otherwise wonderful rendition, and on one recent CD reissue the line was actually removed from the song. Gracie revisited "Reviens" often throughout her career, with notable recordings on her radio series in 1938 and also in a medley featuring "The Last Time I Saw Paris" performed at the Radio City Music Hall in 1941, where she performed the song "straight."

Gracie was back on the air in vauedville on November 12, and whilst out to lunch at the Savoy on November 16, following the success of the Palladium engagements (and during rehearsals for their next revue, *The Show's the Thing*), Archie and Gracie overhead a conversation at the next table. The famous Duncan Sisters, who had made a hit on Broadway with Topsy and Eva, a vaudeville interpretation of Harriet Beecher Stowe's novel, *Uncle Tom's Cabin*, were in London to premier the show on the West End stage. Rosetta Duncan, who played the "blacked-up" character of Topsy, had taken ill with a breakdown caused through overwork and the stress of the self-financed production. Both sisters had made a personal investment of £10,000 each for the musical adaptation, and unless a replacement could be found, the show, along with the two hundred people involved in all aspects of the production, would be cancelled and the sisters would lose their chance to carve a name for themselves in the West End.

Gracie saw this as an opportunity to show goodwill and immediately went over to Vivian's table and told Vivian she would be willing to take over Rosetta's part in the production. Although the mischievous character of Topsy was on stage for almost the entirety of the production, Gracie reassured Vivian she would be more than capable and more than pleased to take the part, and for no personal gain. She agreed to do the show there and then, and went straight to the Gaiety Theatre to begin rehearsals on the 50 pages of script she had to learn, and her new song, "Why Does the Hyena Laugh?"

It was announced by newspapers Gracie was to take over the role, and Gracie stayed awake all night with a vinegar bandage wrapped around her head as she tried to learn the lines and routines. In doing so, Gracie got a stiff neck and Auntie Margaret provided a continual supply of tea throughout the night as she crammed the lines. Rehearsals continued through the afternoon of November 17, with Gracie opening the show that very night after only a day's rehearsal and with only two cancelled performances.

Standing in the wings before the curtain, Gracie's nerves seemed to get the better of her as all the lines went out of her mind, but at her cue to give Topsy's "saucy laugh," which signalled her entrance to the stage, her professional training came to the rescue. Here followed Topsy's first line, "I's a wicked girl, I is!" and as Gracie got on stage the stiff neck disappeared entirely and she went on with the show. Gracie's greatest fear was that her attempt at an American voice would not be too funny, but with the years of honing impersonations this was no great worry. The audience was carried along for the three-hour show by her versatility, dancing, and playing the fool, along with her new comedy number.

For two acts of the show Gracie stuck solely to the script as rehearsed, but in Act Three she lapsed back into her native Lancastrian and performed a solo set of songs as Gracie Fields—but still in black face—singing her popular numbers of "My Blue Heaven" and "We're All Living at the Cloisters." Whilst these bore no relevance to Old Virginia, and more to Lancashire or the music halls of Leicester Square, the audience appreciated them warmly and realised Gracie had indeed saved the show and the Duncan Sister's reputation.

As the curtain came down the audience clamoured for more as Gracie and Vivian had to return to the stage more than four times to take bows. One of Gracie's greatest showbusiness memories is being carried down the entire length of the strand on the shoulders of well-wishers. Though biographers have previously stated it was on the opening night of *Mr. Tower of London* when this occurred, it was in actuality as she left the Gaiety Theatre after her first night covering the role of another performer. A similar event occurred the following night, when Gracie had to stay in the theatre for fifteen minutes and be escorted out of the stage door by a police escort with people climbing onto the roof of her taxi and swamping the car, the driver only managing to shake them off by the time they reached Leicester Square. The newspapers suggested the act of generosity at "considerable personal sacrifice" was typically Gracie, with her secret being "just hard work and determination," which got her through line learning.

The opening night of Gracie's engagement with the show saw takings of over £100 at the box office, however, Gracie insisted she didn't want any salary for her performance. She was only able to stay with the show for little more than a week due to the imminent opening of *The Show's the Thing*, but her well-publicised week saved the show and the Duncan Sisters' investment. She left on November 26 and was replaced by Mimi Crawford. After only two days in the role, Vivian Duncan decided Mimi wasn't right for the role of Topsy, so they switched parts, with Vivian taking a lot of performance tips from Gracie's portrayal of the character. Rosetta Duncan returned to the show on December first and exclaimed, "If any fun the show now yields, the thanks are due to Gracie Fields!" Gracie met up with the Duncan Sisters quite by chance on a New York-bound ship in the early 1940s and posed for a photo opportunity with the pair and a chance to reminisce over the performance from over fifteen years previously.

Taking a well-earned break, Gracie and Archie, with Lillian and Bert and Tommy and Nino, went "oop North" in early December 1928 to spend some time in Blackpool, where Gracie was photographed on the sands riding a donkey, and later on the promenade on a horse and trap. As the year drew to a close Gracie Fields had certainly etched her name as a West End star. It had been the most lucrative and busiest year of her career thus far, and had set her up for the future years to come. There was talk of a specially commissioned portrait of her to be hung in the foyer of the St. James Theatre as a lasting tribute to "one of the most unexpected leading ladies of the West End in serious drama." One newspaper wrote about the portrait, "I know that Miss Fields is making regular visits to a studio in St. John's Wood, where she is having her portrait painted by that well-known Irishman, John Flanagan."

Gracie makes up for the role of 'Topsy.' (1928).

Gracie Fields at the "grand age of 2." (1900)

With Clara Coverdale's Nine Dainty Dots.

With Charburns Young Stars.

Gracie's first publicity head-shot. (1914).

Another early publicity shot.

It's a Bargain tour company. (1916).

It's a Bargain tour company. (1916).

Mr. Tower of London tour company. (1921) (Shaun Hewitt).

Gracie Fields and Archie Pitt's Wedding Day. (1923) (Shaun Hewitt).

The Selinger Family. (1900s) (Jan Steele).

The Fields Sisters. (1923).

Gracie and Irene Selinger. (1924) (Jan Steele).

Studio portrait by Peter North. (Shaun Hewitt).

The 'By Request' company take a break. (1927) (Mervyn Rossini).

Riding a Blackpool
donkey. (1928).

9 Molesworth Street, Gracie's birthplace. (Shaun Hewitt).

Gracie as Lady Kate Weir in *S.O.S.* (1928).

Tower.

With 'Mac' in the garden of *Tower*. (1929).

Another rare publicity photo. (Shaun Hewitt).

The Show's the Thing. (1929).

CHAPTER FIVE

1929 - c.1930

*Happiness, wonderful happiness, where is
your hiding place? Come back to me.*

*Loneliness, infinite loneliness,
out in a wilderness I seem to be.*

- "Born to be a Clown" (1935), recorded by Gracie Fields.

ALTHOUGH IN LATER LIFE Gracie described her marriage to Archie as a "black void" and simply a marriage of convenience, in the early years of their nuptials she often reported to the press she and Archie were very happy together. In one exclusive she wrote, "I wouldn't have let Archie slip by me for anything. He's been a staunch comrade and I don't know what on earth I'd do without him. All our battles for success have been fought together and we've stood shoulder to shoulder to face whatever's been coming our way. I owe to one man all the success, happiness, and prosperity that has ever come my way." In later life Gracie's brother commented on the marriage as "a business marriage as far as Archie was concerned. I don't think he ever really loved Grace, and she certainly didn't love him. She had a lot to thank Archie Pitt for as a manager and as an artist. But as a husband, no."

There were times when the pair were bleakly unhappy. Facing financial troubles in the early years along with the stresses that came from moving a large production from town to town, Gracie said the two ways of keeping her man happy were to "feed the brute" and "keep him laughing." On one unhappy morning Gracie and Archie were getting on a tram and Archie had a face "as miserable as a Lancashire lad at Blackpool who has lost the bob he was going to spend on his winkle supper." As Gracie lurched toward her seat she did a deliberate comic stumble to get Archie and the others on the tram smiling. In the early days of touring together other cast members referred to Archie as "Gracie's young man" even though he was substantially older than her. Film producer Basil Dean remembered Archie in his autobiography, *Seven Ages*, as "a sad, curious little man with a commonplace mind and a shrewd idea of the commercial value of the wife he had acquired." His great-granddaughter, Jan, recalled, "He was a hypochondriac and would have crazy whims like not eating bread until it was three days old or refusing to eat bananas unless they were completely clear of spots. Gracie wouldn't pander to him, but Annie Lipman made a complete fuss of him."

When the young Archibald Selinger left school he thought he would like to pursue a career on the stage, but started out his working life in a Christmas-card shop at fifteen shillings a week. One of his tasks whilst at the shop was to send a batch of sample cards to two hundred different firms with an enclosed stamped addressed envelope to his own firm in case any orders wanted to be made. Two days later the two hundred letters all came back to the factory, each containing the sample card and an envelope addressed to another company. Archie had packed the samples in the "return" envelopes by mistake and he was promptly dismissed.

His next job was as a clerk for an engineering firm, Newtons, which he intently disliked. After work he relieved his stress by writing comic songs and sketches which he later performed at the local pubs and clubs for five shillings or seven-and-six a night. According to his nephew, Tony Parry, Archie got his stage name from two of Britain's most distinguished genteels, taking the name for his act as a distinguishing class marker. Mr. Newton dismissed Archie from his clerking job when he caught the young Archie scribbling down comedy scenes in the back of his ledger, including one joking his hatred for his boss. His next job was as a travelling salesman for plants and flowers, of which he only took one order in four weeks. In desperation, Archie went into the Savoy Hotel and asked to see the manager. Trying his luck, he was greatly surprised that the manager actually needed a rush job of two twenty-five-foot potted palm trees for the front lobby by that evening. Earning fifty pounds for the job, Archie delivered them within hours and the plants remained in situ for many years to follow.

Archie's first sketch was called *Flying*, in which the chief property was the basket of a hot-air balloon, with the plot revolving around a man lost on a flight. A theatre manager booked this sketch, and soon enough Archie was earning seventy shillings a week performing at the Paragon Music Hall on Mile End Road. It was here he scored his first song success with "Simple Willie," which caught on tremendously with the public, and he began to receive bookings of up to £9. A five-year contract from the Oxford Music Hall for £10 was too big a chance to turn down, but during his first performance a bout of nerves stopped him and the contract was retracted as the managers thought he wasn't up to par. His first professional newspaper notices came in 1907, where he was described simply as "The Quaint One" who "knows how to sing a good humorous song and is loudly applauded" and is a "comedian with a sense of character as well as a sense of humour." After touring the country for over seven years with his solo act, including an appearance at the Rochdale Hippodrome in the week beginning January 21, 1914, which Grace Stansfield would surely have seen. His next booking was with Percy Hall and *Yes I Think So*, and it was here that he and Gracie met for the very first time.

From the early days of *Yes I Think So*, Archie seemed to have Gracie's best interests at heart, something she attested to herself, as he arranged a better theatrical boarding house for her in Manchester (on Ackers Street) when he realised Gracie was turning up to rehearsals tired due to the long walk to and from the theatre. In addition to this, being the good houseguest that Lillian Aza spoke about, Gracie had not only started to clean the plates after breakfast and dinner, but had also started cleaning down the house with a bucket of hot water and ammonia. When Archie found out about this he immediately put a stop to it as he felt it would eventually affect her stage work.

Later, when he was setting up his own revue, Archie held auditions for chorus girls from fifteen to fifty, but being so unimpressed with the talent that turned up he realised he would have to find attractive novices and train them himself. Mothers willingly sent their children to Archie Pitt as they knew he would only accept girls who conformed to his standard, training each new girl for three months before she was to appear in a show. His personal interest in the company was only of a practical nature, as he ensured safety for all the girls, including finding acceptable lodgings for them and arranging a bank account for every new member, which is why many chorus girls remembered him as "Daddy Pitt."

Alarmingly, Gracie wrote in her autobiography, *Sing As We Go* (1960), "I don't think I ever hated anyone as much as I did Archie in those first few years. His eyes unsettled me, like the look you get from a customs man. In the early days, Archie was ten years ahead of his time, as his humour was to be giggled at not guffawed. However, I began to feel that I couldn't perform at night if I didn't see his little bald head off stage in the gloom. When I did, I was alright again."

Archie married Bertha Deitchman, whose stage name was Mary

Denver, on March 11, 1912 at Poplar Registry Office. Together they had a daughter, Rosalia Irene, on October 23, 1912, but the couple divorced on May 5, 1922. Bertha wanted to go back onto the stage and take the child with her about the provinces, which Archie objected to. Instead, she took the child to her sister's home at Ilford, and when Archie went to visit her he was refused admission and had his letters returned, torn into pieces. Archie was granted a divorce from his wife on the ground of her apparent misconduct with a man named Max at a hotel in Richmond, and took custody of their daughter, who was looked after when Archie was on tour by his mother, Bertha.

Their daughter began her own stage career as "Little Irene Pitt" with her theatrical debut at the Annual Social Night of High Road Factory, Balham on December 17, 1921. As she grew older she eventually went into her father's touring revues, where she met her first husband, Louis Rosenbloom (Lou Ross), a violinist with Archie's agency who would become Archie's musical director until 1932, when he would then take over as Gracie's personal musical director until 1937. Throughout their marriage Irene and Gracie were on good terms with each other, often taking trips to Paris together, with Irene recalling frequently in later life Gracie's obsession with swimming.

In 1929, Archie told the newspapers, with a hint of protective jealousy, "Everybody seems to have discovered Gracie except me." In the same interview in the *Blackpool Gazette*, Gracie told the reporter, "When Sir Gerald du Maurier saw me at the Alhambra and engaged me, I suppose he thought from my songs that I knew all the passion and stuff. The only lover I have had is that," as she looked at her shortish husband, "I suppose I ought to go and see some sheik films to get passionate?" Although being facetious at her husband's expense, it perhaps hints at the cracks which were beginning to show in their marriage even at such an early stage.

Archie had grown tired of the Islington apartment at Upper Street and had planned his own £12,000 mansion on Bishop's Avenue in Hampstead, informally known as "Millionaire's Row." He had also taken a suite of rooms above the Prince of Wales Theatre for a new set of offices, which had once been the home of Horatio Bottomley, swindler and politician, and had leased the entire tower at the Alexandra Palace for a rehearsal space for his productions in June 1928. His new building venture was just that, a production, as the newspapers delighted in reporting the Lancashire mill girl realising her ambition with a grand palace. Planning every room intricately, including the furnishings and the decor, Archie wouldn't allow Gracie any say in the designing of the house—even of her own private bedroom. An architect specially designed a foundation stone which read, "Gracie and Archie 1923," and work began on the grand house on Millionaire's Row.

During the construction, Gracie's father paid a visit to the building site and exclaimed, "Eeh, Gracie! What're yer building? A maternity home?" inadvertently foretelling the house's future. Archie called the red brick monolith "Tower," after the revue which had made him, and he furnished it lavishly. Situated on two acres of bracken-covered ground, with massive old oaks as sentinels, the red brick mansion was supported with Portland stone pillars which stood next to two imposing mahogany doors at the top of a semi-circular drive, bedecked with cannons. Described as the fruition of a cherished ideal absolutely regardless of cost, the building was constructed by W. Quinnell, who had the task of translating into bricks and mortar the months of Archie's careful thoughts devoted to the planning, even down to the 28 telephone lines and luxurious kennels at the back of the house for their four Airedales.

Parquet floors were so highly polished they reflected the green and cream walls and light oak staircase with a massive dome-like stained-glass window. The dining room was panelled in dark oak and supported by oak beams, reminiscent of a Tudor banquet hall, with two expensive Persian carpets, one either side of the dining table. Antique hide-covered chairs, an old sideboard, and a few unchased silver vases enhance the richness of age, except with the convenience of electrical light. Across the corridor was the small breakfast room in unvarnished oak, with a view of the garden at the front of the house.

The kitchen was sixteen feet square with well-scrubbed deal tables in the centre and fitted with refrigerators and every other known idea to keep food wholesome and relishing. Just off the kitchen was the maids' sitting room, bright and comfortable with deep seated easy chairs, whose only danger is that the bell may not always be heard. Immediately on the left in the hallway was a guilt automatic lift for the benefit of the servants, and a cupboard under the stairs which housed electric vacuum cleaners and mobile baskets for soiled linen. Also in the hall was a telephone casket equipped with a switchboard connected to a telephone in every room. One contemporary reviewer stated: "One of the doors on the other side of the hall admits you to the most beautiful ballroom I have ever seen." The mirror-covered walls were silver and gold panelled, with a sprung floor for dancing and rich mauve and gold hanging curtains. On the other side of the ballroom was the library, again furnished in light oak.

Upstairs, the spare bedroom housed twin beds in green and gold enamel and richly-figured silk counterpanes with a wardrobe hidden behind a curtain. Gracie's bedroom was a spacious room in delicate green lacquer which extended to the baby grand piano. Gold, green, and purple decorated the room, which lead to her own bathroom. White and black-grained marble to the ceiling, a bath, untarinshable fittings, inviting mirrors, and a plate-glass encased shower bath.

The main bedroom, which was used by Archie and Annie, not Archie and Gracie, was thirty feet long and covered in green plush with gold curtains. Two rich oak beds were concealed behind embellished curtains set on a semi-circular platform reached by two steps, with rich counter-panes above the beds. The bedroom overlooked the expanse of the back garden and lead to Archie's own private study. Across the corridor was a sitting room in purple plush, which was the sitting room of Tommy Fields' own self-contained three room flat. Annie Lipman's official room was decorated in blue and gold Chinese lacquer furniture, with her bathroom in white and green, but this was mainly used by Archie's daughter, Irene, although she denied this in later life. Auntie Margaret also had her own set of rooms, and on the third floor were the servant's bedrooms and bathrooms, all tastefully furnished with the acme of comfort which every maid aspires.

Among the large gardens ran squirrels, and at the back of the house was a set of kennels for the Airedale dogs which Gracie and Archie kept. These were later joined by a parrot called Mac, which Archie had picked up in Skegness, and apparently a pet monkey which had its own setting at the dinner table. A Lancashire cook was hired on Gracie's orders, named Maggie Walker. Gracie gave her the surprise of her life when she discovered that Maggie's three brothers, whom she believed had died in the War twenty years earlier, were all in fact still alive. So, Gracie paid their train fare from Glasgow to come and stay for a few days at Tower during early July 1928. Often, Gracie took her meals in her small sitting room with Mrs. Nuttall and Edith. On one occasion Archie lambasted her for having tea with the servants, which he believed was Gracie lowering herself. The mauve and gold chocolate box of a house really was not Gracie's ideal, whilst Archie was enjoying the millionaire's lifestyle. He insisted she stop visiting Woolworths, that she was to have a mink coat, and buy a Rolls Royce. Archie also bought himself an American "hot-stuff" car, and Gracie had her own "pigmy car," a Ford, which she did her own running around in as she did not like the ostentatious cars Archie continued to buy. Along with Auntie Margret, the rest of the staff included Reginald Bettinellie, Henry Lammond, Jessie Lammond, James Collister, David Martin, Vittorio Righini, and Archie's private butler, Reginald Burrows, who would stay with Archie until 1937.

Archie eventually conceded, at Annie's persuasion, and agreed to let Gracie decorate her own room in "all the heart-warming colours that I could find." He was horrified when he saw the results and was thankful it was at the back of the house, yet all Gracie wanted to achieve was to "allow guests to sit in the room in rolled-up shirt sleeves without Saville Row suits or Oxford Street shoes and sit in their socks by the fire." To Archie's further horror, whenever he brought guests to the house they all gasped in polite amazement at the splendor of the rooms, but always ended up sitting in Gracie's crazy-coloured room. Realizing this, he moved Gracie downstairs and made this his own office, giving her a room directly facing the garden. She planted various seasonal bulbs and flowers which could be admired, when in bloom, from the window, and she added brightly-colored watercolours as a contrast to the rich oil paintings throughout the rest of the house. Everybody was soon sitting in the conference drawing room again as opposed to Gracie's old room upstairs, which she counted as a personal victory for herself.

Speaking of her wealth, Gracie told the press, "The material side of success is very pleasant to me. It means that I have been able to set up my mother and father in a farm in the country, and that I can have a beautiful home. In the old days when I was playing a seaside town, I used to have a 'bob ride' along the sands whenever I had chance. Now it is nice to know that if I like I can ride in Rotten Row and swim in my own swimming pool." Gracie remarked, however, "The sad thing is that I can only live in one room at a time."

On December 28, 1928, Archie's new show, *The Show's the Thing*, began its pre-London try-out run at the King's Theatre Southsea before touring the UK in various venues for the next twenty-three weeks. The show eventually moved into the Victoria Palace in London on June 4, 1929, when the current variety season ended. With music and lyrics by Gordon Courtney, scenery again by Roy Parry and George Jewett, and the orchestra conducted by Annie Lipman, this revue promised sixteen unrelated scenes and sets and costumes which to rival the famous *Mr. Tower of London*. One of these, the opening number, was set in a massive circus tent and involved the chorus girls performing tricks with hula hoops and balloons. Gracie was variously featured in the show as "The Lady with the Elastic Voice," "The Maid Victoria," "Spanish Dancer," "The Schoolroom Cleaner," and even Archie's daughter in one scene.

Whilst in Southampton on January 12, Gracie attended a Red Cross Ball at the Bungalow Cafe along with her brother, Tommy, and leading dancer, Monti Ryan. Whilst 'The Show's the Thing' was playing Southampton Empire, Joe Baker, who would later go on to become a comedian in his own right, made his stage debut when Gracie brought him on stage as a six week old baby Another charity event at the Cardiff Empire Ball followed on January 22, and on February seventh Gracie presented the prizes for Best Ankle, Best Head of Hair, and Best Beauty at the Hull Palais de Dance. On March first Gracie and company visited the Ministry of Pensions Hospital at Dunstan Hill, and the following week appeared at the National Union of Journalist's Ball at the Adelphi Hotel in Liverpool, where she performed a solo cabaret spot and was presented with a basket of fruit as thanks.

It was in her part as "The Maid Victoria" that Gracie got the most laughs in the show. Using her Chaplin walk, which she mastered in her early touring days, Gracie served the dinner guests at a party held by Mr. and Mrs. Banktop, played by Mary Ludlow and Archie. In the scene, Gracie's comedy business involved cleaning wine glasses with a feather duster and spilling soup over the guests' lap. So popular was this routine that it was partly filmed for a Pathe newsreel. Gracie even rehearsed how to successfully achieve the "whip off" tablecloth trick, which she included to great reviews, and one evening spied a bicycle at the side of the stage and rode around, setting the table from the bicycle. So hilarious were her escapades with the bicycle they were kept in the show as a regular part. Another scene, "Copper Blues," involved a full company of over forty policemen lining the stage. Two of the songs from the show, "Copper Blues" and "Dancing Shoes," were so successful that various dance bands, including Ray Noble's famous band, covered them on 78rpm records.

As with previous revues, Gracie's numbers throughout the run frequently changed to feature what was popular at the time, and she is known to have performed: "Like the Big Pots Do," "We're All Living at the Cloisters," "Sentimental Fool," "They All Make Love but Me," "I Love No One but You," "The Show's the Thing," "Painting the Clouds with Sunshine," and duets of "Thank Heaven for You" with Monti Ryan, and "Cute Little Flat" with her husband. This was recorded on H.M.V., as were many of the songs in the show, and features comedy patter between Gracie and Archie discussing each other's problems, such as Archie's bald head and bow legs and Gracie's apparent knockknees.

Whilst the show was playing the Liverpool Empire in March 1929, before moving off to play the Manchester Palace the following week, H.M.V. sent a remote recording van to attempt to record Gracie's latest 78s live on stage, and three recordings were made on March 14, only two of which were released. It is likely that H.M.V. did this to keep up with the demand of Al Jolson's "Sonny Boy" record, which was proving to be the fastest selling record ever (the fist million-selling record), and H.M.V. wanted Gracie to be the first artist on their label to record the song.

During the show, Tommy Fields was also given more solo comedy business to do, and even a violin solo and comedy numbers "I Wish She'd Come Along Now," "Connie in the Cornfield," and "I Ain't Certain."

When the show opened at the Victoria Palace for a limited run on June fourth, Gracie was dubbed by some reviewers as "England's Sweetheart," with the only criticisms of the show being the prompt could be heard all too often from the wings, and that Annie Lipman's hairdo got in the way of Monti Ryan's delightful dancing. Annie had a tough task conducting the show, as she told the newspapers, "Gracie's work is spontaneous. She is liable to do things differently without notice, so I have to be purposely alert." Gracie's pianists in later years often commented that she would speed up a song, change a song halfway through, or choose a completely different selection than agreed whilst on stage, so they had to keep awake, and it seems that Gracie was playing tricks on her conductors as early as 1929. One impressive scene, "We're Not so Bad as We Painted," featured the chorus girls in washable dresses being painted on as the number proceeded, inspired by a similar scene in one of Archie's earlier revues.

In London, on May 24, 1929, Gracie appeared in an all-star charity matinee concert in aid of the Anglo-French Ambulance Corps at the Phoenix Theatre alongside Florence Desmond, Sonnie Hale, Jessie Matthews, Vic Oliver, Jack Warner, and Douglas Byng. On June fifth the company took a matinee off and hired a charabanc for a trip to the Derby, and the following week Gracie and her two sisters attended a theatrical charity garden party where Gracie won first prize in the treasure hunt then entertained the guests with songs performed with balloon helium, which was recorded on camera. On June fourteenth Gracie appeared in a high society charity matinee concert in aid of the National Birthday Trust Fund at the Apollo Theatre, accompanied at the piano by Fred Ferris. Along with Gracie on the bill, presented to the Duchess of York, were Stanley Holloway, Ann Penn, the Adams Sisters, Brian Lawrence, Bobby Howes, Ellen Ford, Leslie Hensen, and Sydney Howard, with the show topped by George Burns and Gracie Allen.

In other excursions during 1929, Gracie presented smoking pipes to old music hall theatricals at a charity event and was also made a Life Governor of the London Royal Free Hospital on Grays Inn on December 12. More radio appearances were scheduled, including a solo spot on the BBC on July 30 and an appearance in vaudeville programme on August second, and on November 14 Gracie was again a guest at the Variety Aritst's Annual Ball. On August 11, 1929, Gracie was back for a second Sunday concert at the Folkestone Pavillion with Mabel Constanduras, Marie Dainton, and Norman Clare, and on September 24, attended the wedding of British film star Chili Bouchier to Harry Milton, the juvenile lead in *The Show's the Thing*, at Paddington Registry Office. The next weekend Gracie was at a bicycle race meeting at Herne Hill, where the chorus girls of the company were racing. Having practiced for weeks around London, the Lyceum Cup was presented by Gracie to Millie Hire, "a big girl from Newcastle" who was making her debut on the cycle track.

Gracie made her first return to Rochdale since she had made it big in August of that year. Stopping for a quick visit on the 27th, she performed in two houses as she opened the new Rialto Cinema. For the sake of old associations, Gracie took no fee for the performance, and instead a donation was made to the Music Hall Ladies' Guild, of which she was currently president. Her train arrived at Manchester Central Station at 4:25pm, and a car took her to back to Rochdale—it was the first time she had made the journey through the land of her childhood in an automobile. The emotions of performing for her native townspeople with whom she had played and worked with in the mills got the better of Gracie, and she cried as she walked on stage to thunderous applause from her old friends.

One of the usherettes at the new cinema was a young girl named Annie Oates, who was still trying to find her way around the new cinema when Gracie arrived, as it had only been open a week. Trying to find where the staff cloakroom was, she barged excitedly through the wrong door and straight into Gracie's dressing room. Gracie turned to the young girl from her dressing table, where she was brushing her long auburn hair, and asked, "Is everything alright, love?" Annie explained she was looking for the cloakroom, and Gracie got up and showed her the way herself.

On November first, whilst Gracie and Archie were at the theatre, thieves broke into Tower using a ladder they had taken from a neighbouring house, climbing into one of the upstairs windows. Although the maids were both in the house, neither of them heard the robbery as the thieves made away with one of Gracie's fur coats, trinkets, jewels, and Scotch skirts, wrapping them inside one of Archie's large leather overcoats to make their getaway by car. Ever the optimist, Gracie said, "They were actually quite nice burglars," as they left a large silver mirror inscribed to her from the Duncan Sisters, a gift for stepping into Topsy's shoes.

As the rift between Archie and Gracie grew, Betty and her sister began spending more time together, and frequently visited the Cafe Royal after performances. Gracie and Betty mingled with the theatrical people whilst Betty's husband, Roy, mixed with the camouflage painters from the First World War and other war veterans like himself. Betty remembered, "Some nights these greats, Augustus John, Epstein, the famous model Delores, would get together in a room that looked like a scene from the brush of Tolouse Lautrec: red velvet plush seats, marble tables, and decorative bar complete with colorful barmaid." Whilst Betty's memories of the room were of "a new world," it was here that Roy Parry introduced Gracie and Betty to Augustus John, Henry Savage, and an Irish painter named John Flanagan.

Flanagan had known Roy since the First World War, when the pair were both infantry soldiers together, and Betty attempted to play cupid between Flanagan and Gracie, as "by all accounts, Gracie was a very mixed-up woman" as her marriage had begun its final breakdown. John, born November 24, 1888, was the son of a distinguished civil servant and had left his hometown of Ballinrobe against his family's wishes that he would follow in his father's footsteps and eventually become a politician. Flanagan, however, preferred to live as a bohemian in London. Betty's son, Tony, described John as "a likeable bohemian soul who always had time to joke … and evidently the tonic that Gracie needed."

In her unpublished memoirs Gracie described two men who would have a great impact on her life: Henry Savage, "a small, clever, restless man with a Cyrano de Bergerac nose and sensitive eyes," and his companion, Flanagan, as "a broad Irishman with curly black hair and the saddest eyes I have ever seen." She furthered her description in her published autobiography as "he gazed at me with all the combined pensiveness of good whisky and his Irish nature," and the pair instantly clicked as friends. It was Betty who boisterously suggested John should paint Gracie, who agreed that he saw "pictures in a fire … Joan of Arc praying before a battle, freckled choirboys singing in the snow, Grock the Clown and Florence Nightingale with the Mona Lisa's smile." Henry Savage, who was sitting, stroking a small tea-coloured kitten, blurted out, "The Mona's Lisa's smiling like that because she hasn't got any teeth. That's her secret!"

During this period, on stage Gracie was electric, whilst after a performance she would shut herself down to wait for the next evening's show. At aftershow parties and meetings people stared at her in anticipation of her saying something funny. When Gracie didn't, they were often surprised and sometimes offended. Flanagan agreed that if he was to paint Gracie it would be for "the sorrow behind her eyes" and not for who she was on stage. Gracie was amazed she had known Flanagan for less than an hour and he had already seen right through the facade of a happy-go-lucky performer and seen "the daily grinding of life of Archie and Tower." When Gracie told Archie the next day she was going to have her portrait painted, he was concerned at how much it was going to cost and to get it in writing that Flanagan was going to paint her for free. Naturally, Annie backed up "The Guv'nor," which immediately took all the happiness out of the portrait for Gracie.

What shocked her even more was that Archie stipulated the portrait could not be painted the coming Thursday, as he had arranged a meeting with a solicitor to create a will. It was Annie who told Gracie, "You're an important woman now, dear, if anything should happen to you all your affairs must be in order." Gracie was stunned and realised that this was the final straw. Without time for her to think further, John turned up and began making preliminary sketches of Gracie. "He talked all the time and his voice soothed me," Gracie later recounted. He talked about books, artwork, and bargains in Chelsea secondhand shops, and on every subsequent visit he made he took her a small trinket or curio he had picked up along the way. "These tokens meant more to me than any of the riches which I kept in my 'palace,'" remembered Gracie in her unpublished memoirs.

Much to the annoyance of Archie, the scruffy artist often brought along Savage, who kept Gracie company during the portrait sittings. The two men opened new doors of education for Gracie, which infuriated Archie as the pair began to quarrel even more, ending with him banning the two men from coming to the house at all. Instead, Gracie took secret trips with Auntie Margaret to Flanagan's studio in St. John's Wood, hidden behind a row of terraced houses. He told Gracie, "At night on the stage you look as if you don't know what misery is. You give off sparks and your eyes shine. Next day, you sit and you look half dead." He sensed something was not quite right at home with her, whilst Grace often found herself crying at the studio, eventually telling John everything of her unhappy life.

When Annie found out about this, she reported everything back to Archie and even told Gracie she was being unreasonable by not doing what her husband told her to do. When Gracie told Archie firmly she did not want to make a will, he told her she was "impossible to talk to these days" and left the room, followed by Annie, who rebuked Gracie by shaking her head. Gracie remembered how the arguments between the three of them always left her feeling like a villain, and when her friends announced they were going on a trip to Cannes, Gracie packed her bag and left Archie for good.

This was two weeks before the June opening of *The Show's the Thing* at the Victoria Palace, and as Gracie watched the grey, crumpled sea curdle behind her, she realised she made a mistake in coming away. It gave her no sense of freedom, and when she reached Paris she called Betty. Roy answered and told her bleakly that Betty had gone away to their parents' home in Peacehaven. The whole cast was devastated that Gracie had left the show suddenly, mainly as it was going to be Tommy's big solo break in the West End. Although John told her, "Human happiness is more important than stage shows," Gracie realised that it was her family's happiness that came first, and she returned to London to honour the run, taking the midnight steamer back to England. Annie opened the door of Tower and told her, "I knew you'd come back. I told the Guv'nor not to worry."

Although Gracie still carried on her now not-so-secret relationship with Flanagan, she honored her role in the show, and honored Noel Coward in getting her hair redone to remove the kiss-curl in her fringe, which he said he hated. As the variety season was set to return to the Victoria Palace, *The Show's the Thing* transferred to the Lyceum Theatre on August 19, where, even though the box office was taking in more money than the previous shows, the theatre managers still turned the show out, so it eventually played three West End theatres, the third being the Winter Garden Theatre on Drury Lane, where it opened on November 27. On September seventh, Tommy Fields announced to the press his engagement to Gracie's understudy, Dorothy Whiteside, who he married the following March. During the run John took ill, and Gracie went back to his studio before going home to make sure he had a fire going and to take him round fresh bread and milk to ensure he would eat. "I wasn't in love with John Flanagan, nor he with me, and my sister knew it, but he was my friend, and he was ill," writes Gracie in her autobiography, but many close to Gracie have argued otherwise, that the pair were indeed in love.

Whilst the show was playing at the Lyceum, the great opera star Luisa Tetrazzini came to visit on October 23. She heard that although Gracie clowned half a dozen operatic arias in a mixture of Lancashire, Italian, and French, she was getting all the top notes (which she had learned solely from Gramophone records). Tetrazzini sent a note back-stage asking whether Gracie would sing part of "La Traviata" for her. Horrified at the thought of singing mock-opera in front of one of the greatest stars of all time, Gracie attempted to guy her songs as she did every night, but found herself a nervous wreck in doing so. The bulky dark-haired Frenchwoman eyed Gracie through lorgnettes whilst Gracie agonised over whether to do the song or not. Would it be more of a snub to guy the song or to ignore Tetrazzini's request? Archie decided for her in the interval, demanding her, "Do it. You can't go wrong."

The schoolroom cleaner scene saw Gracie scrubbing the floor in a cap and greasy hair whilst telling earthy jokes, the climax of the number calling for her to throw a wet dishcloth at the audience! Deciding to perform for Tetrazzini, Annie Lipman conducted the number in a higher tone so that Gracie would have to struggle to reach it and naturally be forced to guy the number so even Tetrazzini would realise why she was singing comically. Sweating at the possible onslaught, Gracie took to the stage, and Tetrazzini stiffened when she heard how high the opening chords were played, swinging her lorngettes violently to Annie in the pit. Gracie remembered the audience stirring like the trees in autumn when the wind blows through the bare branches. There and then she decided to sing the number straight, and had reached all of the high notes of "The Polonaise" from Mignon, not the requested Traviata—which she didn't know all the words to.

Rushing to her dressing room, she found Tetrazzini already waiting for her. "My dear," she said, "oh, my dear, you must sing in opera, in good, great opera, not, not this …" And with a wave of her hand Tetrazzini dismissed the whole Lyceum Theatre. However, Gracie couldn't be swayed no matter how hard Tetrazzini tried to persuade her. Although Gracie later claimed she ached to her soul as "I wanted so badly to go with her," she knew it wasn't where her heart lay. The pair were photographed together, and Tetrazzini signed a copy of her recording of the Polonaise for her and asked Gracie to sign a copy of the same disc back.

In the programme for the Lyceum run of *The Show's the Thing* there are two adverts featuring Gracie: one for Sarony cigarettes and the other for "Keeping a lovely skin with Pond's Cold Cream." This was one of the first times Gracie appeared in advertisements, although through the years she appeared in hundreds of advertisements for different products, many of which she certainly wouldn't have used. In the early 1930s every post sack received new advertising offers. "So-and-so's gloves, garters, gaspers, and gumdrops, and I had to turn them all down!" She didn't turn every advertising offer down, however, and she is known to have advertised Potter's and Moore lavender cream, Lux soap, Hurseal heaters, Wayfarer raincoats, Personna razor blades, Tenderleaf Tea, Fizzy Water, Oldsmobile cars, Barnes pianos, Eastern foam cream, De Reske cigarettes, Arrid deodorant, Anona soap, Viennese jumpers, Aquatite raincoats, Marquise hairnets, Norbury shawls, Surf Maid tinned shrimp,

Smiths crisps, Mars chocolate, Wix cigarettes, Macleans toothpaste and chewing gum, Phillips televisions, Jamaican rum, Martini cocktails, Hercules bicycles, Phosferine, Adams caravans, Recumbent cycles, and the LNER.

Gracie and Archie appeared in court on November 13, 1929 in the role of litigant in the Chancery Division in front of Mr. Justice Eve. Sir Patrick Hastings KC acted on behalf of Gracie and Archie and moved ex parte to restrain Walter and Frederick Melville, the proprietors of the Lyceum, from publishing a statement that *The Show's the Thing* was to come to an end on November 23. Although the show had been a continuing success since it had opened in August, the Lyceum was booked for a pantomime season from December, but Archie refused to move to the Melville's other theatre, the Princess. So, the theatre proprietors erected hoarding intimating that the show was closing permanently, when in reality it would only be transferring to another theatre. The judge served that he would restrain the Melvilles from publishing any further notices about the "closure" of the show, with costs in Archie and Gracie's favour. Eventually the show closed on November 23 at the Lyceum and opened on November 25 at the Winter Garden Theatre, Drury Lane. It was estimated that in the 23 week pre-London tour 300,000 people had seen the show, 150,000 during the eleven weeks at the Victoria Palace, and 350,000 in the fourteen weeks at the Lyceum.

For the Winter Garden opening on November 25, Gracie had a wardrobe of new dresses created, with sixteen yards of green chiffon being used in the creation of one dress alone. Two other dresses consisted of twelve yards of black velvet and another in blue chiffon. To fit into these Gracie stuck to the apple diet, and on December tenth she made the chorus girls of the show sign a dietary pledge. "We undertake, in the interest of health and a trim, slender figure, to adhere to a rigid daily diet, not to eat between meals, to smoke cigarettes in moderation, and to drink hot water every morning before breakfast." Some of the girls told the press they had lost up to seven pounds by adhering to Gracie's diet over the past fortnight. Proud of this fact, Gracie remarked, "Personally, I eat everything that should make me fat, but I am very active and my weight has not particularly increased since I was seventeen years old. I am not imposing a strict diet for the girls."

Later that month Gracie presented Banardo's charity with an extremely large Christmas pudding for their charity raffle to help toward raising the £1,000,000 target they were looking for. On December 19 Gracie and Tommy lead the singing of "The Song of the Donjeroos" at a matinee at Olympia at Bertram Mill's famous Christmas circus in front of 6,000 Donjeroos between the ages of 7 and 16. Gracie also appeared in a charity show at the London Palladium in aid of Brinsworth House, the retirement home for members of the theatrical profession, headlining a bill which comprised of Norman Long, Naughton & Gold, Will Fyffe, Will Hay, Talbot O'Farrell, Dick Henderson, Debroy Somers, Billy Bennet, Teddy Brown, Charles Austin, Nervo and Knox, and Lilly Morris.

Archie's next show, *Making Good*, was produced at the New Theatre Northampton on July 22, 1929. Presented in nine scenes, the show was headlined by Duggie Wakefield alongside Betty Fields, Richard Neller, Billy Nelson, Chuck O'Neill, and Clarice Clare. The show centred around Wakefield and Nelson as the life and soul of the entertainment business who play college students expelled for playing a practical joke, much to the displeasure of their fathers who do not wish to see them again until they have made good. The pair try everything from starting a garage on their last month's allowances to trying their hand at builders. In an endeavour to escape a creditor they seek refuge in a Turkish bath, not realising it is only for ladies, they then leave for Paris on a cross-Channel steamer and try their hand as stewards before securing positions as waiters in a Paris nightclub, where they are discovered by their fathers, who eventually forgive them. The scene in the garage allowed the pair to show their skills with an innertube and Nelson's acrobatics on the building site. The show ran until October 1930, when Duggie had to pull out of the show after suffering an accident on stage in Portsmouth and badly injuring his eye.

On January 12, 1930, Gracie broadcast on behalf of the Golden Square Throat, Nose, and Ear Hospital in *This Week's Good Cause*, and so complicated and tongue-twisting was the language that Gracie fell about in fits of laughter halfway through the appeal before checking herself and apologizing and proceeding to sing for them. Three days later, Archie, Tommy, and Gracie performed on the BBC in excerpts from *The Show's the Thing*. On Valentine's Day Gracie presented the prizes and performed one solo number at the North London branch of National Union of Journalist's dance at the Alexandra Palace, accompanied by Irene Pitt and presented with a bouquet of Lilly of the Valley as thanks, coming straight from the theatre to do so. Another charity show followed on February 19 at the Winter Gardens for Orphans of the variety profession, starring alongside Peggy O'Neill, Gerald du Maurier, Ivor Novello, Violet Lorraine, and Naughton and Gold. Gracie was playing that week at the Manchester Palace and caught the train especially to London to honor her promise to star in the show.

Before the London closure of *The Show's the Thing*, Archie presented a national tour which began on December ninth at the Newport Hippodrome with Polly Meadows and Stanley Brereton taking Gracie and Archie's roles. The tour was not a success, as audiences were expecting to see Gracie Fields, but Archie honoured Polly's contract as best as he could, with Gracie taking on some of the shows. After the London closure of the show at the Winter Garden on February 8, 1930, Gracie headed straight to the Manchester Palace for a fortnight from

February tenth, taking over from Polly, and she did the next four weeks at Liverpool, Southampton, and Streatham Hill. Whilst Gracie was in Manchester, she visited the Bolton greyhound track and was presented with a greyhound as a gift, which she donated back to the club. There were some newspaper rumours Gracie secretly visited Rochdale with Annie Lipman one afternoon, to visit old friends, which is highly likely, but probably not with Annie.

On February 23, Gracie was a guest at the Variety Artist Ladies' Guild event, and on February 27, at the Liverpool Empire in the third week of touring, Gracie and Betty Balfour visited the Lancashire Cotton Fair at the City Hall on Deansgate before heading back again to London for a second concert in aid of Brinsworth House at the Victoria Palace. March first saw further charity concerts at the London Palladium in aid of the Sadler's Wells Theatre starring Sybil Thorndike, Stirling Mackinlay, and Leonard Harvey. Archie decided against closing the tour after Gracie had rebooted its success, and when Gracie left to go back to variety in March 1930 the tour carried on for another three years with Peter Fannan, Bert Wright, Peggy Stamula, and Dan O'Shea.

Gracie was at church on March 20 as a guest at the funeral of Harry Weldon. On March 31 Gracie and Annie Croft were the first two female variety artists to be broadcast by the BBC in test transmissions from Baird Company's headquarters in Long Acre. Remembering this event 46 years later in a BBC documentary, *The Birth of Television*, Gracie recalled, "Well they took me in this tiny box and they said, 'Sing!' I said, 'But there's nothing to sing to?' So I'm put in this room, a smallish little room, about the size of a telephone kiosk you see in the streets, well, they put me in there and said, 'You're going to sing through here.' Well, I could see, to me, it just looked like a little brick wall. I said, 'Are you kidding? Are you pulling my leg?' They said, 'No! You sing through there, and it's going to be seen a mile away.' Well, I thought somebody was pulling my leg or something, but I've sang in so many places, so I just thought, *OK, we'll go in and sing.*" The press described the broadcast tests as a success, and although not perfect, they were remarkably clear as Gracie sang "Nowt About Owt," "Son of the Road," and "My Indian Moon." That same evening Gracie appeared at a dinner dance and cabaret in aid of the Oak Hill Journalist's Home at the Greyhound Hotel in Croydon.

During the run of *The Show's the Thing* in March 1930, Gracie presided over one of the stranger contests she ever judged: the winner of the "most shapely foot" from the chorus girls of the review. Standing in ink and leaving an imprint on a sheet of paper for anonymity, Dorothy Whiteside won first prize. May 13 saw Gracie back headlining at the London Palladium, in Greta Garbo makeup, in a bill shared with Johnson Clark, Payne and Hilliard, Jerry and her Baby Grand, the Houston Sisters, Buck and Bubbles, and Gerladine Valliere. Gaining credit for her mixing of the sentiment and the ridiculous, Gracie performed "Three Green Bonnets," "Stop and Shop at the Co-Op Shop," "Body and Soul," "A Couple of Ducks," "Nowt About Owt," "Sonny Boy," "Reviens," and "I'm a Dreamer" during her two-week run at £700 per week.

In April 1930, sister Betty returned from a successful tour of the United States, achieving much more success there than Gracie had the previous year. On May 29 Gracie opened the Clapham Common Women's Committee Fete, and on June sixth Gracie made her third appearance at the Folkestone Marine Gardens Pavillion in their annual Sunday Charity Concert, and a few weeks later Betty did the same. Gracie's roadshow was briefly titled by Archie as *Gulliver's Travels*, starting at the Sheffield Lyceum at the end of May before taking in Leeds, Birmingham, Liverpool, Finsbury Park, Brighton, the Holborn Empire, the Finsbury Park Empire, and finishing in Nottingham, where it was retitled again as *Archie Pitt's Review Shop* in November. During this time

Gracie played the London Palladium from July sixth, then on to the Finsbury Park Empire the following week, the Brighton Hippodrome, and finishing her tour week beginning July 28 at the Nottingham Empire.

It was rumoured there would be a South African transfer of *The Show's the Thing*, so at the end of July, with her concert commitments completed, Gracie decided to finally take the holiday to France she had been promising John Flanagan and Henry Savage—and her first trip abroad in two years. The two men were already holidaying in Cagnes sur Mer near Nice and had been sending regular postcards to Gracie, who was busy reading a copy of Norman Douglas' highly hedonistic novel, *South Wind*, which fellow revue member Edward Chapman had given her. Set on the mythical island of Nepenthe, *South Wind* tells of the fictionalised events of the island's visitors and inhabitants, which caused debate amongst the literate due to its open and frank discussion of moral and sexual issues and open promotion of a hedonistic lifestyle. With £8,500 in her bank account, Gracie withdrew £500 and set off to find John and Henry. It was in April, too, that Edith Fields returned from a successful trip to America where she had appeared in variety for several weeks, but she had already begun to decide the stage was not necessarily for her anymore.

After a few days in the French sun, fed up with too many hills and lack of a "real sea," Gracie told the group she wanted to find Nepthene—which she had discovered was based on the Isle of Capri, fourteen miles off the coast of Sorrento. Although John's passport was out of date, looking like three tramps with a touch of bohemianism the trio set off to find a different world. "I thought Cannes was going to be like Blackpool and I could sit on the sand and the sun would be shining. Instead of that I was in a town and on top of a mountain. I had £500 and we paid our way. We saw Pesta and Rome, bought antiques, and I had an entirely different life by the time I got to Capri."

When they got to the Italian border Gracie remembered, "John went green with fear" as there was a chance he would be refused entry if the customs officials inspected his passport too closely and realised it had in fact expired. Thinking on her feet, Gracie began singing the only Italian song she knew proficiently, "Santa Lucia," and pleased with the rendition the official stamped the passports without even looking at them. Inspecting the map, Gracie recalled, "The first town we seemed to stop at was called Uscita," which the three of them could not place until a frustrated Italian told her that "Uscita" meant "Exit!"

For some reason unknown to Gracie, Henry had decided to wear his old, moth-eaten overcoat for their Mediterranean trip, clearly not taking into account the Italian sunshine, but he was proud of it as it had a lining of fur. During a stopover in Rome a porter mistook the trio for a party of eccentric millionaires and ushered them into the Grand Hotel where rooms cost 500 Lira per night, let alone the £500 Gracie had taken for the whole month! The next day they arrived in Naples and took the boat to Capri for the first time. They stayed in a "neat little hotel" overnight and went travelling by horse and cart the next day around the island's winding roads. Gracie had never seen anywhere as beautiful, with little white and pink villas clinging to the mountainside, colored blossoms and exotic plants trailing along walkways and pathways.

When Gracie first saw the Marina Piccola, the island's small harbour, she instantly fell in love and realised her ideal dream really did exist. Gracie saw for the first time "a blue bay with cloud-capped mountains towering above it" and decided there and then that if she was to ever own even a blade of grass in this shangri-la she would be the happiest person alive. The trio rented rooms for somewhere between five and ten days (different sources cite different lengths of time) in an old English fort. Known as Il Fortino, the former Naval prison was bought in 1880 by a British captain who had married a Caprician girl and had sold it when they moved to Australia. (Gracie met descendants of the couple in Torquay in the 1960s.) It had been owned since 1919 by Marchesa Aldofo Patrizi and her seventeen year old son, Ettore, and Gracie remembered the "broken-down yard where a donkey brayed, two crazy-looking Alsatian dogs barked, and a brood of chickens were clucking wildly." Getting violent indigestion from the Italian food and bitten by mosquitoes, John and Henry returned to France via Corsica. Gracie returned to London for the rehearsals of her next revue, and back to Archie and Annie, who had also been on holiday, together, to Menton in France. However, Gracie had fallen in love with the island, and from then on, every spring Gracie and John would visit Il Fortino together. John got on well with Ettore, and during a period when Gracie couldn't make the trip spent a week in Capri on his own with Ettore in a lodging in the town, spending the week gambling and drinking.

By this time, the Stansfield family became unhappy with the Telford house. In winter the fields turned to mud and they had to trudge over a mile to get to the bus stop or the local shop. So, with plans to once again "move oop," Jenny began to look for a new property for the family. John Flanagan was now a regular visitor with Gracie, and the family was fully aware the pair were "involved" with each other. On one visit John stayed for two weeks and set up his easel and began painting Fred's portrait, but only until eleven each day, when they both cycled over to the Dew Drop. Tony Parry said, "Granddad preferred John to any of Gracie's other choices, as they shared the common interest of the four ale bar at the local pub."

Meanwhile, Tommy Fields and Dorothy Whiteside were married on March 15, 1930 at St. John's Church Hampstead, before the wedding reception held at Tower. Edith Stansfield and Duggie Wakefield were married on May 18, 1930 at the little Norman Church of St. Laurence in Telescombe Village.

Duggie, originally born Albine Holderness Wakefield in Ecclesall Bierlow, Sheffield, on August 28, 1899, began his career in Hull as a slapstick and knockabout comedian, billed in 1917 as "an amusing dude," before he changed his name to Jack Wakefield and began touring with R.R. Taylor's *Joy Flips* in 1920, A. D. McFarlane's *Dinkie Darling* in 1922, before moving on to Thomas F. Convery's revue, *On the Dole*, from January 1924. He announced in March 1925, in order to avoid confusion with another artist, he had changed his name again to Douglas Wakefield. He continued to tour under this name before transferring to Archie Pitt's spectacular and fanciful *Too Many Cooks*, which premiered at the New Brighton Tower on January 17, 1926 under the baton of Annie Lipman.

After touring successfully with this show, Duggie (and his now comedy-partner Nelson) opened in Archie's *Boys will be Boys*, which premiered at the Alexandra Palace on February 27, 1928, where he first met Edith Stansfield, who was also in the company. Duggie had been living with his partner, Amelia Black, also a performer, at 4 Wyke Gardens in London since 1926, but the pair separated in 1929 after he had begun a relationship with Edith. Duggie went on to become a successful comedian in his own right, headlining the Victoria Palace's Pantomime as Dame in 1935 and touring in successful comedy shows as a solo artist and as one of the *Four Boys from Manchester* until his death in 1951.

A whole "posh do" of a family affair was held for the first family wedding in the new home at Telscombe in May 1930, even though Edith told the newspapers, "We wanted no bells or bouquets." Fred was presented with a pair of spats for the first time in his life, which confused him greatly. He proudly walked his youngest daughter down the aisle with spats on upside down, alongside Duggie in a pair of silver shoe-buckles bought for him by Gracie—which he hated—and guests included members from both the *Making Good* and *The Show's the Thing* companies. Duggie and Edith moved into their first home together at 17

Seymour House, Compton Street, and their first child, Douglas Austin Wakefield, was born on December 18, 1931, and their second child, Grace, on July 24, 1933.

Gracie's home 'The Haven' then and now.

Gracie in 'Walk this Way' (1931).

CHAPTER SIX

1930 - 1932

When skies are blue you're beguiling,

And when they're grey you're still smiling.

- "Sally" (1931), recorded by Gracie Fields.

HAVING TIRED OF TELFORD in Peacehaven, Fred and Jenny began to look for a new house to live in which was closer to the shops and a main road. They found a property, in its own grounds, at 29 Telescombe Cliffs Way. The house was only one and a half miles from their current property, but the family thought it would be more suitable to live in. No sooner had the property been bought Jenny began designing rooms in her mind, which were committed to paper by John Flanagan. Before the family moved in, and after an endless amount of building work, the house hardly resembled the property which had been bought in the first place. Both Jenny and Gracie's visionary minds expanded rooms, added balconies, windows, and a perimeter wall, and the back of the house was redesigned to look like a ship sailing on a green lawn. To further the effect, lifebelts and gangways were added to the exterior of the house, which was adorned with railings and a false funnel on the flat roof outside the French windows of Gracie's bedroom. Collecting life rings became something of a passion for Gracie, and whenever she went onboard a new ship she always requested a new life ring with the name on to take back home to Peacehaven, and eventually Capri.

Gracie's bedroom walls were hung with dove-grey mauray silk with an Italian marble and brass washstand in the corner, and her private sitting room was decorated with Art Deco blonde inlayed wood. Her private bathroom was designed in apple green tiles, white plush carpet, and large mirrors to reflect the light. The favourite and most used room in the vast house was the large living room-come-billiards room. In the corner stood a well-stocked bar, an immense fireplace surrounded by oak beams, a grand white Bluthner piano, and at the end of the room facing the garden was a semi-circular bay window to the ceiling. This room was filled with trinkets and souvenirs from Gracie's fans and from her travels, and from this room derived the name of the house, The Haven, with "Gracie's bar" installed at one end of the room. Gracie loved filling the house with guests, musicians, and friends, and often after her shows in London, finished on Friday nights she would come down for the weekend to stay with her mother and father, often bringing an entourage of friends with her on the last train to Brighton.

Fred tended to the garden, which was filled with foreign and tropical flowers, with pride, and a tennis court was added. It was soon realised nobody was for tennis, so Fred kept his chickens on the court instead. A large pond with a small fountain in the middle was also added. The pond was dug so deep it was decided that instead it should become a swimming pool. Coming home drunk from the local pub one afternoon, Fred fell in head first. Luckily Gracie was sitting in the garden at the time and dove into the pool to save her father, who had toppled off a small child's boat which he had been playing with on the pool. A bridge and railings were soon placed around the water and it was never used as a pool again, as Gracie feared that one of the many little children from the orphanage who frequently visited, or her sister's children, would follow suit and fall in. "I didn't care, and I didn't have to care how many rooms and paths and pools and tennis courts Mum built. The place was home, filled with people, noise, laughter, and kids." In the 1960s, Gracie had three small bungalows built in the grounds of the house for her siblings and their families to use.

As a present to her father, one morning Fred and Jenny woke up to a brand new black Austin 7 on the drive of the house. Gracie had arranged for some driving lessons for Fred so he could nip Jenny down to Brighton to do the shopping or visit the other towns along the Sussex coastline. Fred's lessons took place on the flats of the Downs, away from any obstructions or traffic, and the former engineer soon became adept at handling the gears and managing the engine. Tony Parry remembered watching these driving lessons and recalled, "Whatever the procedures were in those days to obtain a driving license are a mystery, but I am quite sure that my grandfather never had one or would have qualified!" Regardless, Fred used the car to take Jenny to the shops and to run himself along to the pub, but never into any congested areas or areas where traffic was likely!

At Jenny's insistence, Fred drove her to see Duggie Wakefield in pantomime in Brighton one Christmas. The hair-raising journey was filled with profanities as Fred had never driven into a town before, especially not over the hilly drive from Peacehaven to Brighton. The pair returned unscathed, except with some damage to the rear bumper, as Fred had selected reverse instead of first gear in the theatre's car park. Deciding to make a solo trip the next week, Fred drove to a series of pubs in a nearby town, then decided to drive back home again, giving his friends a lift in his car. Jenny was woken in the night by a call from the police station saying Fred and his companions had been arrested for drunken and dangerous driving, as he had sped through a crossroad and nearly run over a policeman on point duty in the village of Rottingdean. The policeman had to dive into a nearby doorway to stop the car full of singing revellers from hitting him, and so Fred spent the night in the cells.

Archie had also bought himself a new car, a top-of-the-range Rolls Royce, which Gracie first saw when coming out of the theatre after a matinee show. Press photographers asked her to pose with the car, sit on the bonnet, and even kiss it before she and Archie drove away as the "happily married theatrical couple of the West End." As the car passed the BBC end of Oxford Street, however, Archie ordered the chauffer to pull over and told Gracie, "You should be able to easily get a bus from here," as he was meeting Annie Lipman further down the road. A stunned Gracie watched what the press described as "her dream car" pull away, leaving her standing on the pavement. Gracie's marriage was clearly very strained, but according to Gracie the final straw came when Archie and she were having an argument on Hampstead Heath. Archie told her it was solely due to him that she was a star, so Gracie took off her fur coat and flung it in the mud. He picked it up and started to brush the dirt off it, and it was at that moment Gracie finally realised what Archie actually was. In later years Gracie added, "My inlaws and a fast talking salesman persuaded me I owed a little class to myself, so I bought a maroon-coloured Rolls Royce, complete with speaking tube, radio, fur rug, and liveried chauffeur. You could see it in Calais on a clear day!"

During one interview, when asked by the newspapers what her lucky mascots were, Archie rudely interrupted Gracie and said that he was her only mascot. An embarrassed Gracie quickly apologised for this and explained her real lucky mascot was a stuffed cow named Jessie, which was thrown to her on the stage by Clarice Mayne, a music-hall singer and variety performer. In another instance, Archie scolded Gracie for ordering a port and lemon at the Savoy Hotel. Growing up in Rochdale, Gracie had been told this was the "ladylike" thing to order, but Archie thought it vulgar and common. Still tied to a contract until April 1932 with Archie, Gracie knew that it was not in her interests to leave him and the company of *Walk This* Way so she persevered for over twelve months in a marriage which had entirely broken down.

Gracie busied herself with as many different recreational activities as she could set her hands to. From May 11, 1930, Gracie was at the Brighton Hippodrome with the Green Sisters, Wensley and Dale, Nina and Nora, the Brent Brothers, Norman Carrol, and the Eight Black Streaks of Dance. Next followed a run at the Holborn Empire beginning on May 28, with the Norman Thomas Sextette, Bennet and Wliams, Max Miller, and Al and Val Reno. Gracie added new songs into her repertoire here, including "A Cottage for Sale," "Painting the Clouds with Sunshine," and "The Punch and Judy Show." On May 28 Gracie performed in another charity concert in aid of the Ladies' Guild Music, in an all-star cast featuring Gracie impersonator Jenny Howard, and on June first Gracie opened the South London Hospital for Women's summer fete with Sir John Leigh in celebration of their new outpatients department.

Whilst playing in Plymouth, Gracie had fallen in love with a charming cottage in the little fishing village of Cawsand. Gracie uses the word "little" to describe the house, though on postcards of the day we can see it was in fact a substantial three-story building standing right on the beach at Cawsand Bound. The "tiny little ramshackle place" captured Gracie's heart, and Archie stunned Gracie when he told her he would buy it for her. The pair had been drifting apart, and this little kindness from Archie, which was less than a week's wages for him, "meant more than I could explain." It meant so much to Gracie that she carried the key around in her pocket wherever she went to remind her of her own little holiday home, known as "Ocean Waves."

Some time later when she was again in Plymouth, Gracie took her friends in the company for a picnic to Cawsand to see her cottage, which she had been decorating and furnishing in her mind. When they got there the cottage was gone, and in its place a bare patch of ground where Gracie's dream cottage once stood. Gracie phoned Archie in London, aghast that someone had torn down her home, and it was revealed it was Archie who had done it, at Annie's suggestion, to build a modern house with a fancy garden. "Do what you like with it," Gracie told him, "I don't want it anymore!" Archie eventually built a two-story house, keeping the name Ocean Waves, and sold the property without Gracie having ever stepped foot inside. Gracie would return frequently throughout her life to Cawsand, often staying at the Ship Inn, and becoming close acquaintances with the proprietors there and enjoying many "lock-in" sessions. Many elderly citizens of the town still remember Gracie serving behind the bar of the pub there. Gracie was back at the Palladium on August 18 alongside Kimberley and Page, Gaudsmith Brothers, Mary and Erik, Collinson and Dean, Hidnustanis, and Julian Rose. On the 23rd, Gracie again visited Herne Hill, where she presented a trophy to Mrs. E. Palmer, the winner of that year's Ladies' Cycling Championship.

Coming out of rehearsals for her next, unwilling, Pitt production, Archie had arranged a two week holiday in America, followed by a two week cabaret season in New York. Gracie thought everything in America was ''a big query,'' as she was mainly used to playing a Lancashire comic character. It was therefore likely American audiences would not even be able to relate to it, let alone find it funny. She confessed that on her first visit to the USA she did not want to work, but simply take a holiday and look around with the vision of perhaps working there in the future, but Archie insisted she take the $5,000 dollar contract offered to her, regardless of whether she wanted to do it or not. If the American audiences could understand her dialect, Archie suggested to Bert it may be worthwhile Gracie branch into films. The group, which consisted of Bert Aza, Irene Pitt, Archie, Annie, Gracie, and their maid, Ina Mackay, set off for America on the HMS Berengaria from Southampton on September 6, 1930.

Whilst onboard, Archie had arranged for Gracie to appear in a cabaret show on the ship without her prior knowledge. He signed the contract and took payment, and Gracie only knew about this when she arrived to the restaurant on September 10 and found the program inside her menu card detailing, "Gracie Fields will perform songs from her repertoire with conductress Annie Lipman." Loathed to showing herself up by causing an argument, Gracie performed a few of her old favourites in the First Class Lounge in the 9:15 cabaret slot. The party arrived in New York on September 12 and enjoyed two weeks' vacation before Gracie's stint at the Palace Theatre.

One evening after visiting some of New York's sights, Archie, Irene, and Annie went out for a meal together while Bert took Ina along as secretary to finalise the contracts at RKO's Manhattan office, leaving Gracie in the hotel room alone. Gracie said, "I despise myself when I am afraid," and alone in her hotel room at midnight in New York, she was afraid. She got herself dressed up and walked out along Fifth Avenue, dazed and lonely, among the canyons of the great city. After seeing her name in lights on Times Square, Gracie decided she needed to take a drink. "The drink which my mother used to give me when I was a little girl and feverish." A glass of milk. Opposite the Palace Theatre, she went inside a drug store fountain bar, and in broadest Lancashire, forgetting to talk posh because of her nerves, asked for the glass of milk. "Huh? You'll have to speak in English, baby," replied the clerk, who turned his back on Gracie. Even though the theatrical hoarding across the street proclaimed, "England's greatest star," an average American couldn't understand a word of her native speech, and this troubled her greatly.

Running out of the store, forgetting that American cars drive on the other side of the road to the English, Gracie ran straight into the path of an oncoming taxi cab, whose driver broke hard to prevent running her over. Scared to death, Gracie passed out and woke up in the backseat of the cab. The friendly taxi driver, who Gracie said, "I only ever knew was called Ike Schmolenski," offered to take Gracie on a free journey wherever she wanted, as long as she told him what the trouble was. Gracie found herself in the back of a New York taxi pouring her heart out to a friendly stranger in the middle of an unknown city. Ike swung the cab round to the front of the drug store and told her, "Get in there, Miss Gracie Fields, and don't come back out again until you get what you want!" Gracie went inside the store, slapped the counter and did her trademark errand-boy whistle, shrill and vulgar, which shocked the clerk. She told him she had asked for a glass of milk, and, "If you don't understand English we'll do it in sign language!" She grabbed two ice cream cones from the counter and put them over her forehead, imitating a mooing cow, which got a round of hearty laughter from the customers and the clerk. "That's my baby!" shouted Ike from the cab, and he promised to be at the Palace Show, which made Gracie feel an infinite amount better.

What worried Gracie, however, was the next morning, when the Palace managers told Bert and Archie they were worried she would not be well received and had booked her four evening shows in Flushing, Long Island so she could try her act out in front of a real American audience. Archie explained to her there was more to lose than just the Palace engagement, so in a trance Gracie learned and rehearsed her four new American songs and presented them in a small theatre in Flushing. The audience sat with mouths agape, but Bert reassured Gracie she had outgrown small theatres and when she got on stage at the Palace everything would be fine. The managers at the theatre had heard the reviews from Flushing and were very concerned, even further so when Gracie suggested she sing the black spiritual "Sing You Sinners!" which she had performed in *Topsy and Eva*. Gracie thought that this number would be well appreciated by the audiences and insisted that she keep it in her act for her opening week.

Gracie made her Broadway debut at the RKO Palace on September

27, and made her American radio debut on September 29 when she broadcast some of her popular Lancastrian songs over the air, including "Little Pudden Basin." "They did not know a pudding basin by that name at the time, so each time I sang the song I had to carefully explain what it was all about. They appreciated that no end." She had been seen by a radio producer who visited the theatre and suggested Gracie should perform a few numbers, but not her American ones. Her Palace vaudeville bill was shared with the Clayton, Jackson, and Durante trio, Fields and Dave Apollon, Odali Careno, and the Pasquali Brothers, Ted Healey as master of ceremonies, Cara Barry, Clyde Cooke, and Helen York and Virginia Johnson. Gracie received the top reviews, making it the top bill of the season. Even though Gracie approached her performance cautiously, the press reported she scored soundly in each of the songs she chose to sing. Gracie mainly performed the songs which she had been working on for a number of years, including "Cute Little Flat" and "My Blue Heaven," but added a few new songs to her repertoire especially for the American audiences, which was appreciated by the press.

Gracie, however, remembered this differently when speaking about the performance on Parkinson in 1978. "I was a flop for the first three nights. They scared me to death. One artist told me I had to put a lot of jewellery on, a lot of earrings and jewellery. I looked like a Christmas tree. I always did everything anybody told me. It wasn't me. Then they said, 'Don't change your songs, they're all right. Then after the third night I said I'm changing my songs. Archie told me to leave it, but I put one in and it was perfect. Then I put another one in and it was perfect. I said to the comedian who went in on everybody's act, 'Why aren't you getting in my act?' He said, 'Oh no, no! You're too much of a lady.' I say, 'I'm no lady!' Then he came on in my act, and from then on it was a wow!"

On the Saturday evening of her first week Gracie was met at the stage door by a familiar face in a yellow taxi, and she shocked both Annie and

Archie when she hopped into Ike's taxi and went off with him, leaving them aghast at the stage door. He told her he wasn't too impressed with her performance, as the audience "had her scared," at which Gracie burst into tears. Ike pulled into a side street off Times Square and the pair headed into an all-night cafe. Through their discussions, Ike told Gracie, "Folk are the same anywhere, all you've got to do is make 'em laugh." Gracie realised to achieve this she had to change her numbers in the next week's show, otherwise she truly would be branded a failure.

In later years Gracie recounted, "For the first two days of my Palace show I was stiff with fear." It wasn't until a show on the Sunday evening that Gracie really felt that she had broken American audiences. "I followed Al Jolson, who was at the performance and had been dragged out of his seat and on to the stage to sing his two famous songs, "Sonny Boy" and "My Mammy." Jolson hadn't been in New York for over five years, but had come to the Palace's Sunday night performance, which was renowned to have stars sitting in the audiences on their nights off from musicals. Ivor Novello, who had worked on the same bill as Gracie at the London Palladium in 1928, went backstage to wish her luck and was horrified to find her a nervous wreck.

"It was then my Lancashire blood got up, and I went on stage for my spot before the interval feeling as empty as a vacuum. I said to myself 'Blow you. I'll keep you all here and show you who Gracie Fields is!' And I gave them all I got. Even though I say it myself, it was a magnificent performance, the best of my whole career. I certainly put the 'fluence on them!"

Gracie went on straight after Jolson and parodied him, burlesquing "Sonny Boy," which even got the World's Greatest Entertainer himself chuckling, and Gracie then ditched her carefully prepared American songs and went straight into her Lancashire set.

It was the tradition at the Palace that Ted Healey would burst in on each artist at one point during their act and act some comedy patter with them, but he didn't go near the shy Gracie during her first week. "Perhaps it was the fact that I was wearing a beautiful white evening frock? I believe they half expected to see me fidgeting with lorgnettes."

In her second week, Gracie specifically asked him to do so. "The Lancashire lass with a sharp profile and rebellious buzz of red-brown hair will be grabbed up by the biggies heap quick [...] the lady has everything!" was how one American reviewer described Gracie. Although the comedy business of her opening performance was a little off, Gracie altered this as the week went on to great success. A star in Britain, Gracie found winning the hearts of American audiences required little time and less patience, as she entered the stage to a tremendous ovation—primarily due to the mammoth publicity campaign that RKO had organised, heralding "Britain's Greatest Comedienne's" American debut. After her spot, Gracie was called back regularly during her American stay for "a dizzy amount of encores" as the American audience demanded to hear more from the Lancashire import. After she had obliged by singing "Crying for the Carolines," the audience called her back and demanded she make a speech!

Overall, the problem lay with the show which was "uneven and accentuated by the best of the best next to the worst of the worst." After her two weeks, Gracie was offered a third week at a further $2,500 and agreed to play it until RKO cancelled the engagement, as they had no spare New York theatres to accommodate her at such short notice. Instead, the group set off back to England on HMS Mauretania and arrived to a press reception at Paddington Station on October 22. Arm in arm with Archie, Gracie spotted her mother in the crowd and quickly broke away from him to greet her, the cameras focusing on her and Jenny's pride. Archie, Annie, and Irene slipped by the cameras unnoticed, back to Tower.

When Gracie got home Archie told the papers she worked well and was received well, but for Gracie, "the only snag for me is work. I think

America is all right: the people are wonderful and I've never known hospitality so lavish or sincere." Florenz Ziegfield, of the *Ziegfield Follies*, tried to sign Gracie to return the next year for a stage production, but Archie explained to him she wouldn't be able to fulfill this as she was tied to *Walk this Way*. By the time her contract with Archie had ended Ziegfield had died and Gracie never got the chance to work with him. Instead, George Black engaged her for a three-week run at the Palladium from October, where she premiered some of the songs she had picked up whilst in New York, which were not well-received by the audiences as they were expecting the "Lass from Lancashire," not the New York star. She also performed old and new favourites, including, "Swinging in a Hammock," "Little Pudden Basin," "Stop and Shop at the Co-Op Shop," and "As Long as He Loves Me."

Gracie had played the Palladium twice already in 1930 for £700 a week, but now riding on the back of her New York success her fee increased. In her second week in November, Gracie performed some of the comedy sketches which audiences associated her with. It was during this Palladium run that Gracie introduced a number called "Lancashire Blues," which she had written herself whilst in America. In the song, Gracie sings, "You can keep all your waffles and corn on the cob, give me some hot-pot, straight from the hob!" as she yearns for her native Lancashire whilst away in Tennessee.

After the Tuesday night's Palladium show on December seventh, Gracie invited members of the press to a "hot-pot party" on the stage of the London Palladium. With a menu printed on the invitation stating the party will commence at quarter to midnight, the menu comprised grapefruit followed by hotpot (from Gracie's own recipe), rice pudding and coffee, with tea, beer, and whiskey the drinks on offer. During the party it was announced Gracie had signed a contract with British

International Pictures to star in a £500,000 talkie to be produced at Elstree Studios the following year.

On November 11, Gracie opened the Scenic Golf Club in Piccadilly before heading off on another short tour, *Archie Pitt's Road Show*, taking in the Holborn Empire for a week on November 15, the Finsbury Park Empire on November 22, and the Cardiff Empire on November 29 with Fields and Rossini, Harold Walden, the Laurel Brothers, and the Pitt Girls.

Gracie was back at the London Palladium on December 14 in her second charity benefit concert in aid of Brinsworth House. Many of the previous year's stars were also appearing, but with the addition of G. H. Elliott and Max Miller. Over Christmas Gracie paid a visit to Dunston Hill in Newcastle, where she gave a performance for the patients, and when asked about the film by the enthusiastic patients she told them, "Honestly, I don't know the first thing about it. Archie says he's not going to tell me, so that I can't go about telling other people. I don't know and I don't care what my work is." Tommy turned down a part in the film even after constant begging from Gracie to take the comic part, because, he said, "I don't have a funny face. Give it to Duggie Wakefield instead."

Continuing to tour with the *Archie Pitt Roadshow* in January 1931, the show played the Southampton Empire in the first week of January, immediately followed by a week at the Finsbury Park Empire, the Nottingham Empire, and the Brighton Hippodrome, where she appeared with Lewis and Lawn, Flying Banvards, Will Somers, Jack Joyce, Fields and Rossini, and Harold Walden. Gracie was back at the London Palladium in October for three weeks, where she featured new songs, including, "Swinging in a Hammock," "Little Pudden Basin," "Stop and Shop at the Co-Op Shop," and, as requested by the audiences, "As Long as He Loves Me."

Gracie continued to tour through January 1931 with Lewis and Lawn, Flying Banvards, Will Somers, Jack Joyce, Fields and Rossini, Norman Carroll, Nino and Lawn, and Harold Walden, visiting Southampton, Nottingham Empire, and the Brighton Hippodrome before a week in Rochdale for a charity week. Returning to her native town of Rochdale, with her efforts in aid of local causes, her "Gracie Comes Whoam" week began on January 26, 1931, and was the fulfillment of a long-cherished desire to do something for her hometown. Giving her services and time for free, any money raised was to be distributed between various Rochdale charities, including the Memorial Home for Crippled Children, the Rochdale District Nursing Association, and the Rochdale Infirmary. After a week of civic receptions, hospital visits, and two concerts at the Rochdale Hippodrome, Gracie also kicked off the Rochdale Hornets football match against Wakefield Trinity Football Club.

Accompanying Gracie on this tour was her new personal musical director, Harry Green. Harry had first performed as Gracie's musical director at the London Palladium in 1929, and he would on-and-off conduct for her until My 1934 in between Annie Lipman—who Gracie was trying to move away from—Lou Ross and William Pethers. In an interview in later life, Harry remembered, "I never knew what she was going to do next, and she never gave a poor performance all the time I knew her. She made us laugh, she made us cry, literally, and she was so natural."

He recalled, "We were on the way to do a show at the Blind Institution and she confessed to me she did not want to stay long. 'Be ready to leave quickly, when I've finished,' she told me. It grieved her to be in the presence of so much distress, and that day she felt she could not stand too much of it. I said I would, and when we arrived she explained to the management she couldn't stay long, as she had another engagement . Would they have a taxi at the door in half an hour?

"This was the only time I ever knew her to do this, but it takes great courage to joke and make fun in such circumstances. I didn't know what engagement she was going to next, or if she really had one, but the taxi duly arrived. We packed up quickly and climbed in. And as the taxi started, Gracie said 'Let's go to them pictures!'

"She has a way with her audience which always put them in sympathy with her even when it is on someone else's behalf. As, for example, when she has finished her turn and the audience is clamouring for more. That used to be one of our nightly difficulties. Gracie would do her show, and encore after encore, until her allotted time had expired, and more than expired.

"In spite of the flashing of the number on the number board for the next turn, the applause would go on and on, fading for a moment and starting up again in wave after wave, the way applause does fade and start after a popular star."

In later life Harry Green remembered, "Once I saw her save a situation which was, well, a little embarrassing, with a remark no one but Gracie would have dared make. It was one afternoon at the Alexandra Palace when she was giving a charity show—she was always giving charity shows—and Prince George had been going around an exhibition at the palace and had come to the performance. After the show he came round on to the stage. It was all unexpected. Nobody seemed to know what to do. The manager and the other artists seemed somehow to have got themselves all grouped round in a circle, and as the prince came up there was an embarrassed hush and then 'Ee, I can see it now. I'd never have believed it,' cried Gracie, advancing to meet him. 'Lot's have people have told me, 'e's just like our Tommy.' Which made everybody laugh, including the prince. It was just the way she said it.

"I do not think I have ever known or met a woman, certainly not a variety artist, who lives quite so retiringly when away from stage.

"When she is on tour she does not take the best hotel in the town.

Though she could afford to buy the hotel, she leaves it entirely alone, and books 'digs' in the old, old way. Not necessarily the most expensive digs either, just the ordinary professional digs, such as any other member of the company might book.

"There are four outstanding things about her that alone would put her in a class almost alone amongst women. She never drinks (or hardly ever), she does not smoke, I have never heard her swear, and she never loses her temper. All the time I was with her, I only knew her to have two drinks. Once was while she was playing at the Palladium and she had been invited to a staff party at a big shop across the way. Whether it was she felt like being especially sociable with the girls or that she was extra tired that evening, I don't know, but she had a whiskey and soda. And it certainly surprised me. Another time was at Edinburgh. She had been giving a charity show for the benefit of the Ninth Lancers, quartered there.

"Tobacco she avoids very wisely, for the sake of her voice. Swearing isn't in her nature any more than losing her temper—not even the mild 'hells' and 'damns' now thought so little of by women. There was one night when she would have been perfectly justified in losing her temper with me, but she didn't. It was a little incident that arose out of the fact she carried such a large repertoire. To make it easy for the band to find their parts quickly I had numbered all the different songs, and before the evening's performance I always wrote down a list of the half dozen or so she proposed to sing. I wrote two lists, in fact. One for those members of the orchestra on my right to pass around amongst themselves and another for those on my left.

"This night I accidently omitted one figure on one of the copies, and the result was that when the third song was due, one half of the band started playing "Looking on the Bright Side" and the other half "Sally." And both fortissimo. You can imagine what it sounded like. Even Gracie was startled. But she only laughed and said as she looked down at me,

'Oh, so you're tryin' to muck me up , are you?' And when we managed to sort it out and she had finished the number, she said, taking the audience, as usual, into her confidence, 'Well, you can stay another week!'

"Her good temper is proof against anything. A baby squealed out one night when she was in the middle of one of her opera burlesques. It was her own comic rendering of 'Toselli's Serenade' and, perhaps, it was her top note that incited the baby somewhere high in the gallery. At the sound, she stopped her performance and called out, 'All right, luv, I'll be with you in a minute' and looked down at me, and asked, 'Is that owt to do wiv you?' And when I shook my head, she went merrily on again."

At her performance on Tuesday, the 27th, at the Hippodrome, Gracie was joined by Fields and Rossini and the Pitt Girls dancers. The "Gulliver's Travels" sketch from *The Show's the Thing* was recreated with Fred Heppell taking Archie's original role, and June Meredith, Tommy Fields, his wife, Dorothy, and Mary Ludlow retaining their original parts. Music was provided by the new English baritone popular on the BBC, Ivan Mellodew, and Rochdale's newest entertainer, whilst Norman Evans—who would carve out his own name in variety theatre—also appeared on the bill. Although Archie didn't attend the week with her, more than five of his photographs appear in the programme which was sold for charity, almost as many photographs as Gracie herself! In total, her first Rochdale charity week earned £1,673 9>1, which was split between the charities.

In later life, Norman Evans remembered his first meeting with Gracie. "The first time I met Gracie I'll confess my knees were a bit shaky. I was an amateur and helping to organise our Rochdale Charity Week, at which Gracie had agreed to appear. She was so understanding and helpful that I've never forgotten it—or another day a few years later which made an enormous difference to my own career. I had plucked up courage to give up my work as a textile salesman. I'd gone to London and was lucky enough to get an audition with Stoll at the old Alhambra. Gracie heard I had come down from Rochdale and telephoned me to come out to visit her at the theatre she was appearing at. Gracie spent twenty minutes of her time on stage that evening introducing me as a bright lad from Rochdale, and from a star of such magnitude to someone unknown, that was something, I can tell you!"

In February, Gracie played the Liverpool Hippodrome, Leeds Empire, and the London Metropolitan, where with her on the bill were Fields and Whiteside (brother Tommy and his wife) and Irene Pitt (Archie's daughter) in their own variety acts, but also in the "Gulliver's Travels" sketch from *The Show's the Thing*, with Freda Short and Fred Heppell. Whilst at the Plymouth Theatre Royal, Gracie visited Tor House Blind Charity on February 14 and performed to the patients there, and on February 17 had returned to Rochdale to kick off the Hornets match against Trinity Wakefield. Gracie was back to charity work on February 18, singing six songs at the Alexandra Palace in aid of the Music Hall Ladies' Guild. She told the audience, "I mix a little pathos and a little humour in equal quantities. If I fail to amuse, I sing to the orchestra to try and make them laugh instead!" From February 21, Gracie appeared at the Leeds Empire, and whilst in Leeds attended the West Leeds Conservative Party's fancy dress ball as well as a bazaar in aid of the RSPCA, where she told them about her 12 dogs, 36 rabbits, pigeons, lovebirds, canaries, and parrot she kept at Tower. The following week, at the London Metropolitan, Gracie performed "Fred Fanakapan," "Dancing with Tears in My Eyes," "More than You Know," and "Go Home and Tell Your Mother," in a bill which also starred Irene Pitt (Archie's daughter), Fred J Heppell, and Tommy Fields and his wife, Dorothy Whiteside.

Whilst backstage at the Metropolitan, Gracie described, "In comes this fellow one night, very Cockney, and he tells us all of this song he's just

see p.166

written with some friends." The title of the song was "Sally." Originally titled "Gypsy Sweetheart" and later "Mary, Mary," the three songwriters eventually settled on "Sally," which surprised Gracie, as the title of her upcoming film, *Sally in our Alley*, had not yet been released to the public. After a little work and an audition for Archie, it was agreed the song would be used in the film. "Sally" was written by Harry Leon and Leo Towers and sold by Bill Haines at the recently established Cameo Music Publishing. Bill Haines spent twenty-five years as a music hall performer before he opened his own music shop on Denmark Street. After he had successfully found Gracie a number of songs for her films, she often relied solely on him in the acquisition of her new songs. None would ever be as successful, however, as "Sally," as the song would go on to be the star vehicle of Gracie's new film, appearing throughout the film over six times. Played in the background by an orchestra, whistled by dockyard workers, and sung by Gracie twice, it seems the title song of the film was its star. Even as recent as 1992 the song was still making royalties of £20,000—primarily due to Paul McCartney's inclusion of the song in his *Tripping the Light Fantastic* world tour.

From March 11, Gracie was at the Plymouth Theatre Royal, where on the 14 she attended a Tor House blind charity event, and from March 28, Gracie was back at the London Palladium in a "request week" alongside Debroy Somers, Gold and Raye, and Jack Barty. Sending request postcards in weeks before, Gracie specially selected songs from her repertoire which the audience wanted to hear, and these included "As Long as He Loves Me," "Go Home and Tell Your Mother," "Why Waste Your Tears?" "Stop and Shop at the Co-Op Shop," "Fred Fanakapan," and "More than You Know." Looking radiant in a black, long dress, all sequined, and wearing a beret, Gracie announced to the audience she would soon be making a foray into films. Whilst she was appearing at the Palladium, Gracie and Archie were involved in a car crash in St. John's

Wood on Hall Road, and although Gracie was uninjured, Archie suffered a bruised face, arms, and legs.

The title of *Sally in Our Alley* (1931) was chosen for Gracie's first film, based on Charles McEvoy's play *The Likes of 'Er*, and was adapted for film by Archie, Miles Malleson, Alma Reveille, and Charles McEvoy. Gracie liked the idea of this as her first film, as it was "an original story, and it hasn't just been written for me." Shooting tests began in late February 1931 at British Lion Studios in Beaconsfield, with both Basil Dean and Archie Pitt wanting to direct the film, even though Archie had never stepped foot in a film studio before. Bert had approached and been turned down by John Maxwell, the head of British International Pictures. Before going to see Basil Dean at A.R.P., Gracie said in 1927, "Someday I should like to make a talkie in England. Don't you think it must be great, when you are old to be able to look again at yourself when you were doing your best work and say, 'That's what I used to be like?'" Now was her chance. The film was eventually directed by Maurice Elvey and produced by Dean. Gracie wasn't happy she had to get up to begin filming each day at six in the morning, and compared this with going back into the mill. On her first day in the studio the make-up man inspected Gracie's face and concurred he must shave her upper lip, an idea she loathed and hated, but submitted to, and which Maurice Elvey thought a ridiculous idea when he later heard of it.

The plot is that of a British soldier who goes off to fight in World War I with his girlfriend waiting and worried at home. He is soon wounded in battle and crippled, and he concludes she would be better off believing that he had been killed so she can get on with her life. She gets the news and is devastated, and several years later she is still grieving for him, but he has now been cured and goes looking for her.

The first line of the film which Gracie was to deliver was "Good Morning, George," and she repeated this line for thirteen hours before the crew decided that they must have a take which they could use and moved on to the next line! Archie and Basil were often at odds with each other, with one telling Gracie what to do only to be rebutted by the other. After they had argued, and a few takes had been made, Maurice Elvey, the only one with any real idea of shooting film, offered his advice by asking, "Perhaps we could try it this way?" By eight o'clock, when everyone was too tired to argue, it was usually filmed Elvey's way—and to great result. Elvey remembered of Gracie in the 1960s, "Without doubt the greatest actress I ever directed. I say actress and not variety artist. I did three of her early films before she became too expensive for me."

When it came to Archie's turn to have a cameo speaking role the rehearsals went fine, but when he stood in front of the cameras he began to sweat profusely. The cast and crew thought that he was ill, but it turned out that he was paralysed with fear. The title song of the film was to be shot in a coffee house with a smoky atmosphere, achieved by burning brown paper off-camera. Amongst muffled sneezes from the crew, and her own watering eyes, Gracie managed to get through the song. "I have sung 'Sally' all over the world since, in peace and war, in triumph and disaster, but never in such nightmare conditions as that first time in a film studio!"

In April, and the fourth week of shooting the film, the Gramophone Company experimented by recording the film's theme song whilst the film was being shot, to great effect. (Eighty-one years before *Les Miserables* (2012) achieved critical acclaim for live-recording the soundtrack). Whilst one scene calls for Florence Desmond to smash a set of crockery, this film had to be shot six times with six complete sets of crockery to get the desired effect. While shooting the film Gracie was afflicted with temporary blindness, known as "Kleig Eyes," caused by the blinding glare of the studio lights. Filming had to be halted on Gracie's scenes for three days from April 17, as it was required Gracie wear dark glasses and stay at home. Archie told the newspapers, "It's a temporary affliction, and after a day or two of rest she will recover completely, we hope." Away from the studio, Gracie was honoured by the Criterion's Gallery First Nighter's on April first. Gracie did recover, and the film was finished before Gracie and John Flanagan took a holiday to the Patrizi property in Capri in May.

Gracie first saw the film at its tradeshow premiere at the Manchester Hippodrome on July 11, before its London Trade Screening on July 14. When it was eventually released, the film took £10,000 at the box office and solidified Gracie as a film star. Performing at the Leicester Square Theatre for a week from July third, Gracie presented songs from her upcoming film as a gesture toward British film. When it was complete, Lillian Aza remembered the distributors couldn't get one booking for it despite Gracie's big success in both theatre and on record. Bert offered to buy the rights to the film and remembered the Empire Birmingham had been wired for sound. After a meeting with the bookers and distributors he was determined he'd get it booked in there, so approached Moss Empires, who were grateful for the approach. Seeing then there was a market for the film, the original distributor's stepped up a gear and sold the film to the top theatres. Gracie earned £15,000 more on percentage than the original salary Bert had asked for her. The following week she began a week's run at the Brighton Hippodrome alongside the Green Sisters, Wensley and Dale, Nina and Nora, the Brent Brothers, Norman Carrol, and Eight Black Streaks of Dance.

In the depths of the Depression, *Sally in our Alley* was perfect for its time and appealed directly to the working classes amidst who it was set. Whilst the film was escapist, it is not so farcical that the audiences couldn't believe it. "Drama, melodrama, and a new star, it sounds like the formula for several hundred pictures." Although Gracie was playing a Lancashire girl in London, the setting could easily have been in hometown Rochdale, as the lacklustre plot and neurotic acting of a young

Florence Desmond (in her first film appearance) was simply intended as a vehicle for Gracie.

In comparison to the unfavourable reviews Desmond was getting, Gracie was described, "As well as being the queen of the variety stage, she is also a dramatic actress of genius [...] and set for a promising future in the talkie industry," and "A distinctive personality who shines among London's greatest stage stars." Many background actors were employed for the film to fill up the main scenes in the coffee house, the pub, and in the street. Gracie is clearly at ease in the film acting with her fellow working-class people. Her scenes with her beau, played by Ian Hunter, however, appear quite stilted—especially when the two are attempting to show affection for each other.

In later life, Florence Desmond recalled, "What a dear Gracie was to work with, and what energy she had! She never seemed to get tired. A rehearsal was a performance to her. Many times I heard Basil Dean say, 'Save your voice, Gracie.' To which she replied, 'The more I use my voice, luv, the better I can sing.'"

At this point, Florence Desmond did not have a car and Gracie would pick her up at Baker Street Station every morning at 6:45am to give her a lift to the studios for their 9am shooting start. Florence also said, "I can honestly say that I enjoyed making the film more than any other picture I had made."

Gracie and Florence would often sit together at lunch on set and discuss everything from why Rochdalian leather clogs with brass studs were the only shoes that "rest my feet more than any other kind of shoe," and that Gracie had never had her own children because, "I am almost afraid to own something that I can love. It's a funny thing, but whenever I love something very dearly it is always taken from me. It used to be that way when I was a kid: if I had a dog it used to die. It's been the same since I've been grown up."

Many fans cite this first film as Gracie's best, but it is mainly let down by the over-melodramatic Florence Desmond. Whilst Gracie said both Archie and Basil Dean had no idea about the film business, it seems Florence Desmond had no idea about the acting business. There are distinct underlying elements of class conflict, in which a glamorisation process for Gracie is mocked and played down, and a performance of Fred Fanakapan significantly highlighting class differences. Film business had always been a difficult problem for Gracie, holding off screen offers for a long time, believing herself to belong solely to the world of the theatre. As film companies were badgering her to take a screen test she refused each one and carried on with her theatre work. After box-office profits began to soar the film business came easier for Gracie, who was spurred on by the positive reception of the film. This came as a double-edged sword. "I viewed this with very mixed feelings, for it meant they wanted me to make more, and I had never disliked any work so much." Gracie said, "As soon as they shut the studio, I felt trapped. I never felt it in a theatre. It always seems as though endless waiting to say a few days' work." So, for the time being, both her and Archie decided to not think about any further films and focus on the theatrical production which Archie had been planning, called *Walk This Way*. (Originally titled *Let's Say Grace*).

Away from the studios and the theatre, Gracie and Archie had decided to sell Tower after less than two years living in it. Announced on April 15, the sale went through on June 9, 1931 by Messrs. Hampton and Son. The sale of Tower was really the final death knell for their marriage, and Gracie remembered in later life, "When our marriage disintegrated I felt as though I was a personal failure. It didn't seem right to go round being miserable when I had so much to be happy about; it seemed wicked and ungrateful. So I pushed the dream of a 'someone' to the back of my mind and my heart for a long, long time, and I went to fall in love with an island instead, an island called Capri."

It has long been a myth that Gracie donated the property to become a nursing home for mother's, but in fact, the Tower Maternity Annex of the North Middlesex Hospital was privately bought before conversion into the medical facility, which existed up to the 1970s. By 1936 the extensive grounds had been divided up and another plot built on the far end of the garden, which became the Heinrich Stahl Jewis Care Home in the 1960s. For the maternity hospital, the main house was much-extended with single-story rooms, and in 1968 a further nine houses were built in the middle section of Tower's former grounds, keeping in style with the original 1920s design. The maternity annex was demolished by the 1980s and a huge house was built on the site, again called Tower, without proper permissions and was demolished in 2004, where three blocks of luxury apartments now stand.

Tommy and his wife had already moved into their own home a few months previously, and Auntie Margaret moved to Peacehaven for a while whilst Gracie and Auntie Margaret moved in temporarily with John Flanagan in his studio apartment. Whilst not ideal, it served Gracie well until she found somewhere small and homely of her own. This eventually came in the form of a small studio garret at 2 Queen's Road Studios, St. John's Wood. Built on the back of a four-story house, the place had a stone floor, a bath which doubled as a dining table, and also a small cooker. Upstairs, it had a tiny attic room where Auntie Margaret was to live. Gracie bought a carpet and a Bechstein piano for decoration, and said, "For the first time in London, it felt like home." Her manager, Bert Aza, didn't like the house and was appalled the magnificent **Gracie Fields** was living in a house with a stone floor and keeping potatoes in the bath, having downsized immensely from the ridiculous opulence of Tower.

Following the sale of Tower in 1931, Gracie and John Flanagan took a short holiday to Spain and returned with the ideas for a house in Spanish style, with an old English bar, all spit and sawdust and a red roof.

Originally planned for Highgate, planning permission for this house was granted on Frognal Way on May 30, and construction began.

April 22 saw Gracie honoured by the Gallery First Nighters in celebration to her at the Criterion restaurant, and the following week Gracie appeared in a concert for the Variety Artist Ladies' Guild and Orphanage, at which she made a massive gesture toward the charity. In November 1930, Lottie Albert, the secretary of the Variety Ladies' Guild, asked for any artiste's assistance in locating homes for children of variety artists who had either died or fallen on hard times, and immediately Gracie set the wheels in motion to donate her home on Dorothy Avenue in Peacehaven to the Guild, with the aim of housing up to twelve orphaned children to begin with. After some interior alterations the Gracie Fields Children's Home and Orphanage opened the following year in a ceremony attended by music hall artists Charles Coburn, Rob Wilton, Norman Long, Charles Austin, Sir Harry Preston, and Mr. J.H. Thomas. Run officially by the Guild, the orphanage was financed by Gracie until 1967 and usually housed anywhere between 12 to 25 children. Whenever she was in Peacehaven Gracie would go to the orphanage (often cycling the short distance from the family home) to visit the children who all lovingly referred to her as Aunty Grace. The fees charged for many of Gracie's private and public appearances throughout her career went to the orphanage's upkeep fund, and in later life Gracie said, "The few thousand pounds that the house has cost me was the best investment I have ever made."

On May 11, Gracie took part in her second Royal Variety Performance in front of the king and queen at the London Palladium in an international bill that featured Al Trahan, Alfred Rode, Teddy Brown, Rich Hayes, Jack Stanford, Max Miller, and Johnson Clark. Also appearing on the bill was Gracie's brother-in-law, Douglas Wakefield, and his Boys from Manchester, performing comedy routines. The press described

Gracie as, "Not tethered by talent; she is freed by genius; she roams where she will; she takes all comedy for her province, and to comedy itself she gives a wide definition. There is something fundamental about her that will probably overcome the perils of success just as it outfaced for so long the discouragements of neglect." On June 22, Gracie visited the Northold Park Races for charity, and at a further charity event on July 21 she publicly performed the song "Sally" for the first time to an audience—something which she would thereafter do at every live performance for the next 48 years.

Whilst Gracie had been touring in variety and filming *Sally in Our Alley*, Archie's next review, *The Comedy King*, opened at the Bristol Empire in February 1931 and starred Duggie and Edith Wakefied with Chuck O'Neill, Len Clifford, Alfreda West, Horace Gilbert, Violet Brooks, Fred Louin, and the Pitt Girls and Boys. The story focused on Duggie as the would-be king of Begonia vying for the throne against Boris Brodska (Gilbert). The show ran for less than four months, when poor audiences meant Archie took it off the road and took the majority of the cast for his next big Gracie show.

Appendix Dec 1930

This, as it turned out, was his last show with Gracie, and was scheduled to make its provincial debut at the Blackpool Opera House on July 27, titled *Let's Say Grace!* After two months rehearsals at the Alexandra Palace, the retitled *Walk this Way* promised to be Archie Pitt's greatest revue to date, featuring Britain's latest and long awaited film star. Nineteen year old Irene Pitt had married Lou Ross, Archie's present band leader who provided the interval music, the previous day in Hampstead, and the whole troupe then headed up North, ready to open at the opera hous in the early hours of July 27.

Archie considered this to be his funniest revue, having honed his years of practice to finally achieve a piece to rival *Mr. Tower of London*. Although *The Show's the Thing* had been a commercial success, he believed *Walk this Way* would beat it and keep his star act part of the company even if he could not keep her as a wife. However, compared to the other two shows, *Walk this Way* was prodigal. Norman Newell, who many years later would work on recordings with Gracie, cites his earliest recollection of her was whilst she was playing in *Walk this Way*, and, "she was absolutely magic. I never dreamt I would get to meet her, or even work with her." The show played 18 regional theatres before moving to London in December 1931.

Before the show opened at Blackpool, Gracie could not resist to go and see the bairns at the Children's Sunshine Home at Rossall and visited them for a whole afternoon, where she sang her popular songs and read the children stories. On August first Gracie unveiled a plaque in the Actor's Chapel at St. Stephen's on the Cliffs Church in Blackpool, bearing the names of the donors to the unique theatrical chapel, including herself, Archie, and Archie Pitt's Productions, accompanied by the Bishop of Blackburn. That same week in Blackpool, Archie judged a dance talent competition, announcing Connie Chambers as the winner and signing her to his production company.

All twenty scenes of the revue were separate, with dresses by Madam Ann of Holborn and scenery again by Parry and Jewett. Archie took inspiration from Gracie's civic reception in Rochdale earlier in the year of how best to open the show and introduce the cast members. Gracie had two solo spots in the show in which she makes the transition from grave to gay, but was also featured in many of the scenes with Duggie Wakefield, Tommy Fields, Irene Pitt, and Morris Harvey. Gracie's opening number in "The Town Hall" scene was "The Clatter of the Clogs," a song highlighting the musicality of the footwear of thousands of factory workers toddling to work each morning. Duggie Wakefield and the Boys from Manchester presented a bit of business of being caught up in an inner tube from a garage, which was first presented at the Royal

Variety and later recreated in Duggie and Tommy's film, *The Penny Pool* (1937). In a dress designed by Ella Wells, Gracie appeared in her own solo spot before the act closer of "Way Down East," a Cockney knees-up at a London wharf. Dressed as a pearly queen, Gracie performed "The Lights of Paris" with her brother and a Cockney Jazz number with the entire company in garish blue and orange costumes.

The pinnacle of the show came in Act Two, in a scene where Irene played a doll who befriends Renee Foster dressed as a golliwog. Gracie's singing makes the pair come alive, as well as the other toys in the shop played by the boys and girls of the company. Further comedy scenes took place in a hospital ward, with Gracie playing Tommy Fields's daughter; a convict dance, danced by the male dancers of the company; a tragi-comedy scene on the Embankment; a seedy pub called The Red Umbrella; and a scene played in the trenches of the First World War. Gracie appeared as herself at the top of the bill and performed the songs which she was releasing on H.M.V. at the time. "Tosselli's Serenade" and "River, Stay Away from My Door" were performed throughout the run, as the audience reception for the numbers was excellent. Tommy also had his own solo spot in the performance, where he performed some of his comedy dancing and played the violin.

Boldly handled with a variety of colours, ostrich feather, and pretty girls, *Walk this Way* mainly toured the North of England, branching into Scotland during its few months in the provinces before the show moved down south to Cardiff, Brighton, and Southampton. Whilst the show was playing the Manchester Palace in November 1931, Gracie returned to Rochdale with her brother to watch Rochdale Amateur Operatic Society's production of *Katinka*, and spent the afternoon with her entire company at Rochdale Town Hall at a charity dance in aid of the Rochdale Football Club. At the event, Gracie promised to pay the train fare for the club's next match, as it was looking likely that due to ill funds the team would not be able to continue in the northern section of the Third Division League. So on November 14 Gracie footed the bill for £15 when the team boarded the 7:21am train from Rochdale to Barrow. Whilst playing the Glasgow Alhambra in late August, the male members of the company took part in a charity golf match against professionals in aid of the Wheatley charity. Over Christmas 1931, Gracie appeared in a special BBC variety radio programme as a last-minute stand-in, with her £100 fee for performance being given to her Children's Home in Peacehaven.

Walk this Way was booked to re-open London's Winter Garden Theatre on December 15, where it was slightly criticised in the press for lack of novelty for the rest of the cast, but heralding Gracie with rave review and championing Archie in "the disclosing of the remarkable talent which is hers." Reviewers also lamented the great loss to the comedy stage as her brilliant comedy acting was overshadowed by her even better vocal acrobatics and performances. When the show reached London a bit of business was even written in to show off Gracie's new Pekingese puppy, Topsy, who was receiving media attention of her own, and even featured with Gracie on the front of the book called *Whose Dog are You?*

One evening whilst Gracie was preparing for the show in her dressing room, a bespectacled young man burst past the stage-door keeper and into Gracie's dressing room, where she was sitting with Annie Lipman and Auntie Margaret. This young man was Harry Parr-Davies, who would go on to have a long and fruitful association with Gracie. Since *Sally in our Alley*, Gracie had been besieged with songwriters sending her songs or asking her to try out a few bars of their latest composition. Archie eventually put a stop to this, as musicians were a constant stream both to the theatres Gracie was performing in and their home. "Harry looked so stricken and nervous," remembered Gracie. "I couldn't turn him out so I told him to sit and play the piano." Seeing the piano itself was an amazement for Harry, "as dressing rooms never have a piano, but this was the stage piano shoved into Miss Fields's room for storage." As Harry played, Annie sang the words to the song, aptly titled "I Hate You." Ever charitable Gracie thought hearing the lad play for five minutes was better than snubbing the young hopeful.

To Annie and Gracie's surprise, the tune was surprisingly good and the lyrics fit well with it, but Harry had only composed one verse and a chorus. However, Gracie was so impressed with him she told him to come back to the theatre each night and use the piano in her dressing room, as he didn't have one, and finish the song off. A fortnight later when the song was finished Gracie accepted it into her repertoire, and in the meantime she and Harry had become firm friends.

Born in Neath, South Wales on May 29, 1914, by the time he was in his teenage years Harry had already composed a number of songs and was working on full operettas. Gaining popularity in Neath by playing the church organ, his teachers tried to sway him to go to Oxford to study classical music, but Harry's heart was set on composing popular music and comedy numbers. He had travelled to London to pester the music stores of Tin Pan Alley to try and take some of his numbers, and when he had no success he decided to go to the very top and visit Gracie herself. He didn't believe she had accepted his song until a contract arrived at his parents' house in Neath, and his parents realised, "I had not been conned by some of the big London leg pullers."

1932 began with *Walk this Way* still running at the Winter Garden, and the show took its final curtain on April 2, 1932, and as Gracie tried to leave the stage door it soon became apparent it wasn't going to be possible. The police were called to usher Gracie through the jubilant last-night crowd, and even they fought to get her through. Gracie had an idea, and went upstairs to her dressing room window, gave her errand-boy whistle, and promptly gave a speech of thanks to the waiting crowd, but asked them kindly to "get out'o'the road so I can get 'ome and get mi tea!" Although the show had a big cast and over eleven loads of scenery, it closed on the wrong side of the balance sheet.

Immediately after the revue was finished Gracie and Archie officially parted company, and on Wednesday June 22, 1932, Archie Pitt Ltd. officially closed trading, with all management being handed over to Aza Agencies, although Archie did still produce shows until 1936, and *Walk this Way* continued touring the country until August 1933 with Duggie Wakefield, and following his departure Nat Mills and Bobby took the leading roles. *Walk this Way* and *The Show's the Thing* both continued touring until December 1934, when shortly afterward all the scenery and props from both shows were sold at auction.

A scene from 'The Show's the Thing' (1929).

CHAPTER SEVEN

1932 - 1934

A song and a smile making life worthwhile,
So sing as we go along!

- "Sing As We Go" (1934), recorded by Gracie Fields.

REALISING THAT A SEPARATION was imminent, Archie had begun to plan a smaller house to move into when he and Gracie split up. As it was mainly her earnings which had paid for the building and the upkeep of Tower, a second house was built in Gracie's name—and money—on Frognal Way in Hampstead. The white brick and blue-tiled two-story house was named Blue Tiles, and construction began before Gracie and Archie separated, with Gracie originally wanting a house in Spanish style. Building costs were estimated to be £3,500 but went well over £10,000 by its completion. Although Gracie is listed as living there in the 1934 electoral register, it is unlikely Gracie ever even stepped foot into the building, which was built with the full intention of being Archie and Annie's (and butler Gerald Burrows) home together, which was completed in 1934, two years after Gracie and Archie had separated. Even though she never lived in the house, there is a plaque on the building at 20 Frognal Way,

Hampstead from the Heath and Old Hampstead Society stating Gracie had built the house for herself.

Archie and Annie's relationship had been going on, with Gracie's full knowledge, for many years. Something which was confirmed in later life by Lillian Aza. She commented, "She knew about the setup at the time they got married. Gracie was never a wife in the accepted sense of the word. She had her work, and her heart and soul were in her work. Archie was quite an ill person and had to have a special diet and so on. Annie was the one who always prepared it for him, and Gracie always told Annie to do it. Really, it was Annie who took on the wifely duties."

On the other hand, Tommy presented his sister as a neglected wife and said, "Archie Pitt loved women and money, and that's what he got. It wasn't a happy marriage, but Gracie had her work and that alleviated the tensions and miseries." Archie's great-granddaughter, Janice Steele, recalled, "Archie's requests, like leaving bananas to go black before he ate them or having bread on the side for three days annoyed Gracie, but Annie was only too happy to pander to his whims."

Archie and Annie lived together in the house until 1938, when Gracie received a letter from Archie saying he was terminally ill and he wished to have ownership of the house because it was still in Gracie's name. Instead, Gracie drew up a contract with his lawyers that he was to live in the house until his death. However, he could not afford the upkeep of the house, so Gracie came to a compromise and arranged that he was to be paid £5 a week for the rest of his life. "I knew then that he wouldn't starve and my conscience was undisturbed." Archie was not happy with this idea, and moved to 46 Willingfield Way, Hampstead Garden Suburb. The couple also had a second house in Sandbanks in Dorset, a cottage called Roscombe.

It is fondly rumoured Gracie wanted to see some good come out of Tower and donated the building to be used as a maternity hospital. The truth, however, was that the house was in Archie's name and he sold it for a minimal cost of £5,000 when auctioned on June 9, 1931 by Hampton and Sons. The house eventually did become a maternity hospital, but it was not donated by Gracie. When Tower last came on the market before its demolition in 1992 the house was estimated to be worth £24 million, having undergone recent renovations, including an underground garage, a swimming pool, and self-contained nightclub where the old ballroom used to stand. The house sold for less than half its estimate due to major restoration work which needed to be done, and was eventually demolished. In its place now stands a set of multi-million pound apartments.

Gracie and Archie officially separated in early 1932, not 1935 as some books suggest. Even though the press did not report it, the couple were no longer photographed together and only seen in public at key events when he needed to "keep face" to the public. This ridiculousness stopped in 1933 with Archie's last appearance with Gracie at the lunch to celebrate the pressing of her four millionth pressing. The decision to separate was not easily made by Gracie, especially as she was already contracted to be involved with her next film. In later life, Gracie described Archie like "being married to a balance sheet" and that "if I did not find the courage to break the habit of obeying him, which I had grown up with ever since I was sixteen, I should never be able to make a full and happy life for myself." Following what she wanted for once, Gracie decided to split from him entirely. She did, however, agree for him to continue his involvement with her next film, and even set up a regular income for him from her earnings.

Archie did continue a career in variety, touring revues, and also reincarnating *Mr. Tower of London*. From Monday, February 15, Archie appeared at the top of a variety bill at the Brixton Empress with a new comedy offering titled *A Fleet-ing Acquaintance* co-starring Beryl de Querton. He also had a short-lived and unsuccessful film career, starring in *Danny Boy* (1934), *Barnacle Bill* (1935), and *Excuse My Glove* (1936), all of which made no impact at the cinema. His final turn in review was in a reprise of *A Fleeting Acquaintance*, which was first presented at Colston Hall reopening in December 1936, before touring briefly and unsuccessfully in 1937.

Inspired by John Flanagan's studio apartment, after leaving Tower Gracie bought her own studio at the back of the terraced houses at 2 Queen's Grove, St. John's Wood, not too far from where John was living in his studio. The studio itself, Gracie remembered, "looked like a good storage place for potatoes. It had a stone floor and a little alcove where there was a bath and a cooker. When you didn't need the bath you could cover it over with boards and use it as a table.

"Upstairs there was one tiny attic, and Auntie Margaret, who was living with me, and I shared this as a bedroom. To get to the place you had to go through an unlit alleyway by the side of the house, and Archie's brother, Bert Aza, who was still my manager and my dearest friend, was horrified with the whole setup when he saw it." Gracie decked the studio out in fine carpets and sofas and bought herself a Berchenstein piano." I could lunch at the Ritz, sing at the Palladium, sign a thousand autographs a day, meet the important people who always seemed to crop up, but when I got back to the studio and Auntie Margaret's welcoming smile, it felt like a real home."

On March 3, 1932, Gracie visited Dr. Banardo's home and brought along a giant Easter egg for the children there to enjoy. Various scenes from Gracie's last Pitt revue were played during the second half of her London Palladium engagement during the week beginning April 21. She was rejoined by Duggie Wakefield in presenting his "New Garage" scene, and Tommy Fields in the hospital scene. Teddy Brown also became part of the nightclub scene to "add colour," whilst Helen Grey performed a contortionist's routine. Gracie added new songs to her repertoire, which now included "Sally," as well as the humorous "Grannie's Little Old Skin Rug" and the beautiful ballad "Home." The following week she appeared at the Brixton Empress in a variety bill featuring Max and Harry Nesbitt, Randolph Sutton, and the Valeros Brothers. Following this she returned to Rochdale, where she was appointed Life Governor of Rochdale Infirmary in a small ceremony at the hospital.

Before Gracie had left Capri after her first visit she had instructed Ettore Patrizi to inform her if ever a plot of land was to come for sale at the Marina Piccola. As it happened, Ettore's mother had decided to sell Il Fortino and was giving Gracie first refusal on the house she had fallen in love with. In later life Gracie said, "I'm one of those restless people who're always wanting something different, something new," and Capri was something which she certainly wanted.

Worried at the thought of someone else buying her dream house, Gracie insisted she must have it immediately, even though she didn't know how much money she had in her bank, as she was so used to Archie or Bert arranging her finances. In her unpublished autobiography, Gracie described how earning so much money from stage performances, radio, and films horrified her. To her friends in Rochdale, £100 a week would seem a fortune to earn, which in fact it was, but she writes, "I could spend five pounds on trinkets for friends and have £95 left over for the next week." The truth was that Gracie was earning so much money at this period she couldn't tell to the nearest hundred just how much she was actually earning. Long forgotten 78 records which she had sung only once at the time of recording months before were still making money, and royalties were still pouring in to Bert Aza's office on Charing Cross Road. One distressing problem, however, was the thousands of begging letters which they received daily. Gracie was receiving so much post during this period that the Royal Mail had to supply a delivery van every other day with letters especially for her.

Bert was horrified one morning when he found Gracie writing out countless checks in response to the begging letters, and promptly stopped her from replying to them. After arguing her case, Gracie agreed to let Bert filter the letters and investigate the most worthy ones to see if the poor old lady who would be sent to prison for not paying her milk bill wasn't really a wealthy young businessman—which sometimes was the case. A private investigator was hired, but Gracie was still unhappy as she believed the writers must desperately need the money to have written to someone they didn't even know for help. Gracie received begging letters of all varieties, ranging from requests for artificial limbs, dresses, blankets, and light bulbs, to pleading mothers of apparently sick children who wanted them to be sent to doctors in Switzerland.

Meanwhile, after much confabulation with John Flanagan over the fifteen thousand pounds cost of the Capri property, Gracie decided to look seriously into its acquisition and hired lawyers, surveyors, and architects to go to Capri on her behalf. All of the contractors took expense-paid trips to the property, but failed to report back to Gracie on the matter. She eventually was put in touch with Sir John Serrao, the British Embassy's legal advisor in Rome, who set about helping her with the purchase of the property. The Patrizi's, in need of money, had agreed they would take eleven thousand pounds for the dilapidated building and all its land, but Gracie still was unsure about whether or not she could afford or justify this price.

Agreeing to variety engagements throughout the summer ensured she could live reasonably. After a short break following the closure of *Walk this Way* on April 25, Gracie was headlining at the Palladium, including "Sally," "Granny's Little Old Skin Rug," and a second time in the programme in a scene from *Walk this Way*, titled "A Quiet Sunday," with Morris Harvey playing a harassed neighbour trying to read the newspaper while Tommy Fields practices the violin, before Billy Nelson and

Duggie Wakefield arrive with drums which drive even bedridden invalids into active flight. Syd Seymour also appeared on the bill with the "Mad Hatter's Nightclub" scene from the show alongside Teddy Brown, Scott Sanders, Frank-Le-Dent, and Helen Gray, as well as the Boys from Manchester in their inner-tube sketch routine.

From May second, Gracie was breaking box office records at the Brixton Empress with Morris Chester's 16 Sporting Dogs, Morris and Cowley, Max and Harry Nesbitt, Little Doreen, the Eight Dancing Dominos, and Randolph Sutton. The following week Gracie was back in London at the Victoria Palace, and from Saturday, May 14, Gracie, Fields and Rossini, Leslie Hutchinson, Annie Croft, and Lilly Morris broadcast in music hall, with Gracie again broadcasting from the BBC on May 21. During this week, from May 16, Gracie was back at the Palladium in a special holiday bill starring Will Hay, G.S. Melvin, Talbot O'Farrell, Clapham and Dwyer, Nell Kelly, Gary Leon, Eddie Hanley, and the Kitchen Pirates.

Being out of filming for almost over a year, Gracie agreed to star in a second film to fund her Caprician home, and filming was scheduled to begin at Ealing for Gracie's next film, *Looking on the Bright Side*, directed by Jack Raymond and written by Brock Williams and Basil Dean, with additional scenes by Archie Pitt, on April 25, but due to Gracie's variety engagements was delayed until June second, while *Sally in Our Alley* (1931) premiered during this week to eager audiences in Christchurch, Australia. Richard Dolman, Gracie's leading man, was announced the day before filming began as Basil Dean finally made a decision in selecting him, as opposed to the thirty other actors he was considering for the role to sing and dance alongside Gracie. Shooting began after a succession of disagreements, namely the fact Basil Dean rewrote the majority of Archie's script and took over from Graham Cutts as the film director, as he was not happy with the work Cutts had done on the completed scenes.

Following on from the popularity of her first film, a similar down-to-earth comedy storyline was used in which Gracie plays a hapless beauty technician who falls in love with an up-and-coming songwriter named Laurie. For the first time in her career, Gracie played a character with a name other than Sally ... Although, the name of her character was Gracie! Swayed by fame, martini cocktails, and the highlife, Laurie, played by Richard Dolman, leaves Gracie, and it turns out whilst she can be a success on her own, he is a failure without her. The biggest set ever built in Britain up until that point was built at Elstree Studios and consisted of two blocks of Art-Deco apartment buildings with winding stairways, known as Parker's Paradise, based on Peabody's buildings in Drury Lane. The climax of the film sees the two apartment buildings sliding together in an almost fantasy image so that Laurie and Gracie can finally embrace each other. But before they could do this, Gracie had to run up and down the steps hundreds of times during filming—more often than not singing the film's title song, later complaining that it gave her corns and blisters on her feet. When Gracie saw the film at its Irish premiere in Dublin in September 1932, she told the press afterward how exhausted she was just rewatching the scene running up and down the stairs.

Another scene in the film sees Laurie and Gracie attend a cocktail party, at which Laurie has too much to drink and Gracie doesn't know what to do with the cherry in her martini glass. She suggested to the props team, "Real drinks look more effective on camera than colored water in the cocktails," and much to the fury of the financiers of the film, real alcohol was used when water would've easily substituted on the black and white film stock. Gracie quipped to them, "Don't look on the tight side, but look on the bright side!" as she trilled the film's title tune much to the pleasure of the crowd-scene audience, who progressively got more and more inebriated as the filming of the film's two party scenes went on.

Much like the film's predecessor, Gracie relied on a catchy theme song to carry her through, and this came from composer Howard Flynn. Flynn had spent a significant time in hospital, and wrote the catchy number to cheer himself up through his ordeal. He, like thousands of other writers, sent his song along to Bert Aza for consideration to be used by Gracie, and was delighted when the song was not only picked for use in the film, but chosen to be its title, which, as in *Sally*, appears throughout the film in different incarnations, the most lavish of which was a Busby-Berkley inspired Art Deco song and dance routine in the hairdresser's salon, including pretty manicured chorus girls, moving scenery, a tap-dancing bellboy, and a foppish Italian parrucchiere. One of the film's highlights is when an out of work Gracie decides to join the police force but is constantly reprimanded for playing with her Yo-Yo, singing, playing, skipping, and impersonating Charlie Chaplin.

As with her first film, the popularity of the five songs Gracie performed was publicised with 78rpm record releases and sheet music covers for each of the songs, featuring Gracie's image. One of the most tender scenes of the film features Aunty Grace in a Jolson "The Singing Fool" (1928) Sonny Boy inspired routine, "You're More Than all the World to Me," by Bill Haines, Maurice Beresford, and Frank Sumner. Harry Parr-Davies's first published song, "I Hate You," takes prominence in the film, even though most of the characters comment on its terrible title. Strangely, only one of the songs Miss Fields sings is a broad comedy type, for which she is famous, and this was written by Bill Haines, Maurice Beresford, and James Harper, and titled, "He's Dead but He Won't Lie Down," a song about the antics of a very virile 103 year old.

At the Dominion Theatre in Vancouver, when the film was given its first Canadian tryout, the audience didn't really take to it and houses were half empty. When the film came around for the second time on the circuit, the theatre's manager, Ivan Ackery, "began to do some good promotion work. We worked with the newspaper, giving free passes to the film to cooperative advertisers; we got free window space in shops where we hid free passes among the merchandise and lucky customers would find them on making purchases. I worked with eight music stores in the city, having them feature Gracie Fields records and sheet music, and went on CKMO with a great radio man and Fields fan, Billy Brown. In short, we blitzed it!" The film played three weeks in its return run and received 36,334 paid admissions in the first fortnight, making it the most popular film to that date in Canada.

Whilst filming at Ealing, Gracie was visited on July 8 by Malpas, the globe-trotting troubadour from Melbourne who was cycling his way around the world, and filming spilled into the streets of Ealing when scenes were shot outdoors on Pishtanger Lane to add local color and authenticity to the film.

After the success of this second film, Bert Aza presented Gracie with a contract from ATP for six films at £12,000 per film, but this tied her to Archie Pitt for another six films. Whilst Archie had remained almost entirely in the background in *Looking on the Bright Side*, he had assisted Basil Dean and Brock Williams in the scriptwriting, surrendering his half of the direction to Graham Cutts. Knowing only too well that money cannot always buy happiness, even on the isle of Capri, Gracie turned down the £72,000 contract and told Bert to find her another deal, no matter how small, just so she could pay off the purchase of the house. However, the press speculated that out of the film, Gracie would earn £25,000 for her six weeks' work, taking home 50% of the film's profits.

Filming was completed and Gracie, on July 22, was back at Folkestone Marine Hall in what was turning out to be her annual charity concert, which was cancelled due to filming overrunning, and Gracie was replaced by Flotsam and Jetsom. Next came a week at the Grand in Blackpool, where Gracie premiered songs from her new film before the film was actually released. Whilst here, she was photographed being windswept overlooking the holidaying crowds from the top of the Tower. Her tour continued as she played a week at the Kingston Empire from August eigth in a bill with the Wallington Sisters, Paddy Drew, the Three Eddies, Randolph Sutton, Rome and Ronae, Collinson and Dean, and the Figaros; and at the Liverpool Empire from August 22 with Dinks and Trixie, Rome and Romane, Horace Kenny, Collinson and Dean, Lapp and Habel, Victor Moreton, the Three Eddies, and the Three Rascals.

Whilst in Liverpool, Gracie met J.E. Marsh, manager of bon marche, and filled out one of the store's application forms in attempt to become one of their shop girls. She was engaged right away and started work in the store's stockings department, which was "too much of a doddle," so she was transferred to shoes. Also in Liverpool, Gracie visited the telephone exhibition and used the transatlantic telephone to speak to Mr. Dawe, chief of the radio terminal in Montreal.

From the first of September, Gracie was performing at Dublin's Theatre Royal, and on the seventh Gracie was at the Plaza Ballroom to see the counterfoil sweepstake drum, which, Gracie being Gracie, she got inside the lottery barrel. However, somebody accidentally set the drum in motion and Gracie screamed and jumped out of it as it began its cycle! While in Ireland, Gracie also saw the premiere of her latest film, *Looking on the Bright Side* (1931). Back in Britain, Gracie played the Chelsea Palace from September 12 before *Looking on the Bright Side* went on general release to the public the following week. By October the film had already taken a gross income of £100,000, with cinema proprietors clamouring to book the film even before it had gone on release. On Saturday, the 24th, Gracie sang "Sally" on the football pitch between Chelsea and Newcastle United, and the following day appeared in a special charity concert for the Variety Artist Ladies' Guild and Orphanage charity concert at Daly's

Theatre, where she performed on stage and Archie bid from one of the boxes at the onstage auction, much to the annoyance of Gracie he was even there.

Playing the Chatham Theatre Royal for the week from October 3rd, Gracie starred with Balliol and Merton, Collinson and Breen, Horace Kenny, the Three Bobs, The Hartman Troupe, Freddie Phyllis and Anne, the Wallington Sisters, John Payne and Arthur Gibson. The smallest town on her tour, tickets didn't sell well and advertisements had to be continually pushed in the local papers.

Gracie was again back at the Palladium from October tenth with Rome and Gaut, de Biere, Gerlys and Lysia, Bedni Tafani Troupe, the Two Cottrillos, Claude Lester, Les Woltings, Billy Russell, Syd Seymour and his Mad Hatters, and whilst here, on October 13, appeared in the Metropolitan Charity show in aid of St. Mary's Paddington, where she auctioned baskets of fruit and bouquets presented to her, in a bill with Randolph Sutton, Ernie Lotinga, Bower and Rutherford, Billy Bennett, Peggy Rhodes, the Superb Eight, Harvey and Nervard, Rigoletto Brothers, and Austell and Arthur.

Owing to her success that week, Gracie was retained the following week from the 17th in a completely new bill consisting of the Wolthings Trio, Olsen's Sea Lions, Marie Macquarrie Harp Ensemble, Robb Wilton, Bobby Uke Henshaw, Will Hay, Austel and Arthur, and Teddy Brown. Following this, from October 24, Gracie was on the road in a variety tour which began at the Southend Hippodrome and took in the Portsmouth Hippodrome, Newcastle Hippodrome, the Stratford Empire, and the Brighton Hippodrome before finishing at the Leeds Empire for Christmas, and returning to the stage on Boxing Day at the Brixton Empire.

During this variety tour the acts with Gracie changed frequently, and she had with her: (Portsmouth) Jackson Owen and Co, Three

Rascals, Collinson and Dean, Miss Lutie, Griffiths Brothers, Joe Young, Tex McLeod, Frank Condo's Hot Steppers; (Newcastle) Raymond Smith, Collinson and Dean, Fields and Rossini, Rome and Romaine, Frank Condo's Hot Steppers, the Melvilles, Auntie, Maurice Chester's 16 Famous Dogs; (Stratford) Collinson and Dean, Frank Condos, Jackson, Owen and Co, Three Rascals, Walter Niblo, the Melvilles, Clifford and Rhode, Balliol and Merton; (Brighton) G.S. Melvin, Balliol and Merton, Joe Young, Three Rascals, the Wallington Sisters, the Two Bells, the Griffiths Brothers, and Tony Capaldi; (Leeds) Walter Niblo, Tony Capaldi, Allinson Sisters, Jackson Owen and Company, Raymond Smith, Frank Condo's Hot Steppers, the Three Rascals, Maurice Chester and his 16 Famous Dogs (Brixton) Bert Maddison, Murray and Mooney, Sam Mayo, the Four White Flashes, Balliol and Merton, the Three Rascals, Victor Moreton, and Horace Kenny.

When Gracie was appearing with Jackson Owen, Bert Aza recalled, "He was a well-known comedian with a comedy sketch in which six sailors took part. They had to line up in a row while Jac scored plenty of laughs off them. One evening, Jack couldn't get on with his dialogue and the sailors were doubled up with laughter. Yes, it was Gracie. She had pinched one of the sailor's suits and walked on it with the other five. It fit her nowhere, and she looked a real fright as she went through the dills doing everything wrong."

Gracie was in a special New Year variety concert on the BBC on December 30, with Harry Welchman, Ann Penn, Max Miller, Muriel George, and Ernest Butcher, but this was after a week's furor with the press, as the General Theatre Corporation, who had recently taken over Moss Empires, tried to ban variety artists on the radio as they considered it was taking away custom from the Halls. Bert Aza found a way through the contract, which was signed with Moss Empires before their amalgamation, and so Gracie went ahead and broadcast, and when it was pointed out stars such as Will Hay, Leslie Hutchinson, Billy Bennett, and Billy Russell—who were all fairly regular broadcasters—were under contract with the GTC, the case was thrown out and variety returned to the airwaves.

1933 began with variety again staring at Hackney Empire on the first day of the New Year before moving on to the Edinburgh Empire on January 15, where Gracie visited Henry Ballantyne's wool factory in Walkerburn. Touring continued through Birmingham and onto the London Metropolitan before the London Palladium from February 22, before returning to Rochdale for a second charity week from March first. By February 1933 H.M.V. had issued over 60 Gramophone records of Gracie, even though she said, "Recording is particularly hard work. One may have to sing a song ten or twenty times before it's passed as correct!" From the sales of her recordings it was calculated Gracie had sold over four million records on the H.M.V. label, and that production of her records alone kept 120 factory workers at Hayes busy. In early February she topped a newspaper poll to find the most popular British film star, on the basis of two films alone, and also visited the patients and staff at the Queen's Hospital in Birmingham. To celebrate the pressing of her four-millionth record, H.M.V. executives decided to hold a Lancashire-themed party at London's Trocadero Hotel and invite the press in a novel way—by making a Gramophone record for the invitation.

Recorded on January 23, the single-sided two-minute record features two H.M.V. executives talking to each other—disturbed by Gracie—who are discussing her sales figures. "Good gracious! It looks like my income tax form!" is Gracie's response, and to the suggestion of holding a Lancashire lunch, Gracie agrees, "That's not a bad idea. In fact, it's a good idea. Why not set about pressing another four million?" The lunch was held on February 14 at quarter to one at the Trocadero Hotel, and insisting, "We mustn't forget some of the folks from Rochdale," the H.M.V. executives, press, and Gracie's family were joined by family friend Bertha Schofield, Mayor of Rochdale James Wilkinson Dutton, Bob Brierley the clogger, and Gracie's old school master.

It was promised there would be some surprises in store, and these came in the form of seven large wooden tables in the form of Gramophone records featuring Gracie's latest recording, "Play Fiddle Play," as the centre label. One of these record tables went back to Peacehaven before it was moved to the Rochdale Museum Archives in 1985. Further to this, the drink coasters were also based on Gramophone labels and the waitresses were fitted in clogs and shawl. The place settings consisted of actual Gramophone records featuring a specially recorded musical menu called "The Day We Gave Our Lancashire Do," which Gracie recorded on February sixth. Whilst the recorded sketch may be somewhat contrived and amateurish, the song itself references members of Gracie's family and Gracie's song hits to date, including "The Lovely Aspidistra in the Old Art Pot," "Grannie's Little Old Skin Rug," and "The Little Pudden Basin."

The Lancashire meal on February 14 consisted of soup, fish, chips, and peas with a slab of butter and a loaf of bread placed in brown paper in the centre of the table for guests to "dig out the butter for ourselves," followed by a Lancashire hot-pot, beer in thick pint glasses, apple pudding, and tea drink with the spoon still in the cup. Speeches were made following the meal, with the mayor of Rochdale telling of his town's pride at their daughter, promising, "One day, a statue of Gracie Fields will be erected in her home town." His speech received a hearty round of laughter when he told about "when last she was in her home town the summit of Miss Fields's popularity occurred in the mentally deficient wards of the local hospital." It was suggested at the lunch her sales popularity is only equalled by Caruso, and that both of the artiste's Gramophone records were played on the summit of Mount Kamet in 1932 when members of a British expedition were the first to climb the mountain.

Earlier in the day, Gracie, Jenny, and Harry Parr-Davies visited the H.M.V. factory at Hayes, Middlsex in a publicity stunt to see the pressing of the actual four-millionth disc. In front of a large crowd of factory workers, Gracie pressed herself a copy of "Looking on the Bright Side," which was then promptly put onto a Gramophone player and Gracie joined in with herself in singing the number. After a crowd sing-along of the tune, a surge forward to get Gracie to sign copies of her 78s knocked Jenny flying into Harry Parr-Davies and called for the manager of the factory to restore order so Gracie and her family wouldn't get crushed in the stampede for an autograph.

From February 27, Gracie was back in Rochdale for her annual charity week. On March first, the current ban on variety artist's broadcasting was lifted for Gracie, "owing to the special circumstances connected with the occasion." George Black, the director of the General Theatre Corporation, decided he did not wish to do anything which would adversely affect Gracie's good cause, as her fee from the BBC was to be donated to Rochdale. George Black later remembered, "My most vivid memory of Gracie is on a boat in the bay of Naples singing 'Sally' with half a side of bacon tucked underneath her arm."

Whilst she was sitting in Bertha Schofield's kitchen, at the back of her off-license at 2 Milkstone Road, a telegram arrived for Gracie. Excusing herself into the other room to read it, Bertha and her daughter, Ada, rushed in as Gracie let out a high-pitched scream. Thinking something was clearly the matter with Gracie, they were relieved when she told them it was nothing for them to worry about. The sale of the Capri property had gone through, for £6,000 (400,000 lire), and Gracie now owned the entire Patrizi estate, which left her with only twenty five pounds in her bank account but with some humble buildings, vines, and an expanse of uncultivated hillside and a stretch of rocky beach. With the money from the contract for her second film, Gracie had put her family first and bought Edie and Duggie a house in Hampstead, given Betty and Tony financial aid to sell their home in Cheyne Walk in Chelsea and upgrade to Jessel House in King's Cross, and bought Tommy and Dorothy a house of their own in Edgeware.

Her Rochdale charity week of 1933 netted a total of £1,117 14s and 9d, which was distributed between the Gracie Fields Orphanage, the British Legion, Rochdale Mission, Rochdale Nursing Association, the Children's Convalescent Home, and the People's Services Guild. The *Rochdale Observer*, speaking of this charity week, wrote, "No queen in her own country ever received greater homage nor was more ecstatically cheered and adored by her people." Special souvenirs were sold in Rochdale during the week to add to the funds, which were porcelain compact mirrors with a photo of Gracie with "Look on the Bright Side" written on the porcelain side. When Gracie returned to Rochdale for her regular charity week in February 1933, someone shouted to her on the town hall balcony, "Where's yer Yo-Yo, Gracie?" and she shouted back, "I've had it stuffed!"

At the Plymouth Palace from March sixth, hundreds of people were turned away from the theatre every night as there simply weren't enough tickets for people to see Gracie before she moved on to play the Bournemouth Pavillion the following week, onto the Wimbledon Theatre the following week, and a short UK tour before heading back to the Holborn Empire from April 26 alongside Naughton and Wayne, Five Sherry Brothers, George Hurd, Victor Morton, Earle and Austin, Auntie on the Bike, Rome and Romaine, Payne and Hilliard, and the Four Jokers. While in Plymouth, Gracie stayed with friends at the Unicorn Hotel and attended a football match.

Whilst Bert was looking for a suitable film for Gracie's next, Gracie found her own contract with RKO pictures for one film at £5,000 a week—an estimated £25,000 total for the picture. Harry Parr-Davies signed a contract with her to provide the entire score to the film. Due to the success of the film, and with Gracie's salary dependent on how much the film made, it was estimated she earned over £28,000 in total for *This Week of Grace*. "Bert went green when I told him that it was he who had to tell Archie about it." Furious he was losing out on money, Gracie offered him £4000 as an apology, but he would have none of it.

Now in a very tough situation, as Bert and Archie had managed her career since she was sixteen, Gracie had no idea how to manage herself if the worst came. Bert was naturally very hurt Gracie had sought work behind his back, but he eventually smoothed it over. He agreed to solely represent Gracie for ten pounds a week and five percent on any and all money from other sources, with any money from advertising campaigns going to the orphanage charity.

Although fallen out with Archie, Gracie remained friendly for a few years with his daughter, Irene, and her husband, Lou, remained her personal musical director until 1937, after having his own band in 1933, Lou Ross Aeolians. Archie was annoyed Irene and Lou had taken Gracie's side in the argument, with Irene questioning what Archie even saw in Annie. Irene's granddaughter, Janice, suggested, "It was because she gave him the attention and looked after his every need. Gracie wouldn't bow down to him, but Archie was a great hypochondriac and Annie was only too happy to play nurse to him. He used to have these odd habits of never eating bread unless it was three days old and the like. Gracie would have none of it, but Annie would happily go along."

Eventually, Gracie, Lou, and Irene lost touch, partly at Monty Banks' insistence after a failed property deal in Genoa, with Irene and Lou's marriage eventually deteriorating, leading to divorce and leading to Irene living a promiscuous and full life, according to her granddaughter. Lou sent their daughter, Jacqueline, to a convent during the War, and Gracie sent her occasional things. Lou married Jeanette Isabel (known as Dot) in the early 1950s. Jacqueline lived for them and was very excited about having a stepmother, a mother figure at last. Sadly, they weren't close, although Jeanette and Lou were very close with their grandchild, Janice. The pair owned a restaurant, The Shrubbery, and café in Southend-on-Sea.

Irene's granddaughter, Jan, recalls, "I don't know what Irene did after she left the stage. She seemed to do just what she wanted. She married again twice and had a daughter, Sandra, from one marriage, but she was given up for adoption. (Irene first remarried in March 1947, becoming Irene Dunstone, and again in March 1967, becoming Irene Bevan). Irene lived in the Seychelles and in Whitehaven for a while, also Boulogne-sur-Mer and Leigh-on-Sea. I think Irene enjoyed her life but didn't want commitments—at least that was my understanding. Lou kept Irene away from Mum, but Mum always gave the impression Irene had walked away. Mum had a governess who lived with them who she was very close to."

Although Irene abandoned her daughter, Lillian, Aza still kept in touch with the family regularly, sending a special delivery of smoked salmon in a box shaped like a salmon every Christmas, often to the bemusement of the family. In 1952, when Jacqueline was married, Gracie and Boris sent £20 for a wedding gift congratulating the pair, from their "ready-made Grandma." It was also Lillian who arranged a reunification meeting between Jacqueline and Irene in later life, and also let Jacqueline know she had a half sister. Janice recalls, "Something in the back of my mind makes me think Mum met her first at Lilian's, then Irene did come down to Leigh-on-Sea. My late dad retired in 1990 and we were definitely in touch by then. I found it a rather strange relationship but was interested in some of the letters written between Irene and Mum about everyday things, which was surprising. I think my mum was desperate for stability, and Mum and Dad had an amazing marriage. Sadly, my sister went off and did not wish to keep in touch, so I know Mum felt she had been abandoned all over again.

"My mum never spoke about this part of her life. I know Gracie was good to her whilst she was in the convent and sent her trinkets and things, and I know Lillian kept in touch, but Lou never spoke about his past. Mum and Dad bought me a violin (I was useless), as Lou used to play, but he was reluctant to help me and refused to play himself, so I always wondered why and what might have happened. My mum said when she was born Irene said, "Urrgh, take it away!" But that's only hearsay. She did feel abandoned, Lou never spoke about it. Maybe if I had been older I might have asked. He died when I was about 12/13. I adored him and missed him dreadfully, as he and Dot lived downstairs and Mum and Dad upstairs, so I spent time with him every day. I also know Lillian sent Mum items from Pat, Edgar, and Hilda when they passed away, including a Japanese-style sewing table, which I now have. Likewise a porcelain goat and donkey which Gracie had in Capri. Gracie and Irene only met once more, in 1977 at a birthday party held for Lillian Aza in Brighton, at which they were both guests."

A few months earlier on a train to Brighton, Gracie was introduced to Nell Emerald, the sister-in-law of Stanley Lupino. Nell invited Tommy and Gracie to meet her mother over coffee, and there confessed to Gracie she had written a plot scenario for a possible film, titled, *This Week of Grace*, and asked whether she would be interested in it. Gracie read the scenario, and whilst she liked it, she was constantly snowed-under with scripts to look through. However, after a few weeks she decided Nell's film would be the "perfect film to step out on my own and break away from Archie's scripts," but when she called Nell she was nowhere to be found. After nearly three months of searching, "My Lancashire obstinacy paid off, as I found Miss Emerald and got the scenario from her." Gracie had decided she wanted to do that film and only that film. Whilst the director, again Maurice Elvey, wasn't impressed, as weren't many of the other cinema officials, Gracie demanded the film be made, and her demand paid off when the film was a third box office success for Gracie.

Gracie's Lucky Day was announced as the title for her next film in the first week of March 1933, while Gracie was appearing at the Bournemouth Pavillion, and filming began in the first week of June with external shots at Twickenham, Stoke Poges, and Eridge Castle by kind permission of the Marquess of Abergavenny. Whilst Gracie had moved away from ATP to star in the Radio Pictures film, a dispute ensued over her performance rights to be able to star in the film, but ultimately it was agreed Gracie's contract at the time did not stipulate she wasn't allowed to make a picture for another company. Radio Pictures, based at Twickenham Studios, had already been booked for another film, and so ironically the production had to take place almost entirely at ATP's studios at Elstree. Emerald's original scenario was expanded on by H. Fowler Mear, Jack Marks, and Maurice Braddell, and was titled *This Week of Grace* in a nod to Noel Coward's 1928 revue, *This Year of Grace*.

With the tag-line, "A modern Cinderella story," the plot revolves around Grace Milroy, who loses her job as a local barmaid and takes up a position of housekeeper at Swinford Castle, the home of the eccentric Duchess of Swinford. Whilst Grace and family all take up the housekeeping post, Grace falls in love with Viscount Swinford, played by Henry Kendall, even though in society's terms she is below him. The house's butler, John Stuart, agrees to teach Gracie how to be "reefeend," but this is against herself and her family's own background. Against the odds, Gracie and Lord Clive eventually get married and provide the happy ending as told through Harry Parr-Davies' song.

The film's climax sees Gracie dressed as Cupid on top of a fountain, while the Sherman Fisher chorus girls dance around her. Since she was a child Gracie had prayed for a producer who would make her the "queen of a flying ballet," and she knew this wasn't going to happen with Archie Pitt. With *This Week of Grace* producer, Julius Hagen, however, Gracie's ambition would be achieved, and directed again by Maurice Elvey. This hope for Gracie was born in pantomime, "and now here was the dream come true, but was it a dream or a nightmare for me?" Gracie did the flying Cupid act strapped into a leather thong attached to a length of wire, "and felt for all the world like a sprawling frog instead of the graceful nymph I was supposed to. The morning after we'd shot this every joint was aching and in agony and I was bruised from ankles to chin." The final outcome worked, though, as the scene is one of the most hilarious in the film, seeing Gracie balancing on one leg atop a Grecian column singing "When Cupid Calls." A pesky spider lands on her back and throws her off balance as she tries to itch it with Cupid's arrow. Of course, this sends her spiralling around the stage on the harness, ruining a wedding scene (including removing the groom's toupee and the bride's veil), and causing all-round havoc to the show. Although this seems a particularly stuffy and not widely held view, one reviewer in *The Times* stated of the finished film, "There are too many passages in which a crude and uncomfortable humour is extracted from the awkwardness of the plebeian in high life," in reference to the film's drawing attention to class differences and etiquettes.

Although the film was just as much of an ordeal as the others, with Gracie getting boils under her arms through stress, she knew she was working for a purpose: to earn the funds to pay for her Caprician home. She took her photograph album of her first Capri holiday onto the set with her and reminded herself her Italian dream was obtainable. After filming was completed Gracie told Bert she didn't want to make any more pictures, and to not accept any contractual offers from any other filmmakers. The film received its London Trade Show premiere on September seventh before the premiere at the Plaza London three days later and going on general public release in the first week of October. The film was so popular it was still being shown in provincial cinemas as late as October 1936, and was dubbed, "Gracie's best film to date." Interestingly, in one scene of the film Gracie picks up a ukulele and begins to strum the opening chords of one of the songs before she puts it down and continues to sing. This came a year earlier than her Lancashire counterpart George Formby's playing of a ukulele on film, in his film, *Boots, Boots!* (1934).

Archie asked Gracie to visit him after filming had finished, and apologized for everything he had done previously to upset her. His true colors showed through, however, when he produced a contract for one film in which he was to be part-director and writer, and begged her to sign. Although promising to never ask anything from her again, he needed the finances as he wasn't turning out to be the success he thought he would be without Gracie. Thinking about this, she agreed to think on it, wondering whether the decision to start anything with Archie would be wrong, as she had a new and happy life with John, or did she owe it to Archie for starting her career off?

In an unpublished section of her memoirs, which were recently discovered, Gracie writes a very telling story. "The morning I promised to go to his house to sign the contract, a young lady came to see me and imparted some very valuable information. It was something I'd always worried and troubled about since I was in *Mr. Tower of London*, something Archie knew I was always upset about and he always denied it's possibility. I immediately rang him on the phone and told him never to get in touch with me again. I'd just been told something that had worried me over a number of years, something that he would understand and know what I was talking about. I could not ever see or speak to him again, so 'forget any contracts, to me you're dead.'" A secret which still cannot be revealed to this day. Gracie only ever saw Archie once again after this, although she helped him out many times financially when he was in need.

On June 6, 1933, Gracie took her first aeroplane from Croydon Airfield to Paris, where she stayed for a short break. From June 23, Gracie was back in variety at the Finsbury Park Empire, and on July 1 travelled to Southampton with her sister Edith to wave Duggie Wakefield off to Hollywood. A crowd of friends, family, and fellow Water-Rats had gathered at Victoria Station to wave him off, but Edith and Gracie travelled to Southampton to see him onboard ship. On July 9, Gracie appeared at the Clifton Hall Garden Party where she sang "Sally" without prompting after her audience didn't take too well to "Whiskers and All." Following a week in Bournemouth and a week in Birmingham, from July 26 Gracie was back at the Palladium for a week, in a run also starring Chick York and Rose King, Joe Young, Archie Glen, Donald Stuart, Franklyn D'amore, the Hai-Yung Troupe, the Three Allisions, and the Kirks.

Over July and August of 1933 Gracie toured fairly extensively, including Scarborough, Morecambe, Blackpool, Southport, and the Brixton Empress, and in doing this took a sort of busman's holiday. She bought herself a caravan, a Model 33 Eccles from the London Caravan Co. Ltd. and decided to enjoy her own home luxuries in her caravan, as opposed to lodgings or hotels. "Ee, it's a grand existence!" she told reporters who came to visit her shows and asked her about her caravan. Whilst on the road, Gracie crowned Bessie Robinson "Ormskirk Carnival Queen," presented Miss A. Tasker a trophy on behalf of Wigan Infirmary's driving competition (as well as starting the race), visited Tartleton Village Fair, and whilst in Blackpool went to see *White Horse Inn* as well as judging the Bathing Beauty Competition on August 19. Her director, Basil Dean, told the press, "Gracie prefers the simple life. She has just a simple flat with a serviceable, unostentatious car. No meals among glittering fashionable hotels, among luxury suites and society's darlings."

As much as Gracie liked the caravanning life, the main downside was she and John were woken each morning by scores of wasps, mainly brought on by the glorious sunshine that August 1933 brought. The caravan season passed without incident until the final leg of the journey from Scarborough to Blackpool. Gracie and John were joined by Grace Wakefield and Tony Parry, and the caravan overturned along the Gisburn-Clitheroe road. John and Gracie managed to get the van back up again, calm the children down, and continue on unscathed to Blackpool. Whilst they were at Blackpool, Fred and Tommy joined the pair for a few days and to take the children to the Pleasure Beach, and John on a fishing trip.

Whilst Gracie was out on the road caravanning, her sister, Betty, had decided to use Gracie's car whilst in London. The car had no policy or insurance, which Betty claimed she didn't realise when she was arrested and taken to court over the matter. Betty was held up at Brighton Police Court on August 14, and Mr. F. Howard Collier admitted the offence on her behalf. It was claimed that as Gracie was a very busy woman, she usually left her insurance policies to her agent. The car in question, an Austin Swallow, was not insured as Gracie had just bought a new Humber, and Bert had not insured the old car as he thought Gracie was going to sell it. Therefore, the policy was transferred from one car to the other, as opposed to taking out a new one for the new car, which Betty apparently did not know about. Alderman Gervis accepted this explanation and fined Betty £2 for the matter.

This Week of Grace received its London trade premiere at the Prince Edward Theatre on July 27 before a general release on October 16. After her tour had finished, where Duggie Wakefield signed an MGM contract in April to appear in Hal Roach comedies, on August 3 Gracie signed what was cited to be a £2 a minute contract with Associated Talking Pictures with Basil Dean, a total of £23,000 per film. Although she had not wanted to be in any more films, Gracie realized herself how prudish it would have been to turn down a film contract at this price. On stage she was the second highest earning star behind Sir Harry Lauder, but now at £23,000 per film she was Britain's highest paid film star, and had a contract price which rivalled even some of Hollywood's biggest players. It was rumoured this new contract was a similar salary to what Greta Garbo was earning, and the press worked out that the estimated time spent on a film set divided by her fee made Gracie's wages £2 a minute. Speaking to *Film Pictorial* after the signing of the contract, Basil Dean told, "Many people ask, 'Is she worth it?' Of course she is worth it!" He described how Gracie was an outstanding personality, bubbling with vitality and rich with both comic and serious genius, and about the unexpected success of her first film. "If the box office has proven Gracie is worth her brass, far more has Gracie herself proven by her unselfishness, her right to the very best that life can offer her."

After finishing caravanning Gracie went to Capri, where building and renovation work was beginning to specification on her house. She had agreed the Patrizi family could still live in half of the house, and she was to live in the other half until the time came when they could afford to move out. Ettore and his mother lived there until the early 1950s, looking after the property as caretakers while Gracie was away.

As renovations happened Jenny and Fred came out to visit the property to see what Gracie had frivolously spent her hard earned brass on. She built terrace walks and steps down to the beach below. Oleanders, hibiscus, bougainvillea, and orange trees were planted, and in later life Gracie remembered to Jess Yates that her very own orange tree gave her the greatest thrill and she wanted to show her mother, but by the time she had to see them Gracie had eaten them all, and so sent out for artificial oranges to be hung on them to impress her. A huge mimosa tree was planted in the centre of her terrace. Diamond-shaped blue tiles were laid on the patio, and railings were added to form a balcony over the sea. A grove of orange, lemon, and fir trees were added for shade, and both Jenny and Fred were impressed with the property. Jenny was even more impressed that the locals were addressing her as "Bonny Sarah," but Gracie had to tell her they were actually wishing her a good evening in their native tongue. Jenny also spent many hours in the kitchen trying to teach the Italian women how to make Yorkshire puddings. "The noise could be heard all over the island! Mother couldn't speak a word of Italian, and the cook couldn't speak a word of English!" When the cook achieved the Yorkshire pudding Jenny agreed she had got it and could stay.

"Give me something fresh and plenty of it, and I'm all right, making new beginnings in something or other every day. I like beginnings better than endings. There's such a delight in newness." Capri for Gracie was an entirely new venture, one which would give her the most peace and satisfaction throughout her life. Whilst the initial investment may have only left her with £25 in the bank account, it bought Gracie a slice of happiness previously unavailable or unobtainable for her. Forty workmen had been busy working on the property all spring, and when Fred went over to the island in summer he appointed himself as foreman. He was unimpressed with "those ruddy Italians. I give them a job to do and five minutes later they've gone off swimming or fishing!" So he got on with both the electric and the building work himself. One mishap occurred with his mixing of the cement with seawater, and cracks began to appear. In later years Fred swore he built the house himself, but in actuality only renovation work took place in the early years, not many structural changes. "I'll give my father credit, though, he did put the new windows in by himself, but these were blown out by a landmine during the War," told Gracie years later.

Forty packing cases with her possessions from her studio in London were shipped over in to Naples and on to Capri, including thousands of books, bookcases, two pianos, and a black ebony dresser. "Ettore swore for years that it had been his grandfather's, but me and John bought it from the Caledonian Market in London." A friend of Gracie and John's, Joe Foreman came out to visit and help with the renovations, and over dinner one evening the trio decided to rechristen Il Fortino, which was known on the island as Villa Patrizi. Gracie didn't like the idea of Villa Fields, and Joe scribbled down various ideas, including one which both John and Gracie liked the sound of, The Song of the Sea. They asked Ettore what the Italian translation was for this, and when he told them La Canzone del Mare, the name was instantly settled on there and then. From there Gracie went over to Capri, where building and renovation work was beginning to specification on her house.

Gracie left Capri (she never stayed longer than six weeks in the early years) and returned to England for her annual week's run at the London Palladium commencing July 26. In this performance, Gracie wore her hair a little shorter and a beautiful white dress, and added two new comedy numbers to her act, "Whiskers and All" and "The Rochdale Hounds." The audiences delighted in her beautiful rendition of "Three Green Bonnets" and the current hit at the time, "Stormy Weather." This was something George Black later remembered in his memoirs, as he wrote, "The house was hushed, breathless [...] This was blazing sincerity, a heart speaking to hearts of the world." Even at this point in her career, only two years after first recording it, Gracie was getting tired of "Sally" and told the audience, "Even she's growing whiskers!" But the people chanted for it, so Gracie gave the number as an encore. In subsequent concerts it soon became apparent to Gracie she wasn't going to shake off Sally so easily, as the song had fast become her signature theme.

On September 21, Edith Wakefield and her family left aboard the Europa to New York, where Duggie had film contracts lined up, and on

September 26 Gracie performed for the first time in her life in a football ground. At the opening of the football match between Chelsea and Newcastle United, Gracie took to the microphone set up in the middle of the pitch at Stamford Bridge in Fulham and sang "Sally" to the 30,000-strong crowd. She also took part in a publicity stunt on the roof of the radio offices, where she released thousands of balloons in promotion of the film *The Lost Squadron* (1933), and also opened the Tomb Thumb miniature golf course at Streatham Hill.

Touring again in variety, Gracie was at the Aberdeen Empire from September 3, where on the eighth she attended the Visitors Day Press and Journalist Exhibition at Kittybrewster and sang an impromptu duet with herself when she heard a 78rpm of herself playing on a Gramophone. On September 16, Gracie agreed to be a judge at the Wigan Reliability Trial, where she also fired the starter gun before leaving for Belfast for a run beginning on September 18 with her tomboy grin and a fringe of golden hair. From October third Gracie played at the Brighton Hippodrome in a variety programme with Jackson and Owen, Earle and Austin, the Melvilles, Metro and Goldwyn, the Three Bobos, Payne and Hilliard, and Olsen's Wonderful Sea Lions.

Before shooting began at Elstree on her fourth film, *Love, Life and Laughter* (1933), Gracie visited the British Legion's annual Carnival at Tarleton Rectory in Preston on October 9. Whilst here, she borrowed the vicar's hat and burst into a spontaneous version of "The Rochdale Hounds," incorporating the hat. Her new film contract had put her back in the black after the money spent on her Caprician home, and also gave her enough money to endow the orphanage at Peacehaven so it wouldn't be troubled for funds in the future. This included the erection of a new £5000 wing in 1934 to accommodate more children. "They'll have to fend for themselves one day, but for now they can sleep in comfortable beds and nice rooms. If you make good pictures, you must make a good orphanage." The contract with Associated Talking Pictures, formerly Associated Radio Pictures, now solely tied Gracie to working on film for them and not accepting offers from other British companies, as had happened with *This Week of Grace.*

The following week Gracie was back at the Holborn Empire. This was recorded by H.M.V. on October 11 and issued on a special three Gramophone box set embossed with Gracie's image and the detail, "Recorded at an actual performance." Two different recordings exist of this show, as a different edited version with different comedy patter and song introductions was released on the Regal Zonophone label two years later. The originally issued H.M.V. recording contains Gracie's full performance at the Holborn Empire, and is the earliest surviving full live concert of Gracie's, offering a unique insight into her performance style as she was nearing the reach of her popularity.

Blending the serious "My Cabin in the Pines," which she sends up with "Stormy Weather," comedy was added with the inclusion of "Whiskers and All," which was well received at the Palladium earlier in the year, and also a comedic send-up of "A May Morning." At the end of the concert Gracie gives her errand-boy whistle to stop the laughter and applause and demands a speech, employing a pseudo-posh-Cockney accent. She tells the audience, "Ladies and gentlemen, I do want to thank you so very very much, I do wish to thank you so awfully, no really, honest to Gawd. I do thank you very much indeed, but there are other people working at this theatre, so I'll have to say good night."

Years previously, Gracie had written, "The audience is new every time, and if you can only feel yourself one with it you can keep a real freshness, and your song will go. That's a good piece of psychological thinking." Every performance for Gracie was a new challenge. Her comedy patter with the audience in the Holborn shows make this clear, as she asks, "What would you like me to sing?" knowing full well the response would come back as "Sally." "Sally? Sally! Every blinkin' time, Sally! I'll be singing Sally when I'm nine hundred and ninety nine! Come on then, play oop! Yer having your money's worth tonight, aren't yer!" Halfway through the song Gracie stops the audience and tells them, "Let's forget we're in the Holborn Empire and imagine we're in our front room having a bit of a do," insisting they all know the words as well as her and should join in. The shared bond created between audience and star is part of what made Gracie popular to the masses, and this is evident in the Holborn recordings as a sense of solidarity of our kind is created through Gracie's performance.

Gracie was back in Scotland, playing the Edinburgh Empire from October 16 before heading to the Bradford Alhambra for the end of her tour the following week and her only appearance in the North for some considerable time. Her final public appearance before filming began was at the Annual General Meeting Variety Artists Ladies' Guild on November 25, of which Gracie chaired that year's meeting.

When Gracie told Bill Haines at Cameo Music she wanted a lively and upbeat song for her new film, he did some digging in the office archives and came up with a dusty manuscript in a locked drawer of a number written in 1931 by Leo Tower and Victor Ford. The "dots" were sent up to Gracie at the Palladium, where she had a listen to it on the piano during rehearsals and exclaimed, "That's it! That's the one!" As with *Looking on the Bright Side*, the song proved so fitting to the storyline of the film that it's title was also chosen to be used as the name of the film, *Love, Life and Laughter*.

"I'm a Failure," also included in the film, was written by a Leeds woman, May Thomson, who was introduced to Gracie by the xylophonist Teddy Brown, and Gracie was so impressed by the new talent the number was used in the picture. "Out in the Cold, Cold Snow" (which received it's pre-film tryout at the Holborn Empire), "Cherie," and "Riding on the Cloud" were all penned originally for the film, and the original song sung by Nell Gwynn to Charles II, "How Happy the Lover," was also included.

Written by Eric Dunstan, the film critic of *The Star* newspaper, and Major John Sterndale Bennet, and produced by Basil Dean, Gracie plays a London publican's daughter named after Nell Gwynn, who much like the original becomes romantically involved with a king. This one, however, isn't English, but from a broken down mittle European duchy, Granau, with a lonely castle amidst an alpine-like landscape. They meet while she's selling oranges on the streets, with proceeds for a charity trust. He gets to know her at the pub, and she attends a full-dress affair in his honor at the embassy. The king is informed by his father he must make an announcement that he's going to marry the princess of another royal family in order to acquire badly needed power and funds. Nellie is hurt and runs off, not understanding how much he really wanted her. A telegram with a confusing message is soon received at the pub, and the family leaves to go to the king's side, believing that Nell's to marry him after all. But the truth is evident on arrival, that though his feelings are still with her he must marry the dull and emotional daughter of the wealthy neighbouring monarch. Gracie—that is, Nellie—gamely makes the best of it and takes the silly princess though a crash course in charm, and in no time she becomes more presentable, and the royal wedding will be a success.

The film's male lead was played by John Loder, a dashingly attractive actor who had achieved mild success in Hollywood. Basil Dean thought the pairing of Gracie and John to be "an amusing idea to play his stolid, good nature, and perfect manners opposite the forthrightness of a Lancashire mill girl." Born on March 1, 1898, two months after Gracie, Loder was the son of a general in the Dragoon Guards and was educated at Eton and Sandhurst. War broke out while he was still

THE LIFE OF DAME GRACIE FIELDS

in training, where he saw active service in Gallipoli as a lietutenant in Hussars at the age of seventeen. He also fought in Egypt, Tripoli, and the battle of Somme, and at nineteen was commanding a troop of cavalry in the rank of captain. He was taken as a prisoner of war in March 1918 and interned until Armistice, where he then joined the Military Mission at the Berlin Embassy before moving to Vienna, Budapest, Prague, and Warsaw. In 1924, Loder resigned from the Army and ran a pickle factory in Berlin until hyperinflation and fluctuations in the market ruined the business. A chance visit to Ufa Studios brought him a small part in a German film, and featured roles thereafter followed. After he was spotted by Miles Mander Hollywood roles were offered before he returned to England in 1932, where he was signed by ATP.

So that the early starts and late finishes which the shooting schedule demanded would not take too much of a toll on her, Gracie hired two rooms in Ealing to be near the film studios. John Loder had a similar idea, and whilst he was filming one day his apartment building was ransacked and thieves made away with thousands of pounds worth of antique jewellery which he collected. Gracie had bought a Charles I ring from John a few days previously, which was the only part of the collection which remained. Gracie promptly gave the ring back to John. The British mountaineer, F. S. Smythe, who had played Gracie's records at the top of Mount Kamet, wrote to her during filming of *Love, Life and Laughter* and told her how her recordings were well enjoyed on the Everest expedition, and that the Tibetans at Base Camp thoroughly enjoyed her singing, including one old Tibetan who took off Beethoven recordings and replaced them on the turntable with Gracie's.

During the filming, according to Gracie, one scene had to be filmed sixty-six times before everybody was satisfied. Whilst according to Lillian Aza, Gracie was a "one-take Joe" in the film studio. This seems to contradict the image of the impatient perfectionist. "Tempers go to pieces and nerves fray to rags on occasions like that," remarked Gracie, especially as the sixty-six takes equated to only four minutes of screen time. A further frustration for Gracie in the filming of this picture was her singing of "Out in the Cold, Cold Snow," in which she had to sing running up and down stairs. Whilst not quite such an ordeal as the opening scene of *Looking on the Bright Side* (1932), the whole morning had been set aside for the filming of this number, and by the afternoon, and thirty-five takes later, the song was still not completed.

To promote the film Gracie wrote a letter to *Film Pictorial* stating, "I have enjoyed filming *Love, Life and Laughter* more than any other film in which I have played. It is a film which was made to cover its title, and if it has done that it will satisfy its audience, and it will also satisfy me. I'd like to have played the real Nell Gwynn, as I think she was a most satisfying character, but I have to give my audiences what they like rather than what I like. If I tried to be a high-brow actress I couldn't give my audience so many hearty laughs as I believe this film will give. And as they say up North, there's nowt like a real good hearty laugh."

As with her previous films, shooting was done at the ATP studios in Ealing, a half hour's drive from Piccadilly. The studios self-proclaimed themselves as the most perfectly equipped in the world, partially due to their commodious and beautifully equipped en-suite dressing rooms. For the filming of *Love, Life and Laughter* there were three stages at Ealing, two of which were new for this production set in a seemingly quiet rural retreat, with a pleasant little green in the centre of the road. After a reshuffle from Associated Radio Pictures to Associated Talking Pictures, Basil Dean took the role of chairman and joint managing director with Reginald P. Baker, with fellow directors Stephen L. Courtauld and Major J.F. Courtauld. During the filming, Gracie was visited on set by thirteen year old Eddie Oliver, who had opened his own Penny Cinema in his hometown of Ramsgate. Known locally as the Cinema

Boy King, a letter from the BBC invited him to meet Gracie on set as a reward for all his efforts in his own town.

Filming was completed on February 9, 1934, exactly thirty days after filming had begun, and ran six days over schedule. It was calculated that during the making of the film Gracie had spent a total of 14,400 minutes on the studio floor, hence her earning £2 a minute.

Before filming finished Gracie attended the Hampstead Policeman's Ball on January 26, where she joined in with the festivities and presented trophies to the six best fancy-dressed officers. Following this, she set off on a few month's holiday with John to Capri, via Rome, Venice, and Florence. Shooting did not begin on her next film until early April, so it gave the pair a chance to get away and relax after the hectic and non-stop thirty days of filming.

Gracie on the set of 'Sally In Our Alley.' (1931).

A publicity shot from 'Sing As We Go.' (1934).

CHAPTER EIGHT

1934 - 1935

Every tinker, every tailor,
every soldier, every sailor

They adore you.

- "Queen of Hearts" (1935), recorded by Gracie Fields.

EN ROUTE TO CAPRI via the major Italian cities, Gracie and John were met in Florence by their friend, Henry Savage, and they happened to meet Norman Douglas and his wife, Oriali, the author of the novel *South Wind*, which had inspired their first trip to Capri. Gracie remembered, "We all were together and we all wanted to swap stories, when Norman said, 'You know, Gracie, I'm reading your life story.' Of course, that nearly killed me." Her life story was being published weekly in *The News of the World*, telling her own take on events throughout her life, from her early days in Rochdale to present day filming with everything in between, including a nonsensical column of how she likes to eat the Lancashire delicacy, fatty ducks. The story was written by Brodsky. "It wasn't really that good, and I was getting terrible letters off my mother about the nonsense," and even John was unhappy with it, as it presented Archie and Gracie still having a happy marriage when they had been separated for almost two years.

Gracie and Norman Douglas met many times socially over the years, as they both lived on Capri, and often attended many of the glitterati's Caprician parties together.

Whilst in Florence it was decided La Canzone del Mare needed some gates for the front of the building. Gracie and Henry went off to find some and John went off on his own. Gracie found a grand set which she couldn't afford, and John returned elated he had found the perfect set from an old man in the market. Although John couldn't speak a word of Italian, he had drawn an elabourate set of gates on a piece of paper and presented it to various market traders, one of whom said he had just the set in storage and to meet back in an hour. An hour later, the gates were brought in a handcart and Gracie paid twenty pounds for them. They were instantly shipped off to Capri via American Express, and the large metal gates, with designs of ships' wheels, are still in position to this very day.

When they got to Capri they were joined by Harry Parr-Davies to choose the new songs for the next film, along with J.B. Priestley, who came over to discuss script ideas. Gracie remembered her time in Capri "was always a holiday, but a sort of working holiday." On this trip, Gracie's solicitor came over as she and John had decided they wanted to be married. On his arrival John presented Gracie with a copy of A. P. Herbert's book, *Holy Deadlock*. Not the sort of book for a situation like the one she was in, and Gracie almost immediately gave up on the idea of marriage. "It all seemed hopeless to try and get free after reading this book, so I scrapped my idea of freedom."

Still under contract for another film with ATP, Basil Dean announced during the filming of *Love, Life and Laughter* (1934) in January, that Gracie's next film was to be called *Grace, Darling*, and penned by J.P. Gregson. Based on the Victorian Lifeboat heroine, the film was to be a comedy set against a modern retelling of the Bamburgh lighthouse-keeper's daughter who rescued survivors from the shipwrecked Forfarshire in 1838. Planning began in January for the new film, but it wasn't until early April the idea was dismissed as producers decided the blending of the tragedy of a shipwreck would not work well with Gracie's brand of comedy. Instead, Yorkshire author J. B. Priestley put forward an idea to make a film about Lancashire mill girls. Basil Dean quickly took to the idea, and the pair spent the first week of May at Gracie's villa in Capri discussing the idea.

Harry Parr-Davies had written a tune many years earlier for a song called "Peter the Pup is Twenty-One Today," and although the song had only been featured in one of his early, local operettas, Parr-Davies decided to revisit the tune. "I will tell you a secret," Harry told the newspapers many years later. "I stole those tunes from my own operetta, furnished them up a bit, and there you are." The reworked song became the eponymous "Sing as We Go," and one of the most popular marching pep songs of the 1930s, with the new lyrics apparently written on the back of an envelope while in the back of a shoe shop in Hyde, Cheshire, when Harry and a salesman friend of his were travelling through the town. When Gracie heard it, as she had done previously, she again presented Harry's song to Basil Dean, who agreed this was to be the title of Priestley's film.

Whilst Gracie and John were still in Capri, a court case was held in Peacehaven against Arthur Rowland and Walter Scott, who masterminded a scam around the town in Gracie's orphanage's name. Between November 14 and 20, the pair had gone around Brighton and Hove door-to-door selling raffle tickets for a "Grand Christmas Draw" seemingly on behalf of the charity, selling tickets at 6d each, pocketing the money for themselves. Over 7,000 books of tickets were sold before police arrested the men on November 20 for selling illegal public lottery tickets, and a further 150,000 books of twenty-five tickets were found unsold at their homes as part of the grand scam. Being in Capri, Gracie missed the National Trade Show premiere of *Love, Life and Laughter* at the Leeds Tower before it was publically released in May.

"Gracie's philosophy on life has always been to meet trouble with a smile and a song," claimed Basil Dean when the film was announced in April, which is apparently how *Sing as We Go* received its title. It was also announced at this time that Betty Fields was to star in a film of her own about the seaside town of Blackpool, called *A Lassie from Lancashire*, although this idea was eventually shelved and Betty filmed *Lost in the Legion* for British International Pictures instead, a story about two ship cooks who become stranded in a shipwreck and are forced to join the Foreign Legion, directed by Monty Banks and costarring Leslie Fuller. Betty had previously made two films in 1932, *Old Spanish Customers* (1932) and *Tonight's the Night: Pass it On* (1932), another film with Leslie Fuller. Around this time Duggie Wakefield was propositioned to go to America to star in comedy films as an English rival to Laurel and Hardy. Friend of the family Mervyn Rossini remembered how Duggie was used almost as a bargaining tool to get Laurel and Hardy to sign another contract, and when he arrived in America he was almost sent immediately back home, as he wasn't needed. This was not quite entirely accurate. Whilst in Hollywood, Duggie did make a series of short films for Hal Roach which were released through 1933 and 1934.

The title for Gracie's film was announced on April 14, and Basil Dean stated, "I cannot disclose the details of Miss Gracie Fields' contract for the film, but it includes a salary a little higher than any other salary ever paid before for a film." It was speculated to be a total of £70,000 after salary.

Filming began in Blackpool on May 26 when Gracie was greeted at the Central Train Station by a crowd of 40,000 people. On her arrival in Blackpool, Gracie attended a civic reception at Town Hall and was presented with the largest stick of Blackpool Rock ever fashioned, by the Coronation Rock Company, before filming began for three weeks, at the Tower, on May 30.

Blackpool had long been Britain's top holiday resort, popular with the working classes who Gracie was aligning herself with through her films. As a child she had often visited Blackpool with her family during the Rochdale Wakes week, and whenever her touring company with Archie reached Blackpool she delighted in taking the other members to Pleasure Beach or the South Shore for a donkey ride on the sands. *Sing as We Go* was to be her first real "Lancashire" film, as Priestley saw great potential in Gracie's Lancastrian character on film. Of Gracie's close association to Lancashire, he wrote, "Listen to her for quarter of an hour and you will learn more about Lancashire women and Lancashire than you would from a dozen books on the subject. All the qualities are there—shrewdness, homely simplicity, irony, fierce independence, an impish delight in mocking whatever is thought to be affected and pretentious."

Sing as We Go (1934) planned to bring the atmosphere of Lancashire onto the screen, and in a vivid way show both the workaday side of its life and the Mecca of its pleasures. Blackpool is as central to the film as Gracie, and the film is a unique snapshot of the town in its heyday. Every major landmark was filmed, from the illuminations to Pleasure Beach, the outdoor swimming baths to the Tower Circus, and the Tower Ballroom to the promenade. The camera even takes a trip up the 518 feet of the Tower itself! Whilst many cite this as Gracie's best film, film critic C.A. Lejeune disagreed, stating, "We have an industrial north that is bigger than Gracie Fields running around a Blackpool funfair."

During the filming in Blackpool, the town's mayor and mayoress, Alderman and Mrs. C.E. Tatham, took an active part in the production, appearing in an outdoor beauty contest scene filmed on June 5. The pair were on set from ten in the morning until six that evening, but were more than happy to be so just to appear on film with Lancashire's greatest daughter. Unfortunately for the mayor and mayoress, the scene had to be filmed again on June 11, as during the Beauty Parade, Miss Southport, Mavis Storey, slipped and fell in the pool.

An article in the *Blackpool Gazette* stated, "Blackpool has gone movie crazy, and at all cost the location of the outdoor film work is to be kept secret to avoid the presence of crowds at the wrong time." The crowds included a group of adults and children near the North Pier who narrowly missed being run over by a tram due to congregating to see Gracie.

A similar problem occurred in the crowd scene inside Blackpool Tower Circus. The scene, whose pinnacle is the flooding of the circus floor for the popular "Water Finale," was filmed on Saturday May 19, and Basil Dean put an advert in the *Blackpool Gazette* requesting extras for the film. Dean had always tried to ensure a sense of realism in his films, and the behaviour of the crowds at the seaside atmosphere certainly enabled him to achieve it. The condition of free entry to the set was that sneezing, talking, and unsolicited applause are not allowed. Queues to get into the circus on the day of filming stretched all around the Tower, with an estimated total of 30,000 having turned up to try and get into the film.

A scene at Pleasure Beach which called for Gracie to be dunked into water during one of the attractions had to be reshot to get the angles right, and Gracie's greatest fear was there wasn't enough water in the pool for her to be dunked into and she would hit hard onto the concrete. Because of this fear, the scene needed to be shot five times, including new dry dresses and a rejuvenated hairstyle. After filming was completed in early evening, until 2am Gracie waited inside the Tower for a taxi to come and pick her up to take her back to the Metropole Hotel, as the crowds waited to try and get her autograph. By early morning, however, the numbers had died down sufficiently that she was able to make her escape through a side exit of the Tower. During the first week of filming in Blackpool, the Blackpool Tram Corporation selected the "best driver of the best tram, tested and retested the brakes, and held up the entire town's tram timetable" to ensure a scene in which Gracie narrowly misses colliding with the vehicle on her bicycle didn't end up killing her accidentally!

Doubling as Greybeck Mill, Sir John Holden's Ashley Bridge Mill in Bolton was used for the opening and interior scenes of the film, and Denvale Mill on Union Road in Bolton was used for the film's climax, where the Besses o'the Barn band and Wingate's Brass Band accompanied Gracie in the marching finale. Basil Dean claimed, "Mill lassies were very enthusiastic to see themselves in a picture, and they behaved with complete naturalness." The film production unit was surprised to find hardly any of the mill girls actually turned up for work in clogs and shawl, and Gracie had to borrow a pair of wooden clogs so the sound of the clatter of the clogs was picked up by the microphones. Dean distributed various shawls to try to achieve some of the stereotyped quaint authenticity of what a lassie from Lancashire looked like in the minds of cinema audiences from around the country.

Alongside leading man John Loder, Lancashire comedian Stanley Holloway has a cameo role in the film as a bungling policeman who follows Gracie around Blackpool. Gracie first worked with Stanley in her days as a juvenile, and he had since been taken on by Gracie's agents, Bert and Lillian Aza. It was Gracie who suggested he should be booked into some variety dates, where he became well known for his comic monologues such as "The Lion and Albert" and "Pick Up tha' Musket." Stanley remembered, "I played a policeman and I was appearing at Drury Lane at the time and caught the train on the Saturday night, no sleeper, to Blackpool. I arrived on a lovely morning at five o'clock. The studios sent a car to come and meet me and took me to the hotel, where I had a wash and changed into my police uniform. I was supposed to be directing traffic, and having no sleep I really felt like doing it!"

It is reported Stanley's characterisation was so realistic he even managed to deceive the local police. Dressed in his policeman's costume one lunchtime whilst the unit were filming, Stanley took a break and went into one of Blackpool's penny arcades, where a real policeman stopped him and asked what he was doing that for on the job. "It took some convincing that I wasn't a real bobby and was one of them-there actor-types!" Morris Harvey, who appeared in *Walk this Way* with Gracie in 1931, also had a cameo in the film as a cowboy busker at one of Pleasure Beach's sideshows. As well as this being Gracie's second film appearance with leading man John Loder, Frank Pettingell again starred with Gracie. He played her father, Mr. Milroy, in *This Week of Grace* (1933), and in this film her Uncle Murgatroyd, a hapless clock-mender and member of the Ancient Order of Stag Hunters on their annual parade. The stag hunters in the film comprised of voluntary members of Blackpool Lifeboat Band, who were filmed walking along South Promenade and also in the Winter Gardens' Spanish Bar.

Whilst in Blackpool, Gracie agreed to come back to the town after filming had finished and play a fortnight at the Grand Theatre. Filming was completed in the town on June 11, with the production company moving back to Ealing to finish the interior scenes of the film. On June 22, Gracie accompanied Basil Dean and Victoria Hopper to the opening Gala of the Regal Cinema Southampton in a concert before the showing of *Love, Life and Laughter* (1934).

With filming complete, Gracie opened at the Southport Garrick on July third alongside Levanda, May Vaughn, Tom Payne and Vera Hilliard, Haver and Lee, Stella and Orpwood, and Turner. Her brother-in-law, Pat Aza, was the Garrick's manager, and when he asked Gracie what she wanted as her programme notes she told him, "Oh, put me down as a stick of rhubarb!" Following Southport, Gracie moved back to Blackpool to take part in the promised shows, where demand was so high she had to extend for another week, finishing her four-week run on August 30. Each week in Blackpool consisted of an entirely different variety bill, but the audiences only really cared about seeing Gracie. For her second week, from August 16, Gracie was joined by the comedian Max Wall and supported by Bartlett and Ross, Eve Drury and Ramond, Stetson "The Mad Hatter," the Three Rascals, the Dale Sisters, and Harver and Lee.

When the record season was finished Gracie celebrated by taking out all the artists from all other of Blackpool's shows for a day out at Pleasure Beach as she hired three Corporation buses to carry them all down to South Shore. As opposed to going on one of the buses, it was arranged Gracie would travel to Pleasure Beach via a donkey, "a tawny-haired little fellow who was waiting for her at the stage door." She also took a trip in a Blackpool lifeboat, captained by Coxswain Harry Parr (not Davies!), who dressed Gracie in traditional oil-skins and heavy life jackets just in case they capsized. Another event patronised by Gracie at this time was the drawing of the winning tickets for the Irish Sweepstakes.

Gracie's persona of an unsophisticated Lancashire mill girl enamoured her to the working classes as she aligned herself directly for and from the working classes. Because this solidarity of the classes, when the film opened it proved to be Gracie's biggest box office hit to date, and it is reported she took a salary of over £30,000 for the film. During her Blackpool run Gracie treated 450 Bolton millworkers to one of the happiest and most joyous evenings they had ever experienced as a personal thank you for their help and hard work during the making of the film. Gracie personally sent an invitation to the mill workers for the dinner and dance at Bolton's Palais-de-Dance, where Gracie arrived to massive applause at midnight following her Blackpool show, as the crowd serenaded her with "She's a Lassie from Lancashire." After being presented with bouquets by some of the film's extras, Gracie took to the stage to perform five numbers, including "Sally," "Little Man You've had a Busy Day," and her latest film's theme song, which the millworkers had all come to know very well during filming.

After leaving Blackpool Gracie opened at Margate on September 3, Bournemouth Pavillion on September 10, the Liverpool Empire on September 17, the Dublin Grand on September 24, and finishing in variety for 1934 at the Bradford Alhambra on October first.

Straight away, when not on stage Gracie was back doing her charitable visits which she so loved, such as visiting the Bradstock Lockett Children's Home for Crippled Children and Birkdale Home for Blind, where Gracie forgot the words of "The Punch and Judy Show" mid-song and swapped to "Love's Last Word is Spoken" instead. Whilst performing in Southport on August 29, Gracie visited the Sunshine Home for Blind Babies in Birkdale, where she insisted all twenty-three children call her Aunty Grace. Having memorized more words and music than almost anyone else, Gracie was surprised to be corrected by the children as she sang to them "Peter, Peter, Pudding and Pie," instead of "Georgie Porgie." Gracie graciously accepted her mistake, made a joke of it, and continued her afternoon singing their requested songs, such as "The Punch and Judy Show" and "Fred Fanakapan." On September 5, building work commenced on a new extension wing at the orphanage in Peacehaven, and on September 6, Gracie sang to a group of disabled children at the Cliftonville Oval in Margate, and appeared at the Grosvenor House Variety Ball on November 15.

A call from Bert Aza in London urged her to return to London for a "special meeting" on September 20. The meeting was with the famous American film producer Mack Sennett, who wanted to take Gracie filming in America. Gracie was not keen on the idea, as she said, "Often at the end of a hard, long day at the studio I ask myself, 'Grace, old girl, is it really worth it? Why don't you get out and retire?'" Tying herself to an American film contract was not something she wanted to get herself into.

At the commencement of this tour a statement was issued to the press saying, "Gracie Fields announced today that she would bring suit against any actress who imitated her on stage without first procuring permission to do so." Gracie remarked, "I have been forced to take this action because people hear these impersonations and say, 'Well, if that's what Gracie Fields is like I wouldn't pay to go and see her.'"

As early as August 1928 Gracie was being imitated on the stage. It was reported in the *Brighton Standard*, "Gracie Fields stands quite alone in her vocally fantastic art. And even the cleverest mimics may study her in vain ... When Jenny Howard and Percy are at the height of their caprices, you might think, as far as she is concerned, you are hearing a prelude or mixture of Gracie Fields. For Miss Howard has many queer vocal pranks and gifts of mimicry closely resembling those of the more famous artiste. There is no suggestion of plagiarism, of course. It just happens so." By 1934, however, Gracie had clearly had enough, as "one day last week she was mimicked in no less than four different broadcast programmes," and "a few weeks ago at a well-known London variety hall she was impersonated by three out of the eight acts on the bill." The only exemption which was allowed, at "special dispensation by Miss Fields' manager, Bert Aza, was the impressionist Beryl Orde," and quite possibly Gertie Gitana, who Gracie had once aspired to be and was now performing in music hall routines as Gracie.

Gertie, who from a very young age Gracie cited as one of her greatest inspirations, had performed alongside Fields and Rossini at the Brixton Empire in August 1931, and again in Edinburgh in October 1932, but from 1933 was touring with a show called *George, Gertie and Ted*, where she had teamed up with Ted Ray and G.H. Elliott. During the show there was a section where they all impersonated famous stars. At a charity concert in Chelsea in the 1930s, Gracie heard a voice that was distinctly familiar, but singing one of her own songs. When she went to see who was on stage, she found that Gertie Gitana was impersonating her. Gracie cried as she later remembered, "That wasn't right. She was such a big star and she shouldn't be mimicking me, I'm just Gracie Fields from Rochdale."

From September fourth, Gracie was back at the London Palladium with the Boys from Manchester, Billy Caryll and Hilda Mundy, Smith Rogers and Eddy, Vic Oliver, Michel and Arnova, Norman with Violet and Ray, Tommy Brookins and Sammy Van, and Billy Bennett. The following week at the Brighton Hippodrome from September 11 with the Four Jokers, Wright and Marion, Kadex Four, Three Rascals, Stetson, Victor Moreton, Auntie, and Earle and Babette.

Sing as We Go (1934) received its trade show premiere in Leeds on September 11 to rave reviews, and on September 15 Gracie appeared at a cinema ball at the White Rock Pavillion, Hastings, where she arrived from Margate at 1am and was greeted by the Plaza Cinema manager and Archie Pitt's old tour manager, Fred Heppell, for whom she had specially agreed this appearance. The Mayor of Margate introduced, "Tonight we have with us the queen of all hearts," before Gracie sang "Sing as We Go," "Little Man You've had a Busy Day," and "Sally" before joining the party for supper.

By popular demand, George Black retained Gracie from September 19. Gracie opened in her annual variety week at the London Palladium with Vic Oliver, Joe Phillips, Wright and Marion, Chilton and Thomas, Hollywood Four, Jack Edge, Mary and Erik and Harvard, and Mortimer and Kendrick. Her popularity was so great the run was extended to three weeks, with Gracie still going strong, with booking extended owing to the phenomenal demand. Gracie heard that there was a party of over three hundred Welsh people in the Palladium on September 27 who had specially come from Wales to see her, and she surprised the London audience by stepping in front of the curtain after her act and sang an encore of "Hen Wlad fy Nhadau" entirely in vernacular, Lancashire, Welsh. The secretary of the Mold Chamber of Trade enthusiastically lead the rounds from the audience, and George Black was so impressed he quipped, "We'll book him for the next variety season!" Not to be outdone by Gracie, Will Fyffe recounted a visit to a Welsh party where he once performed a song in Welsh, and he presented the audience with their second Welsh chorus of the night in "Bugeilio'r Gwenith Gwyn," which was met with further applause. In the same house were 400 members of the northern branches of the Co-Operative Wholesale Society, so Gracie duly obliged in singing "Stop and Shop at the Co-Op Shop" to them.

The following week at the Palladium Gracie was with Smith, Rodger and Eddy, Chilton and Thomas, Payne and Hilliard, Bonhair Gregory Six, Will Fyffe, Dave and Joe O'Gormon, Monro Bros, Calienta and Lolita, and 16 Palladium Girls. During this run, on October sixth, Gracie paid a visit to Monarch, the Post Office's cable ship at Tower Bridge Pier, where she attempted to conduct the band in a chorus of "Sally," but threw her baton overboard and said "I'll Sing it Instead!" Whilst on board, Gracie chatted for over an hour with the Tars and joined in with a game of spinning the yarn, at which she beat them at their own game. Before she left the ship, Gracie offered to buy the band six new instruments—an offer which was promptly accepted—much to the delight of the band's secretary, Mr. Watkins, who was surprised at just how much interest Gracie had taken in them.

Gracie was at the Holborn Empire from October tenth with Lassiter Brothers, Billy Danvers, Leslie Weston, Auntie on the Bike, Bennet and

Williams, Kadex Four, Griffiths Brothers, and Earle and Babette. Gracie's artistry, pathos, and comedy are beautifully defined in her wonderful act. She is variety's queen with her subjects bowed in adoration.

Earlier in the year Gracie had bought a house at Frinton-on-Sea, a popular summer retreat for many stars. The house on Connaught Avenue in Greenway was called Tinkerbell, and Gracie wanted to ensure it was kept private. It is debated, however, by local residents, whether or not the house was owned by Gracie or Lillian and Bert Aza, and Gracie was just a regular guest there. It is also rumoured Archie Pitt had another, private house, Playbox, on Ladygate Drive in Greyshott, Hampshire. It is rumoured by local residents the house was named as a bolthole for Archie and his mistresses, and after the breakdown of their marriage Gracie gave all the furntiture away to local families. On October 21st, Gracie appeared alongside Florrie Forde at the Gresford Colliery Disaster charity concert at the Lyceum Theatre.

In 1928 in Frinton, Gracie spotted the talents of a young Mary Lawson, who was employed by Archie in one of his touring revues at Gracie's request and would appear in the *Lido Follies* summer season, which Archie would host annually in the area. Whilst the newspapers reported Gracie had bought a new house, "those closest to her are sworn to secrecy about it." She explained herself, "I simply must have some privacy when I am not working. My home has been a kind of road house, but now I hope to have some haven of rest."

Whilst the whereabouts of this house were kept secret for many years, Gracie made it publically aware that she had bought Augustus John's old house at 28 Mallord Street in Chelsea, and is listed on the 1935 electoral register as living at the address with John Flanagan, Margaret Livesey, and Mary Barratt. Although she bought it early in the year, as an upgrade from her studio flat, by November she had still not moved into the address and decked it out with fine furtniture and porcelain, including a rare

Laura Knight designed Clarice Cliff 48-piece circus dinner service, originally bought from Harrods, and which is now in Manchester Art Gallery. (Minus one plate, which Gracie remembered in 1968 being broken at Mallord Street when her niece Grace was asking about the set.)

In early November Gracie threatened court action, so Augustus John made a hurried removal from the Chelsea studio as Gracie demanded immediate possession. The Dutch-inspired house was built in 1913 by the Russian architect Boris Anrep from designs by Robert van t'Hoff, and contained a large studio with parquet floor, which Gracie had the downstairs for an artist's studio for John. In 2010, Mallord Street was recognised as one of Britain's most expensive streets to buy a property on, along with Bishop's Avenue in Hampstead—both streets Gracie had a home on, and as of 2018 the Grade II listed building is currently on the market for more than £9,000,000.

Also listed as living at the property is Mary Barrett, born Mary Edith Valentine Barrett, the daughter of Jerry and Catherine Barrett, in December 1909. She had written to Gracie previously before she first met her in Blackpool during the filming of *Sing as We Go* (1934). Mary was working as a housekeeper for a wealthy family in Lytham, but after meeting her and realising what a genuine person Mary was, Gracie insisted she come and work for her. Mary remembered, "Apparently I was a fan, and she thought my letters were funny and interesting. I lived in Lytham and I went to see her in a show, and when she asked me to come and work with her you could've knocked me down with a feather." Mary told Gracie she'd love to join her but couldn't leave her current employer in the lurch, which Gracie thought was very admirable.

After she worked her notice Mary moved into Mallord Street with Gracie, John, and Auntie Margaret, and stayed with Gracie for the next forty-five years. "She said I just fitted in completely. I was the maid of all work. I did her hairdressing, I was her maid, did her cookery. I did anything! I even washed the car, the lot." Born and raised in Stockport, Mary's first job was helping her mother and father on their stall on Stockport Market before she got a job in a local mill in Reddish. Soon realising this was not the kind of work she wanted to do, Mary found a job in service at a house in Stockport before taking up the position in Lytham, where she eventually met Gracie.

During her run at the Holborn Empire Gracie was visited by the songwriter Jimmy Kennedy. He had read in the newspapers, "Miss Gracie Fields has made some wonderful new recordings before going off to her villa on the isle of Capri," and this subconsciously gave him the idea for a song. He penned the lyrics to "The Isle of Capri"—which were put to music by Will Grosz—with Gracie specifically in mind. However, the publishers "didn't get the idea of 'I Love Capri' being a pun of 'Isle of Capri,' and it was turned down." Another reason was the lyrics tell of a sailor who proposes love making to a lady with a plain golden ring on her finger, so Kennedy was asked to take the line out. He refused to do so, as he liked the line, and argued the lady in the song may have been a widow. The song was eventually accepted by the Peter Maurice Music Company and advertised as a "Tango-Foxtrot Ballad." Kennedy presented the song to Gracie himself and "made a tremendous effort to make Miss Fields sing it, and she kindly agreed to record it, which contributed greatly to its success." The song became a staple part of Gracie's repertoire and has been widely covered by many artists in the years since it was first written. In 1979, when speaking about the song, Gracie admitted, "The song was written for me, but I didn't want anyone to know that I'd fallen in love. But the songwriter knew."

Before she and John headed back to Capri, Gracie played in a benefit concert for the Printer's Pension Corporation on October 21 at the Palladium, in a bill starring Jack Hylton, Bobby Howes, Caryll and Mundy, the Crazy Gang, Ronald Frankau, the Three Radio Rogues, and Eve Becke, and Gracie was back at the Finsbury Park Empire from October 22 with Les Pierrotys, Kadex Four, Leslie Weston, Earle and Babette, Griffiths Brothers, Olsen's Sae Lions, Bennett, and McNaughton.

Following this engagement, Gracie headed back to Capri for a break before her scheduled charity week in Rochdale in early December. Whilst in Capri, Gracie jokingly wrote to Basil Dean on November 15: "My dear Basil, Bert has just informed me of your great generosity in sending along twenty-five guineas to endow a bed at my orphanage. This entitles you to send along any strays if we have a bed vacant, so don't be afraid, I promise I won't tell Victoria! Gotcher! But really, Basil, it was very very nice of you and it is highly appreciated [...] We're having rain a lot here. I'll be leaving next week to start me good work again."

John and Gracie enjoyed a month's holiday in Capri before making their way back to England, deciding to take in some European cities en route. Whilst Gracie was in Capri, J.B. Priestley, on behalf of ATP, visited Arizona to gain some "local color for Gracie's next film," which was to be titled *Say Grace!* and feature an American Wild West setting. Although publicity material was published for the film, both Basil Dean and Gracie agreed they did not want to weaken Gracie's popular British image by featuring an American accent in an American-set film.

With Gracie on her leisurely way back to England via Switzerland and Monte Carlo, the newspapers back home printed advertisements asking, "Where is Gracie Fields?" as her sister Betty had fallen seriously in Peacehaven. The press tried to get Gracie to come back to England to see Betty, who it looked likely was not going to survive her illness. The police of three European countries were searching for Gracie and John whilst doctors in England fought to save Betty. On November 23, Betty had an internal operation and was reported to be in no imminent danger, but there was still no word from Gracie. Frontier stations, border patrols, airports, and ports were all notified to try and find Gracie.

Earlier in the year Betty had signed a contract to star in a series of films to be made at Elstree, but now it was looking unlikely she was going to survive to see them made. Duggie Wakefield came out of his show at the Newport Empire to be with his sister-in-law as the family waited for Gracie.

Gracie was eventually found in Switzerland, and she immediately made her way back home, landing at Folkestone shortly after three in the afternoon on November 26, where she was met by the harbour master and Bert Aza, who assured Gracie Betty was out of danger. From there, the trio took the train to Victoria and on to Brighton. Gracie found a very weak Betty but was pleased to learn the operation had been a success and her life was safe. This episode made Gracie realise that her hectic schedule had meant she had abandoned her family over the past few months. "All I knew was that I was getting very tired and that I wanted more time to spend with my family." In 1951 Gracie recounted, "I'd been to Switzerland for only two days in my life. I remember sunshine and diamond mountains. Some business brought us back to London's murky winter, and each year I have promised myself a week in Switzerland. I've just never gotten round to it."

In Monte Carlo, Gracie had met up, quite by chance, with Stanley Holloway in a casino. He recalled, "It had started to rain and I popped into the casino to get out of the wet. As soon as I entered I heard a familiar Lancashire voice saying, 'Put it on t'black.' Sure enough, it was Gracie. She told me that she'd come out of the rain too and was trying to break the bank, 'so I'm giving a half a crown the run.' Sure enough, she was gambling with five franc pieces while those around her were playing for very high stakes indeed."

Gracie's next Rochdale charity week commenced on December third and was billed as *Hello! Here I am Again!* When booking for her concerts opened in November, the *Rochdale Observer* was bombarded with letters from the public complaining that many of the tickets had been pre-allocated and pre-sold to Rochdale dignitaries. Gracie's schedule of events was a hectic one, including visiting the blind at Milton School and patients at Birch Hall Institution and Rochdale Infirmary, as well as hosting a dance at the Carlton Super Ballroom and kicking off the football match between the Rochdale Hornets and St. Helen's on the Saturday afternoon. Between this, she was appearing at the Hippodrome alongside Jack Daly, Billy Matchett, Victor Hopwood, Joe Adami, and Raymond Smith, whilst *Sing as We Go* (1934) was playing at the Rialto cinema all week.

The BBC nationally broadcast her December fifth performance from the Hippodrome, including a special relay from her dressing room before the show, which Gracie thoroughly enjoyed, as she had previously said, "Broadcasting is a particular strain on the nerves. After all, an audience is part of our show, and to perform without an audience is an almost eerie experience." Broadcasting live with an audience of her townsfolk worked much better for Gracie.

In 1937, Guy Fletcher wrote, "Although her broadcasts are regular, they are comparatively rare, and since December 1934 she has only made one radio broadcast." It was during this show in Rochdale Gracie heard the story of a local orphan girl named Eva Stott. Her father, a local solicitor, had recently died, leaving the young girl in the care of her ninety-year-old grandmother, who visited Gracie's show on December fifth to ask if she would perhaps visit the young girl, who had been ill in bed for many months. The next day Gracie visited the young girl at her home, spending ten minutes talking to her and signing the photographs which the girl had collected of her favourite star.

On Saturday morning Gracie visited the Rochdale football ground and kitted herself out in the blue and white stripes of the Hornets. She shook hands with the players from both teams, mucked about with the referee and the linesman, and cartwheeled her way around the pitch before the referee ordered her off the field—at which point Gracie stuck her tongue out at him and waved goodbye as she headed to the theatre for her matinee performance. At the end of her final performance that evening at the Hippodrome, Mayor J. W. Dutton announced Gracie had made £2,142 17s and 6d for her charity week, and she was presented with a silver tea-service inscribed, "From your Rochdale friends" as a thanks for all her hard work for the town. Gracie told her audience, "I am very happy that I can give so much happiness—as you have told me I do to so many people. God has been very good to me." The tea service remained at Peacehaven until it was bought by the Rochdale Museum Service at auction in 1984, where it is still proudly displayed in their museum.

Three thousand people came to cheer Gracie as she left to return for London on Saturday evening, as the next day she was to appear in another charity gala show at the London Palladium in aid of Brinsworth House. The packed bill also starred the Crazy Gang, Max Miller, Jack Hylton, Elsie and Doris Waters, Dick Henderson, Leslie Sarony, and Billy Caryll, amongst many other acts. Monday morning of December tenth, Gracie returned North to Manchester, where she headlined a week at the Palace Theatre with Violet Ray and Norman Courtney with Peggy and Sylvia, Griffiths Brothers, Kadex Four, Three Virginians, Nosmo King, Red Fred, Dixon, and Pal.

On December 15, Gracie recorded a special record for a post-Christmas release for the News Chronicle, who aimed to provide every voluntary hospital in the country with an up-to-date wireless set. The record, Radio Hour in the Children's Ward, has Gracie on one side and Paul Robeson, Ciceley Courtneidge, and Marriott Edgar on the reverse. Gracie agreed to help, as she "probably knows the inside of hospital wards better than any other variety artist," telling the News Chronicle, "In my weekly visits to hospital wards to sing to patients I have seen how the radio has revolutionised hospital life." Whenever Gracie did have a spare moment from working commitments, she would indeed visit hospitals, homes, and orphanages, often without publicity of warning, to sing for patients.

Later that day Gracie visited the East Lancashire Disabled Soldier's and Sailor's Home, where she gave a performance for the men before returning to London for a last-minute booked pre-Christmas appearance at the Holborn Empire for a week from December 17, with the Houston Sisters, Fields and Rossini, the Melvilles, Calienta and Lolita, Duncan Gray, Scott Courtnay and Peggy Sylvia, Keith Clark, and the Radio Three, and Gracie introduced "Shall I be an Old Man's Darling?" into her live repertoire at this concert. The following day Gracie attended the christening of Leslie Fuller's twin daughters, as she had agreed to be the children's godmother, along with Rene Houston of the Houston Sisters.

Gracie admits in her autobiography, "It seemed so long since Betty had called me up, since Edith had been round to see me." But Edith paid Gracie a visit whilst she was appearing at the Holborn Empire. A row ensued between the two, which saw Gracie writing three checks for £10,000 each to her brother and two sisters. Although Gracie writes she had intended to do this act of charity as a Christmas gift anyway, it certainly seems in retrospect her charity may have been spurred on by her sister's angry visit, and from what Gracie hints at in her book, Edith was envious of her success and a potential reason why she had stayed away from the stage.

However, the episode brought Gracie and her family temporarily closer together, and that Christmas Gracie bought cards, got all [her] groceries at Fortnum and Mason, kept an open house, and generally didn't know how much she owned. Her film contract was due for renewal, but she was reluctant to sign anything just yet, enjoying spending time with her family and John too much. Tommy remembered in later life, "She gave us hundreds of pounds. I mean, it was embarrassing really at times. She didn't have to do it. We never wanted any money, we were all independent, all of us. But she thought nothing of giving us £500 for Christmas. It was very nice, but a bit embarrassing, because what could we give her in return? What could we buy her? She had everything." Regardless, Tommy and the rest of the family continued to accept Gracie's gifts until a family argument in the 1970s when she told each member of her family that they would not receive anything else from her until after her death.

Following a family Christmas at the orphanage and at Peacehaven, on December 28 Gracie visited the Kennington Oval for the annual Variety Artists and Ladies' Guild Christmas Party before she took up a ten-day engagement at the Hippodrome, Brighton for ten days, the *Gracie Fields Christmas Roadshow* with Robb Wilton, Olsen's Sea Lions, Griffiths Brothers, Harver and Lee, Phyllis and Anne, and Jasper Maskylene. During her run, on January fourth, Gracie threw a party for 450 children at the King's Cliff Cinema in Brighton, which comprised of the showing of *Love, Life and Laughter*, then the personal appearance of Gracie as a special surprise, where she sang to the children for fifteen minutes.

Before Gracie moved on to her next venue, she visited the Brighton Astoria to see Anna Neagle and Sir Cedric Hardwicke in *Nell Gwynn*, to see their interpretation of the original story which Gracie's *Love, Life and Laughter* was based on. Gracie also sent a donation, along with Isaac Foot MP and the earl of Mount Edgecumbe to two Cawsand fishermen whose livelihoods were hanging in the balance as their boat had been smashed against some rocks during a stormy sea.

1935 opened with a week at the Metropolitan Theatre, Edgeware Road from January seventh, playing to packed houses. Gracie's Metropolitan Theatre show was billed "the greatest attraction in the variety world," and was Gracie's only London show of 1935. She headed the bill of Ramond and Nala, Stamford and Taylor and the Three Rascals, Joe Young, Leslie Strange, Cliff and Rhodes, Fields and Rossini, and the Kadex Four before moving on the following week to the Birmingham Hippodrome, where her repertoir of carefully selected numbers exploits every phrase of human nature and emotion, from the liveliest to the most depressed.

A week at the Birmingham Hippodrome was spent with the Three Emeralds, Herbert and Hatton, the Five Marywards, Raymond Smith, Buck and Chic Co, Olsen's Sea Lions, Duncan Gray, and Young and Younger. Following next from January 14, demand was so high in Birmingham, as Gracie again broke the box-office records, an extra matinee had to be added on Friday afternoon in addition to the two scheduled for Thursday and Saturday. It was reported crowds of thousands were turned away from the theatre, and that those who had managed to procure a seat were "delirious with delight" by the time the curtains opened. In a spare moment, and in another act of charity for which she was becoming widely known, Gracie visited the town hall on January 18, performing to 1,500 children in the mayor's annual tea party for underprivileged children.

The following week, Gracie was at the Stratford Empire with Calienta and Lolita, Ramon and Nada, Tom Fagan, David Poole, the Three Rascals, Herbert and Hatton, Joe Young, and the Kadex Four. As soon as her week at Brixton's Empress Theatre bill was announced for her run commencing on January 28, all the tickets sold out in the first morning of their sale, in a bill with Stanford and Taylor, Leslie Weston, Ramon and Nada, the Three Rascals, the Kadex Four, Rio and Santos, Joe Young, and Fred, Phyllis and Anne.

It now seemed that in every town Gracie visited another charitable engagement called on her support or patronage, and Gracie rarely refused. Throughout 1935, when she couldn't attend one of the many events she was invited to, Gracie would often send along a token of appreciation or an item to raffle or auction off for funds. Tea-cosies were a favourite item to be received by charities from Gracie, as well as signed photographs, desk-blotters, jigsaws, bars of Anona soap with her image on them, and often an expensive toy doll for children's charities. Around this time, *Eve's Own* magazine offered a gift of a brass clog pin badge with Gracie's signature embossed as a promotional lucky mascot with the magazine. Occasionally, at events when Gracie had nothing to present she took off her hat and auctioned that. When she first arrived in Blackpool during the filming of *Sing as We Go* (1934), Gracie refused to give her prop bicycle back to the properties department, and instead auctioned it off for charity. One little girl wrote to Gracie whilst in hospital and received a jigsaw with the star's image and a signed note inside the box, and Gracie was always only too willing to respond to requests— much to the dismay of Bert Aza, who actually hired a private detective to vet and check some of the thousands of requests his office was getting.

On January 29, 1935, Gracie took to the boxing ring in aid of St. Dunstan's Charity for the Blind, a charity she had a close association with, where she performed for twenty minutes inside the ring in their annual tournament held at London's Stadium Club. Gracie was presented with a large bunch of roses and carnations, which she immediately insisted were to be auctioned off, and which were sold for 22 guineas to a Lancashire fan of Gracie—who promptly presented them back to her.

With the ideas for *Say Grace!* and *Grace, Darling* shelved, Basil Dean announced on a trip to Coventry on January tenth that filming was to begin the next month on a modern-day Lady Godiva story, "where the gallant lady will be played by none other than Miss Gracie Fields." The film was to be called *Up with the Lark* and shot primarily in a farmyard which the mill-girl Gracie had visited during her holidays and is somehow forced to play the part of Lady Godiva in a local charity event. The film promised new surroundings and new situations for her inimitable joking in a story unequalled in the history of comedy and was to be directed by Monty Banks.

In a press release for *Film Pictorial,* Maud Miller posed the question, "Why can't Gracie Fields be given more serious parts?" To which Gracie responded, "If I tried to be a highbrow actress I couldn't give my audience so many hearty laughs." The idea of bearing all as Lady Godiva didn't appeal to Gracie, so a film alternative had to be found instead. Priestley had the idea of setting a film in his own native Yorkshire, as opposed to Gracie's Lancashire, and the idea was set as he returned North to gain some inspiration and ideas for the film, which was due to begin production on March fourth.

On February first, Gracie renewed her contract with ATP to star in four films to be completed by the end of 1936 for £150,000, with her pay now being £3 a minute, but with revenue and film income it was expected "Miss Fields's income will be considerably more," as she was estimated to be making over £1,000 a week. This placed her as one of worldwide cinema's highest paid stars, taking home a larger salary than Greta Garbo, who was only paid £60,000 for her latest film, *The Painted Veil.* "I'm frightened of all this responsibility," Gracie told the press in Basil Dean's office. "What I want is a house in the country at 10s and 6d, not all this responsibility." The next day, Gracie was presented with a leg of lamb for the children at her orphanage, one of the 1,100 gifts of lamb which were presented to the newsboys of London from the newsboys of Adelaide. The lamb was handed to the branch manager of British Empire Films, who had it sent to the orphanage at Peacehaven.

Before filming began, and whilst Priestley and Dean worked on the script for what was to become *Look Up and Laugh* (1935), Gracie took a trip to Capri which was cut short when it was suggested she appear in the Crazy Gang's final record-breaking week at the Palladium, beginning February 25. Gracie returned to England on the twenty-third in time to rehearse before joining in the Gang's frivolity and antics, including being blindfolded and strapped to a spinning wheel whilst Jack Carson proceeded to throw knives at her, carrying on absurd advertisement boards, and appearing in a comedy sequence wearing Bud Flanagan's straw hat and Jimmy Nervo's trousers. In her own section, Gracie performed her usual routine of comedy and straight numbers, burlesquing "Love in Bloom" dressed in flannels and wailing "Shall I be an Old Man's Darling?" whilst the gang proceeded to come on stage and interrupt her. Her knockabout entrances and exits were hailed with enthusiasm as Gracie "worked as hard as any other member of the company in the craziest show London has ever seen." It was suggested Gracie should take a full-time placement as a member of the Crazy Gang, but her contractual obligations prevented her from doing so, despite her wishes to join in permanently with the frivolity.

Also in February, Archie staged a reproduction of *Mr. Tower of London* at the Derby Grand Theatre before it began a successful UK tour. The new version starred Betty Driver as Sally Perkins—the part made famous by Gracie—and Norman Evans as Archie's character. The show ran successfully for over two years, riding on the fact Betty was "discovered" by Archie and Norman was "discovered" by Gracie.

On March sixth, at a luncheon given by ATP at the Savoy Hotel, the title of Gracie's new film was announced to the media, and it was confirmed Gracie would stay with ATP for at least another three films. Filming began later than planned, on March 21, on *Love on Wheels* (which later became *Look Up and Laugh* (1935)) at Ealing, written by Priestley, with extra scenes added by Gordon Wellesley. The film featured cameo appearances from Betty and Edith Fields, Harry Parr-Davies, Nino Rossini, Duggie Wakefield, a fleeting shot of Gracie's mother, and

246

an early starring role for Vivien Leigh, who one film critic wrote had a "promising future ahead of her on screen."

During this film, and the next, Gracie had a stunt double for some of the scenes, Zetta Morenta, whose real name was Lillian Tollis. The story concerns Yorkshire comedienne Grace Pearson, who campaigns to save her local town market from demolition, to be replaced by a department store. On March 11, one of the parts in the film had not yet been cast, and the casting director and Huddersfield playwright, Mr. J. R. Gregson, told the newspapers he wanted "a middle-aged Yorkshire woman with a determined expression and sharp features." He was subsequently inundated with requests, photographs, CVs, and actor profiles, but eventually the character was cut from the script, as he had too many to choose from and no time to do it.

The entire fictional setting of Plumborough Market was recreated following the designs from Kirgate Market in Bradford, with a number of fully-stocked stalls being used, whose shots were matched up with a number of Schüfftan shots. Extras for authenticity in the market's crowd scenes were real Huddersfield and Bradford market workers who were sent to London and put up in a local Ealing hotel. As opposed to being astonished by the brightness of the Kleig lights, the Yorkshire locals were amazed at the stability and structure of the market stalls. After shaking them and pushing them to see if they would collapse, they were announced by Bradfordian Mr. T. M. Moffatt to be "a lot better than the ones we have in Bradford Market ... I wish the people there could see these ones. It would do them a bit of good to see what a decent stall's like." Selfridges in London was also used for the filming of one particular scene on a Sunday when the store was closed.

Tommy Fields made his screen debut in the film as Gracie's stuttering brother with a gambling problem, and Duggie Wakefield appears as a local flower seller in his usual, gormless role. Grace, "a theatrical," returns to her ill father after her review of *Mind those Legs* closes, and she turns down a part in a West End production as she vows to help her father and townsfolk, who all seem to know Grace personally. Grace takes over running her father's music shop in the market hall, a stall stocked with sheet music of a one "Gracie Fields." This gives Gracie the opportunity to sing the latest song releases, including the film's cheery title song, "Love is Everywhere," and the comical "Anna from Annacapresi" in a department store's music section. There are even impromptu performances of "Looking on the Bright Side" and "Sally" during the course of the saving of the market.

Another song is performed by Gracie, disguised as the Italian opera singer Madame Bellatrini, accompanied on the piano by Harry Parr-Davies, in attempt to ruin the opening ceremony of the new wing of Belfer's department store. The mock-operatic number shows how Gracie could easily have been proficient singing grand opera and is a performance reminiscent of what Madame Tettrazini would have witnessed in 1928. Amidst the perfect top notes, Gracie pulls grotesque faces, puts the band parts in, and generally "mucks up" the song. As a sign reads, "You Can't Beat the Market," that is the main ethos of Gracie's character throughout. She is certainly one of the people in this film, which is another film showing her solidarity with her native townspeople. A lock-in at the market, and the discovery of a charter signed by Edward III, eventually saves the market from demolition, only to be spectacularly exploded by accident.

The comedy in this film certainly seems dated compared to Gracie's other films, including a scene with a bungling town mayor, played by music hall star Robb Wilton, in a boxing-ring style argument which takes the metaphor too far, as Gracie, a representative of the market-stall holders, goes to battle against the shop-keeper's alliance. A scene with an overflowing vat of Andrews' Liver Salts, whilst funny in the 1930s, doesn't hold as much comedy as some of Gracie's other films. One of the film's highlights is Gracie's antics during the flying of a gyrocopter in a last-ditch attempt to reach the mayor before the final fate of the market is decided. Frequently throughout this film, Gracie breaks the "fourth wall" by winking at the camera and pulling comical faces and aside, something she did previously to characters in other films, culminating in a final address to the audience in the finale of *Sing as We Go*. However, throughout this film Gracie directly involves and addresses the audience with winks and gestures, again reinforcing the solidarity between audience and star. The film also features cameo appearances by Tommy Fields' theatrical partner, Nino Rossini, and future film star Kenneth More.

On April 16, the Lord Chief Justice Hewart visited the Ealing film set, and the two Lancastrians were introduced to each other. Hewart had told the newspapers how he had twice been lured from his Lewes home to a dinner of the Association of Lancastrians in London, believing Gracie was to be there. After hearing of his disappointment, Gracie arranged for Lord and Lady Hewart to visit the filming of a scene in the fictional department store, in which Gracie is dressed up as a Boy Scout. After spending some time watching her film, Gracie broke the filming and told them, "Come this way for the buns and the cake," which Lord Hewart told the newspapers "was the most homely remark I've ever heard!" Around this time Gracie offered the Salford author, Walter Greenwood, the use of her villa on Capri for his honeymoon with wife Alice Myles shortly after Walter had completed his third book.

The final shots of the film to be completed were the scenes of Gracie in an aeroplane, and during the filming a second plane was used to give the cloud effects. Cameraman Gordon Dines nearly fell out the open cockpit holding the camera whilst trying to achieve the necessary shots. Following the completion of filming on Gracie's sixth film in early May,

no immediate plans were set for her next, although her contract stipulated two more to be made by the end of 1936, and so Gracie left to take
a holiday in Capri. "The downside to filming," said Gracie, "is that every
town the production is to be filmed in, I am said to have bought a house
there." Having recently purchased Augustus John's studio, Gracie's next
move was to buy herself a bigger house to accommodate herself, John,
Mary, Margaret, and eventually Harry Parr-Davies, his parents, and the
Italian maid, Flo-Flo. She found the perfect property, named Greentrees,
at 36 Finchley Road, just around the corner from where her sister, Edith,
and family were living at 9 Cornwood Close.

The exterior of the house was mellow red brick with a large garden to
the rear. Instead of designing the interiors herself, Gracie left it to professional designers, whose idea for the **"richest working girl in the world"**
was to give her a Hollywood set for a drawing room. Under the great
chandeliers, the walls, grand piano, and furniture were all white with
gold thread in the upholstery. There was a yellow, fitted carpet and pink
damask curtains at the building's huge windows, and Gracie loathed to
remove the wrapping from the furniture in fear of **"mucking it up."** The
house had a constant stream of visiting composers coming to use her
piano, who were forbidden by Aunty Margaret to enter the best room.
So Gracie bought another piano for the dining room, then another for
the library, and finally a fourth to go into her own bedroom. Eventually
Gracie got fed up of composers constantly traipsing through the house
and had the pianos, a billiard table, and a bar moved to her "gold and
white tomb," where she "let them get on with it." Even then she had to
put a **2am** curfew on them trying out their new songs, because **Aunty
Margaret** wasn't getting any sleep!

One of the only surviving descriptions of the house comes from
Maud Goldthorp, a newspaper interviewer who visited Gracie at her
home and focused part of her report on the house itself. Goldthorp

wrote, "Gracie's 'office' is a large room with long windows at one end, opening on to a surprisingly large strip of garden—large for London, that is—but retaining the essential homeliness of the rest of her house. It has warm, buff walls, the most admirable paintings, plenty of books and flowers, and is very, very comfortable. In one corner is a large workman-like desk in light-coloured wood, and in the entire room I see only one portrait. It is of the late Gerald du Maurier. The office, Gracie explains, was originally situated upstairs, but as bits of it were continually creeping downstairs into the lounge it was moved in its entirety to this room. In the garden and hall are brightly colored little fishes—goldfish among them. Apparently when the hall fish grow to a certain size (and they are always growing, says Gracie) they are transported to the fishpond in the garden." Tony Parry remembered visiting the house many times after Fred, Jenny, and himself took the afternoon train from Brighton to London to see Gracie at the Palladium that evening and spent the night in "Gracie's big, great house on the Finchley Road."

The newspapers proclaimed, "Gracie has conquered every field of entertainment, and has won herself a unique place in the hearts of the British public," and announced an eight-week tour of South Africa, commencing in the autumn, earning Gracie an estimated £12,000. Following on from her sister>s success in the country a few years previous, Bert Aza thought now the right time to send Gracie to the Union, but not before completing some other engagements lined up in England first. The first of these was seeing the £5,000 extension wing of her orphanage opened on April 29, which could now accommodate up to 25 children. "I wanted an orphanage that did not look like the usual ones, and I think we have got it," explained Gracie at the opening ceremony.

When asked about her next film, and the likelihood she would go to Hollywood to film it, Gracie told reporters she hadn't even considered Hollywood, especially after her self-proclaimed failure of a fortnight in New York four years previously. "Hollywood and New York are just whistling stations to a red-haired woman who has made more than $750,000 dollars a year for almost a decade." Films which starred Gracie constantly outdrew Hollywood productions in local cinemas, running three and four weeks over their allotted time due to the demand for Gracie, but Gracie still did not enjoy the gruelling schedule of filming. Her sister Betty, who had achieved minimal success with a small recording career of thirteen songs, had recently completed filming *Lost in the Legion* (1935), directed by Monty Banks. Having had so much fun on set, Betty suggested to Gracie that Basil Dean should try to get him on board for Gracie's next film after his first project with her was cancelled. Gracie said that she'd give it some thought but had other commitments to focus on before filming was to begin on her next picture in October.

On the roof of Cameo Music Publishers, with Bill Haines and Jimmy Harper (Shaun Hewitt).

On deck of RMS Berengaria en route to America (1930).

Gracie and her mother on returning from America. (1930) (Shaun Hewitt).

Tommy Fields' wedding to Dorothy Whiteside. (1931) (Shaun Hewitt).

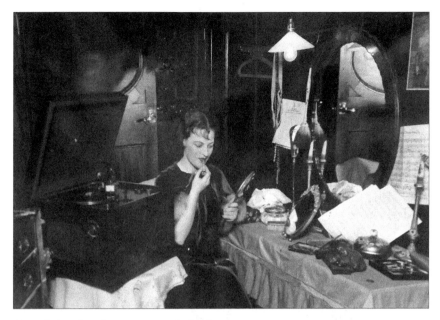

Gracie's London dressing room. (1931).

The trade show premiere of *Sally in our Alley*. (1931).

On set of *Looking on the Bright Side*. (1932).

On set of *This Week of Grace*. (1933).

Rochdale Charity Week. (1933).

Rochdale Charity Week.(1934).

On set of *Sing as We Go*. (1934).

Relaxing in Capri, taken by Basil Dean (1934).

Gracie, Duggie, Michael, and Grace.

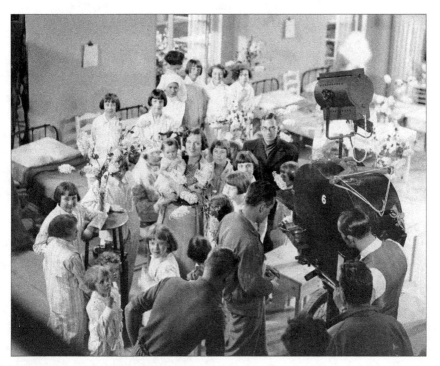

On set of *Look Up and Laugh* (1934).

The company en route to South Africa (1935).

Arriving in South Africa. (1935) (Mervyn Rossini).

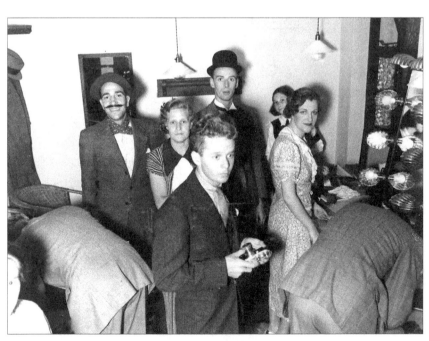

The company backstage in South Africa. (1935) (Mervyn Rossini).

Some free time in South Africa. (1935) (Shaun Hewitt).

An unusual portrait of Gracie. (Rochdale Museum).

The Fields Sisters on the set of *Queen of Hearts* (1936).

A still from 'Queen of Hearts.' (1936).

Gracie in Capri. (1935). (David Bolton).

CHAPTER NINE

June 1935 - 1936

And when I grow too old to dream,
That kiss will live in my heart.

- "When I Grow Too Old to Dream" (1935),
recorded by Gracie Fields.

IN LATE JUNE 1935, after opening the new wing of the Saffron Waldon Hospital, Gracie and John travelled to Connemara in Ireland with film director Brian Desmond Hurst. After reading John Millington Synge's play about an Irish woman who had lost her husband, father-in-law, and five children to the sea, Flanagan had the idea to film a version of the play himself. Gracie agreed to finance it, although she is unaccredited in the film's titles, and Hurst agreed to direct the short film adapted from the play by Patrick Kirwan and Denis Johnston. Filming began in Renvyle on July second in what Hurst claimed to be the most beautiful country for filming he had ever seen, whilst chief cinematographer Nicholas Debaiheaff was overwhelmed at the seascapes, which he spent hours filming. Gracie busied herself around Renvyle by visiting shops and cafes as a tourist and catching up on fanmail in her hotel. A local ceilidhe band was approached to be in the film, and filming was so low-budget that part of it was actually filmed in the cottage of local Connemara girl (and one of the film's stars), Bridgit Laffey.

In Britain, newspapers reported that on her busman's holiday, Gracie "has visited the set herself in this effort to bring something fresh to British pictures," as she busied herself following the camera team across the vales and hillsides. It was even reported Gracie helped the team rescue the sound-recording van from a bog. After filming was completed in Ireland, the production company moved back to England in mid-August to film interior scenes in a disused church on Marylebone Road. Gracie visited the set to see the filming of the final scenes, and had it not been for Gracie's financial support the film could not have been completed, as members of the Abbey Theatre Company, including Sara Allgood and Maire O'Neill, had to come over to England to finish the final scenes. In total, the film cost only £6,000 to produce, and Gracie was so pleased with the venture that she, Flanagan, and Hurst considered a second film based on Epstein's famous model, and someone who Flanagan had painted, Dolores.

The forty minute *Riders to the Sea* (1935) received its trade-show premier in late September of that year, where Gracie explained the director "knows his knitting, that's why I engaged him to do it. I thought the story a great subject for the screen, and I could see despite their financial handicaps the producers meant to do their utmost to make a fine film out of it." Synge originally wrote the play for his fiancée, Maire O'Neill, who had a cameo role in Gracie's *Sing as We Go* (1934), and her sister, Sara Allgood, and the two actresses reprised their roles from the Abbey Theatre's production in the film production. The film had its official premiere at the Theatre Royal in Dublin the following year, which Gracie was present at, tying in a week in variety in Dublin at the same time.

Elsewhere on cinema screens, unaware Gracie and Archie Pitt had been living apart for over four years, cinema managers at Bristol thought it would be a good idea to showcase Archie's latest film alongside Gracie's screen debut, *Sally in Our Alley* (1931). On July 16, the Bristol Hippodrome put Mr. and Mrs. Pitt for the first time together on the same cinema bill. Archie's film, *Barnacle Bill* (1935), featured the character Jack Tar (which he originated in *Mr. Tower of London*), a breezy seaman who, with his sailor friends, gets a girl out of her romantic troubles as he tries to balance his own family life with his time spent at sea. The film, directed by Harry Hughes with a script by Avling Ginever, was based on Archie's own character devised from his early reviews, and ultimately was a critical and box office failure for the City Film Corporation.

As opposed to wasting her time seeing Archie's film, in July Gracie travelled back from Capri, where the issue of British tourists on Mediterranean cruises was becoming an increasing problem for her privacy. Gracie came back to England and her kinfolk for a fortnight's stint in Blackpool. Although the increasing crowds visiting Capri were often an intrusion on Gracie's privacy, she used this to her advantage and often secured herself some "proper English bacon" from the cruise ships docked in the harbour. Gracie visited the Balaclava Hall in Surbiton on July 27 to watch a performance by the Excelsior Players from Surbiton Modern School of their latest show, *Port of Call*, before opening her two-week summer season at the Blackpool Grand from July 29 with Ford and Seagrave, Allan and Lavoie, Griffiths and Miss Lutie, Fields and Rossini, Three Virginians, Eve Drury and Raymond, Leslie Weston, and the Two Lidners. Gracie complained, "I do want to go down to South Shore and enjoy myself, but I dare not."

Her popularity in her native Lancashire was so high she thought herself to be a prisoner in her own hotel room as "[the fans] crowd round me, dig me in the ribs, slap my back, and all make a souvenir out of my dress." Even though on occasion she tried to disguise herself with horn-rimmed glasses and old clothes and hats, as the image became more frequently seen in newspapers and film magazines, and her cinematic output widened, her disguises were proving to be less and less successful. Therefore, Gracie had to resort to being "a prisoner in my own hotel room." Performing alongside Gracie in the packed houses at the Grand were the Macdonald Twins, Duncan Gray, Nicol and Martin, Ivor Vintor, Harry Hemsley, and Olsen's Crazy Sea Lions.

Due to demand, Gracie performed two houses each day, and whilst in Blackpool the Bishop of Blackburn, Dr. P. M. Herbert, visited Gracie and all the other artists of Blackpool theatres on his annual charity mission. Gracie stressed how much she thought Blackpool and the rest of Lancashire was "reet grand." On August fourth, *Look Up and Laugh* received it's official Leicester Square premiere, along with a simultaneous Northern release in Morecambe. Gracie deceived the Morecambe crowds by slipping through to the cinema along the Promenade unnoticed until she got to the cinema steps of the Astoria, where the thousands of people who had been waiting more than two hours to see her surged forward to get closer to their idol. Police had to rescue Gracie and control the crowd. From the rooftop of the cinema Gracie shouted to the crowds below, "I did it on yer that time! I'll show you how to crib in for free!"

The next week Gracie was back at the London Palladium for a three-week run, where one critic wrote, "Without her this week's programme would be enjoyable; with her turn added it becomes an artistic experience, marred only by a momentary uneasy feeling that she is squandering gifts that might have enriched grand opera or fine plays." With Broadway passion, rollicking humour, and Lancashire dialects, Gracie once again won the London audiences over as the established successor to Marie Lloyd, only more impish and neighbourly. Gracie told the newspapers every time she played the Palladium her first-night nerves were at their worst, as this was often where she introduced her latest songs and worried how well they would be received. During her August

1935 run she sang "Sing as We Go," "Sally," "The Rochdale Hounds," and three of her upcoming releases on her new recording label, "Turn 'Erbert's Face to the Wall," "South American Joe," and "When I Grow too Old to Dream." Gracie was retained at the Palladium for two weeks in bills starring the Chevalier Brothers, Will Fyffe, Ray Hurling and Seal, the Juggling Melvilles, the Mito Trio, Gene Sheldon, Senator Murphy, Venita Gould, and the Four Whirlwinds during the first week; and during the second week, Sherkot, Carl Shaw, Ray Hurling and Seal, the Four Whirlwinds, the Five Canadian Wonders, Venita Gould, George Hurd, Payne and Hilliard, and Cadd Mack Owen and Topsy.

Gracie had taken the decision to leave her recording contract at H.M.V., where she had been for the past seven years, and move to Rex, who promised a guaranteed 2,000,000 record sales on records priced at a shilling, instead of H.M.V.'s half a crown. Whilst the bosses at Rex admitted, "Our contract is just pin money to Gracie," Gracie explained her change of record label was because her people couldn't keep up with the output of her recordings at the prices they were currently at. The records promised to be "equal in every way to what Miss Fields has previously made" and were on sale to the public from August 29. This coincided with Gracie's last public appearance in England before filming her next picture and the upcoming African tour.

During her first Rex recording session in July, Gracie recorded "Turn 'Erbert's Face to the Wall" by Max Kester. He later remembered working with Gracie: "I never knew if she was going to be very funny or a great singer. But it happened that she turned out to be both! Though they always wanted to hear Gracie's pure singing, they also wanted her broad Lancashire accent and a sense of fun which she could only do in the funny song. In and out the studios I used to have songs and ideas in my pocket. Sometimes she was difficult if she didn't like it, but if we were in a jam she was such a sweet person and she would sing them. She didn't expect both sides of the 78 to be great commercial successes. One with me was 'Turn 'Erbert's Face to the Wall,' which, bless her darling heart, the result of that was that I was able to put down the deposit on the first house I had. Ronnie Hill and I wrote it together. There were several others we did at the same time. She always used to call me 'Mr. Hemmingway,' and sometimes we used to have large cups of strong tea and have dripping toast. Harry Parr-Davies played the piano, and I used to natter away with Gracie, and both coming from the North, we got on fine." In another recording session for Rex, for "South American Joe," Gracie cartwheeled around the studio.

Appearing for a week in Brighton at the end of August, following a week at the Manchester Palace, Gracie starred alongside brother Tommy, Payne and Hilliard, the Kadex Four, Leslie Strange, Patricia Rossborough, the Two Lindners, Michael Kerry, and the Juggling Demons. As she was in Brighton, Gracie could not attend the Lytham St. Anne's annual festival, and instead sent a trophy for whoever was to be crowned Best Child Comedienne in the show. The trophy went to Mabel Pogson from Dukinfield in Tameside, who won the competition out of 400 children for her comedy dance routine, and a radio broadcast on the BBC followed on September third.

Having completed all her theatrical engagements before her South African tour, Gracie spent some time in Peacehaven with her family, and the new introduction, Michael Frederick John Stansfield. Michael was born to Tommy and Dorothy on Christmas Eve 1934, and this was the first time Gracie could "make a real proper fuss of him" away from any contractual obligations, films, or tours. Tommy and Dorothy had lived at 117 South Alexandra Mansions, South East Saint Pancras, since 1932, but in 1936 bought a house at 27 Longcrofte Road in Stanmore, next door to Nino Rossini and Babs Rossini, calling their home Whitefields as an amalgamation of their names. Mervyn Rossini remembered, "This was ideal for my mother and Dorothy because they both had a young son and they had each other's company when the men were on tour." Stanmore was chosen because these houses were just five minutes' walk from Stanmore Station and the Bakerloo Line, which would take them straight into the heart of the West End theatres.

Mervyn also remembered, "Dad and Tommy were great practical jokers, and many a theatrical landlady was at the sharp end of their jokes. They told one landlady they would like one of their friends to join them for lunch, so could she lay an extra place? They went on to say he was a very nice chap but she should only give him a fork and a spoon because he couldn't be trusted with a knife. She agreed to that and he turned up the next day for lunch. Nobody else was in, so they had the dining room to themselves. She had cut up his meat into small squares and just laid a spoon and a fork on the table. He looked puzzled and asked for a knife. She ignored him. He asked again and she refused him. He asked several times more and she just left the room. Dad and Tommy then explained the joke to him, and the landlady came back into the room and he again asked for a knife. She just folded her arms and glared at him, at which point he threw a fake fit on the floor and she ran off terrified!"

On September third, according to Guy Fletcher in 1938, Gracie made a rare radio broadcast performing a number of live songs—which would be her last broadcast (other than her contracted radio show in 1937) for a number of years. The fifteen minute broadcast was Gracie's longest to date, and on October sixth she was first heard live in Australia and New Zealand, when in her dressing gown over her pyjamas she broadcast from the drawing room 28 Mallord Street at 8am. In a programme of anecdotes and songs, specially set up by the GPO, Gracie and Harry Parr-Davies, introduced by Basil Dean, were heard over 11,000 miles away and on over 65 different stations, who reported back the reception is perfect.

During September, Gracie performed another of her kindly acts, which were quickly earning her notice. She heard that a horse belonging to a young greengrocer in Peacehaven had been killed in a road accident. The young man couldn't afford another and his livelihood seemed lost. Gracie bought him a new pony, and one night after a theatrical performance she presented it to him.

Gracie and John took a small break to Capri before her next engagements were to begin. Although she did not realise it, John wasn't happy in Capri and he began to hate the place. "He felt he was in prison, stuck on an island with only two boats leaving every day for the mainland. He loved London and pottering around the secondhand shops or going to the greyhound races." That is why Gracie bought Augustus John's house in Chelsea, in the hope John would be happy and turn out some good work there inspired by the renowned artist's studio in the home. But her own work was beginning to dominate him too much. On this visit to Capri she decided to surprise him and ordered a box of artist's materials to be sent over from Naples, including expensive brushes, paints, and canvases. When she presented them to him he flung them across the room and categorically told her he did not want them, as his painting equipment was precious to him and now she was even trying to take over that.

On a walk to the lighthouse in Capri, John finally told Gracie they could no longer be together, as they lived completely different lives. The pair stayed friends throughout their lives, occasionally meeting, such as at the Irish premiere of *Riders to the Sea* in August 1936. Gracie often helped John out financially, such as when he opened a gentleman's club in London for artists in the 1950s, The Renaissance Club. Whilst Gracie helped to finance it, she didn't go to the opening night of the club, and instead Betty and Tony Parry went on her behalf. Years later, Lillian Aza commented, "John was very fond of Grace, but he couldn't accept the glamour and everything that went with it, or the fact she could afford to buy things for him. He didn't want it." Gracie's brother, Tommy, reiterated this when he described, "John would go around and sell a picture for £35 or £40, and then she came home with two or three thousand pounds and chucks it all onto the bed. Well, where do you go from there?"

On returning to Peacehaven, Gracie decided she would meet Monty Banks at both Betty and Bert's insistence, with the proposal of him directing her next film, due to begin shooting in October. John Loder, Gracie's onscreen leading man, had also worked with Monty in *You Made Me Love You* (1933), and probably also helped persuade her to try working with him. With John out of her life, Gracie wanted to fill the void with something else to keep her mind occupied, and although she hated it, filming seemed a reasonable idea. In her autobiography, Gracie recalled their first meeting: "I dreaded filmmaking, but Monty was already renowned for his skill at handling comedy pictures [...but] when I first saw this short little Italian with curly black hair, overdressed in a too-perfectly pressed suit and a silk shirt, I wanted to giggle."

Monty came down to Peacehaven for Sunday lunch, something Gracie was already "put-out" about, as Sunday was her rest day and a day which she spent in her plain, everyday clothes, from playing with the pets and the children in the garden. Meeting the renowned director would be no different, and she stayed in her slacks.

Having just read how Gracie was one of the highest paid women in the world, he was surprised to find her in dirtied, everyday clothes with her hair wrapped up in a turban. In an unpublished part of her memoirs, Gracie writes how after the clashingly dressed pair had looked at each other for a while, she said to Monty, "You look like an overstuffed settee, lad!" To which he replied, "And you look like an old kitchen cloth, but I bet you'll clean up rather well." Gracie knew immediately that a firm friendship would develop between Monty and herself.

Born Mario Bianchi on July 18, 1897, in Cesena, Italy, Monty was the son of famous bandleader, Leopold Bianchi. Monty first arrived in America in 1915, where he spent a number of years before returning to Italy. He passed through Ellis Island on December 12, 1920, with the intention of seeking a cabaret job as a dancer. In 1927 Monty told a trade press writer that in 1917 he was working as a dancer in the Dominguez Café in New York City. Although working for Fatty Arbuckle by 1918, he seems to have moved on before the Arbuckle-Rappe scandal rocked Hollywood in 1921, after appearing in over 35 Arbuckle shorts. Monty achieved success as a slapstick comedy actor and director in many silent films for small studios, including the famous Keystone Cops. He achieved success and fame working alongside the likes of Fatty Arbuckle, Laurel and Hardy, and Alfred Hitchcock. He later established his own companies, but moved to live in England in 1928 after the invention of talking pictures effectively stopped his acting career due to his thick Italian accent, where he worked for Warner Brothers and British International. By this time his role was more as a producer.

Remembering that first Sunday meeting, Gracie said, "My two dogs liked him, the children liked him, my mother and dad liked him. He helped cook the lunch and did the washing up afterwards, and [I] told him that you look better with your jacket off and sleeves rolled up." Gracie knew that aside from his hearty and friendly laugh, Monty was not quite the type of personality she was used to working with. "When we shook hands later that evening after agreeing to work for each other, I was still a bit watchful of what was to come, and I had no idea that Monty would take over in my life where Archie Pitt left off."

Still in Peacehaven on September 29, Gracie visited the Vera Garbutt Juvenile Operatic Society's production of *The Mikado* in Hove, where she was presented with a bouquet by the Mayor Loadsman for visiting the show. During the interval, Gracie took part in an auction on behalf of the Sussex Maternity Hospital, where she bought a five-guinea box of chocolates in aid of the charity. With *Queen of Hearts* (1935) lined up to be Gracie's next musical comedy, the public's demand to see her play a straight role brought the announcement on October fifth that Gracie had signed up to take part in a film biopic about Madame Sans Gene, the eighteenth-century figure who started life as a washerwoman and became the wife of the famous French General Lefebvre. Basil Dean believed the idea to be "a great success, as casting is perfect and production is set to begin next year." As with many of Gracie's proposed film projects, this one also did not get past the announcement stage.

Another proposed idea around this time was Gracie's desire to sing grand opera, specifically the part of Madame Butterfly. In an interview with Hettie Grimstead of *Windsor Magazine,* Gracie told of her desire to study the piano and play the classics properly instead of just picking out the easy bits. Gracie went on to tell Hettie, "My greatest professional ambition is to play in my favourite opera, *Madame Butterfly*," as she went on to give an impromptu performance of "One Fine Day" to Hettie. "Not so bad when I sing without mucking about, is it? You'll see me wearing that kimono yet, mark my words! I practice my scales while I'm dressing in the morning. The dogs don't mind, but my parrot always cusses me. He can sing a bit himself, so I tell him it's professional jealousy. He's a rum old bird. Harry Lauder gave him to me some years ago." This is another dream which was never realized for Gracie, although it is reported that in later life a private recording of Gracie singing "One Fine Day" materialized, although this claim has not been substantiated.

On October seventh, Gracie and her family visited the Telescombe Cliffs fête near their home, where as the guest of honor, Gracie cut the blue ribbon to announce the fair as open. As opposed to a formal speech, she turned the opening into a conversation, saying, "I've done my bit cutting t'tape, it's up to you all to make it a success. I've declared the doings open, so let's get to it and make it a success!" Later in the day, Gracie arranged a coach to pick up the children from the orphanage and let them have an afternoon at the fête too. The children formed a guard of honour for Gracie and escorted her around the event, as she took them around to every stall on the fair as requested, buying eggs, sweets, chocolate, and Madeira cake for them before letting them all have a turn on the coconut shy.

Other appearances in October 1935 saw Gracie performing in the opening night gala of the Granada Theatre Wandsworth on October 13 and at another cinema opening at the Dominion Cinema in Southall on October 15, where she had to be driven to her car after the performance by a black Maria police car. This was the first time Gracie had ever ridden in a police car, which she thought was "a reet great thrill, having to be rescued like David Lloyd-George." A dense crowd had been gathering outside the theatre since three that afternoon to see her, and not the two films on offer, (John Beal in *Laddie* (1935) and Elizabeth Bergner in *Escape Me Never* (1935). Four days later, on October 19, Gracie made a whistle-stop ten-hour round trip back to Rochdale to open a bazaar at her old church, St. Chad's, arriving at the bazaar at 2:30 before spending an hour with Bertha Schofield at 2 Milkstone Road for a cup of tea and a catch up, before getting the 4:45 train back to London.

Filming began on *Queen of Hearts* (1935), written by Douglas Furber, Clifford Grey, Anthony Kimmins, and Gordon Wellesley, at Ealing Studios on Monday, October 21, two weeks later than planned due to last-minute script changes and new writers. The filming schedule was due to be completed before Gracie's South African departure on November 23, and from the very outset everything was tight. The newspapers made a great deal that Monty Banks was to direct Gracie, with one journalist writing, "What these two will do, thus teamed, almost encourages me to think that Gracie may at last have a film which attempts to do justice to her great talents."

Although not needed on the first day of filming, Basil Dean had previously instilled it into Gracie she was to be present during all aspects of filming. "I decided to come an hour early to see Monty Banks at work and what I was letting myself in for," remembered Gracie. Surprised to see her when she was not called to the studio, Monty ushered Gracie to a canvas chair, which she promptly jumped up from with a shout as he had lit a bonfire of newspapers under her seat, much to the delight of the other cast members. As the Kleig lights flashed on and the players moved into their opening scene, Gracie fished around in her oversized handbag in search of a pair of sunglasses to shield the glare, but she was beaten by Monty, who presented her with a set of glasses from his top pocket.

With his deliberate clowning from the very start of production, Monty relaxed the actors' apprehension and Gracie described him as "so slick and sure of himself. He seemed to know exactly what he was trying to do and how best to achieve it." Although Gracie was fascinated watching the other actors under Monty's spell, she later admitted, "My mind easily wandered, especially to my Greentrees garden and the grass that needed mowing." Two days later, Gracie was required for her first scene, and when she turned up to begin her scene she asked the whereabouts of "Little Caesar." She was told he always turned up exactly twenty minutes late to the set, and chased the missing twenty minutes for the rest of the day to ensure he always finished his films ahead of time. Sure enough, punctually twenty minutes late, Monty arrived and threw himself straight into filming. "Monty knew comedy like a mathematician knows calculus. My face ached with laughing as I took off my dark glasses and stepped in front of the cameras."

Although Gracie's first filmed scene was a short one, which she had learned the lines for, after the dialogue was completed Monty sat silent. Not knowing what to do, Gracie began to ad lib the next scene as much as she could remember and continued to rattle on like this all morning.

With the script turned into nonsense, Monty lit silent cigarette after silent cigarette as Gracie carried on. "At the end of the first day my nerves were frazzled." Thinking that the slick, slapstick professional had enough of her version of comedy acting, Gracie was surprised when Monty told her, "You just keep doing what you're doing, Miss Fields. The stuff you're doing naturally at the end of each scene is wonderful, and the only part of the film I'm going to keep so far!"

Ever the perfectionist, at the end of each day's filming Monty spent hours going through the "rushes" and all the takes to choose the best clips and the best angles, often staying at the studio until two or three o'clock in the morning. The filming of *Queen of Hearts* (1935) rattled on quickly to keep up with Gracie's scheduled South African sailing date. Under orchestration from Ernest Irving, one of the film's key songs, "Do You Remember My First Love Song?" written by Harry Parr-Davies, took fifty-six hours of work by Irving before it was recorded "live" on the stripped-down soundstage at Ealing, accompanied by a stripped-down studio orchestra and chorus. Whilst the soundstudio was being set up Gracie entertained the other cast members with mock arguments with Monty, which she stormed off from by high-kicking her way around the studio before the orchestra was ready to record their first take. Two hours later the song was finally recorded. On a break from filming, Gracie filmed her own short film to be used as an advertisement for her African tour, to be shown in local cinemas and played over African radio stations, and on November 17 was a guest at the annual Variety Artist Ladies' Guild and Orphanage meal at Savoy Hotel.

One scene in *Queen of Hearts* (1935) called for John Loder to be involved in a car crash with Gracie in the boot of the car, and word from the studio was John crashed so well, you would've thought he has had years of experience in doing it. Another scene in a coffee shop called for a background crowd, which Monty acquired one night on London's

Embankment. After finding six "down-and-outs," he paid for their fares and breakfast at the studio to achieve a sense of realism and offered them three guineas a day each for their time. One of the men had to pretend to eat a cake at a coffee stall, but forgetting he was acting he ate the bun anyway, causing havoc for continuity. During the filming an Irish fan sent Loder six unlabelled bottles of whiskey as a gift, which at first were regarded with suspicion. At the end of the day's filming John invited Monty, the assistant director, and the cameraman to his dressing room to test the drink, and six empty bottles, countless card games, and a lot of money lost later, it was decided that there was nothing wrong with the whiskey and it had indeed been a thoughtful present from a fan!

One of the last scenes of the film which Gracie filmed was her infamous "Apache Dance" with famed gymnast and dancer, Carl Balliol. Gracie had worked with him earlier in the year on her variety tour before her Palladium engagement and remembered his "Dangerous Acrobatic Act," and thought it perfect for the film. She insisted she do the scene herself as opposed to employ a stunt double, and after being thrown around the studio for a few hours the scene filmed is easily one of the funniest and best remembered in any of Gracie's films. There were rumours that Gracie and Balliol had a relationship, and in the 1970s her friend Ettore Patrizi expressed, "She had become enamoured with a British ballerino. She did not have an affair with the dancer, only sent him passionate love letters [...] The dancer blackmailed Gracie and Monty for the return of her letters, which they bought and destroyed." Perhaps part of the payoff was his inclusion in the film?

The film itself is about Grace Perkins, a working-class seamstress from Barnsley who is mistaken for a rich patron of the arts and cocoa magnate, Lady Vandeleur. After striking up an unlikely friendship with stage idol Derek Cooper, played again by John Loder, Gracie eventually takes the lead in the next production—even though the police try to stop her. The soundtrack, provided once again by Harry, is largely unremarkable, except for the film's love ballad, "Do You Remember My First Love Song?"

It was during this film Gracie acquired a new personal assistant, in addition to Mary Barratt and Auntie Margaret. As Margaret had to stay and look after Greentrees whilst Gracie was to go on her South African tour, and Gracie didn't want to take Mary, as Margaret may cause a fuss, she chose to take her hairdresser from *Queen of Hearts* to accompany her. Maud Rowe had done such a good job on Gracie's hair that she told her she wanted to take her to South Africa with her as a personal hairdresser and aide and stop any arguments between Mary and Margaret. Whilst not much is known about Maud, except that she has a very brief cameo in *Queen of Hearts*, her private photographs which sold at auction in the early 2000s of Gracie's South African tour provide a unique snapshot of Gracie's private life. Harry Parr-Davies also accompanied Gracie in South Africa, and he also has a cameo in the film in a crowd scene as an out-of-work pianist.

Filming went quickly ahead of schedule, until the last week of production when one of the actors fell ill, and on the final allotted day of production there was still a lot left to do. Gracie was due to leave for South Africa at six the next morning, and Monty still had over a week's worth left of filming to complete in one day. Even though the schedule was tight, a lot of the usual larking about and good humour was encouraged by Monty, especially as he stepped in front of the cameras himself. Early in the film he has a small cameo—as he did in all his films—as a drunken passerby, but was forced to step in again in a later scene set on stage when the actor scheduled to do it couldn't be found in the studio. With the scene needing to be filmed, Monty did the scene with whitened hair and a false moustache and completed the short scene himself, credited as "Montague Banking"—a name he would use in later productions. After an amazing amount of work was completed in the morning, the flow of production stopped in the afternoon as the cast were celebrating someone's birthday over lunch. Gracie remembered, "They came back in the kind of giggling mood where they don't seem to realise where play stops and real work begins."

Monty had worked eighteen hours a day on this film, fuelled with hundreds of cigarettes and countless cups of coffee as he watched every inch of footage in the cutting room. Now, in the last few hours of filming, the cast weren't holding it together and were even squirting him with soda siphons. Regardless, he carried on, swelled with fatigue and kept awake by pills. In his drowsy state he knocked his eye against a piece of scenery which someone had left in the way, which was the height of merriment for the cast as "little, good-natured Monty had got a black eye! What a comical little chap!" With his assistant director next to him, filming was completed long after midnight when the boisterous players had calmed down and were now feeling a little bit sorry for themselves. Gracie realised, however, Monty was having difficulty and couldn't actually see out of his damaged eye. As everybody began to leave the studio for their taxis to the West End and to various parties, all Gracie was concerned about was the state of Monty's eye. She asked various cast members if anyone was at home to look after Monty, and great giggles about the rumours of Monty's "mad wife who wasn't really his wife" who was living with him passed around the cast.

Monty had met actress Gladys Frazin in a lift at the Piccadilly Hotel. In 1929, he said, "I did not speak to her at the time. I noticed her because she was wearing a red rose as a buttonhole—a flower I particularly like. Two weeks later we were formally introduced in the lounge of the hotel, and I recognized her because she was wearing the same kind of flower I admired on our first meeting. Sometime later we both played at Elstree in the silent picture, *Compulsory Husbands*. It was at that time we fell in love. The sequel is certainly curious—we now return as man and wife to make talking sequences in *The Compulsory Husband* (1930), for which we formerly acted as single folk." Even though the pair were married in 1929, and Monty adopted her son, Leo Junior, they were divorced on April 29, 1932 in California, granted by Superior Judge Lester Roth, as the unhappy marriage was fuelled by Gladys' schizophrenia and severe depression, while Monty frequently returned home to find she had once again run away, returning highly intoxicated. In 1932, Gladys had disappeared for several days and returned to live with her parents. When she had become too much to handle, scared of being institutionalised, and with nowhere else to go, Monty and Gladys still lived together and had even announced in 1934 they were to remarry, but this did not happen.

Although not bothered about the intricacies of Monty's marital arrangement, with her only concern whether anyone was at home to tend to his eye, Gracie got on the phone to Lottie Albert. A few months earlier, one of the children at the orphanage had an eye infection and a very good specialist came and sorted the child out quickly. Lottie arranged for Dr. Ryecroft to go straight to Monty's house, ignore anything the crazy wife may say, and see to Monty immediately. By the time everything was arranged it was almost four in the morning and Gracie only had two hours to get to Peacehaven and sort her luggage out for a four month tour of South Africa. Luckily, however, the sailing was delayed a few hours, but even luckier, Dr. Ryecroft rang Gracie and told her that even though she had woken him in the early hours, she had saved the vision in Monty's right eye.

Monty had arranged a farewell party to meet Gracie at Waterloo Station on November 23, but because of his eye injury he did not turn up. The rest of the film crew, however, were there to surprise her, along with Gracie's family, Basil Dean, the Azas, and Charles Coburn—the man who broke the bank at Monty Carlo. Edith, Duggie, and the Wakefield children were not there to see Gracie off, as they were on holiday themselves in Madeira, accompanied by their maid, Maud Donald, having travelled on the Cap Morte on November fourth. The very tired Gracie was bombarded with flowers and greeted at Southampton by a crowd of hundreds as she boarded the ship, Windsor Castle. She told them, "Hopefully the journey will be a complete rest, and happily I am a good sailor." Having worked herself flat out, with only two hours sleep, Gracie went to bed and stated, "I slept for the next four days." Whilst the rest of the party, including Tommy Fields and Nino Rossini, were exploring the ship, Gracie eventually materialised out of her cabin when the ship had reached Madeira, where Duggie and Edith came aboard as a surprise before they returned home on the Windsor Castle from Durban on December ninth. December fourth was Nino Rossini's birthday, and a party was thrown in his honour on board.

During the filming of *Queen of Hearts* (1935), Gracie's hair had been made a pinkish tint so it would show up better on cameras, but on board the ship, Maud was unable to procure the right materials to make Gracie's hair it's natural colour again. Although Gracie was naturally brown, for fifteen years her hair had been dyed dark red, but Monty wanted to make it lighter, as red hair filmed black. Ultimately, the film itself, after cutting and editing, was completed on December 11, and the newspapers reported Gracie worked herself into the verge of a breakdown and how nobody else other than Gracie could achieve her best picture to date running on so little energy and to such a tight schedule. It was given its trade-show premiere on February sixth the following year, and whilst the reviewers indeed thought it was Gracie's funniest and best film to date, their only criticism was the 18th-century costume and wig Gracie wears in a number of scenes on the stage made her unfamiliar to her native audiences, and they hoped she will not do something similar in any of her next films. The film's official London premiere was given on March seventh at the New Paramount Cinema, Tottenham Court Road.

Doubtful of any reception at the dockside in Africa, "I didn't think they'd have seen any of my films or heard any of my songs," the ship arrived in port at Capetown on December 20, where Gracie was met by a crowd of thousands, wearing a vivid green velvet dress, even though Tommy tried to persuade her against the unlucky color. This aversion to the colour green is something which seems to have been part of Gracie's family, as David Timmins, Tommy Fields' grandson, remembers his grandfather as hating a green carpet so much in the 1980s that he stood on boxes to avoid touching it. When David came of age to have his first car, his mother, Tommy's stepdaughter, was horrified to find he had bought a green car, and was convinced that he was going to crash it!

On the dock, despite having a sty in her eye, Gracie cheered and smiled to the thousands who had gathered to see her in South Africa, much to her surprise, as she was driven through the streets in an open car as confetti and flowers were thrown on the group from the throngs of both Blacks and Whites and from the rooftops of buildings. The initial reception of thousands had frightened her. Even though she was used to large crowds turning out to see her at the opening of a building or crowding around the stage door of a theatre for an autograph, this was something entirely different.

With the reception totally staggering her, Gracie's first concert in South Africa was not a success, as nerves were shattered. She had taken sheet music for 150 different songs out to South Africa, along with a steamer trunk of band parts just in case she was requested a song she didn't know. However, after her first concert the blame was put on the orchestra and not Gracie, as her reputation meant it could not be her fault the show was a failure. At once she wrote to all of the Capetown newspapers it was solely her fault and not the orchestra, and if management would give her a second chance at her own expense, the critics could come back the next night and she would show them "just what Gracie

Fields was all about." They all accepted to re-review the show, and were astounded at the difference in performance, stating Gracie's forty minutes passed all too quickly as she mesmerised the audience the second time around. Her supporting company were also well received, which consisted of Tommy Fields and Nino Rossini, Doreen the Xylophonist, Jack Daly with Irish songs and stories, and Raymond Smith in a ventriloquist act, Payne and Hilliard, and Raymond and Lolita.

At the end of the show, the orchestra all stood and cheered her, presenting her with a silver plaque which read, "To Gracie, from the Orchestra"—a totally unprecedented event in South Africa. As she left the theatre Gracie was overwhelmed by a crowd of over 1,000 people who had gathered at the stage door to see her, and a police escort had to be called to drive her back safely to her hotel. During her stay in Capetown, Gracie could not resist visiting a children's orphanage, and she agreed to give a free concert to the children and staff on the morning of December 16 at the Capetown Opera House.

Johannesburg was the next stop on the tour, and the train carrying the company—which was on an ordinary schedule—stopped for a prolonged time at each station. All the local people crowded onto the train platform to see Gracie, and they all demanded a song, so at every station Gracie got out and sang two songs before the waves of the people parted and the train could continue onward. When she eventually arrived in Johannesburg over six hours late, the theatre's manager, Mr. H. Lyell Taylor, fought with great difficulty to get his car through the crowds to get her to the theatre. In Johannesburg, the orchestra was led by a Mr. White, a South-African Welshman who had constant arguments with Harry, as each thought the other was impersonating him, not realising that in fact they were both native to Wales!

For many weeks it had been heralded by the BBC that Gracie was going to join their Christmas Day party via a link-up from her dressing room at Her Majesty's Theatre in Johannesburg. The demonstration broadcasts all worked perfectly, but when the show went live on Christmas Day a power failure meant Gracie's English listeners could not hear her. Gracie did not realise something was wrong as she sent her Christmas message and two songs to England until a radio engineer from the local station dashed up to the theatre and told her all that was being transmitted back home was dead air. The next day Gracie apologised to the newspapers. "I wanted to give a special message of Christmas cheer to Britain, especially Lancashire." Gracie promised to have a second attempt on New Year's Day, "as long as the atmospherics don't mess it up again!" Instead, she let off hundreds of balloons with raffle tickets attached to them to be returned to the local theatre to claim prizes, and on Christmas morning visited a local orphanage to distribute presents and gifts to the children, dressed as Father Christmas

From Johannesburg, Gracie wrote to Basil Dean in England on December 23: "Basil, my dear, thank you for your nice letter, and sorry to hear you're all alone in the cold cold snow. You should be playing principal boy. I'll bet you'd look good in tites [sic], almost as good as me. We think they cover your hairs up. Well we certainly are having a real royal welcome in this country, too much so, I've only to sing sitting in a la la, then I'll have sung from every kind of stage, platform, or room. Still, it is so really wonderful how all the English folks are so thrilled to have us here, and the show is going marvellous, which is so good, as when we have such a terrific reception it's a bit scaring if you're going to live up to it. Tonight is another fresh audience for us. So glad to hear the film is OK, sorry about my stand-in. Hope this OK. My love to you and Vicky. Grace"

Alongisde Gracie on her South African tour, as well as her brother Tommy with Nino Rossini, was Jack Daly—who Gracie had previously worked with in variety. Although his wife, Flora, accompanied them on the trip, it is rumoured in the Daly family that he and Gracie were romantically involved. His grandson, Michael J. Burn, recalled, "I recall being told by my mother that Jack and Gracie had an affair. However, at the risk of being thought disloyal, I always thought there were a lot of quite daft stories floating around our family. Daft, but quite interesting and amusing! I am told by my sisters that our mother had a distinct memory of Gracie giving her a doll and saying she would be her new mother. The timing would have been around the time of that South Africa trip, but it is all quite anecdotal and unsubstantiated, of course."

Thoroughly enjoying her stay in Africa, buying as many rugs, skins, tribal masks, and souvenirs as she could lay her hands on, Gracie rang Bert on January third and asked him to consult her existing contracts to see whether the tour could be extended by another four weeks. Delighted that it could, Gracie scheduled in more time sightseeing and was photographed sitting on top of Table Mountain, visiting the Goudini baths, and riding in a Johannesburg fire engine when she took part in a fireman's cabaret show. She also extended her run at Johannesburg's Her Majesty's to six weeks, as opposed to the allotted four, and frequently visited patients at Johannesburg's Central Hospital. On January seventh, the company visited the East Geduld Gold Mine, where they all went underground on a tour of the mine and Gracie was photographed with a large block of gold. The mine's manager told her it was worth over £30,000, and if she could lift it with one hand she could keep it. "I couldn't stir it! But as a consolation prize they gave me a piece of gold quartz with veins of precious gold running through it."

When Gracie had woken up in Madeira, a bouquet of flowers and a telegram had arrived from Uncle Sam Alexander, a well-known South African figure and lover of all things theatrical. Another bouquet was waiting at her hotel in Capetown, and when the company did eventually meet him, he played a great host for them all. A collector of precious and rare diamonds, on her 38th birthday Sam presented Gracie with a small golden diamond and threw a party for her at the Orange Grove Hotel. The company presented her with a large wooden inscribed box, and Mr. White, the orchestra leader, bought Gracie some more South African artefacts for her increasing collection. Shortly after her birthday, Gracie moved onto Pretoria, where she was received by the St. Dunstan's After-Care Fund for Blinded Soldiers, who threw a reception for her at Polley's Hotel. Mayoress H. W. Delley presented Gracie with a bouquet of flowers, and Gracie stood on a chair during the reception to sing "When I Grow too Old to Dream" and "Sally" to those present. Whilst at the event, Gracie took off her hat—which Bert Aza had sent to her as a birthday present—and auctioned it off for a total of £5 for the charity.

After visiting the Society to Help the Civilian Blind's fancy-dress party for 500 children at Langham Hotel, Gracie was photographed back at the hotel enjoying a whirling dervish routine dubbed "Insurance against the Blues" on January 17, presented at the Western Province of the Life Assurance Representatives Association of South Africa's second annual dance to aid the Mayor's Unemployment Fund. Next, the company moved onto Vaudette for three shows, and then to the Theatre Royal in Durban, opening on February seventh for a fortnight before playing the Maritzburg Grand Theatre for a week. A big crowd of visitors came to see Gracie when she visited the Doonside and the Valley of 1000 Hills, and she was photographed sitting among the natives—who presented her with two tribal shields as a memento of her visit. During her final week in South Africa, Gracie returned to Cape Town to board the ship back home and agreed to give one final week's performances in the town, who were rather upset she had spent so long in Johannesburg!

Not bothering about suspicion, the party set off back for England on the Stirling Castle on Friday, March 13 (another omen Tommy didn't like). Gracie was content she and her company had enjoyed a successful tour of South Africa, and was returning with a steamer-trunk full of mementoes. In response to an article in the *Film Pictorial* extolling the virtues of Marie Dressler, one Gracie fan wrote, "Pay a visit to the stage door of a theatre where Gracie Fields is playing. You will see, not fantastic hysteria, but a genuine love and admiration for one who is loveable, unspoiled by success, and cares for those who are less fortunate than herself. That is the secret of Gracie's charm. She is one of us."

Whilst Gracie had been in South Africa, back at Peacehaven her mother and father had taken part in a local Peacehaven charity concert, where Jenny performed "Daisy Bell" and "You Made Me Love You"; Fred performed his party trick, "You'll Never Miss Your Mother"; and Tony Parry took part in a comedy Astralesque dance. In the afterparty at a local hotel, Fred was amused to be asked whether he had ever thought about taking part in films as a Lancashire comedy character.

As soon as she was on board the Stirling Castle Gracie cabled ahead to England and promised the variety director of the BBC, Eric Maschwitz, as soon as her ship docked in Southampton she would take the train to BBC's broadcasting house to make her return broadcast, accompanied by the BBC Variety Orchestra, conducted by Lou Ross with Harry Parr-Davies at the piano. On board ship, Gracie rehearsed her routines and performed three shows: one for the crew and two for the fellow passengers. She arrived back home on March 30 at 10pm, and in her twenty-minute broadcast announced, "I feel like a big kid who's been on an outing," as she told the listeners all about her wonderful time touring the continent and visiting the Zulus with all their nothings on!

After a short break catching up at Peacehaven with her mother and father, and helping her sister Edith set up her new home, Oak Wood, on Hendon Avenue, London, Gracie was back into performing on April sixth, when she kicked off the charity football match between Press and Boxers at West Ham's Upton Park, and two days later she was in

Southampton to launch a new paddle steamer owned by the Isle of Wight and South of England Royal Mail Steam Packet Co Ltd.

Building of the ship began in late 1934 by I. Thornycroft & Co. Ltd. of Southampton at a cost of £35,000, but they waited for Gracie to return from her South African trip before they officially launched the new Red Funnel packet steamer, PSS Gracie Fields. The ship was unusual in that it was named after a celebrity as opposed to a person of nobility or royalty. Originally with a raised deck and open bridge, alterations in 1937 added a wheelhouse, enclosing the captain from the spray. At 396 tonnes and measuring 195'11" x 24'11", Gracie launched the ship as she sang "Sing as We Go" on the dockyard to the thousands who had turned up to see her christen the ship with a bottle of champagne. After letting go of the bottle someone on the podium had to remind Gracie to verbally name the ship, at which point she announced loudly, "Gracie Fields goes to sea!"

At the luncheon held after the launch, Gracie was presented with a silver christening cup, an inscribed lifebelt, and a flag-shaped platinum brooch featuring diamonds, rubies, and sapphires spelling out "G.F." in international flag symbols. Gracie frequently wore the flag brooch throughout her life, and Joan Moules erroneously states the item was stolen later in Gracie's career. (This was not the case, as existent photographs clearly show Gracie wearing the badge as late as August 1978, and throughout the 1950s.) The brooch came up for auction at Bonham's Auction House in January 2010, where it sold for £1,560 after being sold by Gracie's nephew. Throughout the summer months the Gracie Fields acted as a pleasure steamer from Brighton and Southampton to the Isle of Wight, but out of season it acted as a pilot ship at Southampton for the American cruise liners.

Before leaving for South Africa, Gracie recorded a number on Rex called "Look to the Left and Look to the Right," instructing children about the importance of road safety. She first recorded the song for the Public Address Company with Sir Malcolm Campbell, and the recording was played constantly through towns and cities on a van with a tannoy system. Upon returning to England, Gracie found her Rex recording was one of the BBC's most requested songs in their children's shows, and her chanting of "look to the left and look to the right and you'll never never get run over" had actually saved the lives of many children. The record, set in a fictional children's ward, features the popular Corona Babes in sketches with Gracie as they tell Miss Fields how they have been run over. The record perhaps should've been played to Gracie's chauffeur, Harold Edgar Head, who was fined £1 in Oxford for breaking the speed limit along Iffley Road on April 23, 1936, whilst Gracie was appearing at the New Theatre in variety alongside Stetson, the Four Jokers, Billy Russel, Joe Young, the Velma Four, Young and Younger, and Balliol and Tiller—the same Balliol as referred to earlier.

From a week at the New Theatre Oxford, beginning the April 20, Gracie began a short tour with Fields and Rossini, Balliol and Tiller, Kouple of Komics, Collinson and Dean, Four Jokers, Felovis, and Duval. They went on to play the Manchester Palace from April 27, the Finsbury Park Empire from May 4, the Brighton Hippodrome from May 11, the Chiswick Empire from May 18, and Gracie was back at the Holborn Empire from May 25 with Fields and Rossini, who had added a new scene into their act, dressed as two girls dancing around the Serpentine to the Blue Danube. From June first the company played the Lewisham Hippodrome with Payne and Hilliard, Rio and Santos, the Hollywood Four, and Calienta and Lolita.

Whilst in Manchester, Gracie opened a new aquarium at Belle Vue Zoological Gardens on May first, and was photographed holding two dingoes. Her company for her 1936 tour also included Fields and Rossini, Pepino's Miniature Circus, Rio and Santos, the Hollywood Four,

Caliente and Lilita, the Despardo Duo, Balliol and Tiller, George and Jack Dormande, Murray and Mooney, Collinson, Dean and Scott, and the Vardel 4. (With different artists appearing at different engagements.)

A new cinematic role was planned for Gracie's next film, a proposed film about the St. Neots quadruplets to be filmed in Morecambe. As with many of the other rumoured films associated with Gracie, this one did not come to fruition, but on April 18, Gracie's new film title of *The Show Goes On* was announced by ATP. On Sunday, May 30, a variety concert was given at the Phoenix Theatre for the Variety Artist Ladies' Guild and Orphanage with Lucille Benstead, Elsie Carlisle, Lee Donne, Norman Evans, G.H. Elliott, Pat Hyde, Ronald Frankau, Howard Rogers, Robb Wilton, and Syd Kaplan, with the orchestra conducted by Jack Trevor.

Achieving success on theatrical bills with their double act on both variety and pantomime, including appearing in a summer season with Gertie Gitana and G.H. Elliott in 1936, Fields and Rossini travelled, like everybody else, by train from town to town almost every Sunday. Mervyn Rossini remembered, "At one time they bought a three wheel Morgan, and this was a lot of fun and more convenient than the train. They got lost one day and were in a country lane and drove through a ford. The water was deeper than they expected and they had to open the doors to let out the water." Later, the pair bought a saloon car and were driving through Bedfordshire. It was January and the roads were covered in ice. Tommy was driving and skidded into a ditch. "Unfortunately the suitcases were piled on the back seat and came forward, propelling my father's head through the windscreen. That was not too bad, but when he came back into his seat the glass almost cut off his nose. The ambulance took four hours to arrive, on chains, and took him to a local doctor because they wanted quicker treatment than another four hours to a hospital. The doctor was out of his depth and made a mess of stitching it up, but it was later redone by Sir Archibald Mackindo. They should have taken the train!" Gracie and Tommy's nephew, Tony Parry, was taking dancing lessons from Vera Garbutt in Brighton around this time too, which did not amount to anything, as Tony decided against a career on the stage, like his family.

On June sixth in London, Gracie herself was involved in a car crash on Marylebone Road. Although "a little shaken up," as she put it herself, Gracie was uninjured as her car took the worst of the impact in the three-car pile-up. After six weeks of stage work straight out of her South African tour, Gracie headed to Dublin on July 12 to see the premiere of *Riders to the Sea*, along with her conductor, Lou Ross, and Harry Parr-Davies. Whilst she did not travel with John Flanagan, she naturally met up with him and Brian Desmond-Hurst at the premiere, but did not spend any large amount of time with him, as she was appearing at the Theatre Royal in an unusually attractive variety programme also starring Lou Radford, Bobby May, Olsen and Jean, and Jimmy Campbell. Whilst in Dublin, one of Gracie's first visits was the Children's Hospital, and later the local radio station, where she broadcast to the Irish public and surprised the interviewer by stating, "Dublin audiences are just like any other. If you provide entertainment that pleases them, they are pleased." Gracie's own *Queen of Hearts* (1935) was commercially released on July 22 to audiences.

Before completing her summer engagements and returning to Capri with Harry Parr-Davies, Gracie visited the paddle steamer named after her. The steamer made a special journey on July 26 to Brighton to pick up Gracie, her family, and the orphans from her home, where it took them on a day's trip to the Isle of Wight and back again. Gracie was photographed at the helm of the ship, and when asked would she like to retire to take up a life on the high seas, Gracie joked, "Nay, lad, I shan't retire until I've endowed my orphanage." Gracie told the reporters she yet wanted to make £200,000 solely for the orphanage so it could be self sufficient for the future. "The theatre is my first love, but the trouble is that if I stand by the theatre I will be working until I am 90 if I am to get that orphanage endowed."

The following day Gracie was back at the London Palladium and had dyed her hair blonde for the occasion, which was a surprise for both the audiences and reviewers. Some audience members reported they didn't realise it was Gracie on stage until she began to sing, and Gracie joked, "It's wonderful what the African sun can do to yer hair!" Offering the essence of each of her sombre ditties, and then laughing at the audience for taking her seriously, Gracie performed over six new songs in her repertoire to the Palladium audience, including "Poor Little Angeline" and "Queen of Hearts." Wearing a frilled Spanish gown of black and white with an elegant piece of black tulle which is transformed by a twist to make a Lancashire shawl, Gracie was showered with flowers at the end of her performance. Alongside Gracie on the bill were the Eastern Brothers, Archie Glen, Earle and Fortune, Bud Harris and Bert Howell, Giovanni "The Man who Baffled Scotland Yard," the Four Ortons, Murray and Mooney, and again with Fields and Rossini.

After a series of shows at the Margate Pleasure Gardens from August third, Gracie's annual run at the Blackpool Grand followed from August tenth. On August 13, Gracie appeared in the BBC's *Top O'th' Tower* programme, billed as, "A Blackpool night's entertainment, arranged and presented by Victor Smythe." The show started with Gracie in her dressing room at the Grand before moving to other entertainment venues, including, the Tower, Palace of Varieties, Opera House, Empress Ballroom, Tower Ballroom, Tower Circus, Central Pier, South Pier, and South Shore Pleasure Beach, including an excerpt from Jack Taylor 's 1936 Season Revue King Fun at the Opera House with George Formby, Frank Randle, Randolph Sutton and the Savoy Junior Band, and Max Miller from the Palace Theatre. On August 16, Gracie delighted a crowd of 10,000 who had gathered on the Promenade outside the Metropole Hotel to see her sing from her hotel balcony. After Gracie had waved them all goodnight the police used megaphones and loudspeakers to disperse the crowd.

Alongside her at the Grand was Sherkot, Joe and Young, as well as Ivor Vintor. At the end of her fortnight's run, Gracie presented the new mayor of Blackpool, Alderman Newman, with a check for 100 guineas to help with the Barnsley Mining Disaster Fund at Wharncliffe Woodmoor, where 58 miners died. On the afternoon of August 13, Gracie gave her services for free for the charity as she took to the stage of the Grand to auction a series of collectables and antiques, including a first night programme of *The Wrong Box* from London's Royal Olympic presented to Queen Victoria.

A trip to the Glasgow Empire, from August 17, saw a Horden girl performing in front of Gracie, twelve year old Thelma Bennett, who won a place in a local talent competition to be presented to Gracie. Whilst in Glasgow, an offer from Hollywood came through to Gracie, as her contract for ATP only scheduled for one more film, to begin production in October. The first Hollywood offer Gracie received was £65,000 from Twentieth Century Fox. Not thinking about work, however, Gracie ignored the offer at Bert Aza's suggestion, as he felt that a comeback offer would be made if the company really did want to procure Gracie.

On August 15, Tommy Fields was in Brighton Magistrates' Court for parking offences on the day Gracie and the orphans went to sea. Tommy, who was living at Longcroft Road, Cannon's Park in Middlesex, had given Gracie a lift to the pier, where he parked his car and went along with her at the last minute. "I left the car there because I did not think the trip was going to be very long, but when we were out the sea began to get very rough, and most of the passengers very sick. I would not have left the car so long in the normal way," Tommy claimed. The magistrates dismissed the case for payment of costs. Around this time, just as Bert had guessed would happen, Twentieth Century Fox came back with another offer, this time more than doubling their previous attempt, now at £150,000. Gracie knew this would endow her orphanage and stated, "I want money for the kids. I'm not bothered about all that Hollywood glamour stuff, I'm doing alright over here—nothing to grumble about."

Gracie attended sportsman Sir Harry Preston's funeral on August 22, where she gave a reading about his charity work, and subsequently held the traffic up near North Walsham when she decided to visit the local market on the way back to Peacehaven. Before heading to Capri with Harry Parr-Davies, Gracie attended the second birthday party of Leslie Fuller's twins at their home in Middlesex, where she played with her godchildren for a number of hours and was filmed by Pathe reel. Her last job before going back to Capri, much to the heartbreak of Bert Aza, was to decline the £150,000 contract from Twentieth Century Fox.

Gracie testing out her new Barnes piano, which she gave to the Rossini family.

CHAPTER TEN

1936 - 1937

A song in your heart means your in love
With someone who's in love with you.

- "A Song in Your Heart" (1936), recorded by Gracie Fields.

EVER SINCE HARRY PARR-DAVIES had first come into Gracie's dressing room and thrashed out the few uncompleted bars of "I Hate You," the pair became firm friends. Harry was Gracie's personal accompanist for over twelve years, and the pair often holidayed and socialised together. Gracie remembered, "When we all went down to Peacehaven for weekends everyone took it for granted that Harry would spend most of his time at the piano playing like an angel and shouting like a devil for his breakfast right up till tea time." Both Mary and Jenny obliged by providing him breakfast throughout the day, and Gracie admitted, "I felt like his big, doting sister." It was always Gracie's personal wish that Harry would complete a musical score just for her to star in, but this is something which was never achieved. Harry had massive success in writing songs for George Formby, Flanagan and Allan, and Evelyn Laye, and even brief success in later years with musicals, but none ever with Gracie in mind for the lead role. Gracie wrote in her unpublished memoirs of Harry, "We are both very proud of each other, and we would sock any person who criticized each of us—although we do row like the dickens sometimes when I think I should sing a song one way, and Harry the other."

Shortly before his death in 1955, Harry wrote an article for the *Red Star* newspaper detailing his relationship with Gracie, describing her puckish sense of humour. He wrote, "I remember mimicking her once, and she didn't think it the least bit funny ... Then there was the night at the Palladium when the curtain went up to show Gracie sitting at the piano while I made a grand entry at the top of the staircase. And I'll never forget a trip I made with Gracie up Vesuvius on the funicular railway. Suddenly, she leaned her head out of the window and started to sing. Out trilled her voice at the top of her lungs. The Americans and the English in the car looked embarrassed and tut-tutted. I thought she shouldn't be wasting her voice on them, but the Italians loved it!

"Normally, Gracie seems sure and confident, with neither doubts nor fears of life, and then something happens, and for a fleeting moment she is a different person. I visited her when she first went to Capri. We were walking down a lonely road in the moonlight on our way to a musical festival conducted by Toscanini. In the silence the music wafted to us of Beethoven's Fifth Symphony. Gracie stopped dead and shivered. 'Oh this is a terrible moment.' To me it was awe-inspiring music, but to Gracie it was something much more—something she couldn't explain. Gracie's response to music is something that never ceases to astonish me. One note on the piano and her mood changes. To me, Gracie is a puzzling personality, but still I think she is the greatest artiste I have ever known."

It is an often-quoted fact that Harry told Gracie that any pianist of hers would have to be a mind reader to keep up with her, as she frequently changed her repertoire whilst on stage without notifying her accompanist. "Whenever I rehearse with anyone, I know that as soon as I set foot on that stage I am just as different as day and night, and Harry, having been with me all these years, knows when I am day and when I am night!" Harry had his own room at Greentrees, which became infested with African bugs contained in the furs and ornaments Gracie had brought back from Africa. After a heavy fumigation, Gracie didn't want to take any more chances and burned most of her mementoes in the garden and shopped some of her untouched favourites down to Peacehaven.

When Gracie and Harry left for Capri in late August 1936, Gracie had the full intention of selling the property and moving back solely to England. Monty Banks, having never visited, offered Gracie twice what she had originally paid for it, and this was a tempting offer. When she arrived, however, it looked as beautiful as it ever had, and she fell in love with the island all over again, spending the summer relaxing and rehearsing new songs.

Gracie returned to England in September, where it was announced she had signed a contract with impresario Charles Corchran to appear in a musical in January, although this never went ahead. In early October, Gracie visited Basil Dean at his country house to discuss the script for what was to be her new film, to be titled *The Show Goes On*. Earlier in the year, Gracie told the press she was looking for a story which mixed laughter and tears, but was not like her own life story. The script which Basil presented her, incidentally, had more than one passing resemblance to the real story of Gracie Fields.

On her return with Harry, Gracie brought with her Ettore Patrizi, who it has been rumoured was in a relationship with Harry, as she promised to show him parts of England—including Blackpool—as his first foreign holiday. Amazed at just how many chimneys there were in England, Gracie remembered, "After the three weeks Ettore was glad to get back to Capri after his three weeks of hell, as he told people!"

Returning home, however, Gracie found her Greentrees house had been burgled. Auntie Margaret had set up correspondence with an old

Sunday School friend from Rochdale, having met up with him after one of Gracie's charity concerts in the town. John Fielding was an undertaker, and Margaret had gone to visit him for a few days and to see her family. Whilst she was away a thief with a bicycle had entered the kitchen and other rooms and left dirty tire marks on the floors. One of Gracie's mink capes and a large quantity of silver was taken, but some of the silver, including the tea service from Rochdale, was found thrown in the greenhouse, as it appeared the burglar was disturbed. The thief was thought to be the elusive "Flannel-Foot" who London Police were chasing all around the city, and who was not disturbed by the yapping of Gracie's dog, Ming. On the very same day, Gracie discovered her own pleasure motor-cruiser yacht, which she rarely used, called The Vigilant, moored off Chelsea, was damaged by a passing barge. Realising the theft could have been much worse, Gracie joked to the press, "Guests wipe their feet before they come into my home, I only wish robbers' would wipe the tires of their bikes too!"

On November sixth, Gracie's voice was heard at the Glasgow City Business Club luncheon, where Sir Ian Hamilton played the businessmen a specially recorded Gramophone message from Gracie, "who spoke in moving terms of the men who had come back broken and disabled from the Great War, and how they deserved compassion and sympathy" from the committee.

Gracie's return to England meant a return to filming, as Basil Dean announced her next film, *The Show Goes On* (1937), would feature scenes from her own life. With a script by ex-Naval officer turned playwright Anthony Kimmins, Basil Dean insisted he was to direct this film—which was looking likely to be Gracie's last with ATP, and if it was going to be her last, the man who directed her first wanted to do it. With musical scoring by Ernest Irving, Harry Parr-Davies' songs appear in the film, with "A Song in Your Heart," "We're All Good Pals Together," "My

Love For You," "In a Little Lancashire Town," and the popular "Smile When You Say Goodbye," which proved to be Gracie and Basil Dean's swansong. Jeffery Richards wrote of the comedy, "Basil Dean's approach is markedly and characteristically different from Monty Banks'. Dean's is of character and situation, eschewing Banks' penchant for slapstick."

Shooting began at Ealing in early November 1936 after script alterations, and one visitor to set reported how Basil Dean's film studios are the quietest on earth, as the technicians spoke in whispers, and Dean himself directed quietly, as if he was in his study. A large theatre set was built at Ealing to accommodate some of the scenes shot in a pantomime setting. One of the much heralded scenes occurs when Gracie performs "Smile When You Say Goodbye," which was to become one of her standard repertoire songs, from the bridge of the RMS Queen Mary to a nearby ship full of soldiers chanting her name. In the film, Gracie's character name is Sally Lee, reverting to the name of Sally after appearing in the past few films as Grace.

The semi-autobiographical film tells of factory girl Sally Sowcroft's, later Lee's, rise to stardom in the theatre, and her working relationship with an asthmatic songwriter, Martin Fraser, played by Owen Nares. Featuring her rise from pantomime to music hall and eventually the West End stage, the story shares the backstage rise to Sally Lee, ending in the glamorisation of Gracie at the climax of the film in a big Hollywood-style song and dance number. Many have alluded to the biographical similarities within the film and Gracie's own story, even to the point of Sally Lee and Gracie Fields appearing together in a theatrical bill headed by a troupe of sealions!

On November 8, Gracie organised a charity concert at the London Coliseum in aid of Charing Cross Hospital, with the ambition to raise £3000. Sir Oswald Stoll loaned Gracie the theatre for the night, and a host of stars loaned their services. The bill comprised of Carroll

Gibbons, Ann Lenner, Mantovani, Herman Finck, Harry Welchman, Peggy Cochrane, Tommy Handley, Parry Jones, Magda Kun and Steve Gerary, Leslie Sarony, Leslie Holmes, Arthur Fear, Sutherland Felce, and Bertha Wilmot.

The next day, Gracie took a specially chartered train from London to get her to Belfast for the opening of the new Ritz Cinema, which she had promised earlier in the year on her last visit to the city. Her stage performance was broadcast live on the BBC, with one reviewer writing, "She can sing a top D with any prima donna I know [...] the heartbreak voice and the Fields personality put new life into some established favourites," which included "Would You?" and her new comedy song, "A Feather in her Tyrolean Hat." Exhausted after travelling, Gracie stated, "Eeh, I feel like a wet week!" So popular was her rendition of "Did Your Mother Come from Ireland?" that on her return to England she recorded the song to be issued on record, much as she had done earlier in the year with the popular "Laughing Irish Eyes." On her return, Gracie visited the Carlton Theatre in Norfolk for a charity performance of Madame Osina's Juveniles to help with the Norfolk Blind Fund.

Before filming recommenced on November 31, November 16 saw Gracie donning rugby stripes as she kicked off a rugby match at Mitcham when the Rochdale Hornets visited Streatham, and the following week she played at the Brighton Hippodrome. On November 19, Gracie visited the Variety Ball at Grosvenor House, where she performed alongside Les Allen, Kitty Masters, Elsie Prince, Flanagan and Allen, Helen Raymond, Sam Browne, and John Watt in a programme which was also broadcast by the BBC, and December sixth she gave her services in an all-star cabaret at the Savoy Hotel for the Variety Artists Ladies' Guild and Orphanage, appearing with Jacky Hylton, Robb Wilton, Sophie Tucker, Elsie Carlisle, Florrie Forde, Nervo and Knox, and Naughton and Gold. Her Christmas donation to the Guild that year was £1000. December 11 saw Gracie at Ealing Town Hall, at the Mayoress's Christmas Market for Charity, where she donated £10 toward the fund.

On December 16, news broke Gracie was to receive the Freedom of the Borough of Rochdale, in May 1937, along with asbestos manufacturer, and former sherriff of Lancashire, Samuel Turner.

Gracie told the newspapers, "I could cry, because though I've got used to having a bit of a fuss made over me wherever I go, I feel so grateful that the people who are my own kith and kin have decided to honour me in this way. I went into the mill in Rochdale and was brought up amongst the people who are offering me the Freedom of the Borough, and I know how undemonstrative they usually are. That's what makes it all the more difficult to tell them how touched I am. I know how sincere their tribute is, and I shall always treasure the memory of their invitation. I was astonished when the mayor, the town clerk, and Alderman Bryning approached me to see if I would be willing to accept the Freedom. Willing to accept it!? It means all the more to me because it comes from my own home, although I'm sure I don't know that I've done much to deserve it."

Christmas that year was spent quietly at Peacehaven, spending Christmas Day at the orphanage and hosting a Christmas Day party at her home. With her whole family, Gracie served tea and cakes and presented dolls and soldiers to all the children, who had been taken to see *Aladdin* at the Brighton Hippodrome on Christmas Eve, and were taken to see Gracie in *Look Up and Laugh* at the Brighton Pavillion on Christmas Day night. It was also the first Christmas Gracie and Monty Banks had spent together, as they grew increasingly ever closer. Gracie told the papers, "My New Year's Resolution for 1937 is to carry on being Gracie Fields." This began on January second, when she "carried on" by throwing herself into more charitable causes, broadcasting on the BBC's *This Week's Good Cause* in an appeal on behalf of the London Child Guidance Clinic.

Her resolution began as she sent a message to the Elkins congratulating them for their excellent charity work and wishing them continued success through 1937. On the set of *The Show's the Thing*, 52 tonnes of sand were used to create a beach scene at Ealing Studios before filming finished in early February.

In January, Twentieth Century Fox chased up on their refused contract offers, arranged a meeting in London at the hotel of film executive Joe Schenck, who was visiting London with the aim to persuade Gracie to sign on the dotted line. Gracie took Monty with her to the meeting, on January eigth, but she was so set in her mind she did not want to go to Hollywood. "He had a chin like Mussolini and a very direct and powerful stare," recalled Gracie, as Schenck offered her a contract for eight films. She told him to forget eight, as she didn't want to do one, but when he presented her with the paperwork for eight films at a quarter of a million dollars, she stopped herself in her tracks.

Bewildered at the large figure, Gracie instinctively said, "It's ridiculous," which the American took for the negative and told her it was just an opening offer, and that Darryl Zanuck wouldn't let a few thousand dollars get in his way of procuring the star he wanted. A compromise was agreed, and Gracie got the eight films down to four at £50,000 per film. "I was so scared I made the pen nib cross its little gold legs and splutter. And there was it, I'd been purchased by Twentieth Century Fox of Hollywood!". The deal was announced to the press, who gleefully remarked it was an early birthday present for Gracie, although the official paperwork was not completed and finalised until January 23.

With a potential move to Hollywood looming, Jenny and Fred thought the time had come to sell The Haven, and on January 15 they told of their idea to sell the property and move somewhere in London to be closer to Gracie. Again, this was something which did not come into fruition, and the house was kept by Gracie until the end of her life.

King George V had died at Sandringham in January 1936, and almost a year later Gracie was one of the first variety stars to send her "spare shillings and pence" to a National Memorial Fund, urged by Pathe News. The committee, set up by the lord mayor after the king's death, sought to promote and to assist in the establishment throughout the United Kingdom of Great Britain and Northern Ireland of playing fields for the use and enjoyment of the people in the late king's memory. At the end of January, Gracie took a brief holiday at the Grand Hotel in St. Mortiz, accompanied by Monty Banks, her mother and father, and Harry Parr-Davies, who could not comprehend the "little Italian's ways of kissing both the women and the men when he greets us!" Interestingly, there is a photograph of the group in a horse and carriage outside the clinic of Doctor Nagali, advertising his specialism in X-ray. Perhaps Gracie was in St. Moritz for her, as yet, unidentified illness and to seek some kind of medical advice in Switzerland?

From St. Moritz, Gracie wrote to Basil Dean on February first. "Basil, my dear, It was so very sweet of you to send the telegram on Saturday afternoon. I do hope and pray our film will be the best we've both made. We are having a lovely few days here. Have you been here? I hope when I get back you and Vickie will come and have a meal with me. Thank you again for everything. Yours very sincerely, Grace."

Gracie and Monty discussed her next film role and planned a visit to Hollywood during March. Around this time it was rumoured Gracie was to return to London to star in a new West End musical, honouring her contract with C. B. Cochran, to open in early March, with book by Eric Maschwitz and music by Henry Sullivan and Will Haines. This was the first musical offer Gracie was to receive and turn down in 1937, as later that year she was offered the leading female role in Noel Gay's

Me and My Girl, set to open with Lupino Lane at the Victoria Palace in December. Gracie turned down both roles, with the role of Sally Smith in *Me and My Girl* instead going to Teddie St. Denis.

Cutting her holiday short to honour a promise made to her old friend, George Black, Gracie returned to England just for one day on February 16 to visit the opening ceremony of Black's Picture Palace in Gateshead. She arrived in Newcastle from London at 2:45pm, where she took a car to Gateshead to attend the ceremony and sang to the crowds from the roof of the cinema. She returned back to Newcastle, leaving for London on the 4:30pm train, where she travelled straight back to St. Moritz to resume her holiday. Gracie was back in England on February 20, as she performed in the 43rd version of John Watt's popular radio show *The Songs from the Shows* for the first time in six years. Gracie even brought along with her a special guest, a twelve year old schoolgirl from Mitcham, Irene Price, the winner of a local competition for her Shirley Temple impersonations. Cinema box office managers around the country complained to the BBC as takings were low on the Saturday evening that the broadcast went out, as people were staying at home to listen to Gracie. It was estimated that £150,000 nationwide was lost in cinematic takings on that one evening alone. So popular was the broadcast, however, the BBC decided to include Gracie in a special guest appearance the very next night, much to the further upset of cinema managers!

On February 21, Gracie was elected "Chief Minnie Mouse" alongside the Regal Cinema's owner, Mr. W. Fuller's "Chief Mickey Mouse" at the cinema in Golders Green, for the "best good, charitable deeds of 1936." "Does this mean I have to marry Mr. Fuller?" joked the new Mrs. Minnie Mouse. Returning "up North" on February 26 saw Gracie as the guest of honour at the Manchester Royal Exchange, who were hosting the annual Manchester Press and Panto Ball. Gracie told the crowd, "No matter what rewards the world may offer, what far journeys I may have to take, there can never be any reward or journey so welcome after months of hard work as a trip to Lancashire—especially when I have a good pair of Lancashire clogs to go walking in!"

Returning to the Holborn Empire during the last week of February before her trip to America, with Billy Danvers, the Four Ascots, Low and Webster, and the Three Acronas, Gracie joked with the audience on her opening night. "My voice is not so hot tonight, but even I must have a cold sometimes." The audiences would never notice when Gracie was having a slight off-show, as she always gave her all, from high drama to low comedy, including new numbers from *The Show Goes On* (1937). During her run at the Holborn Empire, the mayor of Rochdale, J.P. Dutton, visited Gracie to arrange a suitable date for her to receive the Freedom of the Borough. With contractual arrangements scheduled in her diary already, Gracie and Bert Aza decided upon Wednesday, May 19, exactly one week after the new king's coronation. To celebrate her "Freedom," the *Rochdale Observer* arranged on the Saturday following the Freedom ceremony, twenty specially chartered trains would take 9,000 Rochdalians to London to see Gracie perform at the Alexandra Palace.

Gracie and Harry Parr-Davies left for Hollywood on March third "to have a look around," sailing from Southampton on the Queen Mary—which featured in her latest film. Plans were already in place for Gracie to make her first Fox film in England, with Monty directing, but Gracie was to meet Darryll Zanuck in Hollywood to finalise plot and story details. Monty had gone on ahead to work through some ideas. As she boarded the train at Waterloo Station the mobbing crowd surrounded Gracie, clamouring for "Sally," which she, for once, politely declined, and was presented with a miniature cricket bat signed by the England Test team, who were currently touring Australia. Gracie told her family, "You needn't expect me to write to you all because I shan't do it. I'm going to write a general letter and you'll have to pass it round to the next one, so don't get fussy if each of you don't hear from me!" This was a tradition Gracie continued when writing home during her Far-East tours of the Second World War, which are reproduced in this book.

En route to America, on March seventh, Gracie gave two performances in the main lounge of the ship, accompanied by Harry. On the trip, Harry leaned over the railings of the ship during the journey and lost his only pair of spectacles overboard. Although she thought it was hilarious, Gracie knew Harry depended on his glasses and sat him in a deckchair whilst she went to the shop to see if they sold any spectacles which would last him until they could get to an optician in America. On the way, Gracie spotted a sign on board which said, "Found: A pair of glasses, apply purser." Gracie did so and gave the glasses to Harry to try on and was surprised to find that they were actually his glasses which had been found. By a very strange chance of fate, the man who had found them had put his hand out of his porthole on a lower deck to see if it was raining at the exact time the glasses fell off Harry's face, straight into the man's open hand!

While Gracie was away, on March 16, Betty, Roy, and Anthony left England aboard the SS Normandie, headed for their new life and home in Los Angeles. Roy had got a job as a scenic painter in Hollywood and the family moved to 236 West Channel Road, Santa Monica.

When she arrived in New York, Gracie was met at the dockside by Monty, who had been waiting all night, as the boat arrived late in port. Gracie remembered, "I had rested on the journey all the way and felt I didn't look too bad on my arrival in New York." Monty, however, suggested otherwise and told her she needed to get her hair fixed. "He told me, 'My God, Gracie! What've you been doing? You look a mess!'" Monty forebade the Movietone camera and the press photographers from taking any close-up shots, or any "cheese-cake" shots showing Gracie's legs, as she agreed to "get it all put right while there's still time."

Monty took Gracie to the Ambassador Hotel and called up the chief hairdresser. "When the girl had finished with it, I looked in the mirror and it looked like a Chinese pagoda! I've never seen anything like it. I looked like Stan Laurel!" Harry Parr-Davies agreed with the hairdresser that it certainly looked the latest and best, but when Monty saw it he was as shocked as when he met Gracie off the boat, and annoyed that she had her photograph taken with a hair-do like that. An irritated Gracie went to the bathroom and threw her head under the taps, dried it roughly with a towel, took a hat and covered her hair and left for the scheduled press conference still dripping.

The conference was in the shape of a banquet thrown by Twentieth Century Fox at the Waldorf Astoria for the 200 most influential journalists and critics to see Fox's new acquisition. The newspapers reported how they were "startled by her bluff Lancashire accent." Gracie responded, "I'm not so sure what yer were expecting from that there Gracie Fields!" In later years Gracie remembered, "Poor Monty wanted so much to make me a success on that first trip that he made himself sick with worry." She also remarked how she "felt ugly and awkward at that conference. My mouth froze into a silly smile. I wanted to run away and cry." Robbin Coons, a reviewer at the conference, wrote, "She was late, and she breezed in as naturally as a gust of wind. She flashed a big, honest-to-goodness smile, acknowledged this introduction en masse, pushed her hat back with a broad comedy gesture, saying, 'This makes me feel like a bally queen!'"

Having been told the sun always shines in Hollywood, Gracie was disappointed to arrive at the Beverley Wilshire hotel in California during a thunderstorm, where it preceded to rain for the first five days of her visit. Prepared to find a place like Blackpool or Broadway, with all the film studios next to each other, she was surprised to find great distances between Movietone City where Fox was based and the locations of Paramount, Radio, and Columbia. Gracie's hotel was on Wilshire Boulevard, and she remembered, "From the window I could see the hills to the North, all grey and green in the sunshine, and the clear, blue ocean at the end of the boulevard." Monty was amused when Gracie asked him to take her on a tour of the film stars' houses, so he drove her to Norma Shearer's French farmhouse in Santa Monica, and the Malibu beach homes of Merle Oberon and Miriam Hopkins. When they returned to their hotel room Gracie's room was covered in flowers, which were deliveries from the studio, fellow film stars, and from "people whose name I'd never heard!"

Gracie wrote to Basil Dean from her hotel. "My dear Basil, Thank you for your very nice letter. Well I'm so glad our film went well. I had letters from my family and they seemed to have passed it, and they're a tough lot as you know. I'm having a lovely time here and meeting some wonderful people. Constance Collier has been sweet to me and showing me off a bit. I'll be back at the beginning of May, so I'll give ye a ring. Hope you've summat good up yer sleeve for our show together. Love to thee from me. Grace."

Monty had arranged for Gracie to have a teeth bleaching with Dr. Schneck before a party to be thrown in her honour by Constance Collier on April tenth. "My own teeth were okay, but I had gaps in between each lower tooth, and when I made my earlier films I had worn a contraption made by a London dentist." Although her teeth were healthy and good looking, Dr. Schenck decided Gracie must lose at least four teeth, as they had phyorrea. Gracie had suffered with ulcers quite frequently but had not associated it with this before, and when the first four teeth were pulled Dr. Schneck pulled out another four to give Gracie a "perfect Hollywood smile" with a new set of dentures, which he applied directly onto the bleeding gums. The same afternoon Gracie was sitting in her hotel room being interviewed by Luella Parsons when an invite came for dinner with Charlie Chaplin and Paulette Goddard that same evening. She said that she'd accept if it was soup they were having, to which the interviewer laughed and called for Harry to give Gracie a glass of Scotch for courage, and to get rid of the tea she was drinking. Instead, with her newly fitted dentures in place, Gracie was served a traditional English roast beef dinner served in her honour, cooked by Chaplin's Japanese chef. After dinner, at which the pair got along famously, a tour of Chaplin's lavish estate ended in his music room, complete with pipe organ, and Gracie and Charlie sat around the piano playing music hall songs.

In an interview with *Picturegoer*, given over the telephone from America, Gracie told the reporter, "Hollywood is trying to make me beautiful, so I am going to oblige. I fear my British admirers won't approve, as they prefer me as a diamond in the rough—or so they say!" Photographs appeared the next day in the *Daily Sketch* of Gracie's Hollywood glamorization, with one horrified caption reading: "Just look what Hollywood's done to our Lancashire lass! Gracie Fields hardly looks like 'Our Gracie!'" Gracie, however, was unhappy about all the reception her beauty treatment was getting in the papers and retorted with a statement: "All this talk of these beauty processes, you'd think that I was an old hag when I left for America!" Having been beautified, Gracie was taken to Gene Kornman's studio and had a series of highly stylised and glamourous photographs taken of her, which were immediately sent to the British papers, who declared, "Look what Hollywood has done to OUR Gracie!"

The party given by Constance Collier for Gracie was dubbed Hollywood's most exclusive party of 1937, and was attended by Cole Porter, Ray Massey, Rex Evans, Charlie Birkin, Auriel Lee, Felix Young, Charlie Chaplin, Tilly Losch, Ethel Barrymore, and Max Hart. "I found myself growing more and more overwhelmed and backed myself up at the piano," at which sat George Gershwin, who was mid-playing "Some

Day He'll Come Along." Remembering part of the tune, Gracie began to sing along to Gershwin—who seemed to pick up—until she dried and apologised for forgetting the words. "As far as Gershwin was concerned, Gracie Fields had come and gone." The meeting with Daryl Zanuck was scheduled for the next day, and Gracie "made herself up" for it, to be held in the restaurant of a local hotel. Monty and Gracie sat together for over two hours, and with still no sign of Zanuck, Monty left to give Fox a call to see what the problem was. "A little man with fuzzy hair, partly bald, a smudge of a moustache and a short upper lip that vainly struggled to hide the two rabbity teeth protruding from underneath it" came into the room, and a dry-throated Gracie was worried that Zanuck may appear to find this man cluttering up the place. After mistaking the small man, who was none other than Zanuck himself, Gracie began to talk business with him.

"After a few minutes talk I began to see the bigness inside the little man. In a city of shrieking personalities, hair-tearing ideas, and million-dollar epics, Mr. Darryl Zanuck burned quietly like a small, grey light-house firmly fixed on dangerous rocks. But he wasn't at sea. Darkness and daylight came and went. Mr. Zanuck sat firmly on his rock, tending his lamp. Some men give you that feeling—it's like having tummy ache and sending for the doctor, and as soon as you hear him thump on the door the pain goes and gets a bit better. In the throbbing headache that was Hollywood, Mr. Zanuck was a human aspirin tablet."

In the crazy whirligig of Hollywood, scripts were presented to Gracie, worked on, eventually tossed aside as unsuitable by the company. Day after day scripts were thrown away, and the only reasoning came when Gracie visited Mr. Zanuck's house for dinner. Whilst Gracie was enjoying the Hollywood hospitality, she didn't enjoy the remarks about her being a simple person enjoying all that America has to offer. Reporting on herself and Harry Parr-Davies going to beach, shopping, and taking in the sights of Sunset Boulevard, the reporters loved the fact Gracie was using a public beach and public transportation.

Wanting to know more about her life, and being so impressed at persevering with her teeth at Chaplin's house, Luella Parsons invited Gracie to take part in her radio show, *Hollywood Hotel*, which was broadcast from a cinema on Vine Street. In the show, Gracie sang "I Never Cried so Much in all My Life" and "Do You Remember My First Love Song?" Tuning in that evening, April 30, was Eddie Cantor, who had heard on the Hollywood grapevine that England's finest comedienne was in town. He was impressed with her radio performance and sent a bunch of red roses to her hotel with a card inscribed: "A bunch of American beauties for an English beauty." He also sent an invitation for Gracie, Monty, and Harry to have dinner at his home, and also for Gracie to appear on his radio show. Both Twentieth Century Fox and Monty jumped at the idea, which would be excellent publicity for Gracie, even though Cantor had told Gracie he had some important advice to give her about her technique. Monty, Harry, and Gracie dined at Cantor's beautiful home, and after dinner he explained to Gracie the differences of American and English audiences and how Gracie must change her technique in America to really capture those audiences.

Harry and Monty both nodded sagely, but Gracie was still unsure as to what Eddie was talking about and nodded along so as not to look daft. In a little drawing room, all out of context and set to impress Eddie Cantor, Gracie forgot the word to every song she had ever performed and opted instead to sing "Sally" as a sort of audition piece. "When I am badly nervous I go right back to the type of singing my mother taught me." Loud. The more the nerves, the louder the singing. Shrieking her way through the song, Gracie realised she could not take any advice off him and instead decided to leave, politely refusing to appear on his radio show, much to Monty's disappointment and embarrassment. Eventually,

Monty realised Gracie was right and neither of them could really understand what Cantor was talking about. The press saw Gracie's refusal to appear on Cantor's show, at a reputed £5,000 per song, as "Gracie turning down all radio bids!"

Around this time, Mae West took to the press and declared, "I earn more money than Gracie Fields!" She told a specially arranged Hollywood press conference, "Everybody knows I'm the highest paid actress in the world, and I don't have to make four pictures a year, make personal appearances, and take part in radio broadcasts either. They say Gracie Fields is to make a million dollars a year (£200,000). I could make two or three million if I wanted to." This didn't stop the masses of support for Gracie, however, as the Lancashire Society of Hollywood reported an almost tripling in numbers—from their initial 600 members, 2,000 English people in Hollywood now claimed they originally hailed from Lancashire. The Macabbee Temple threw a special gala for Gracie and Deanna Durbin, where President John Broadbent introduced Gracie to the 700-strong Lancastrian audience, who serenaded her with "She's a Lassie from Lancashire."

On April 23, Gracie was a guest at Shirley Temple's ninth birthday party, which the Movietone announcer erroneously stated was her eighth. "Aunty Gracie" helped Shirley cut her birthday cake before she told the cameras how she had "a very wonderful time while I've been out here, and I shall be very very sorry to leave. Still, I've got to get back home for the coronation—can't miss that, lads! I'm going to make my first film in England, for this Twentieth Century Fox Company, and I hope it's going to be a good 'un!" After the photographers and cameramen had all gone Gracie sat on Shirley's sun-lit patio with her facing the sea, where Shirley showed Gracie her pet parrot, Red, who shouted "Fire, Shirley! Fire!" which amused Gracie. Gracie gave Shirley some Royal Family mementoes from England as a souvenir, as Shirley was well-known to be a collector of all things royal. Shirley asked Gracie, "Would you like to be a queen?" Gracie told her, "Not much", and Shirley agreed with her, "although I wouldn't mind being a princess." Gracie couldn't resist but to hug her and tell her she was already, which made Shirley give one of her famous dimpled smiles. Later on, Shirley did an impression of Gracie. "It was disturbingly clever for such a young child!"

Before coming back to England, Gracie and Monty took a trip to Lucien Hubbard's ranch in the Coachella Valley in Palm Springs, B. Bar H. Dude Ranch, for a Hollywood barbeque. Gracie remembers this in her autobiography: "I enjoyed my first barbecue—broiled steaks and chops, beans and bacon, ranch-cooked muffins, salads, coffee, home-baked pies, all spread out across a desert garden, with a big moon shining above." Gracie returned to the ranch over New Year 1938, but in her autobiography, she amalgamates both visits into one. After the barbecue in the dessert Gracie sang under the stars for the guests, which the newspapers got knowledge of and elaborated that "she is offered £5,000 in radio appearances for ten-minute spots, but she sang in the dessert for an hour for free!"

The next day a horserace took place over the desert sands, and Gracie had to race Joan Crawford for a mile on horseback to win the prize of a rare, red cactus plant. The pair finished level as the crowd shouted a "dead-heat" but the adjudicator, Franchot Tone, awarded Joan as the winner. Monty would not hear this, claiming the race was a fix, as Franchot was Joan's new husband. "She stood there panting, looking wickedly beautiful in riding breeches while her big eyes stabbed dark fire." Sparked by injustice, and jeered by the laughing crowd, Monty kicked up an argument as the pair squared up to each other. Both Gracie and Joan pulled their partners off each other before a fight broke out.

Setting off back to England on May second on the HMS Berengaria, the ship which first took her to America six years previously, Gracie had promised to appear in the Variety Artist and Guild's charity concert at the Phoenix Theatre on May ninth in front of the Duke and Duchess of Kent. A delay in the sailing schedule meant Gracie could not appear at the Phoenix Theatre, as her ship didn't dock in Southampton until May tenth. Gracie wrote to Basil Dean from the ship on May fifth: "Dear Basil, Thank you for your wire and good wishes. Up to now everything is OK. It was nice of you to show me *The Show Goes On*, and I do hope it will be our best. My love to you and Vickie. Grace." Gracie was also set to appear at a charity concert at the Grosvenor House on May 13 for the Scottish Empire Ball in recognition of the coronation, in a show which was broadcast by the BBC with Jack Payne, The Pipe Band 2nd Bn., and The Royal Scott's Fusiliers.

Arriving back in England, Gracie told the newspapers how delighted she had been by the reception from stars ranging from Tyrone Power and Charlie Chaplin to Loretta Young and Burns and Allen, but "not to think I've gone all-American. I still say 'By-Gum' and not 'Gee-Whizz'! I haven't gone all glamour. I'm still plain old Gracie Fields." Wearing a red, white, and blue scarf and sporting her new blonde hair, Gracie waved to the army of photographers that had arrived quayside to greet her, before heading to London to begin rehearsals for her upcoming appearances.

Gracie and Sandy Powell were both selling well on Rex, and record producers had an idea for the coronation. Sandy remembered, "I was doing very well with my comedy sketch records, so one of the directors said, 'I've got a brilliant idea, let's put them both together on one record. We're going to be millionaires.' We did this double record, [which was recorded in February before Gracie went to America], and it was alright, even today it's respectable, but the amazing thing was that we were both selling big and we were both on the one record, and we didn't sell half as many as when we were doing singles. I shall never understand that." The pair recorded a number of "party" records together, and the special coronation record, *Gracie and Sandy at the Coronation,* was issued with the new king and queen's photograph on the record label.

On May 19, Gracie returned to Rochdale for what was set to be "the proudest day of my life," as she was to receive the Freedom of Rochdale. The mayor set aside his own drawing room to be decorated in flowers and used exclusively for Gracie until the ceremony at noon in the Great Hall of one of the country's finest municipal buildings. Before the ceremony, Gracie was photographed in front of the mayor's fireplace as she presented a rug made by the Disabled Men's Handicraft bearing Rochdale's coat of arms, and interviewed in her dressing room by the BBC interviewer Richard North, followed by her act from the stage being broadcast.

In the ceremony, Mayor Crowder spoke: "It is resolved unanimously that this council do hereby, in pursuance of the 'Local Government Act 1933,' confer upon Miss Gracie Fields the honorary freedom of the borough of Rochdale. With her exceptional gifts of humour and song, she has carried joy into the homes of our people, and by her constant devotion to good works and her constant readiness to be of service to others, she has endeared herself to the hearts of all. And, not least, to the hearts of those who are proud to call themselves their fellow townspeople."

When presented with the Freedom Casket by Alderman Bryning, Gracie held her casket high and told, "It is a red-letter day, the most wonderful and proudest day of my life. I am never happier than when I am telling people what gradely folk there are in Rochdale. Wherever I go in this big world this casket is going with me. I am never so happy as when I am telling people how proud I am of Rochdale, and of its gradely folk."

Thousands of people crowded around the town hall, and traffic had to be stopped throughout the town to accommodate them along the Esplanade. Signing the Freeman's register, Gracie couldn't resist making a joke and sniffed the ink pot before dipping her pen into it. Following this, she went on the balcony with her mother and father to wave at the thousands that had gathered to see them. "We stood together on the balcony of the town hall with all Rochdale cheering us below, and if ever I felt proud, I did that day, not of myself, but of my mother and dad, standing there and being honoured like a king and queen by the town where they'd married, worked, struggled, and reared us kids."

A photo opportunity arose for Jenny, Lillian Aza, Bertha Schofield, and Alderman Brynning when they took a trip to visit Molesworth Street and the house where Gracie was born. Gracie didn't visit, though, as she was whisked off to the local fire station where she donned a fireman's outfit and helmet and went parading through the town dressed as a fire chief. Later in the afternoon a complimentary luncheon was thrown for the Gracie at the Fire Brigade Hall. Samuel Turner, the other investee, was too ill to make the journey over from South Africa but sent Gracie a congratulatory telegram. The five-course menu consisted of chicken or tomato soup, followed by trout with meuniere sauce, then roast duck, with a choice of a quarter of lamb, roast veal, or Devonshire pie for the fourth course, finished with ice cream and pineapple flan and cheese and biscuits. From the town hall balcony Gracie called to the audience, "Ain't it wonderful what the sunshine does to your hair!" in relation to her new Hollywood-blonde locks, and opened her coat "just to show you all it's a two-piece."

Following the Investiture, Gracie appeared at the Theatre Royal for three charity performances, where she changed from the dark blue outfit she had been wearing throughout the day into a white satin and an ermine coat "for show," before returning back to London for midnight, to start the first leg of a six-day cycle race from Wembley as fifteen teams represented eleven nationalities in the contest. The next Saturday, Gracie presented the winning trophies at the Wandsworth Dog Races at the stadium's coronation gala, which was packed to capacity. The following day,

May 22, in celebration of her Freedom and her love for her native town, the pre-arranged concert at the Alexandra Palace for Rochdalians took place at the Alexandra Palace. 10,000 Rochdalians travelled in twenty-three trains to London to see Gracie. Earlier in the evening, Gracie broadcast in a test transmission by the BBC, singing "Nowt about Owt" and "The Coronation Waltz" before moving to the tea party to "see mi own Rochdale folk." During the transmission, the BBC achieved their "closest close-up" to date, with "the visual impression of intimacy reinforced for viewers by the conquering personality of a great artist."

Spending most of the day in Windsor on tours of the castle, Runnymede, and various other landmarks, including pubs which had extended licenses, in the evening 118 specially chartered buses took the visitors to the Alexandra Palace to tea with Gracie. Over 18,000 bread rolls, 18,000 cakes, 9,000 meat pies, 270 gallons of milk, and 136 pounds of tea were used in the party. A special concert was given, topped by Gracie, and also starring Leslie Fuller, Horace Sheldon, Cora O'Farrell, Earle and Babette, Calienta, the Three Hiltons, and Archie and Bert's brother, Pat Aza. During the train journey down to London a voluntary collection raised £200 for the orphanage, and the cash was presented to Gracie on stage at the end of the concert by Charles Cockroft, the organiser of the trip.

Around this time, a script for Gracie's next film was finally agreed on, and the press reported that her first film for Twentieth Century Fox was to be called *He was Her Man*. Based on a story by Phillip Dunne, the film was to be produced in England with Monty directing and supervised by Sam Engel. Before filming began at Denham, Gracie began a short tour of England, *The Gracie Fields Road Show*, starting at the Manchester Palace during the last week of May in a bill starring Billy Russell, Stetson the Juggler, Blondie and Gurlie Hartley, the Holls Brothers, Billie de Woolfe, and Leslie Weston. "There's somebody posh round here!"

shouted Gracie to the audience as she asked them to join in the chorus of Fred Fanakapan as she took to the stage in a light golden, sequined gown to match her hair. Whilst in Manchester, after performing in a midnight charity performance in aid of the Cinematograph Trade Benevolent Fund, Gracie visited the White Heather Holiday Camp set up in Manchester's Heaton Park on June third. A hundred boys were inspected sergeant-major style by Gracie on the holiday camp's first day, and after visited Manchester Town Hall to sign the visitor's book and take a tour of the building.

After finishing in Manchester, Gracie moved on to Liverpool with the show with Joe Young, Simmeck Four, 7 Elliots, Dean Ernest and Shannon, Blondie and Curley Hartley, White and Swagger. In Liverpool, Gracie was honored by a luncheon at the town hall on June ninth, and then given a tour of the new Mersey Tunnel and Barker and Dobson's Chocolate Factory. On June tenth Gracie visited the Liverpool Trocadero Cinema with members of her family to see her brother, Tommy, in his solo film debut of *The Penny Pool* (1937), as she joked, "He'd better not be better than me!"

The next day, June 11, Gracie opened Squire's Gate Holiday Camp's new ballroom. Supported by the bishop of Blackburn, who had recently dedicated the theatre inside the holiday camp, and the Mayor of Blackpool, Gracie signed the visitor's book at Blackpool Town Hall before moving to a luncheon held in her honour at St. Anne's before going on to open the holiday camp's ballroom. As she was leaving the camp an old soldier stopped her car to present her with a bunch of lucky ivy. Delighted with this, Gracie got out of the car to have her photograph taken with him.

The next week saw the Roadshow playing at the Shepherd's Bush Empire, where on June 12 Gracie visited the Prince of Wales Theatre in London's West End. The old theatre had been demolished, and building was underway on a new Art-Deco theatre to take its place, but keep its name. Gracie laid the foundation stone of the building and joked around with the builders and the workers on the construction site, fooling around, pretending to eat cement off a trowel and climbing a tall ladder to sing to the workmen who were sitting in the girders of the new building. For many years the foundation stone lay hidden inside the theatre, but today it stands proudly on display on Oxenden Street.

Gracie visited the East Ham Memorial Welfare Society's Garden Party on June 19, and on June 20 performed to inmates of Pentonville Prison with bandleader Jack Hylton, and the following day in Kent at Maidstone Prison, where the newspapers reported, "Our Gracie sent to prison—but they didn't keep her very long!" The following week the company moved on to Finsbury Park, then to the New Theatre Oxford and the Birmingham Hippodrome with Robb Wilton, Fred Sanborn, Collinson and Dean, Blondie and Gurtley, Joe Young, Red Fred, and Pop, White and Sagger.

On June 23, Gracie visited the Oxford Reform Club at their YMCA annual fete and took part in an "Aunt Sally" skittles match. Two days later, Gracie visited the factory of Potter and Moore, one of the companies she advertised for, as they opened a new factory for their lavender face cream in Leyton. After cutting the ribbon of the ceremony, Gracie sang to the guests, "Who will buy my loomin' Lavender?" in a tune she improvised on the spot.

The Roadshow was performing at the Birmingham Hippodrome when thousands of people lined the roads between Kings Norton and West Heath on July first to catch a glimpse of Gracie as she was to open the new "Bath Tub" lido. It was estimated over 30,000 people turned out to see Gracie, who refused to address or sing to the crowds due to a sore throat, but instead climbed to the top of the pool's diving board and lit a rocket to mark the opening. Mantovani conducted his radio and recording orchestra at the event, and Gracie commented, "Eeh, the whole place is grand!" at the spectacle of one of Britain's brightest entertainment spots.

Whilst on her tour of all the major cities, as she did each year, Gracie donated a further £1,000 to the orphanage in Peacehaven, and whilst at the Glasgow Empire from July fifth, Gracie presented the Children's Holiday Camp with £82 and 16 shillings. Whilst in Glasgow, a young female fan who wanted to meet Gracie landed herself in court and was charged £2 for posing as a member of the CID to get close access to Gracie. Jean Walker, a hairdresser from Sheffield, was holidaying in Glasgow specially to see Gracie, and when she couldn't get into the packed Empire, she told the stagedoor keeper she was a member of the CID. After an argument the keeper rang the police as it was clear the woman had been drinking and was subsequently arrested.

Gracie's latest film, *The Show Goes On* (1937), received its cinematic premiere on July 17 at the London Hippodrome after having a successful press viewing in March whilst Gracie was in America. After completing all her UK tour dates, Gracie's next film, *He was Her Man*, written by Phillip Dunne, was announced before Gracie headed back to the Palladium on July 19, in a bill starring Duggie Wakefield, Billy Nelson, Nat Gonella, Douglas Byng, the South China Troupe, the Monroe Brothers, Stone and Les, Fred Culpitt, and Frank Delrosa. At the Palladium, Gracie added into her repertoire "I Love the Moon," "September in the Rain," "Carelessly," and "When My Dreamboat Comes Home." After the curtain Gracie was called back for an extra encore of "Smile When You Say Goodbye," which was quickly becoming one of her theme songs.

Ding Davey, who would later marry Gracie's companion, Mary Barratt, remembered being in the audience: "She came back from America and George Black starred her at the London Palladium. George Black was the most wonderful showman. He gave her the most wonderful setting of very pale blue drapes and a staircase at the back and lovely soft lighting with the most beautiful music. Everyone was waiting to see the glamourized Gracie, and you saw her through a mist of blue curtains, opened one lot and then another and another. She walked very, very slowly down the steps to the front of the stage with enormous applause from the audience, and it was absolutely true. She looked wonderful. The hair, the makeup, the dress, the white fox-fur around her shoulders, and when she got to the front and she managed to shush the audience, she managed to say, 'They might have changed the color of my hair, but they'll never change me!' and it got a yell from the audience."

Admitting that was a limit to her popularity, Gracie returned to Blackpool during the last week of July for her yearly season at the Grand. Following the chanting outside her hotel the year previously, Gracie kept where she was staying this year a secret and specifically told, "It is a case of no autograph hunters, no telephones, no interviews, and no photographers, by request." It was unusual for Gracie to turn down autograph hunters, as she always obliged signing things as she left the theatre, as she had once been an autograph hunter herself when she was younger but was too scared to ask for George Formby Senior's autograph. "Though I love everyone who comes from Lancashire, the strain of constantly being in the limelight has been too much for me."

After the Palladium, Gracie headed for her annual summer stint in Blackpool for three weeks from July 13, with her supporting artists for 1937 including the Elliotts, Ernest Shannon, Blondie and Gurlie Hartley, Pop, White and Swagger, Harold Walden and Wheeler and Wolson, the Dawn Sisters, and Rio and Santos. Gracie gave the holiday audiences the songs they wanted to hear, all their favourites, and lead a communal singing of "The Rochdale Hounds" and "Sally." Whilst in Blackpool, Gracie visited Senorita Anita Lizana at a tennis match at St. Anne's and attended the Lytham Hospital Gardens Fete on August fifth.

Back in London, Gracie appeared in the BBC's *Radio Rodeo* from the Union Cinema in Kingston upon Thames on September 16, and in summer it had been announced that popular bandleader Henry Hall was to leave his post at the BBC to head into variety on September 25, and Gracie agreed to take part in his farewell show, where she performed "Smile When You Say Goodbye" to him and welcomed him now to the music hall. Before that, however, Gracie paid a visit to Madame Tussaud's waxworks, where the completed statue of her was unveiled on August 12. "Ee, by gum! If that's me, I'm proud of myself!" exclaimed Gracie on the unveiling. She had been to visit Bernard Tussaud on a number of occasions to have casts of her face and her arms completed, and when Bernard told her the casting operation may be a little painful, she told him, "I can take it!" and promptly burst into song. As with other stars, Gracie donated an outfit for the model—a sleeveless black-lace evening dress—but she promised to furnish the model with new clothes as times and tastes changed, and the model was displayed in the Gallery of Celebrities.

At the Radio-Olympia fair on August 24, Gracie took her mother and father to choose a new all-wave radio and wireless set to be presented to the children at the orphanage. Following this, Gracie returned to Capri for a fortnight, accompanied with Monty, as further extension and building work had been taking place on her house throughout summer and was nearing completion.

On September fourth, 400 Rochdale children enjoyed a day out at the Blackpool Pleasure Beach, and when Gracie heard about their trip, she sent a check for £50 to the organisers to help the costs. The sixteenth saw Gracie broadcasting in a special *BBC Radio Rodeo* from the Union Cinema in Kingston following her visit to the opening night of Sonja Henie's new film, *Lovely to Look At* (1937) at the Phoenix Theatre. Radio broadcasts were being censored at the time, but Gracie and George

Bernard-Shaw refused to have their scripts sent in for censoring before they broadcast. The day before the Henry Hall farewell show, Gracie joined the Speedway fans at Custom House Stadium in aid of St. Mary's Hospital, Plaistow. The big event was a challenge between West Ham Hawks and Norwich, and Gracie presented the winning team with the trophies. Cramming as much as she could into her schedule before filming began, Gracie attended the Pageant of Sport at West Ham Stadium on September 24 and the Bicycle and Motorcycle Show at Earl's Court on September 27, where Gracie presented eight "Margaret Rose" bicycles to children with the same birthday as Princess Margaret. The seven seven year olds were given the bicycles by the manufacturer's union, and a further fifty bicycles were given out. Gracie presented the first seven children with a bicycle, gave them a short riding lesson, and sang "Daisy Daisy" to each child.

Two days later, on September 29, Gracie opened the Granada Theatre Greenwich. Gracie was a late stand-in at the Greenwich opening, as it was actually Maureen O'Sullivan who had been due to open the theatre but had to withdraw due to flu. A crowd of 10,000 came to see Gracie on the opening night, and upon arrival Gracie went straight to a roof balcony and performed "Sing as We Go" and "Sally" for the fans on Trafalgar Road. At the gala inside the theatre Gracie was piped on stage by the Dagenham Girl Pipers and described the cinema as "proper posh," exclaiming, "Well, I don't suppose you want to hear me talking, you want to hear me sing. Shove a piano on the stage, lads!" She proceeded to sing "Sing as We Go," "I Never Cried So Much in All My Life" and "Sally." Due to her popularity with the audience at the cinema's opening, the chain booked her again on October fourth for the opening of the Birkenhead Ritz; October 19 for the opening of the Dominion Theatre in Acton; and less than a week later for the opening gala of the Granada Theatre in Harrow on October 25. On October tenth, Gracie and nephew Michael were the special guests at the Maylands Golf Club at Harold Park in Romford, where she flew in by plane specially to take part in their afternoon tea celebrations in aid of funds for her orphanage.

Filming on *He Was Her Man* was scheduled to start early October, and on the sixth, Victor McGlaglen and Brian Donlevy, Gracie's co-stars, arrived in England. A cocktail party was thrown by Gracie in their honour, and on their meeting in front of the press, Gracie shook Victor's hand and explained she didn't know how to properly pronounce his surname, and her maternal grandmother's mother was called McGlaglen as well. When Victor told Gracie, "I think we will make a great picture," Gracie agreed. "Well, we better had do, lad—after all the fuss we've been having!" On Sunday, following the party, Gracie took a trip to Mayland's Aerodrome, Harold Wood, where she opened the new headquarters of Romford Flying Club. At the formal dinner following the opening ceremony, Gracie was presented with a check for £50 for the visit, to be gifted to the orphanage, and in her speech stated, "God has been good to me, and I always try to do to others as I would be done by," as she was thanked for her great services both to charity and entertainment.

Remembering filming years later at Denham Studios, Gracie wrote of Victor McGlaglen: "It puzzled me why he kept moving slowly around me during dialogue, so that to keep my face toward him I had to show the twisted sinews of my neck to the camera. I tried to speak my lines sincerely, whether they were over my shoulder or not." He would also forget his lines and give Gracie the wrong cue lines. Every time a climax developed within a scene a mistake on his part meant it needed to be re-shot. Whilst Gracie didn't understand what the famous Oscar-winning actor was playing at, Monty did. He told Victor, "We'll keep taking this scene until you're both helping each other. Grace will stand it as long as you can, and I shall stand it longer than either of you." The next moment, Monty was acting a gag out for the production crew with his tie caught in the reel of a typewriter in an impromptu slapstick routine to cheer the team up, and Victor caused no further problems.

We're Going to be Rich (1938), with the working title of *He Was Her Man*, was written by veteran Western writer James Edward Grant, directed by Sam Engel, and set during a South African Gold Rush in the 1880s. For the filming, 36 tons of mud were put down in the studios to recreate Johannesburg in the 1880s. In the film, Gracie plays the "Lancashire Lark" music-hall artist, Kit Dobson, torn between her abusive husband, Dobbie, Victor McGlaglen, and American saloon owner, Yankee Gordon, played by Brian Donlevy. One reviewer of *Film Weekly* wrote, "The tremendously vital Gracie Fields of the music halls, and even of her earlier films, has been toned down to such a degree that one can say, for the first time, Gracie is part of the film, not its impetus and reason for existence." Nevertheless, the score features some of Gracie's best-remembered songs, "Walter, Walter! (Lead me to the altar)," "The Sweetest Song in the World," and "The Trek Song," written by Harry Parr-Davies and adapted from the South African traditional anthem, "Sarie Maraise."

Also included is a number about sheep, "Will You Love Me When I'm Mutton?", "There's a Tavern in the Town," and also the dialect-identifying "Ee By Gum." Ted Smith plays a young boy, Kit, whose adoptive relationship with Dobbie is evidently modelled on Jackie Cooper's role in *The Champ* (1931). One number, "My Only Romance," was recorded for the film but eventually cut in place of "The Sweetest Song in the World." The song, although never commercially released, exists as a demo copy.

Whilst filming, a letter arrived by special delivery for Gracie at the hotel she was staying at with "O.H.M.S." marked on the envelope. Monty joked it was a summons from the income tax and opened the letter as Gracie was too nervous to do so. The letter was from the Earl of Clarendon, Lord Chamberlain to the King, congratulating Gracie on being selected to be part of the king's New Year's Honors List, as she was to be awarded the CBE for services to entertainment and was the first female variety artist to receive the honor. Lord Chamberlain sent Gracie another letter during October asking to make a contribution to that year's Royal Variety Show, which was to be her third appearance. Taking place on November 15 at the London Palladium, the 1937 bill was reported to be 97% British. Before the show, on November 13, Gracie threw her second party at the Savoy Hotel in aid of the Variety Artist Ladies' Guild and Orphanage.

On the night of the Royal Variety, the Royal Box was decorated with white chrysanthemums and red carnations and was graced with the presence of the king, queen, and Duchess of Kent. The London Palladium was packed to its three thousand capacity, and for the first time was set up for recording by the BBC to be broadcast live to the Empire. Taking seventh spot on the bill and wearing an elegant white evening gown, Gracie was accompanied on the piano by Harry Parr-Davies and had Lou Ross conducting the orchestra, which he would do for the last time for Gracie.

She performed "Sally," "I Never Cried so Much in all My Life," "The Organ, the Monkey and Me," and a new number she had recently recorded called "Little Old Lady," with bonnet and shawl. Teddy Holmes of Chappell Music later remembered, "Melvo Giddeon phoned me and asked if I had seen the song written by Hoagy Carmichael, which hadn't impressed me. I had another look and thought who best to launch it? Gracie was scheduled to appear in the first command performance to be broadcast, and she sang it on that broadcast. She made it one of the biggest hits of all time." During the performance, Queen Elizabeth "gaily joined in the chorus of 'Sally,'" who persuaded her parents to also join in with a few bars of the song, much to Gracie and the audience's surprise, impressed at "her introducing of gay irrelevances into would-be solemn songs." So loved was Gracie on the bill, the audience shouted her back for two encores, and "Sally" had to be resung at the top of the show.

Playing alongside Gracie and the galaxy of stars that evening was Norman Evans from Rochdale, who made the Royal Box physically rock with laughter in a comedy sketch about a visit to the dentist. Gracie had heard him many years before performing at a church concert in Rochdale, and he made his professional debut at the Theatre Royal in Rochdale during one of Gracie's charity weeks. Also nervously waiting his turn in the wings was fellow Lancastrian, George Formby. Talking to Gracie, George showed her his diamond and sapphire tie pin given to him by his father for luck, who was presented the pin by the king in 1913 for his performance in a private party for the Earl of Derby.

From October 18, 1937 until April 1938, Gracie had her charm and wit expressed in cartoon, as the *Daily Mail* began to feature a comic strip with Gracie's image. Coming straight from the film set at Denham, still wearing a Victorian bustle, Gracie opened the new Granada Theatre in Greenford as well as taking part at the Associated British Social and Sports Club Annual Film Ball party at the Albert Hall on November 14, and the Variety Club Ladies' Press Dinner with Monty Banks on December 12, where she told the guests, "I'd much rather sing for my supper than talk!" when asked to make a speech—which she replaced with four songs instead.

In December, Gracie and George Formby both appeared together again, this time at the opening of the Gaumont State Cinema in Kilburn, alongside Larry Adler, Carroll Levis and his Discoveries, Vic Oliver, Stone and Lee, Alfred Van Dam and his State Orchestra, at the organ Sidney Torch, in a special gala performance on December 20, which was broadcast live by the BBC. This event was the only known time the two Lancastrian stars with the same initials were photographed with each other. (Whilst two photographs were known to exist of the pair, a further two were uncovered in the research for this book, with one of them included in the photograph section of this book).

During December, Gracie recorded the first sessions for her *Fairy Soap* series, which she had signed a contract for. The weekly half-hour radio Luxembourg shows (broadcast on Sunday, repeated on Wednesday) were backed by Fred Hartley and his band, and were issued to radio stations over a series of four 78rpm sides per show. In the series, which was advertised to last a year, Gracie sings her old favourites as well as introducing new songs to her repertoire, one of the more obscure choices being "They Call Me Mimi" from Puccini's *La Boheme.* The shows were prerecorded either by Rex or Decca (by this time Decca had bought out Crystalate, who owned the Rex label) at Rex's Crystalate studios in London or Decca's East Hampstead studios, and each show featured an advertisement by Gracie about Fairy cleaning products. The shows premiered on January 2, 1938, as Gracie introduced, "Hello, folks, this is me. You know me? Maggie dripping! And as I can't possibly tell you all how glad I am to be singing to you today, I think I'd better just sing, eh?" Gracie's last job of 1937 was the opening of yet another cinema, the Caledonian Cinema on London's Mayfair Road at a gala charity concert for the opening night on December 27.

With filming on her first Twentieth Century film finished, Christmas 1937 for Gracie was spent at home in Peacehaven in a large family party. Monty and Harry Parr-Davies both cooked an excellent Christmas dinner for the family, although Harry and Monty made a pitiful attempt at a rice pudding, which resulted in Gracie going to the kitchen after dinner and making her own and Monty being chastised for forgetting to make the gravy. Edith and Betty and their families were there (Betty had retired completely from the stage in early autumn and had come over from America to spend Christmas with her family), and in the afternoon they all celebrated Christmas with the children at the orphanage, as was becoming the regular Christmas tradition.

CHAPTER ELEVEN

1938

They said I'd make a movie star my
figure was so good,
I drew my savings from the bank
and I went t'Hollywood.

"I Haven't Been the Same Girl Since" (1935),
recorded by Gracie Fields.

NEW YEAR 1938 WAS another year which began with charity work, when on January second Gracie broadcast an appeal on behalf of the London Child Guidance Clinic as a replacement for Canon Dick Sheppard, who had died in October. On January 8, 1938, the *Rochdale Observer* started a campaign for the commission of a painting of Gracie to be presented to her from her townspeople as a fortieth birthday gift. A request of ten thousand shillings was made, and by January 22 there were over 1,000 subscribers to the fund, with over 4,000 shillings having been raised. By February second the 10,000 had almost been achieved, and a week later a total of 15,046 shillings had been raised for the painting's fund. Scottish artist Sir James Gunn was approached to complete the painting, to be presented to Gracie at the end of the year at a civic. Celebrating her fortieth birthday the next day, Gracie told, "I think it's daft not to admit your age. Even if you don't say it, you look it probably!"

Although initial filming was completed before Christmas, some scenes of *We're Going to be Rich* (1938) had to be reshot and overran on the average twenty-eight days of her ATP films. Gracie was in the recording studio as late as January 18 recording the songs from the film to be issued on Rex, as filming came to its ultimate completion in late January. Gracie had told Bert Aza not to arrange any contracts yet for the year, as she had not visited Capri in a number of months and desperately wanted to get back to see her home and take Monty on a proper tour of the island.

This was not before a week's run at the Holborn Empire from January 10 with the Two Dancettes, Red Fred, A.C. Astor, Maurice Colleano and the Colleano Family, Five Cleveres, Leo Sax, Mitzsuko, Joe Young. On January 16, Gracie was back in prison again, this time at Holloway Women's Prison, where she performed a repeat of her repetoire from the previous year's Royal Command Performance. The following day Gracie had opened at the Brighton Hipporome for a week with Fields and Rossini, Laurie Joy and Graham, Terina Palmer, Gaston Palmer, Red Fred, Jackie, Leslie Weston, Six Gridneffs, before a week at the Brixton Empress from January 24, and costarring Jack and June Melville, Almaer and Carmen, Pop, White and Swagger, Don and Dorette, A. C. Astor, Harry Jerome, the Holls Brothers, and Ellis and West. Whilst in Brixton, Gracie attended the News Chronicle Schools Exhibition at Dorland Hall, where she had her clothes waterproofed in front of the cameras.

From January 31, Gracie was appearing at the Birmingham Hippodrome with Frank Boston, Leslie Weston, Brown and La Hart, Tex McLeod, the Grindeffs, Wilson, Dake and Hayson, Calienta, and Edwina Styles. Whilst in Birmingham, Gracie opened the Disabled Men's Handicraft factory in Smethwick on February second before a charity concert at the Princes Theatre in Manchester on Sunday February sixth in aid of the Lord Mayor's Unemployment Relief Fund and the Denville Home for Aged Actors and Actresses.

At the concert, which also starred Duggie Wakefield and Norman Evans, the Lord Mayor, Alderman J. C. Grime, congratulated Gracie on being part of the New Year Honours list, and she promptly gave him a kiss on the cheek at his request. Gracie told the Manchester audience, "This will be one of my last theatrical appearances for a number of months. I am going to take a rest and I shan't appear in variety for perhaps a very long time, except for a few charity shows and the two pictures I have yet to make this year." Following the Prince's Theatre concert, Gracie returned to Rochdale for a one-afternoon concert at the Rochdale Hippodrome before returning to the Prince's to watch Duggie Wakefield as Widow Twankey in their production of *Aladdin*.

Bert Aza recalled at this time Gracie's private investments in a firm that made bullets, sewing machines, and other "useful articles" displeased her and told him she wanted "no benefit from a company that makes things to kill people." A few months later, when Gracie asked Bert again, and he told her he had not sold the shares as he thought she was not really serious the first time round, this was one of the only times Bert saw Gracie angry, so he sold the shares immediately and gave all the proceeds to the orphanage.

Gracie still had one week in variety left and was playing the Brighton Hippodrome from February seventh, and on Sunday, February 12 for a show in aid of the School Children's Boot fund. As Gracie was travelling through Cilfynydd with George Hall, the M.P. of Aberdare, they passed the Albion Colliery where men were leaving work. Remembering her time in Wales with *Mr. Tower of London*, Gracie joked with the MP, "What a lot of chimney sweeps you have in Wales! Every time I come, I see chimney sweeps!" From February 13, Gracie honored a promise she had made in 1937 to Arthur Barlow to play the Grand Derby for two weeks to help the Arthur Barlow extension fund for Derbyshire Royal Infirmary. So as not to disappoint those who could not get tickets to Gracie's sell-out two-week run, Gracie agreed to two charity concerts at the Central Hall in addition to her performances at the Grand.

Returning back to London in preparation of the awarding of the CBE, on the morning of her investiture at Buckingham Palace on February 15, Gracie arrived in a large fur coat and hat and joked with the sentries on the way into the palace at how cold of a morning it was. Earlier that morning Gracie's new dress was revealing too much under-skirt, and without having any time to stitch it, Jenny fastened two safety pins to hold it up. Unable to take any family members into the event with her, Gracie was ushered up the crimson-carpeted Grand Stairway to await her Royal reception, praying her dress would hold up. Native Rochdale seemed a long way from the opulence and the grandeur of "Buck House," and Gracie remembered, "It was all stamped on my brain like a photograph. Army generals, colonels, Navy admirals—all in their battledress." Ushered into the ballroom, where an usher pinned a hook to Gracie's dress, the crowd was ordered to sit in rows of gilt and crimson chairs to await the arrival of the king.

"I felt my heart go bump in the bottom of my shoes when I watched the first to receive their awards. It was the first time I'd thought about having to curtsey." Whispering to Harriet Cohen to ask about the cor-rect way to bow before the king, Gracie was even more horrified to learn Harriet had been taking lessons for two weeks on how to curtsey cor-rectly. At precisely eleven o'clock, one hour after the ceremonial wait-ing time, the Guards Regimental Orchestra played "God Save the King" as the king appeared in the blue and gold uniform of the Admiral of the Fleet. "I watched Harriet perform three elaborate curtseys, which looked like part of the ballet about the dying swan," Gracie recalled as she waited her turn to be called. As the awards were being read alphabetically, and Gracie was still officially Grace Selinger, she had plenty of time to watch and try her best to imitate the bows.

When they got to Gracie the band unexpectedly struck up "Sing as We Go" as she lurched nervously forward to receive her honor. "I would give a great deal to know what it was he said to me, for he was so obviously trying to be very kind. But I was so shocked to hear his voice that was so familiar on films and radio that I couldn't grasp a thing of what was going on, nor what I said in reply. I think I must have said something comical, as I can remember that he laughed and gave my hand a good-natured squeeze, and a smile that was half a wink. And that was that! I'd got my medal." Even the two safety pins were still holding up her underskirt.

Waiting outside the palace was Jenny, Edie, and Bertha Schofield. "They stood freezing there for me for more than an hour. I had come too early, so I drove round and round the park till it was time. I'd like to have been one of the servants there and seen everything with my eyes open, but going as one of the people that had to be done up, why, I just couldn't walk straight. I dazed myself in and I dazed myself out of Buckingham Palace. I, who never seem nervous to anyone, was as nervous as could be."

Arriving back at Greentrees, Gracie showed the Movietone cameras what the king had given her. "Well, my feelings are very very happy and contented. I am very proud to have received this honor. I am more happy, because, for my mother's sake, it gives her such a thrill. Also, for the little town that I came from, Rochdale, they're just tickled to death. Well I might tell you all that it's going to cost you half a crown to talk to me now!" That evening a party was held in Gracie's honour at the Dorchester Hotel, where the maître'd, Marino Patresi, created a special dish for her: Pêches Gracie Fields. At the event, Gracie made a speech and told her mother, "Really, it was you who the king should've pinned the badge on." Gracie removed the honor and put it on her mother's coat.

Following a brief trip to Capri, not the long-awaited holiday she was still yearning for, to oversee the building work on her new seawall, on March third Gracie set off for a brief holiday in America with Harry Parr-Davies and Monty aboard the Queen Mary, departing from Southampton with British figure skater Cecilia Colledge, and arriving in New York on March ninth. On this journey they were photographed dining with Charlie Chaplin and Paulette Goddard aboard the ship. Owing to the fact she was in America and could not appear personally, Gracie promised to fund Castleford's "Reet Neight Aht," a night of marbles, darts, and other games, on March first. For the event, three large glass marble trophies to the winners of the competition were created, and a set of specially commissioned marbles bearing a painted-on version of her signature, which Gracie paid for.

In America, on March 24, the group was joined by Jenny and Fred, who boarded the HMS Berengaria at Southampton on February second and set off for America to visit Betty and Roy, who had taken up a home in Hollywood two years previously. Betty and family moved to Hollywood, where Roy had accepted a job as a scene designer for one of the Hollywood film studios, and were renting a small apartment in Santa Monica. This was only Jenny and Fred's second trip to the States together. Gracie, who was there to greet her parents, told the press, "Fred knows all about America! He went to Masa-choo-chits as a mechanic, but he had a very loving mother. He loved her a lot, so when she said, 'Come home,' he came." With her parents in America, Gracie set off back to Capri as preproduction began on her next film for Twentieth Century Fox, the title of which was announced in March as *Picadilly Circus*, which was scheduled to begin filming in the first week of May at Pinewood Studios, still determined that her American films be made in the UK.

Specially written for Gracie by Hollywood scenarist William Conselman, with dialogue by Rodney Ackland, the story of the film is about a group of out-of-work theatricals who try their best to rise out of unemployment and secure themselves regular theatrical work. After singing Afrikaans songs in her previous film, Gracie was now to play a Cockney character with the name of Gracie Grey, who lets her theatrical friends lodge at her uncle's farmhouse whilst they look for work. Filming began on schedule at Pinewood Studios at the end of May, with Gracie having returned to England earlier in the month in search of new songs to be included. She told the *Radio Pictorial*, "I like human songs, when they are romantic or comedy. I hate cynicism in songs. There is far too much of it in real life." One of Gracie's only public appearances before filming began was at the opening of the new Twentieth Century Fox building in Soho Square on May 15. With Monty at her side, Gracie signed the registry book of the opening of the building with a fountain pen presented by one of the company directors, Mr. Hargreaves. Not realising the importance of the pen, Gracie took her own pen out of her handbag before stopping herself and picking up the ceremonial pen to sign the book. "I might not be able to write so well with yours!" she joked. "Not so nervous as I was when I first signed an insurance paper. I sloshed it all over."

Over Easter, Gracie visited the little fishing town of Cawsand for the first time in a number of years, with Harry and Monty, visiting old friends before she opened at the Palladium for a week's run on April 24 and a week at the New Hippodrome in Coventry from April 30.

We're Going to be Rich (1937) opened to the public on May seventh, before Gracie was back again at the Palladium on May ninth for a week in a bill also starring Vic Oliver, Batie and Foster, the Five Talo Boys, Murray and Mooney, the Three Rays, Teddy Brown, and fellow Rochdalian Norman Evans with his "Over the Garden Wall" sketch.

In a break from filming on May 20, Gracie travelled to St. John's Gate in Clerkenwell, where she was made a sister officer of the Most Venerable

Order of the Hospital of Saint John of Jerusalem. For her charity work, Gracie was recognised by the St. John's Ambulance Brigade and presented with the small white cross which she frequently wore alongside her ship's brooch throughout her life. On the way back home from the ceremony, Gracie's car whizzed past an old lady waiting inside the gate to get a closer look at Gracie. When Gracie saw the woman she stopped the car and got out to show the old lady up close the medal she had just received. Almost exactly forty years later to the day, one of Gracie's closest friends, Anne Taylor, received the same award as Gracie. In a letter to Anne, Gracie wrote how proud she was and that they were now sisters together in the service of mankind.

Whilst at the Palladium on May 16, Gracie appeared on the radio in *Monday Night at Eight*, performing a medley of songs from Disney's *Snow White* and a medley of hits from her latest film release, and on July 14, champion rose-grower George Frederick Letts of Hadleigh introduced the "Gracie Fields hybrid tea rose," buttercup yellow with a fruit sweet-briar scent. The glossy, mildew-proof leafed rose won Letts a gold medal and sold for 2s 6d per bush, or 24 shillings a dozen. Onl July 15, Gracie opened the children's fair in aid of the League of Mercy and its work for hospitals at Bedford College, Regent's Park.

Back in the film studio, Harry Parr-Davies had once again composed some of the music for the picture, including "Giddy-Up!" and the lively "Swing Your Way to Happiness," with his music alongside the religious "The Holy City," the comedic "Mrs. Binns' Twins," "You've Got to be Smart in the Army," "A May Morn," and the highly dramatic "Peace of Mind," written by London stockbroker Gerard Paul, who committed suicide shortly before the film's release.

So popular was the comedy number "I Never Cried so Much in all My Life" in *Queen of Hearts* (1935), it was again used in this film. Alongside Gracie in the film in cameo roles are Tommy Fields and Nino

Rossini, with Peter Coke, Mary Maguire, and Roger Livesey, who all take starring roles. The film sees Gracie in a number of exploits, ranging from milking a cow to captaining a sinking pleasure barge. Although Gracie told Maud Miller of *Picture Post*, "I hate cows and I run a mile when I see them," one of the most comedic scenes of the film sees Gracie trying to milk Claribelle. On June 13, the pre-production title of *Piccadilly Circus* was scrapped, and executive producer Robert T. Kane announced the film's new title was to be *Keep Smiling*. (The film was to be the last project that Fields and Rossini worked on together, as after the filming the pair parted company as Tommy wanted to try his hand at a solo career).

In the film, as the *Keep Smiling* company put in a bid for the summer season at the Brightboune Pier Pavillion, a rival theatrical manager, Sneed, tries to thwart the company's plans. The climax comes when the company's star pianist, and Gracie's love-interest, Victor Sigani, is kidnapped and held hostage in a fairground's crazy house. One scene is filmed on a floating houseboat which the company transform into their very own theatre, which is sunk by Sneed in one of his attempts to overthrow his rivals.

At present, the film is the only of Gracie's feature films to have never received a home-video release in any format. One of the only known surviving copies of the film, held by the British Film Institute, is incomplete, with the routine of "Mrs Binns' Twins" missing from the reels. As with his previously directed Gracie films, Monty Banks has a cameo in a hilarious hotel scene in which the lost dog, Mr. Skip, played by the popular wire fox terrier Asta, has gone missing and Gracie tries to return the dog to claim a reward set by his owner, the renowned pianist, Victor Sigani, who becomes part of the company and later Gracie's husband— in a rare film where Gracie gets her man!

During filming, one of the cast developed measles, which worried a lot of the other members of the company. During the collapse of the houseboat, Gracie and most of the chorus girls wore a swimsuit under their dresses, and when Gracie climbed out of the water, with her dress caught up over one shoulder, she revealed her tummy covered in what appeared to be red measles. "Oh! I've come out in spots!" cried Gracie to a horrified Monty. In reality this was just a practical joke on Gracie's part to cheer the cast up, as filming this scene the day previously the boat had slipped into the water at the wrong time and had injured a number of the cast members. Coke, who trained at the Royal Academy of Dramatic Arts, apparently never got used to the comedy and the jokes on set and often retired to his dressing room until he was called to film, not associating himself with the cast.

As far as American audiences were concerned, *Keep Smiling* (1938) was no better than Gracie's last film, but Monty Banks argued it at least gave Gracie an opportunity to show her wide versatility of comedy and singing, even though the story may not be a particularly original one. In America, the film was retitled *Smiling Along* (1938), as another film with the same title as the British version had been released earlier in the year.

Whilst her fellow Rochdalians were celebrating Whitsuntide in June, Gracie was still busy filming and quipped, "I'll bet there wasn't a tackler in Lancashire up before me this morning!" as she was alternating between staying at Pinewood and returning back to Greentrees. During the filming, Gracie was spending a lot of time on the set next door to where *Keep Smiling* was being filmed—the set of Victor Schertzinger's interpretation of Gilbert and Sullivan's *The Mikado* (1938). Gracie met Kenny Baker, a young American who had been brought over to England to play the part of Nanki-Poo, and the pair had a mock rehearsal of Gilbert and Sullivan songs, which was apparently recorded by Monty on a home-movie camera. Enamoured with Gracie, the press reported how Kenny Baker wanted to order every recording Gracie had ever made up to that point.

David Steadman, the current renowned conductor of the D'Oyly Carte Opera Company, remarked, "Gracie could easily have played in Gilbert and Sullivan, and would have made a perfect—" It has been suggested many times over the years Gracie could've been one of the greatest coloratura sopranos of the twentieth century, but she sacrificed this ambition. When not on the set of *The Mikado* (1938), Gracie paid a visit to Barbara Tribe on set, who was making a sculpture of Gracie's head. The young Australian girl had previously won the New South Wales Travelling Scholarship for Sculpture and had been selected by Gracie to model her head.

With filming completed at midnight on July 20, the cast of the film retired to the set of *Brightbourne Pier*, where they were met by Gracie, who had completed all of her scenes early, and presented the cast with a buffet to celebrate. Whilst the cast enthusiastically toasted the star with champagne, Gracie refrained from drinking anything but tea, as the next day she was due in Maidstone.

Visiting Sir Gerrard Tyrwhitt-Drake's Zoo at Cobtree Manor, Gracie had the honour of christening a ten month old, three-foot-six-inch Burmese elephant who hadn't been given a name. Hearing about this, Gracie visited the zoo, and in front of a crowd of hundreds announced, "I'm going to christen this elephant my lucky name, what I consider my lucky name has been. Sally." (Although Tyrwhitt-Drake had hoped she would be called Gracie.) Wishing "good luck and good health to our Sally Ma-Chaw," (Ma-Chaw meaning Miss Darling in Burmese) Gracie shared a glass of Cornish champagne cider with the elephant, drinking some herself and pouring the rest of her glass over the baby animal to the delight of the audience of 10,000. "Oh! She's gonna be a drunkard!" joked Gracie as the zookeeper gave the elephant her own glass of champagne to drink before Gracie retired to the manor for tea. The next day, Gracie was in Rochester as she visited the young boys at Rochester

Borstal Institution. She remarked to them, "There are some bright boys among you, and I bet you can guess what name I gave to the elephant?" before she gave them a round of her title song.

Gracie was back at the Gaumont State Theatre in Kilburn on Saturday, July 23, in a benefit midnight matinee to support Eddie Cantor's appeal for funds for Jewish refugee children. Although the gala was only announced four days before the actual event, the Hyams Brothers managed to get together an all-star concert, compered by Cantor and starring Billy Bennett, Vic Oliver, Flanagan and Allen, George Formby, Douglas Byng, Leslie Hutchinson, Holland and Hart, Beatrice Lillie, Teddy Joyce, Ambrose and His Orchestra, and Lupino Lane and the entire company of *Me and My Girl*. Over £9,000 was raised for the fund, and was only the third, but final, bill the two great Lancashires, Gracie Fields and George Formby, appeared on together. With both Eddie Cantor and Darryl Zanuck being in London at the same time, Cantor proposed the idea of a film with himself and Gracie in, who was reportedly as equally keen as Cantor was to do it. "One of the snags would be to try and not make Gracie too Lancashire for American audiences," reported Cantor.

Ultimately, Zanuck vetoed the idea and no further plans were made for any such film. Instead, plans were underway for Gracie's next film, to be set in Ireland in an Irish sea-saga, *Paddy Darling*. This plan also fell by the wayside, and in July the title of Gracie's next film was announced as *Sally Goes to Town*, to begin preliminary filming in October, with a scheduled budget of £25,000. Filming, however, did not start until 1939, as by October Gracie had other plans and was in America.

After a successful run of sixth months, Gracie's Fairy Soap sponsored radio show changed format in July, as it was decided the next episodes in the series should be recorded live. Recording took place at the Scala Theatre in London, presented by Thomas Hendley, with the intention to give the feel of a live theatre atmosphere in her broadcasts. Gracie also visited the school's exhibition at London's Dorlands Hall around this time, tucking many of the children up to sleep in makeshift beds at the event.

After taking a short holiday with Monty in Blackpool to see Duggie Wakefield performing in the town on July 30, Gracie arrived in Scotland on August fourth for her first sitting with Scottish artist Sir James Gunn for her portrait commissioned by the people of Rochdale at Gunn's Glasgow studio. The next day, Gracie and Harry travelled on the Night Scot train from the Glasgow's Central Station, where she went to visit the Bellahouston Empire Exhibition. The LMS Railway put on extra services to Larnarkshire so fans could come to the exhibition in plenty of time to see her arrival at 10:30, as Captain S.J. Graham welcomed Gracie into the city with a royal salute. Arriving with Harry, Gracie spent over five hours visiting the exhibits and taking afternoon tea in the Empire Pavillion before a broadcast for the BBC at 3:30 with Jack Payne and his orchestra. Whilst at the event, Gracie met Billy Butlin and was photographed with him trying out a new roller coaster for one of his holiday camps. Whilst here, Gracie agreed to visit one of Billy's newly opened entertainment camps, in Skegness, on August 21, where she judged the final of a beauty pageant which had attracted 10,000 anxious mill girls.

Gracie honoured this promise after returning back from a short trip to Capri on August 25, when she visited the camp after a brief stopover at a Monster Gala at Whittle-le-Woods in Chorley on August 20 to celebrate the completion of the building of a new government factory, the Royal Ordnance Arsenal, in record building time. Organised by Sir Lindsay Parkinson, and cheered on by a reported 80,000 people, Gracie gave an impromptu performance of "Sing as We Go," during which she forgot the words and was helped along by a young girl standing next to her at the microphone until she changed her tune to "Walter." Retiring inside to Cafe Collette, Gracie made an appearance on the BBC in the

Lisieux Hall, and during this performance premiered a new song, "The Biggest Aspidistra in the World," which one critic wrote, "If it's not a song which Gracie will be singing for years, I am prepared to eat the aspidistra, and the antirrhinum, and the hollyhock." After the songs, Gracie was presented with an oversized stick of rock and went on her way to honour her engagement in Skegness. She stayed at Sir John Jackson's house in Wheelton overnight before travelling south the next day. Arriving at Butlins, Gracie met with champion boxer Jack Doyle in preparation for his next fight before the pair were given a tour of Billy's camp in an open-top car, judged a bathing-suit competition, and played on the roller coasters.

Travelling via a short break in Boulogne with Monty, Gracie left England for Capri on August 26, foregoing her annual summer appearance at the London Palladium and breaking her seven season's successive run in Blackpool. Whilst she was holidaying in Capri, *Keep Smiling* (1938) received its London Trade Show premiere at the Century Theatre on October sixth after a press preview on September 26 of the unfinished edit. It was reported Gracie had them guffawing in the aisles right from the very start, which resulted in a crescendo of laughter as the comedy business of the film progressed. Some critics heralded it a personal triumph for Gracie, but it was unanimously agreed the film dragged and became quite boring when Gracie was not on the screen, with plaudits for the new Australian actress in the film, Mary Maguire. This resulted in some heavy cuts before its official premiere on March 27 the following year. It was around this time both Gracie and Sophie Tucker had been offered, and subsequently turned down, the role of Glinda the Good Fairy in Twentieth Century Fox's upcoming film *The Wizard of Oz* (1939), due to begin production in Hollywood in October. The famous role eventually was given to Billie Burke.

Gracie was back in England for the beginning of October and appeared at the premiere of the new Irving Berlin film, *Alexander's Ragtime Band* (1938), at the Regal Cinema Marble Arch on October first. At the film premiere, alongside a host of other stars, Gracie told, "How delighted I am to be back this evening to see this picture, because I think I've sang more of Irving Berlin's songs than anybody else. He hasn't written me one yet, one especially for myself, but I'm still hoping." The evening was dubbed the Spirit of Peace Night in the West End, as the previous day Prime Minister Neville Chamberlain had returned from Germany with the Peace for our Time document, signed by Adolf Hitler, with Chamberlain making the famous speech at Heston Aerodrome.

Following the showing of the film, Berlin himself took to the stage to lead the singing of "Alexander's Ragtime Band" before Gracie was invited to sing "Land of Hope and Glory" and "The Lambeth Walk," which she had recorded recently on Rex with a chorus of children. On October fourth, Gracie travelled to Liverpool where she spent fifteen minutes selling tights in Lewis' department store, much to the amusement of staff and shoppers. Later that evening Gracie performed at the opening ceremony of the Ritz Cinema in Birkenhead, accompanied by her sister Betty and performing alongside Steffani's Silver Songsters.

Having been with the recording label Rex for a little over three years, Gracie completed her last recording session with the budget company before her holiday to Capri in August. On October 8, Gracie made her first recordings for the Regal Zonophone Company, a budget label for EMI's recordings, with records selling for 1/6—a slight increase on Rex's "money for jam." In her first recording session for her new label, Gracie recorded another one of the songs which was to be forever associated with her, "The Biggest Aspidistra in the World." The story of how a commonplace houseplant typically found in any Northern working-class home is watered each day with half a pint of Guinness became one of Gracie's most popular and requested songs. In later years, Gracie would often say in concerts, "I'd love to drown Sally and Walter with the blinkin' aspidistra on top!" But she knew they were the songs which audiences wanted to hear.

When interviewed by the BBC in the 1970s, the song's composer remembered how he came to write the song. "As I came through Peckham, I suddenly saw a curtain thrown open wide, and there revealed with a lady with a green watering can which was nearly as big as half the window. But nearly as big as that was the plant she was watering, and I was saying to myself, 'My God! That's the biggest aspidistra in the world!' And by the time I got to the tram the first verse had been written. By the time I got to London and Jimmy Harper, he asked, 'Have you got something on your mind?' And he said, 'For God sake let me do this with you!' He was working with Gracie's pet publisher, Billy Haines. The lyrics went up and I did the song with him. He said to me, "If Gracie agrees to do it, you can have it." Obviously very excited about this song, Bill Haines immediately rang Gracie at Greentrees and sang the song down the phone to Mary Barratt to ask her opinion before she passed the phone over to Gracie. "It was obvious that the comeback was acceptance on the other end."

What spurred Gracie to return to England so early, as she didn't have any contractual arrangements firmly scheduled until November, was a telegram from Clemont Butson, the booking manager for the Blackpool Grand Theatre. After her appearance there the previous summer, Gracie had promised Clemont she would return again in 1938 "no matter what happens." No matter what personal inconvenience it meant, Gracie was loathe to ever break a promise—especially to Lancashire—and she began her run at Blackpool on October ninth after only a week's preparation whilst back in England. Gracie was pleased to be appearing in Blackpool during October, as it meant she could enjoy taking in the resort's famous illuminations, which were to be the last held for the next ten years due to the blackout of the Second World War. "This time I should not only have the opportunity of renewing some very dear friendships, but can do what I have always wanted to do—look around at the lights o'Blackpool!" Accompanying Gracie were Archie Glen, Fred Walmsley, Frank Randle, the Lorch Family, Reco, and May in the "Bumper Show of 1938" in replacement for their summer season.

Gracie got to see the lights on October 11, when Mayor and Mayoress Quayle took her on a tour in their own car after her concert at the Grand after a spectacular ten curtain calls. Accompanied by 100 disabled ex-soldiers in cars following down the Promenade driven by public volunteers, the mayor ordered the illuminations stay lit longer than usual so they could be enjoyed after Gracie's show. In admiration for Gracie, one of the old soldiers presented her with an antique sword belonging to Captain Raphael Semmes of the CSS Alabama, which nearly caused Britain and America to go to war during the American Civil War. Disabled service-man W. Robinson had turned down many lucrative offers for the relic, but instead presented it to Gracie in gratitude of all her work.

During a matinee-free afternoon on October 14, Gracie travelled to Blackburn at the request of the bishop to open the Chamber of Trade Exhibition at King George's Hall. In front of the 20,000 that had turned up to witness her open the exhibition, Gracie sang "The Sweetest Song in the World" and told, "I hope that I shall continue to have health and strength to do the work which God has sent me to do."

That same evening, Gracie made a special appearance at a "Grand Charity Dance" at Fleetwood's Marine Hall, with all proceeds going to the Fleetwood Fishing Industry Benevolent Fund and Fleetwood Social Welfare, where she was given kippers for breakfast. Presented with a box of kippers from Mr. H. Eastwood after arriving at the Hall at 1am following her show in Blackpool, she told, "I love Fleetwood kippers. They are so fleshy, not like those frizzled-up things you get in London. I often sing for my supper, but I don't ever remember singing for my breakfast before." Stepping from her car, Gracie greeted 300 people with "Eeh, you are stopping out late!" and urged the audience, "Let's imagine we're in a tripe shop having a bit of a do," as she sang "The Holy City" from her latest film. With Gracie was her mother, and crowds broke through barriers and separated her from her mother. At the event, Gracie handed out a bicycle to eight year old David Bentley and urged the policemen with a second rendition of "Smile When Say Goodbye" for police to move her—and her box of kippers—through the crowds.

Following Blackpool, Gracie played a week at the Cardiff New Theatre from October 17 before she was made life governor of London Hospital on the October 25. After a presentation by Sir William Goschen, Chairman of the Hospital, a luncheon was held for Gracie, after which she paid visits to various wards, spending over an hour in the children's ward handing small presents out to the children and singing their favourite songs. She told one little boy, "Every time you see a policeman give a reet big smile or touch your hat to him." The honour was the second that year recognising her charity work, and in return Gracie offered her services in a charity concert to be held at the Royal Albert Hall later that same week.

The Gracie Fields Tribute Performance for the London Hospital Bicentenary Appeal at the Royal Albert Hall took place on October 28. In two half-hour sections, Gracie was to perform before Queen Mary. Tickets went on sale in late August for the event, which was to be Gracie's longest single solo spot to date. To coincide with the performance, the *News Chronicle* opened a £1,000 competition to aid the appeal, where readers had to write in suggesting the top seven most popular songs from Gracie's repertoire, to win two tickets for the performance. Accompanied by the Princess Royal, Lady Maud Carnergie, Lady Desborough, Margaret Wyndham, Lord Claud Hamilton, and Captain

Arthur Paget, Queen Mary took to the Royal Box to watch the proceedings. Also at the event were the Mayor and Mayoress of Rochdale, and most of the members of Gracie's family, except for Betty, who was still in America.

Speaking to the press in her dressing room after the show, Gracie remarked, "Oh, Queen Mary was sweet. Perfectly sweet. The choice of songs gave me a little bother. You see, I had to try and please Queen Mary and I had to try and please the customers. I had to put in some of the comedy even though I'm afraid some of it is a little crude. I had to do some of the old things as well as some of the new ones. I sang "The Holy City" in my last film, and when I heard it was King George's favourite, I thought I'd sing it tonight." Gracie claims she never had courage to sing in front of the Albert Hall before, and during the rehearsal alone she was a bag of nerves. "When you do something for other people, you can do for them what you can't do for yourself. When I first came onto the platform I was so scared and I felt so small I should have liked to have gone onto my knees on the stage." In total, Gracie performed fourteen numbers during her act, including a "Snow White Medley," "Sally," "My Blue Heaven," "Little Old Lady," "The Dicky Bird Hop," "We've Got to Keep Up with the Joneses," "The Holy City," "The Biggest Aspidistra in the World," "Walter, Walter," and finally, "Land of Hope and Glory." Many remarked afterward that "The Holy City" was the pinnacle of the evening, performed on the Hall's large pipe organ and accompanied by twenty choirboys.

Gracie had selected four different dresses for the event, only at the last minute choosing which she was going to wear. A few days previously she had been photographed by *Picture Post*, who had done a whole article of "A Day with Gracie," in a dress fitting for one of possible stage outfits, which was the one she eventually chose to wear on stage. Alongside Gracie on the bill, which was broadcast by the BBC and relayed to

America, were the Kneller Hall Band, Reginald Fort and Walter Widdop with Harold Williams and Lance Dossor, in a programme otherwise consisting of classical and operatic music. Major H. E. Adkins specially composed "Theme for a Celebrity" to be played by the 50-strong Kneller Hall Band at Gracie's entrance to the stage. Another reporter at the event was told by Gracie, "Her Majesty asked me how I managed to sing so beautifully and make all those rough noises and shouting. I told her I was a good, strong, hearty girl from the North!" After the event, which Gracie considered to be her best performance to date, as her "voice never felt better and I could feel it like a fine, perfectly tied string," her family all went back to Greentrees for a small party where Harry Parr-Davies presented her with a set of records of the performance from the BBC, which they all listened to.

Years later, Gracie recalled about the performance, "Just after the hospital, authorities took out £3,000 insurance against my non-appearance. I was nearly drowned off Capri, but I kept the story quiet until now because of a superstitious feeling that it might lead to other accidents. I'm a strong swimmer, but a current caught me and kept drawing me out to sea. The shore seemed to get further away and I thought, *My God, I'm going*, until two gardener boys jumped in and dragged me to shore."

The next day she was back at Alexandra Palace for her second broadcast. The special broadcast, with J. B. Priestley, took the form of an after-dinner speech and cabaret concert for the Festival Dinner of the Royal Photographic Society. Gracie and Priestley were at Alexandra Palace, and the society was dining at the Dorchester Hotel with the live-camera action relayed to them on a television set.

Another cinema opening was presided over by Gracie at the Dominion Cinema, East Barnet on October 31. The cinema's manager, Albert Bacal, introduced Gracie to the audience, to whom she performed a few of her favourite numbers, including "Sally" and "The

Sweetest Song in the World," and expressed, "Very glad I am to be able to come along this evening and open this new theatre. I hope you will have a lot of very happy hours here, I'm sure you will. I'll go on choking myself trying to make good films, and you'll choke yourselves coming to see them. So we're all choked!" Following her performance, Gracie had tea with the directors before going onto the roof canopy of the cinema to greet the crowds thronging the streets outside who were not lucky enough to procure a ticket for the opening ceremony.

The next day saw Gracie open a bazaar at St. Alban's Hall in Fulham, where she had to physically fight her way through the crowds to get into the event. Inside the hall, Gracie took to an upper-floor window and sang "Sally" to the crowds outside. In the newspapers that day, Mr. A Harold, President of the Wolverhampton Greengrocer's Association, expressed distaste at the BBC broadcasting "Stop and Shop at the Co-Op Shop," as it flouted the regulation of advertisements being broadcast. As an apparent advertisement for the Co-Op, the Association agreed it was harmful to independent traders. "Eh, lad, it's daft. Those songs are more than ten years old! I sing them on request. The words don't even make good sense. Advertisements? Nay! It's daft," was Gracie's response.

Taking a break from rehearsals for her upcoming recording sessions, Gracie returned to Rochdale on November fifth to be presented with the painting in oils commissioned by *The Rochdale Observer*. Taking to the stage at the Regal Cinema in the afternoon, Mayor of Rochdale, Mary Duckworth, introduced the "wholly unspoilt" Gracie and presented her with the painting in front of 2,000 of the 30,000 subscription contributors. Gracie told the audience how pleased she was the artist had made her, "right nice looking! And by gum, some days I need it. But you don't want me to come here and stand, talking all day. You think, 'I wonder if she's brought her pianist?' Well, I have! So that'll come later on." Impressed with the portrait, Gracie sang "'The Sweetest Song in the World" before she presented the painting back to the people of Rochdale, to be hung in the town's art gallery.

After tea with the mayor at Town Hall, Gracie waved to the crowds from Town Hall balcony, singing "The Biggest Aspidistra in the World" unaccompanied, before visiting a group of Boy Scouts in one of Town Hall's rooms, where she sang "Walter" to them. Gracie returned to London that same evening with a check for the orphanage with the remainder of the balance from the portrait fund. In the first week of the portrait being hung in the gallery, over 14,138 people came to visit. After restoration in 1947, for many years the portrait hung in the foyer of Rochdale Town Hall. In 2013, the portrait was hanging in the mayor's private sitting room, but it's usual home is the Touchstone's Museum Archival Store, where it currently resides.

Following a week at the Holborn Empire with Reco and May, GS Melvin, Anita Martell, Michael and Arnova, Harry Hemsley, Six Resua Sisters, Fields and Rossini, and George Prentice from November seventh, Gracie's proposed trip to America for the latter end of the year was brought forward earlier than expected, and so as not to disappoint the Variety Artists Guild and Orphanage, Gracie brought their annual ball forward. Initially scheduled for December fourth, President Gracie brought the 32nd annual ball forward to November 13 at the Savoy Hotel. After the meal, dancing, and a series of card tricks, Gracie took to the stage with the Harry Musiknat Band to perform "Mrs. Binns' Twins" from *Keep Smiling* (1938), and "Music, Maestro, Please" before a chorus of the statutory "Sally." At the event, Gracie spoke to Irish prima donna of the Universal Grand Opera company, May Devitt. Gracie told her desire to "sing in opera like you." Devitt replied she would give opera up if it meant she could earn a salary like Gracie's!

The following morning Gracie flew to Holland for two shows in promotion of the opening of *We're Going to be Rich* (1937) in Rotterdam and

Amsterdam. One critic wrote after Gracie's first show at the Grand Cinema in Rotterdam, "Lynch the timid soul who kept Miss Fields from us so long on the grounds that we wouldn't appreciate her peculiarly English style of humour ... We insist that hereafter the English tacitly include us in the possessive whenever they refer to Our Gracie!" After her first performance the audience began to chant "Ooze Gracie," the Dutch equivalent of "Our Gracie." Whilst here she was presented with a pair of clogs—Dutch clogs—and was photographed wearing them and a traditional Dutch klenderdracht. "I can't help it," she joked, "I just love me clogs!"

Back from Holland, Gracie, Mary, and Harry Parr-Davies went to Woodhouse Eaves and spent an evening with Tommy Fields and Nino Rossini, who were playing in the pantomime of *Aladdin* in Leicester. The comedy duo were renting a local property known as Beacon House during their run, and Nino recorded part of their first Pantomime appearance on his home-movie camera. Tommy Fields and Nino Rossini parted company after the pantomime, after over eleven years successful partnership together. Tommy had been venturing out on his own a lot, including the successful London review *Paris Fantasee* in 1935, and Mervyn Rossini remembered the split. "Tommy thought he would do better on his own. It was a shame because they had lots of very good bookings as a duo which were then cancelled." Their last appearance together in variety was the week beginning November first at the Croydon Empire, in a bill which also starred bandleader Ambrose alongside Vera Lynn.

In London, Gracie attended the ninth annual Film Ball at the Royal Albert Hall on November 18, where she took charge of the microphone and gave an impromptu quarter of an hour concert. On November 20, Gracie sailed to Southampton Water in the paddle-steamer named after her, to join the French liner Normandie, which was to take Monty, Mary, and herself to America—joining Harry Parr-Davies, who had already gone ahead. Discussing the logistics of filming of *Sally of the Shipyards* was to be part of Gracie's agenda whilst in America, including reports about a possible termination of Gracie's contract.

One of the stars who was in talks to sign up to the film, set in a Clydesdale locale, being Scottish entertainer Will Fyffe who was under contract with Gainsborough. Arrangements were not met for him to appear with another company, so an alternate actor was sought for the film, which did not occur until Gracie had begun filming her own scenes. On board the Normandie with Gracie was Marlene Dietrich, who it was reported "drifted along the passageways in a tailored suit and furs, all glamour and orchids," whilst Gracie sat on deck in a checked suit enjoying a cup of tea watching the star progress to her table.

On December 15, the Santa Monica Police Department presented Gracie with a gold badge declaring her an honorary police chief in a ceremony presided over by Mayor E. S. Gillette. At a Christmas party held in Gracie's honor in San Francisco, the mayor also presented her with the keys to the city, as she told him of her intention of buying some American property whilst she was out in America. The same evening, back in England, the Duke of Gloucester made his first public appearance since he fractured his collarbone in a hunting accident. In his appearance at the League of Mercy at St. James's Palace, he announced Gracie had consented to become the lady president of the Wanderer's Branch of the League upon her return from America.

Whilst in Hollywood, the British and American press broke the story that "Gracie Fields is Broke." It was announced an unexpected income tax bill had arrived for Gracie before she left for Hollywood, which it was expected she would deal with on her return to England, with some even suggesting she had fled England and the taxman. With property in two countries and an estimated personal salary of around £1,000,000 a year, Gracie told the press, "Most of my income seems to go to the British government in taxes, and most of the rest seems to go, you know, to my family and charity. So, really, I have always been stoney. It doesn't matter too much." Income tax was the reason Gracie didn't want to make any of her films in Hollywood, as she would have to pay both American and British income tax, "and probably still owe some money when the taxes had all been paid! I'd be working for toffee apples!"

Before Gracie left for America, she had personally edited the Christmas 1938 edition of the *Movietone News*. With a script written by Howard Thomas, Gracie both acts as commentator and actor in the ten-minute reel as she ousts regular reporter Leslie Mitchell from the reel to take over the job herself. Disrupting his performance by humming "The Trek Song" and then bursting in to sing "The Sweetest Song in the World," Gracie takes to the microphone, stopping Leslie with, "Hang on a minute. What did you call me? Miss Gracie Fields? Oh, Leslie, dahling! I do wish you wouldn't be so quite BBC. It's Gracie, luv, Gracie!" She asks the cinema-going public, "Don't you think it's a shame they overwork this poor little lad? Poor chap. One week he's dodging and chasing the bombs in China, the next he's helping a Duchess launch a lifeboat in Weston-super-Mare. Then when he's back from picking beauty queens in Miami, well then they send him off to Mount Everest where he gets cold feet. It's a shame!"

After dismissing Leslie and breaking the Movietone camera, Gracie announces the news are going "oop North to Rochdale" for their first stop, for some real "happy-go-lucky stuff. None of your mayors laying foundation stones or your Lady Godivas at charity bazaars." First stop is a scene of the Rochdale Hunt, which Gracie had been singing about for years, which gives her the chance for some vocal acrobatics in her voice-overs. Blackpool appears next, showing scenes in the Tower Ballroom, "Eeh, I've been squeezed many'a time in there, haven't you girls?" before moving onto Pleasure Beach, followed by Blackburn. Policemen are shown enjoying a cup of coffee before a female football match at Preston "with a bit o'sex appeal in it!"

"Here's a site of one of Lancashire's famous holiday resorts," announces Gracie as the cameras pan around Manchester, and then, "Liver-penny-pool." Shots of Salford Police's Christmas Pantomime, Lancashire Wakes Weeks, and the "London gasworks" of the BBC before the final shots of bury black puddings being made, completing the tour. After the tours and voice-overs Gracie is joined by Victor Silvester for her dance practice, as they dance "The Trek Song." To coincide with the new dance craze, step-by-step photographs of Gracie and Victor dancing the number appeared in film magazines and periodicals teaching how to dance the routine.

On Christmas Eve, the Fairy Soap Charity Fund closed their offer to pay a farthing for every "Fairy Soap Baby" cut from their cartons and sent to the Gracie Fields Charity Fund. Beginning at the start of the year, Thomas Hedley and Co. enabled charities to raise money for themselves without any work, as listeners to the show collected the cut-outs and sent them with information about their favourite charity. Meanwhile, reports came in from Hollywood that Gracie was again being glamourised by the film studios. Twentieth Century Fox, in an attempt to protect their biggest asset, issued a statement. "Such reports are pure invention. Gracie's popularity is based on her long-established style of comedy and no changes will be made to endanger it."

Having enjoyed her last trip to the Lancashire Society of California, Gracie paid them a second visit on December 17. As she entered the building, all 580 members present serenaded her with "She's a Lassie from Lancashire" as she took to the stage herself and gave an impromptu thirty-minute concert, culminating in "The Holy City," which she preceded by saying, "My 'Holy City' is my hometown of Rochdale, but I'm sure you Lancashire lads and lasses all think the same about your towns back home in Lancashire." After signing autographs for two hours solid, Gracie thought, "I've earned my slice of apple cake." The following night, Darryl Zanuck hosted a party at the Trocadero for Gracie, attended by Claudette Colbert, Clarke Gable, Carole Lombard, Loretta Young, Tyrone Power, Robert Taylor, Barbara Stanwyck, Joan Crawford, and Bing Crosby. At the party, Gracie was asked to sing and told the crowd, "I'm not going to sing a note until I've got a piece of that there chicken pie in my throat," which followed a shrill scale of notes and an impromptu performance in front of Hollywood's brightest stars.

Before spending a quiet Christmas at the Coachella Ranch she had visited on her previous visit with Monty, "while all you back home were snowed under!" Gracie appeared on the Eddie Cantor radio show. Having patched up their friendship at his charity show at the Kilburn Empire, Gracie agreed to broadcast on his show. A gap in the schedule, however, meant she had to sing longer than was arranged for, even though she had run out of songs. The only other sheet music Gracie had with her was "The Biggest Aspidistra," and she was reluctant to sing it as she feared Americans did not know what an aspidistra was. Eventually persuaded by Cantor to sing it, Gracie prefaced the song with a description of the plant, likening it to an American rubber plant, before she performed it. The audience loved the song so much the radio station was inundated with telephone calls and requests asking Gracie to sing it again. In Hollywood, Twentieth Century Fox showed their latest star the American studios in an attempt to persuade her to film there. Gracie paid a visit to the set of *Sing and be Happy*, where she was photographed with Allan Lane and met up with the Ritz Brothers and clowned around on set with them and was photographed sharing beauty tips with Joan Davis.

Gracie once again enjoyed sitting in the desert around a campfire and singing with the cowboys over Christmas at the ranch, and they enjoyed "a gay, wonderful party on New Year's Eve. The ranch hands were ripping out Western music with guitars, violins, banjos, saxophones, trombones, and a piano—it was a glorious mixture!" During the party,

Monty announced he wanted to call in and wish a Happy New Year to Joseph Schenck, the assistant chief of Twentieth Century Fox, who lived in a mansion nearby. Gracie remembered, "It was alive with film stars. But alive is the wrong word. It was like a waxworks." Gracie tried to liven the party up by singing and dancing, including performing an Apache dance with Buster Keaton, but nobody seemed bothered about any of it. Eventually Monty drove Gracie back to the homely party at the ranch and he returned to Schenck's, where Hollywood's largest card game was about to begin.

In her unpublished memoirs, which significantly differ to the published version, Gracie recalled, "I knew that Monty, like most Italians, was fond of a bit of gambling, and so we carried on with our party and I went to bed." The next morning Monty had not returned, and Gracie presumed that Monty had stayed there after the game. At lunchtime his car pulled up outside and he announced he had lost "more than he could afford to." In Gracie's published memoirs she cites Monty had lost $7,000, however in the unpublished draft manuscript the figure cited is $25,000.

Gracie got Monty a cup of strong coffee whilst he shaved, and eventually Darryl Zanuck rang. "The game's still on, Monty, why not come back and have your revenge? I'm afraid we took rather an advantage of you last night." They had to, because the night before Monty had been well and truly festive, and all at once Gracie began to understand why there had been such icy calm and lack of gaiety at the Schenck's party. Nobody had wanted to expend any energy, as they'd been saving it all for the card game. "It's your brass, lad," Gracie said, "please yourself, I think you're all barmy." Monty went back to the party, believing his luck to have changed, and stayed away overnight.

On the third night Gracie drove herself to see if the game was still being played, and found that it was. In a room thick with smoke, and a table cluttered with ashtrays, coffee cups, whiskey glasses, pep pulls, and sandwiches, she found "Pressburger rubbing his eyelids with an icecube and a white-coated masseur stood behind Gregory Ratoff rubbing the nape of his neck." In the middle of all the stubbled men sat Constance Bennett "like an alabaster statue, with fortunes being won and lost around her. She looked like a lily on ice." Although Monty won back some of the money, he still lost in the end, in one of the longest card games Hollywood had ever known.

Whilst in Hollywood, Gracie took a walking tour and allowed a press cameraman to follow her whereabouts, including buying celery and meat at a local market, having her shoes shined, visiting the Brown Derby restaurant, and taking a "Homes of the Movie Stars" tour, which took her to Loretta Young's house. Before returning to England, Monty persuaded Gracie to buy some property in Santa Monica. Although the press were dubbing her as being broke, this cannot entirely be accurate considering the huge amount of money she was being paid for one film alone. Whilst it is likely an unexpected tax bill had caught Gracie off guard, it is certainly unlikely she faced bankruptcy, as some sources have previously suggested. Gracie recalled, "I bought cars, got all my groceries at Fortnum and Mason, kept an open house, and just didn't know how much I owned, or, as I was to find out soon enough, how much I owed to the tax men [...] By the time the tax people had sent in all their bills Monty reckoned I'd have to sell my big house, Greentrees, and all its trimmings, to help pay some of the debts I owed to the Inland Revenue."

Whilst in Hollywood, Gracie's relationship with Monty reached the press, as Walter Winchell wrote, "Gracie Fields and Monty Banks have been romancing quietly by the malls since they met recently." An outraged Gracie remembered this later. "Nobody could have possibly known that unless someone close to me told the press, or somebody else read my private letters. I hadn't told a soul about me and Monty." The first property she bought in America was a hilltop castle, The Castle in the Air, in Beverley Hills. A Hollywood producer had first bought the site as his dream house, but lack of funding meant he could not finish the job, and Monty agreed to buy it with Gracie as a favour to the film producer. After viewing the house, Gracie had dinner with Constance Collier, who she told to keep it a secret she was going to buy it. A furious Gracie rang Constance the next day when it was all over the newspapers, to which Constance replied, "Dear, these things happen in Hollywood. I didn't tell them, but every servant in the house is a news-gatherer for one columnist or another."

Immediately thinking the British press would think she was deserting her country for buying a property there, Gracie called up London and explained, "I really bought the house to help a friend who needed the money, but I thought it might come in useful if I had to make films in Hollywood. Then the Twentieth Century Fox people decided that I should make my next film in England, so I was left with the house on my hands. I shall probably retain it for a time in case I do have to make a film in Hollywood sometime. But all my friends here can rest assured that if I do ever live in the house it will only be a temporary measure while filming. I have no intention of ever deserting England." Just in case Gracie was to move to America, she and Monty also bought a block of five apartment buildings, which they leased some out and kept others for family members at 53 Peck Drive/9601 Olympic Boulevard, Beverly Hills. In his biography, David Bret makes a further erroneous report of Gracie falling for an auctioneer during her time in America whilst she was looking for furniture to decorate the apartments. No evidence has ever been located to confirm this relationship, which certainly seems highly unlikely given the close involvement of Gracie and Monty at the time. Before she left America Gracie recorded *The March of Time* programme for the Blue Network, where she was presented with an award from NBC, which was broadcast on February 17, 1939.

Back in England, the baby elephant which Gracie had named the year previous, Sally Ma-Chaw, unexpectedly died at its zoo in Maidstone. On January 9, 1939, Betty and Roy threw a 41st birthday party for Gracie at their cottage in Santa Monica, attended by many Hollywood film stars. Gracie, Monty, Harry, and Mary set off on their return journey to England on January 14, where they took a train from Hollywood to New York, on a journey accompanying Janet Gaynor. On the platform at Pasadena, Gracie performed for a group of kindergarden children who were also waiting at the station. Staying over in New York for a few days gave Gracie the chance to see some of Broadway's shows and take a trip up the Empire State Building. In an interview in New York she said, "Your American comedy is based on sex. In Britain we draw a lace curtain around our sex comedies. Maybe I am old fashioned, but I do not approve of some of the things I have seen on Broadway!"

Gracie in
Hollywood. (1937).

The James Gunn portrait of Gracie. (1938). (Rochdale Museum).

CHAPTER TWELVE

January to September 1939

Wish me luck as you wave me goodbye,
Cheerio, here I go, on my way.

- "Wish Me Luck (As You Wave Me Goodbye)" (1939),
recorded by Gracie Fields.

WITH THE RUMBLINGS OF war faintly echoing in the European distance, one British newspaper wrote, "Personality defeats the psychologist,
and despite their politics, Hitler, Mussolini, and the rest of them have it
in abundance. So, for that matter, has Gracie Fields. And Gracie Fields,
perhaps, could lead us if she turned her mind to it. She arrived back in
Plymouth aboard the Champlain on February fourth at 4am, where
she proudly displayed her police badge from Santa Monica, inscribed,
"Captain of Detectives," to the crowd which had arrived early to see her.
"It was given to me by the mayor after I had given a charity concert, and
I believe it carries such privileges such as immunity from traffic regula-
tions." When questioned about the American people, Gracie answered,
"They are just like English folk, and the right people are always all right all
over the world, whatever their nationality."

Arriving off the train at Paddington Station, Gracie gave the crowd which had gathered to greet her a few seconds of "The Trek Song" before stopping herself with, "By goom it's cowd out here, in't it?" Wrapping her headscarf around her head, telling the cameraman, "Eh, you can't take a close up of me now, I've been up for two nights!" and again flashed her police badge, warning, "You'd better be careful what you say to me now, lads. I'm one of the force!" Gracie also told about how the American rubber plant would now probably be rechristened an aspidistra, and how Hollywood photographers asked if they could photograph her legs. "I don't get a living with my legs, but they took the picture just the same." That afternoon Gracie had a request to appear on the BBC's *In Town Tonight* with Anna Neagle, which she agreed over the telephone to do. When the producers rang Bert Aza to finalise the details, he told them he had already spoken to someone about it and told them Gracie was not going to appear. "They would take Gracie and spring her as a surprise. People want to know beforehand when she is to appear." However, when he announced Gracie had told him she wanted to do it, Bert immediately rang up Mike Meehan at the BBC and told him Gracie could go on the show. Unfortunately, the bill was full and the compromise was either ninety seconds of broadcasting or to appear on the show the following week, with the latter option chosen.

With rumours of her American film contract being terminated, Gracie told a press conference at the Savoy Hotel on February seventh this was not the case. "They wanted me to make films in Hollywood, but I fought against it and won. I want to give employment to the girls and boys in the studios over here." She also told, "From now on Gracie isn't going to do quite as much in the future." Pushing her "Hollywood-born golden hair," Gracie sat in splendour as pressmen, cameramen, and producers stood around in a semi-circle of admiration. Clad in an American black-wool suit, Gracie talked about "how Hollywood is like an American film set, and you expect to wake in the morning and find it gone."

Travelling to Leicester with her mother the next day, Gracie went to see brother Tommy playing Widow Twankey at the Opera House. When Gracie and Jenny arrived in Leicester, they spent some time backstage with Tommy as Silver Street and Cank Street around the theatre became packed with hundreds of people and the opera house management were forced to call in police reinforcement. Watching the pantomime from the Royal Box, before the curtain rose Gracie shouted, "I've come to see how my little brother is doing, and if he lets me down, well, Heaven help him!" Tommy took to the stage in the second half and introduced the audience to his sister, who joined him on the stage. "This is a holiday for me, and I want to escape the crowds and spend some time with Tommy." Without makeup, and wearing the outfit she travelled in, a black crepe-de-chine skirt and white blouse, Gracie took to the stage to sing "The Umbrella Man," "The Biggest Aspidistra," and "Danny Boy." As the crowd shouted for "Sally," Gracie shouted to them, "You lot want a lot for yer money, don't you?" as she obliged with her signature song. As the final bows of the show were taken Gracie came on for the curtain call, gave her brother a kiss, gave her own bow to a standing ovation, and joined in the closing choruses of the finale.

Still in panto-mood, Gracie travelled to Nottingham the next day to see Duggie Wakefield playing Buttons at the Theatre Royal. At the Station Hotel as Gracie arrived, the manager's daughter, Joan Linton, wearing a white ballet dress, went up to Gracie to ask for her autograph. "You know, I always wanted to be a fairy, but they made me a comic instead. I expect if I had played in *Peter Pan* I would have been Captain Hook." Met by Duggie at the train station, the pair worked their way through the autograph hunters before having a cup of tea at the hotel. After the performance, at which Duggie was worried "Gracie would criticise me too much and take me down a peg or two," Gracie appeared on the stage and gave a repeat performance of the four songs she had sung the night previously at Tommy's pantomime.

On February 17, Gracie and June Clyde were the guests of honor at a carnival party held by the London Hospital in aid of its bicentenary appeal, hosted by Vicountess Dawson. At the Grosvenor House event Gracie showed her prowess at throwing darts—"My Father taught me in the pubs o'Rochdale when I were a lass!"—before taking to the stage in front of the audience to perform seven songs. After the performance, phrenologist Mr. Barr read her bumps in front of the microphone, much to the delight of the audience.

Whilst in Nottingham, Gracie agreed to return to take on a week's work at The Empire beginning February 20, accompanied by Harry Parr-Davies. A theatrical circus booked in at the theatre had cancelled at the last minute, and rather than the house staying dark, Gracie stepped into the breach. Gracie's supporting bill featured Elsie Bowers, Billy Rutherford, Marjorie Stevens, Jack Marks, Leslie Pearce, Henry and Desmond, and Alec Foster, with Act Two taken up with a revuette called "Hitting the High Spot."

One evening, Paul Robeson, who was playing in another theatre in the town, was in the audience and Gracie invited him on stage to sing "Ol' Man River." By day, Gracie retreated to the peace and tranquillity of Sherwood Forest and to her quiet hotel twenty miles away from Nottingham's centre. On the afternoon of the 24th, Gracie visited Ollerton Colliery Company's clinic before performing at the local Electric Picture House cinema in an afternoon charity concert. In her forty-minute charity performance, Gracie sang her old favourites and a new song for the first time, "Addy Day." After a vote of thanks from Montague Wright of the Butterley Company, *Queen of Hearts* (1935) was shown to the audience and Gracie returned to Nottingham for her evening's performance. At her last performance she told the Nottingham audience, "I've had a lovely week and I just hope it won't be another six years until I'm back here again," referring to her last appearance in the city.

Attempting to raise 2,000 guineas for a new extension of the Derbyshire Royal Infirmary, the climax to Mr. Arthur Barlow's charity venture, the pinnacle came at the Derby Assembly Rooms on Wednesday the 21st, when Princess Helena Victoria presented the infirmary with a check for the full amount. The previous February, Gracie had performed in two concerts on behalf of the fund, at which she raised £400. Earlier that afternoon Gracie opened the new extension of the Arthur Barlow Ward and promised to return for the party after her evening's performance in Nottingham. Shortly after 11:30pm, Gracie and Harry Parr-Davies arrived unceremoniously and wasted no time in taking to the platform as "Sally" played, to be introduced to the dancers by the mayor. "Where's little Arthur Barlow? I am very happy to be able to come along and do my little bit, for I think Mr. Barlow is one of the finest men I have ever met. He has done something very wonderful—and I don't know what he is going to do next! I am going to sing you a few songs, not very much though, because I have got to look after this little money box of mine," added Gracie as she pointed to her throat. Nevertheless, Gracie performed "The Umbrella Man," "Mrs. Binns' Twins," "Music, Maestro, Please," and "Sally." After the dancing the mayor presented Gracie with a Crown Derby dish, which she thanked him profusely for, exclaiming, "Eeh, you don't half-produce some grand stuff in Derby!"

In her last theatrical variety show of 1939, Gracie was at the Brighton Hippodrome in Tom Arnold's revue, *Switzerland*, where the first half of the show was an ice show and the second half a cabaret show headlined by Gracie. With 1,200 square feet of two-inch-thick ice, the event was both a theatrical and engineering achievement, as a false floor was applied during the interval to cover the ice. Gracie is served up on ice, with a dash of homely Lancashire brogue to relive the expansive Swiss atmosphere, and each evening Tommy Fields appeared on stage to sing "Two Sleepy People" and "The Umbrella Man" with his sister—which they recorded together on Regal Zonophone. Gracie admitted, "It's quite true I like to try out my new songs on a Brighton audience, because they don't miss a thing and you don't have to shout to put things over. It's much sticker in the north."

During the run at Brighton, Gracie consented to sell her Greentrees home on Finchley Road, primarily due to the tax bill she received earlier in the year. "I just hadn't realised that I ought to have saved at least half of all the money I earned to meet this tax, though Bert had warned me and tried to explain it to me often enough." Needing the money for the Inland Revenue straight away, Gracie sold the house at a loss, but refused to let the new owners keep her goldfish or the tiger lilies in the garden which she had planted. Undaunted, Gracie, in typical spirit, said, "I always knew everything was barmy, but they're not going to have my goldfish, or my tiger lilies in the garden. I planted them myself, they're mine." So under the cover of darkness Monty drove Gracie back to Finchley Road and the pair fished out the goldfish and dug up the lilies which she had planted. Speaking of her decision to sell, one newspaper reported, "Altogether, it is a charming house in mellow red brick and oblong shaped. The ceilings seem to be the only reason for this decision, for every year with clockwork regularity they start to crack till they resemble a very old and very wrinkled forehead. Apparently it is something to do with the ground, which moves about one hundredth of an inch (or something like that) every so often," with no mention of her tax bill.

In January 1939 it was announced Gracie's next film would begin filming at Gainsborough Studios on March 26, after being postponed from October, with a working title of *Sally Goes to Town*, with Gracie playing an Irish character. This title was then changed to *Sally of the*

Shipyards and relocated to Scotland, before eventually being shortened to *Shipyard Sally* (1939).

On March second, before filming began at Islington and Gainsborough Studios, Gracie personally selected her songs for her upcoming film with musical director Louis Levy. Her choices included the lively "The Jitterbugs" and "In Pernambuco," as well as old favourites from her repertoire, "Danny Boy" and "Land of Hope and Glory." One of the songs to be included was Gracie's new farewell song, "Wish Me Luck (As You Wave Me Goodbye)." Before the sale of the Greentrees house, Phil Parks remembered, "We were in the drawing room of Greentrees and she wanted a new song on the spot and wanted a farewell song. Harry was lying on the carpet under her white piano as I played a few chords on the piano. Instantly, Harry said, 'That's a bugle call,' and he got to the piano and played with one finger the key. A few hours later, the song was finished." It would become one of the songs closely associated with Gracie, except for in Holland, where Vera Lynn had a hit with it and it became her signature tune.

Gracie opened at the Holborn Empire for a week on March seventh, accompanied by Georgie Wood, Gauter and Steeplechase, A.C. Astor, Three Jokers, Elimar, Velda and Vann, Clifford Stanton, Marion Pola, and the Fisher Girls. Among old favourites, Gracie added her new "Deep in a Dream." On her opening night, Gracie persuaded Tommy to come on stage out of the audience and join her in a duet of "Two Sleepy People," which was described by one reviewer as a harmless but inspired reductio ad absurdum.

On March ninth, Gracie and Bert Aza visited 10 Downing Street in conjunction with the Dowager Duchess of Devonshire's "At-Home" afternoons, in association with the Toc H movement. Throughout the summer season a set of parties were prearranged, including a garden party at Hampton Court on July 19, and parties similarly arranged by the Duchess of Marlborough, the Duchess of Rutland, Viscountess Allendale, Vicountess Curzon, and Gracie. The next day, March tenth, Gracie gave her afternoon to Bernardos in conjunction with Finchley Habitation at their annual charity market at the Kind Edward Hall in Finchley. Spending time wandering around the stalls, posing for photographs and signing autographs, Gracie's only official duty was to award a prize for one of the competitions and to take part judging the children's pet show.

A few days later, March 13, saw Gracie in attendance at the fourth annual Gaumont British Ball alongside Will Hay, Moore Marriott, Graham Moffatt, and Adele Dixon. At the event at the Royal Albert Hall, the arena was filled with troops from members of each service, with the proceedings brought to a conclusion by Ian McLean reading the "Peace Toast" from Noel Coward's *Cavalcade*. Aside from joining in the dancing and revelry, Gracie performed for the audience alongside the Louis Levy Orchestra. She was back again at the Royal Albert Hall on March 20 at the Centenary Ball of Newsvendors Benevolent Institution Hall for the presentation of the most magnificent cabaret spectacle London has probably ever known. The event was also attended by Cicely Courtnidge and Frances Day, the Crazy Gang, and a host of drummers, pipers, and the Knelier Hall band in an *Empire Peace Parade*. Music was provided by Billy Cotton and his Band and Jan Ralfini and his Broadcast Orchestra.

Earlier that same evening, Gracie had appeared in a broadcast in conjunction with Poste Parisien in a gala performance in honor of the state visit of the French president to Great Britain. Titled *Paris-Londres*, the first section from Broadcasting House saw Gracie in a ten-minute section of her own followed by a live telephone conversation with Maurice Chevalier in Paris and then Chevalier's ten-minute set. During Gracie's section she performed "Grandma Said," "Reviens," "The Family Tree," and a medley of songs from *Keep Smiling* (1938), and joked, "I know what you Paris boys are! I'll get my mother to come and look after me!"

Whilst the radio broadcast was a success, the "genuine telephone conversation" was spotted by one keen-eared listener from New York to have been prerecorded, as it featured the voice of a female telephone operator. At the time, all female telephone operators finished work at 8pm, which was before the broadcast began. A member of the Birmingham Daily Dispatch team went to the BBC to ask about this, and they all confirmed the telephone call was genuine, and until the reporter presented his trump card, continued to admit it was real. This was not the first time the BBC had experienced controversy with one of Gracie's broadcasts, as earlier in the month one of her new recordings was played without an announcement of who was singing it, contrary to their own regulating standards. Over 600 listeners wrote in to say they had heard the announcer say "That was Gracie Fields" before the next record was played. Many newspapers carried the insignificant debate as to whether or not the BBC had or had not ignored telling the public, until the BBC engineers confirmed from their broadcast acetates once and for all the outro was faded too early. All that keen listeners heard was "THAT was Grac..." with the words being faded too early. The 600 people who wrote into the daily newspapers swearing and ascertaining they had heard the announcement were proven to be wrong.

In an unpublicized appearance, Gracie was the guest of honour at the City Livery Club's luncheon at Leatherseller's Hall on March 27. Another event that same month, Gracie went backstage at the Royal Opera House to visit Eva Turner and was photographed applying Turner's eyeliner with Turner wearing her famous Turandot headdress.

Although Will Fyffe was replaced with Owen Nares in Gracie's next film, which was now retitled *Shipyard Sally* (1939) as production began, it was announced in March that Fyffe's new film was also to have a

Clydesbank setting called *Rulers of the Sea* (1939), an epic about steam versus sail on the North Atlantic. Filming began on *Shipyard Sally* in early March at Islington Studios, and during May the production company moved to Scotland to film some exterior dockyard shots. Whilst in Scotland, fellow comedian Will Hay visited the set. Written by Don Ettlinger, a promising 25-year-old Hollywood film writer selected especially for this film, the story concerns the plight of Sally Fitzgerald, a failed music hall performer whose father buys a pub near the John Brown and Company factory with her own money. With the factory threatening closure, Gracie takes a petition signed by the workers and residents of the Clyde to Lord Alfred Randall in London to try to make the government reconsider the closure. After getting nowhere Sally pretends to be someone else to get to meet the great and the good, and of course saves the day, though losing the love of her heart. Overall, the moral of the film was if workers and bosses worked together they would see things through.

Around this time Basil Dean had begun preparations for what would become the Entertainments National Service Association (ENSA) as war in Europe echoed in the distance. Basil had met Gracie to discuss the idea of a charitable war effort with her, and she had agreed to take a leading role as part of the organisation's Central Committee, whose intention was the voluntary mobilisation of all branches of the profession for the provision of entertainment for the armed forces and munitions workers of a country at war.

However, there was a turnaround, as on April fourth Bert Aza wrote to Basil: "I am to tell you that with regard to this matter, Gracie would rather go about it in her own way should, unfortunately, anything of this nature be necessary. I am sure there is no necessity at the present juncture to prepare for this side of things, it will take it's natural course, as before. However, there ain't going to be no war for a long time to come, and business is going to take a turn for the better and you will see a gradual return to prosperity." Although Gracie did eventually take war-work with Basil Dean, their close relationship never fully recovered following this, and letters remained cold, sometimes nasty.

On May sixth, Gracie and her costar, Sydney Howard, attended the Rugby League Cup final between Salford and Halifax at Wembley. It has been said the two stars had their own "War of the Roses" frequently in jest on the set, and they were going to the Cup final to see whose native county would come on top. For the event, Gracie had bought large Salford rosettes and rattles which she distributed amongst the rest of the cast to wind Sydney up on set, and at the Cup final, which most of the cast and crew attended. Halifax won, beating Salford twenty points to three.

Around the same time, a London-based newspaper ran a story on John Flanagan and his plight to paint the poor people of London. Dubbing himself a "London Bohemian," the reporter and John took in a film at a London cinema, where John was shocked when a critic wrote it was mediocre. "I've watched that same film, marvelling at the technical brilliance of it, the uncanny naturalness of the actors, the money and worry that went into its making, and that fellow says mediocre. As if it meant no more mental strain than it takes to produce a meal-ticket gossip column." John did an "Alice in Wonderland" on the journalist and dived into his studio, telling him, "You live in a madhouse. Do you know there is a new aristocracy in this land and the chief aristocrats are George Formby, Max Miller, and Gracie Fields?"

Gracie had been fooling everyone for months, including herself, into believing she was fit and well, when really, "I wanted to topple forward with my head between my knees, with a dizziness that made everything seem to be happening far away at the end of a long, cotton-wool corridor." At the very start of filming, Monty had asked Gracie if she wanted to proceed with the film, as it was better to stop a film before it got started than to leave it half finished. Pretending she didn't know what he was talking about, Gracie dismissed this and began shooting, when really, she was in a tremendous amount of pain. "It had been with me for about two years. The Freedom of Rochdale had been given to me in a daze. My Royal Command at the London Palladium had been done through a mist that made everything seem like one of the very early cinematograph shows. Even when I performed at the Albert Hall in October, it had been with the same sensation of wanting to double up slowly, and with voices far away as when you are waking from anaesthetic."

One scene in the film calls for Gracie to dress up as a man in order to gain entry to a gentleman's club, a scene which cinema historian Jeffrey Richards cites as "a masterly display of her total control of comic gesture, expression, and timing." Fitted out in a magician's suit from a theatrical costume shop, the particular scene where her costume explodes with flags, handkerchiefs, toy snakes, and eventually falls off to reveal her true sex had to be reshot and reset, all the time with a cigar under Gracie's nose. "I never liked using a stand in," remembered Gracie. "If I was getting a fat wage packet, I liked to do the work. When I began to feel sick, I blamed it on the cigar. A weight inside me, trying to fold me up. I had to keep pulling myself back, like a man nodding off to sleep in a crowded train." On set, Gracie began to stumble and had to catch herself on any props or scenery as she could, although she often tried to make a joke of it. Whilst Monty watched her thoughtfully, he didn't say anything, although he could see something was wrong with her. Gracie put this down to, "not having much time to see each other. At the end of a day's filming I went home and Monty stayed behind, as usual, to drink coffee and to watch the day's 'rushes.'"

Toward the end of filming the conjuror's suit scene Gracie knew she had to faint and made her excuses to leave the set so she could do it away from anybody else. "I remember slipping to the floor and how comfortable it felt: the cool, hard, concrete corridor." Gracie awoke to find Monty beside her and tried to pass her illness off by asking for a glass of water and an aspirin. Monty attempted to reason with her to end the filming, as it was clear to Monty she was very ill, but Gracie didn't want to put everyone else's jobs on the line with only three weeks of filming left to go. She would not see reason, however, especially not after the unbroken run during *Mr. Tower of London* and returning from Paris after half a day in 1929 in her only bid for freedom to see the show would go on. "I was not going to spoil a half-finished film for the sake of a dizzy spell."

An argument erupted in the corridor between the two, with the weak Gracie shouting, "I've got guts if you haven't! We'll finish the film without you if you're such a coward!" This shocked Monty as much as it did Gracie, and she began to sob in the now-silent corridor. "The only noise I can remember hearing is my sobs and the ticking of Monty's wristwatch. I was too weak to push him away." Instead, he consoled her as he feared her illness to be more than the "rich suppers and late nights" which she put her dizzy spells down to. Monty was known on set and amongst his friends as a slight hypochondriac, carrying medical books around with him and having a knack for correctly diagnosing illnesses, although he refused to tell Gracie what he feared. "For you, Gracie, the film is already finished," he told her as he explained how the filming schedule was to be edited and different scenes shot and replaced so that Gracie would not have to film any further scenes, and they would work with the takes which they already had. "That is how I came to know Monty Banks. In little matters he was voluble and excitable, but in deep things, Monty's mind ran deeply too."

Gracie agreed to this, and Monty immediately drove her down to Peacehaven, where Mary Davey looked after her and put her to bed. When Gracie awoke the next day she was ready to put the pain down to nothing and head back to London to continue filming, but Monty had arrived with a surgeon to see her. All Gracie remembered from her first meeting with Mr. Searle was his prowess at tying his shoe laces. "He bent down whilst talking and without looking at them and tied two perfect loops with one hand! The man clearly had skill in his fingers." Over the next two days a constant stream of doctors and physicians arrived at Peacehaven to try and determine what was best for Gracie. "It was bloodcurdling", she remembered. Lord Dawson of Penn, the king's personal physician, arrived, as well as the famous Lord Horder, and ultimately it was decided Gracie needed a preliminary exploratory operation to ascertain for certain what was wrong with her. She was given the choice of which "Lord This and Sir Horace That" would do the operation, and she pointed to the quiet Mr. Searle in the corner of the room. Lord Dawson agreed and offered to help in any way he possibly could. Whilst the initial exploratory operation was a success, the doctor's worst fears were confirmed, and it was revealed that Gracie had cancer of the cervix and required a further operation immediately. Without the operation, it was cited Gracie would die within seven months.

The talk of nursing homes and hospitals reminded Gracie that she had a "Good Causes Appeal" radio broadcast to do on behalf of the Manchester Royal Infirmary, but Monty assured her Tommy was to do the broadcast on her behalf the coming Sunday. Too weak to argue with Lord Penn, Mr. Searle, and Monty, when Sunday arrived Mary helped Gracie get dressed and acted as her bodyguard when the frail Gracie walked into the living room at the Haven to the astonishment of her family. Determined she was going to do the broadcast, regardless of whether or not Tommy was already at Broadcasting House, Fred agreed to go with his daughter in the car. "Since she's out of bed, she may as well do something useful!" agreed Jenny, as the car arrived to take them the 61 miles to London. They arrived at the BBC two minutes before the appeal was to go live, and Tommy was already sitting with the script and glass of water at the microphone table ready to broadcast. With Mary holding Gracie up on one side, Fred on the other, and Monty and a crowd of anxious BBC officials behind her, Tommy was as shocked as everyone else to see his sister in London and not in bed at Peacehaven.

Straightening her back through the pain, Gracie made a joke of the situation. "Lads, I'm here, aren't I? What's all the fuss about? Can't a lass enjoy herself even if she is ill?" Near-wrestling a delighted Tommy away from the microphone, Gracie did the broadcast, and the husky-voiced appeal brought in over £2,500 for Manchester's new ward, but not the £20,000 she cites in her published autobiography. The next day, doctors put Gracie into a nursing hospital, as they wouldn't let her stay on a public ward, despite her wishes "to have a gossip with the other people in the beds." Mr. Searle would not allow it.

That same week, on June third, the SS Gracie Fields berthed at Southampton Docks with passengers from the Normandie, including Betty, who had come over from America to be with her sister, along with Tony Parry. They were greeted by Jenny and Edith at the quayside and were delighted to have been met by the "Gracie Fields" ship, which they took to be a good omen for Gracie's wellbeing and upcoming operation.

On June fourth, Auntie Margaret Livesey was to marry the undertaker from Rochdale who she had been back in touch with, John Fielding, at Telescombe Church. Whilst Gracie had arranged the wedding and sent the invitation cards out, she was unable to attend the wedding herself. She requested that on the morning of the marriage Margaret was to visit Gracie in her nursing home in her wedding dress. The surprise for Margaret was that all of Gracie's family had arrived half an hour before, bringing balloons, flowers, and champagne for a pre-wedding party. If Gracie couldn't be at the ceremony or the party at The Haven after the wedding, she was going to spend time with Margaret and family before the ceremony.

Spending half an hour at Gracie's bedside before the wedding at two o'clock, Gracie softly sang to Margaret "Here Comes the Bride" in her very weak voice as she entered the room. "I couldn't get the voice out properly. It was like singing through cotton wool." The preliminary operation the next day was a success and Gracie was sent to Chelsea Women's Hospital, "for the main event," the removal of the infected cells and complete hysterectomy to prevent the spread of the cancer. Even if Gracie pulled through the dangerous operation the doctors only gave her a 50% survival rate. In the 1930s, such operations were described by the press as "a serious internal operation" and "a dangerous abdominal operation," and it was not until the late 1960s that the full nature of Gracie's operation became public knowledge.

Gracie confided to friends in later life that her greatest sadness was never having any children of her own. She did not want a child with Archie Pitt, as she knew that he was not the right man for her, but with Monty she felt something different. " I had always kept my own private dream that one day, even though I was now forty-one, there'd be a husband and children of my own for me, to make my home a real home." Having seen her nieces and nephews born and grow up with a happy family life, and the many children who passed through the doors of the orphanage, it is certain Gracie would've been a great mother to any child. She was "Aunty Grace" to hundreds of children over the years, but never "Mama Grace." The hours in which she had to tell herself, "Well, you can't have everything," were some of the hardest of her life as she resigned herself that the operation to save her life would prevent the life of any children of her own.

Dressed in her surgical robes prepared by Sister Southgate, Fred, Jenny, Tommy, Betty, Edith, Bert and Lillian Aza, and Mary Davey all watched as Gracie was wheeled down the corridor for her operation on Tuesday, June 13. A wry smile and "D'you think I look smart in my Ascot clothes?"

brought wild laughter from all in the corridor, in complete juxtaposition from the situation they were all currently in. Jenny blew her nose hard. "Our Grace, you always were a damned fool!" Which Gracie remembered, "The nearest I have ever seen her come to showing emotion."

Gracie was in a coma for three days and came around to the smell of roses. "A heavy scent like chloroform, like a red blanket soaked in chloroform all around me with Monty's booming voice ordering them away as the scent was taking the air." As Gracie was half awake Monty brought the Bishop of Blackburn to pray with and for her. Unable to do so herself, Monty placed Gracie's hands together for her, and the bishop prayed. Gracie tried to pray along with him but was unable to. "I was too tired to listen. But I knew the words. I didn't need to listen. I said my own prayer. Didn't mean to be rude ... I just didn't have the strength. I think God always knows. Inside me, where the operation had been, it began to tingle like blood flowing into a cramped foot." Monty told her, "All the good bugs are fighting the bad bugs" as Gracie slipped in and out of consciousness.

"One of the most wonderful things I remember about that long illness was the sight of Mary there whenever I opened my eyes." This was something attested to by Mary herself. When Gracie first opened her eyes she smiled at Mary and asked for some custard with two eggs, "Just how I like it." Mary ran out of the room crying, realising Gracie was going to be fine. Mary later remembered, "It was a matter of life and death, and they weren't going to operate at first. One of the most dreadful things for Mr. Searle, having to operate on someone of her name. She looked like everyone else after an operation. She suddenly had a relapse, and it really was touch and go. I used to grill pieces of meat and put them through a duckpress and put them in earthenware dishes and feed them to her. She needed food, but she couldn't eat food. They said she was very anaemic and she needed blood. She wouldn't eat raw beef sandwiches, so I gave her this steak blood with a few breadcrumbs in it and leave the steak for the nurses for their supper. Then I gave her brandy and milk mixed with an egg, then it became too rich for her and she came out in a rash. After the bishop of somewhere came she seemed to take a turn for the better … I used to stay all day, take what I thought she would like, then go home at night. The only time she got uncomfortable was when she was coming round the bed—they took out the new-fangled rubber mattress and gave her an old mattress. It was the only time she complained."

In the days after her coming round, the British press constantly wrote articles about her, Queen Mary enquired about her health through Lord Dawson of Penn, and Lord Nuffield, who had never met Gracie, called specially at the hospital with a bunch of roses for her. Roses also came from Clement Atlee, who himself was facing a major operation, as well as from George Formby and hundreds of other members of the variety profession. The Queen Mother sent a message saying, "Don't try and get well too fast, because when one begins to get well one is apt to forget to take care." Monty was one of the few people allowed to see Gracie regularly, and he told the press it was Gracie's "iron will that is keeping her going. The other day there were a few tears, but she was smiling bravely." Every different age group and denomination of religion sent Gracie goodwill messages, with one little girl sending a block of chocolate and two oranges with a note: "I hope that these will be good for you," and a little boy sent comic books for her to read. Churches and synagogues held special services for Gracie, and hundreds of admirers kept a silent vigil on the street outside the hospital, with straw and coats being laid down on the road to muffle the noise of the crowds outside. Tommy Fields remarked, "I don't think it's ever been heard of before. I mean, the whole country was praying. Such was the love for this woman that everybody felt as though she was part of their own lives."

Given only an even chance of pulling through by the doctors, Gracie was helped through by her indomitable spirit and the sincere and loving thoughts of millions of her admirers. "Though her courage and cheerfulness are still 100 percent, she knows in heart of hearts that she is fighting for her life," commented a nurse at the hospital.

Over the years, the figure of letters and telegrams sent to Gracie has varied from quarter of a million to half a million, but what is certain is that the public's love had never been shown quite so prominently as this to any other artist. The hospital was besieged with flower deliveries, and Bert Aza's office was stacked with letters in hundreds of crates. In the first few days he began to make a scrapbook for Gracie with the letters in so she could read them, but as they arrived by the thousand this task became impossible as they mounted up tremendously.

On June 15, Archie told the press he wanted to see Gracie. In April, Gracie had announced she was suing him for a divorce on the grounds of misconduct with Annie Lipman. "I want to see Gracie as soon as I am allowed, I hope that we can be friends again. I wrote to her when I first heard of the operation and I sent some roses and carnations. She wrote back to me and thanked me and hoped that all this nonsense would soon be over." Admitting they had a "very happy time together" but just drifted apart, Archie wished her the very best and hoped as soon as the time would be appropriate, "she only needs to say the word and I'll be there to visit her."

The famous image of Gracie's illness was a cartoon which appeared in the *Daily Express* on Saturday, June 17, drawn by Sidney Conrad Strube. Strube's famous figure in a bowler hat was drawn standing, looking up at Gracie's hospital window holding a bunch of flowers, which echoed the sentiments of a nation. The caption simply read, "Our Gracie." Moved and touched by the image, Gracie sent a request to see Strube and asked to be presented with the original sketch, which she presented as a thank you to Mr. Searle. "This eloquently summed up the popular adulation she enjoyed throughout the decade," writes Jeffrey Richards. One of Gracie's most treasured keepsakes was a hand-stiched version of the cartoon, sent in by a fan, which she kept in Capri throughout her life.

As Gracie began to recuperate, Monty and Mary took over completely with her meals. Borrowing a duckpress from the Dorchester Hotel where Monty was staying to be near Gracie, they prepared an "invalid broth" which consisted of the pressings of six pounds of beefsteak, and as she got stronger the pair brought over meals from the Dorchester and Gennaro's Restaurant as opposed to having Gracie eat the hospital food. "The nurses clustered like seagulls around the tray when I had done with it, picking among Monty's heaps of artistic delicacies. I shall never forget the sight of him strutting urgent and proud along the hospital corridor with his tray of steaming savouries." Her strength built up as time went on, and by early July Gracie was able to walk around her room with the aid of a nurse. The newspaper updated readers every day with bulletins direct from the hospital, such as, "Gracie has passed a comfortable night," "fairly satisfactory," and "Gracie is getting on quite well."

Following the excitement of a throng of Saturday afternoon visitors, Gracie rang Edith at home in Finchley and asked if she and Mary would bring a piece of trout fried in butter. "It was the quickest meal I've ever made," remembered Betty as the pair shot off back to Chelsea with the food on Mary's lap. Thinking something was wrong with Gracie at the unorthodox evening visit from two closest to her, the press regathered outside the hospital fearing bad news. Edith came out to allay their fears and explained, "Gracie had a very poor night last night and is still in pain, but the doctor is quite pleased tonight. She has only just realised how serious her operation was and would never have got through it if she had known before what to expect. But now she's making a big effort to get well." On June 26, Elisabeth Bergner came to have tea with Gracie in hospital. The pair had met when Gracie was making *Keep Smiling*

(1938), and Elisabeth, *Stolen Life* (1938). Elisabeth often gave Gracie fruit salads on set made from her own recipe, one of which she took into hospital to cheer her up. She told the press afterward, "Gracie was very happy, and her eyes were shining and sparkling."

With every ward of the hospital covered in Gracie's flowers, fans began to send her small mascots and trinkets for luck—which included dozens of sprigs of lucky heather, miniature horseshoes, black cats, and even lucky pigs. Thousands of Romany charms were sent to Gracie to put under her pillow and to wear around her neck. Messages even arrived from the inmates of Wakefield Prison, who all wrote letters to Gracie which were sent to her by their prison officer. "The boys don't forget you, and without exception their question every morning is 'How is Gracie?'" As her strength improved, Gracie began to pay visits to other patients in the wards. Tommy remembered, "She was going round hobbling with flowers and fruit and distributing it to all the patients. She's a woman that can't help but give." Visiting a nursery school in Hadfield, Derbyshire on June 20, Lady Astor told how she was not "everybody's darling. There's only one woman who's ever been that, and that's Gracie Fields. I'm sure every one of us is thinking of and hoping and praying for her. Once when I spoke in Rochdale, I was told by an old man that I was nearly as good as 'Our Gracie.' I felt very proud."

One thing which Gracie could not give, and which she desperately longed to do, was the birth of a child. She was mocked by this through the white wall that divided her hospital room from the next, as she very occasionally heard the sound of a newborn baby crying. "They were thin, little cries, like lost lambs on a hillside. They tugged at my heart." As soon as she was well enough to move around Gracie went to visit her neighbour, as she wanted to see the baby. Gracie found a young girl propped on white pillows feeding her baby. Gracie told her she was not supposed to be up and about yet, "and if Sister Southgate catches me there'll be trouble—but I couldn't resist having a peep at your baby." The six-day old baby, Michael, was too busy to meet anyone, even Gracie Fields. "He was guzzling his milk, eyes blissfully shut. I took his hot, wrinkled little fingers. They curled instantly around mine and held on tightly. The whole world was his friend. I said, 'You're lucky, love. It must be wonderful to have a little chap like that, of your own.' She would not be leaving hospital emptyhanded, never be in need of somebody to love. Women should have babies. No matter how successful she is, how much she seems to be loved, a woman who has never had a baby has lost her way along the road.'"

Gracie went each day to visit her tiny neighbour, which gave her comfort that such miracles could still go on in life, although they would never happen in hers. "I became his godmother. Each year I still remember my little hospital neighbour, wherever I am in the world. It's all very well being rich and successful. I have a hospital of babies—they make me realise how lucky I was to have a mum and dad to have given me a shove when I needed it. But for all this, I knew it was too late now for me to have a baby of my own, like this lass who lay with a wisdom in her eyes that I could only guess after." This is contradicted by Lillian Aza, who suggested in the 1980s, "Grace always said she'd have liked children of her own, but I don't think she really took much interest. There were some wonderful kids at the orphanage that she could have taken under her wing and educated and looked after, but she didn't."

On July 13, an accordion player stood beneath Gracie's window and began to play "Sally" and "Sing as We Go," which delighted Gracie, who mustered up enough strength to get out of bed and wave to the player below. The next morning, escorted by Edith and Jenny, Gracie hoped to escape from hospital unseen, but a crowd of 150 had gathered on July 14, including Movietone cameras, to see Gracie leave for Peacehaven. On the morning of her departure a reception was held in her hospital bedroom, where she told the nurses, "Don't worry. I'm going to be good and do as you have all told me, because I don't want to undo all that you've done since I've been in here." She thanked each of them before saying goodbye to baby Michael. After signing the visitor's book Gracie heard the cheering crowds and had to stop as she had filled up with tears. The nurses and staff all lined the hospital as she left through the front doors, and the clearly weak and fragile Gracie cried as she told, "You all affect me so much with this love you give me. It's wonderful and I do thank you all ever so much." Leslie Mitchell came to her assistance, to prevent her from breaking down, and spoke for the nation when he told how "delighted we all are to see you back."

Unlike quoted in other biographies, there was no moving moment where all the men in the crowd raised their hats in unison to Gracie—a fact attested to by the existent newsreels which cover the whole event. Sister Southgate and Nurse McDonagh helped Gracie into the car, which was being driven by Monty. Arriving at Peacehaven, Mrs. McDonagh and Betty handed Gracie over to Tommy and Dorothy at the front gate as she told them, "I'm tickled to death to be home." Before going straight to visit her new kitchen and newly decorated bedroom, which had both been installed whilst she was in hospital, Gracie went to have a cup of tea in the garden. A shower of rain sent her back inside the house, and she made a telephone call to the orphanage asking about all the children and having a brief conversation with the matron, who assured her all was well and to continue to focus on her own recovery, as the place was in good hands. Before retiring to her newly-colored bedroom, Fred King, Gracie's tour manager for many years, visited her with Bert to see how she was settling back in at home and to reassure her that all scheduled contracts had been cancelled for the remainder of 1939.

Shipyard Sally (1939) had its London previews on July 13 at Century Theatre, attended by Twentieth Century Fox executives, including

Francis Harley, Robert Kane, and Monty. After the showing the public was asked to fill in opinion cards on the film, and the response was this was Gracie's best film to date—as every previous film had been billed. However, the press were not as enthusiastic, with Graham Greene writing, "The picture has the embarrassment of a charade where you don't know the performers well." On July 19, Bert Aza attended the Toc H Garden Party at Hampton Court Palace, which Gracie was meant to attend and scheduled to host her own party later in the year. "It had me proper bothered. They could have my home, they could have me singing for them, but if I had to be the hostess, I knew I'd be nervous and do something wrong! I dreaded it. When the doctors said I must have a minor operation I thought this was a wonderful way out. I can still remember my relief!"

At the Hampton Court party, which Gracie should have attended, Bert Aza was introduced to the queen and, "I told her how sorry Gracie was to miss what would have been the biggest event in her life, for she was to have been presented to the queen, and I said how disappointed she was that she was not well enough to come." Fully aware of Gracie's recent near-death illness, the queen told Bert she was, "glad to know that Gracie was going on well, and to tell her not to try to get well too quickly, because when one commences to get well one is apt to forget to take care."

Exactly a week after her returning home from hospital, Gracie made her first public appearance as she attended court to the divorce hearing of her marriage to Archie at Carey Street. Before Justice Bucknill, Archie gave his address as 46 Willifield Way in Hampstead Garden Suburb, presided over "Selinger, G. v Selinger, A." Gracie was granted a decree nisi with costs going to Archie. Mr. Norman Birkett KC and Mr. Aitken Watson appeared on behalf of Gracie, with Mr. P. M. Cloutman representing Archie. Gracie was accompanied by sister Betty and Nurse McDonagh, who had been living at the Haven all week with the family to look after Gracie in the immediate period following her illness. Pale and nerveless, Gracie sipped from a glass of water as she sat in front of the bar wearing a black astrakhan coat over a dark blue dress and blue-trimmed hat, as the judge allowed her to remain seated during the trial. She did walk to the box with the aid of a stick, where another chair was presented to her for her six minutes in the box. The petitioner's case was that Gracie had left her husband because of unhappiness in 1932, and in October 1938 he had committed adultery with Annie Lipman in a Hastings hotel and had been living with her ever since in Hampstead. There was no mention that Archie had openly been having an extramarital affair with her since before Gracie left him, and no mention of Gracie's relationships with both John Flanagan and Monty. There was also no mention that Annie and Archie had been living in a house built and paid for by Gracie, and how Gracie noted, "In July 1932 I felt compelled to leave my husband." Evidence was given by Ada Elizabeth Skinner, a chambermaid at the Alexandra Hotel in Hastings where the misconduct was reported to have taken place.

As Gracie left the court, the small crowd, which included theatrical friends, cheered her and offered shouts of good luck. She was driven to Edith and Duggie's home in Finchley to rest—with Fred and Jenny living next door. Early evening, Edith came to speak to the press and explained Gracie was kissing Duggie Junior and Grace goodnight and she would be staying the evening in Finchley. Instead, she travelled to Peacehaven later that night after the reporters had dispersed.

Condition permitting, Gracie agreed to do her return broadcast on Sunday, July 30 at 9:20pm from her bedroom at Peacehaven. For weeks before, newspapers were speculating as to "when we will hear her magnetic voice again," and so the BBC planned a special "bedroom broadcast." Some newspapers reported, however, Gracie was making a rapid improvement, managing to walk around her Peacehaven garden with ease, and so it looked possible she may have returned to Broadcasting House on Sunday, July 30. The Lord's Day Observance Society sent a letter to Gracie asking her specifically not to make her variety broadcast on the 30th as planned. They stated, "Any music-hall programme including worldly songs on the Lord's Day would cause the deepest distress to multitudes of people. I therefore confidently look to you to give to Sabbath-breaking theatrical advisers." Accompanied with a bouquet bearing a card marked "With Christian good wishes for a speedy recovery," a copy of the letter was also sent to the director deneral of the BBC, Mr. F. Ogilvie, as well as Bert Aza, requesting not to let the broadcast go ahead.

It was agreed to eventually do the broadcast from London, arriving from Peacehaven at 8:30pm to crowds outside the BBC surrounding her car as she went inside to plan and check her speech for the special broadcast. After a last-minute rehearsal of the Paul Rubens song, "I Love the Moon," written for Phyllis Dare before Rubens' early death in 1917, so many people tuned in to Gracie's broadcast of thanks that Regal Zonophone dubbed the BBC's master-discs the very next day and issued the entire broadcast on a 78rpm record. Before the broadcast, Gracie told those in the studio, "I am a lot better, but still a bit dithery. The singing's going to be a bit of a strain, my throat is all right bit I've not got the old tummy puff yet." John Watt, Director of Variety of the BBC, introduced Gracie at the microphone and Harry Parr-Davies at the piano, to, as one newspaper reported, an estimated 40,000,000 eager listeners.

" *Hello everybody.*

My goodness, but this is wonderful to be back at this old microphone again, and to be able to speak to and thank all you wonderful people for the great love and affection you have shown for me during what has been the most dreadful ordeal of my forty-one years. I felt something was wrong for the past three of four years, but I've been taking little short holidays and thinking to myself, well maybe it's just a rest I needed and saying to myself, 'Well, really, it's impossible for a strong, hardy daughter of the North to have owt wrong with her.'

"But, after completing my last film, Shipyard Sally, I said to myself, 'Grace, lass, tha'll have to go and see a doctor. Tha's much worse. I never dreamed though that it was going to be such a do as it's been. But thank Heaven, and Mr. Searle my surgeon, and all those wonderful sisters and nurses at the Chelsea Women's Hospital, I've pulled through.

"Mind you, I'm not quite fit yet, you know? I mean, I don't feel like riding a bicycle to Rochdale or anything like that, but it's really grand to feel as well as I do after the ordeal. I want to say a special thank you to the Bishop of Blackburn. The day he came to see me was, I think, the most critical day of my illness. I felt all the fight had gone out of me, and I could feel myself slipping fast. But after your prayers, dear bishop, if you are listening, a miracle seemed to happen. For I found myself slowly gaining strength again. It was wonderful. And I do thank you from the bottom of my heart for coming to see me.

"And now I want to say thank you to all you wonderful people from all over the world who have written me such beautiful letters, and for all the lovely flowers and telegrams and countless other presents. I tell you, you've made me cry. I've been so overcome by your devotion. See, I always thought you liked me a little bit, but I, I didn't think you loved me—well, not so much anyway.

"My only wish now is to try and please you with my work in the future, as I seem to have done in the past. I'm going to Capri to get some sunshine, and I hope that in two or three month's time, with God's help, I shall be my old self again. Now I feel you'd maybe like to hear the old voice? They haven't been mucking that about, so I'm just going to sing a verse of a song which I think you all know. The words express all that I feel that I'm trying to say to you now.

"Come on Harry, lad, do yer stuff."

(Following the song): "And now, I want to thank you all again a thousand times and thank you, Mr. BBC. Goodnight, and God bless you all."

Loosely based on the life of Marie Dressler, Gracie's next film for

Twentieth Century Fox was already lined up and ready to go before Gracie went into hospital and was announced to the press in early July. Based on Frances Marion's book, *Molly, Bless Her*, the story originally intended for Dressler was expected to be Miss Fields' next film, which was to begin shooting in the first week of August. With her illness getting in the way there was now no guarantee for Twentieth Century as to when she was going to be able to begin filming and return to work, as the doctors had ordered her to take at least three years' recuperation. In August, during her recuperation, Gracie explained that film had been postponed while she recovered until at least May 1940.

Gracie remembered, "After a bad illness, the days of recovery are like being born again—nursery days. The air tastes vividly of grass and clover, the sky seems big as it did when you were young, the fields are greener than you remember. It is as though dust of years has been wiped away. I can never remember England being more lovely than in those sunlit, warm July days after my operation and the divorce." With the wind blowing in from the Channel, and the flat green Downs behind them, Monty visited Grace every day and confessed his love to her, and that he would like to live with her in Capri. The couple left England to begin this period of rest on August first, accompanied by Mary, Dorothy, and young Michael, as they returned to Capri via the Continental platform at London's number two platform at Victoria Station, boarding the Golden Arrow train at 10:45am.

Returning to Capri after thirty-six hours of travelling, Monty had bought gifts for everyone from England, as he always did, usually bundles of English cloth for his sister and farmers in his hometown of Cesena. When he went to England, gifts for his friends and Gracie's family often included rolls of silk, Italian potteries, and inlaid tortoise-shell and wood music boxes. He had bought Gracie a surprise gift which was waiting for her onboard the boat from France to Naples—her own motor launch for errands between Capri and Naples and Sorrento. Monty had packed all the holiday gifts carefully into it and bribed a couple of sailors to paint it brilliant white for him before the ship docked in Naples. Customs officials took one look at the still-wet boat, and rather than dirty their suits by inspecting it, let Monty, Gracie, and the boat through without question. Through the 90-minute boat ride from Naples to Capri, with Vesuvius in the background and the sun of an Italian August beating down, the couple arrived at Capri "with only a few paint smears on our oldest clothes and gifts for everybody!" remembered Gracie. "We seemed to be leaving behind us in our own white froth all the dirt of divorce, like filth left behind in soap suds. I was lucky to have my villa on Capri, and such good, gay friends in both England and Italy—particularly Monty."

Gracie spent August enjoying the sunshine at La Canzone del Mare, cherishing her friendship with Monty and enjoying her first real holiday without songs to learn, scripts to read, and concert programmes to work out. Monty went to spend time in Cesena, where he had employed architect Gualtiero Pontoni to build Villa Bianchi for them in the Belvedere area of Cesena. Countess Barbara Haugwitz-Reventlow rented the Villa Esmereldo for two months over the ummer, and American socialite Mrs. Harrison Williams took up summer residence at her villa, Pallazo al Mare. Gracie was photographed by the British press during August looking relaxed in a large sunhat with her dog, Hooligan, with her appearance markedly healthier than her last photographs leaving Britain, with photographs taken of Gracie and Michael enjoying swimming and eating watermelon. Tommy arrived to join his wife and son in Capri after his run at the Nottingham Empire finished on August 18.

From Capri, Dorothy wrote to her friend, Babs Rossini, "With the help of Maria, that friend of Gracie's who speaks English, I have been going out a bit at night dancing and the English picture twice a week." After suffering from mosquito bites, stormy nights of sheet lightning and driving rain, "Grace is improving and feels stronger on her legs every day, but still doesn't feel up to going out at night, although occasionally feels bored and very sorry for herself [...] Her will and courage are strong but her legs won't let her. Having her womb out has really upset her. She always fondly expected to have a baby, and now all hope has gone and she has odd weeps about it."

Writing cheerfully to readers of *Film Pictorial* on August 19, Gracie explained she was doing well in Capri. "Well, here I am in Capri, where I have come in search of sunshine. It was rather scarce in dear old England when I left a week or two ago. However, I hope by now the weather is being good to you all and that you too are enjoying some sunshine, which is so necessary in these hectic days. I hope it will not be long before I am with you all again, and if you go to see my latest picture, I sincerely hope you will enjoy seeing it as much as I enjoyed making it. My love to you all." She told one newspaper how it was the "happiest holiday of my life" and that she was singing a little every now and then "to keep the old voice in trim. The village children are the only people who will listen." To test herself, Gracie set the challenge to swim from one bay to the next before she would self diagnose that she was actually well, and also "walk around the 2 1/2 mile village without losing puff."

At the end of August, with Europe teetering on the brink of war, Gracie wasn't concerned about the crisis, as the newspapers reported, "It will take something more than an international crisis to send Gracie Fields scurrying from her convalescence on the isle of Capri." Gracie telephoned her family from Rome, where she waved goodbye to Tommy and his family, to say she had "not got the wind-up and that there was no scare in Capri." Getting stronger every day, taking regular swims in the sea and walking, Gracie intended to remain in Capri until she was well enough, and if the worst did happen in Europe she would be "adequately protected." On the last day of August, Gracie and Monty drove to Capri Harbor to meet the evening mail boat to see if any post had arrived from England for them, whilst Mary remained at La Canzone. Mary had stayed on at Capri to assist Gracie in answering some of the thousands of letters she was constantly receiving wishing her well and to recover quickly.

That same day, the British Government temporarily banned British ships from docking on the island, and fears in Britain began to arise that Gracie would be kept prisoner in her "Mediterranean castle." In Rochdale, a worried Bertha Schofield told how she was, "naturally anxious about Gracie. I haven't heard how she will be able to get away if she has to—or whether she is trying to do so already." On the morning of the 30th, Gracie, Monty, and Mary headed back to England, travelling to Naples on their own motor-launch captained by Ettore Patrizi. Worried they would be caught, Gracie was surprised when one of the guards threw a rope to the boat and helped them climb ashore. "Having seen our little boat come from the direction of the anchored battleships, I think he had mistaken us for some Italian V.I.P.s!" As Ettore returned to Capri the trio took the train to Paris and then on to London, arriving back at Peacehaven on September second. Gracie told her local Brighton paper, "I am feeling very much better, but I shall not be working for some time yet. With the situation getting worse I thought it was about time I returned home, for it is better to be with one's own folks under such circumstances."

In her autobiography, Gracie writes "The three of us sat silently, hearing Mr. Chamberlain's tired voice declare that we were at war with Germany. All the lights in Naples Harbour went out that night, but I was thinking of the lights along Brighton Seafront and Peacehaven, along the whole of my home coast. Britain would be in darkness too, and I wanted to be there, doing something." As Chamberlain delivered his "We are at War" speech on the morning of September third, Gracie was already back in Peacehaven, not in Capri as she writes in her own memoirs.

Relaxing in Capri (1935) (David Bolton).

Hollywood glamour Gracie. (1937).

Performing on stage in the mid 1930s.

Broadcasting to Australia from Mallord Street. (1936).

Having her hair made-up on set by Maud Rowe (1936) (Shaun Hewitt).

Gracie meets Gracie at Madame Tussauds (1937).

Receiving the Freedom of Rochdale (1937).

In the mayor's parlour with her father (1937).

"The proudest day of my life" (1937).

Gracie and George Formby at the Gaumont State Kilburn (1937).

The Stansfield family en route to America. (1937).

A family gathering at "The Haven"

On set of *Keep Smiling* (1938) (Mervyn Rossini).

On set of *We're Going to be Rich* (1938) (Shaun Hewitt).

Gracie and Duggie Wakefield backstage (1938).

Gracie and Monty in Hollywood.

Gracie and Monty on the set of *Shipyard Sally* (1939).

The illustration of "Our Gracie" by Strube. (1939).

Gracie leaves hospital after her major operation (1939).

Gracie leaves hospital after her major operation (1939).

Gracie arriving home after leaving hospital (1939) (Shaun Hewitt).

Archie Pitt and Annie Lipman (1940).

Archie Pitt and Annie Lipman (1940).

ARCHIE PITT'S THEATRICAL PRODUCTIONS

1916:   It's a Bargain (February 7, 1916)*

1918:   Mr. Tower of London (October 28, 1918)*

1921:   Lump Sugar (October 3, 1921)

1925:   By Request (September 21, 1925)*

1925:   A Week's Pleasure (January 12, 1925)*

1925:   Mr Tower of London (With Barbra Bartle and Albert H. Grant) (February 15, 1925)

1926:   Too Many Cooks (January 18, 1926)

1926:   False Alarms (June 28, 1926)

1927:   Safety First (February 13, 1927)

1927:   Orders is Orders (October 31, 1927)

1928:   Boys Will Be Boys (February 27, 1928)

1928:   All At Sea (September 16, 1928)

1928:   The Show's the Thing (December 26, 1928)*

1928:   The Lido Follies (July 9, Frinton Lido, Summer Show for six weeks)

1929:   Making Good (July 29, 1929)

1929:   The Lido Follies (June2, Folkestone Pavilion, Summer Show for two weeks before UK tour).

1930:   Archie Pitt's Stupendous Road Show*

1930:   The Revue Shop (March 15, 1930)

1930:   The Comedy King (December 26, 1930)

1931:   London Revels (April 27, 1931)

1931:   Walk This Way (July 18, 1931)*

1931:   Gulliver's Travels/The Archie Pitt Roadshow (Gracie variety tour)*

1932:   Whose Baby Are You? (Planned, did not open).

1932:   Archie Pitt Limited closed and passed all over to the already existing Aza Agencies

1933:   Archie Pitt's Road Show (Gracie variety tour)*

1934:   Bang Bang (February 1934)

1934:   Savage South Africa (Zulu performance, directed by Archie)

1935:   Mr Tower of London (With Norman Evans and Betty Driver) (February 25, 1935).

1936:   We've Arrived (February 9, 1936)

1936:   A Fleeting Acquaintance (Starred Archie, first presented at Colston Hall reopening in December 1936, before touring briefly in 1937)

1940:   Entente Cordiale—renamed "Formby with the Forces" (June 2, 1940) *Closed due to Archie's death.*

1949:   *Mr. Tower of London* (Posthumous) (Tommy Fields and Ethel Manners) (May 9, 1949)

NB: Archie also managed two Dance Bands, Archie Pitt's Busby Boys and Archie Pitt's False Romantics during the 1920s.

NB: Archie Pitt did *not* produce *Yes, I Think So*, as has been suggested by other biographies.

*Featured Gracie Fields

APPENDIX B

Gracie Fields Filmography

1931:   Sally In Our Alley (Associated Radio Pictures)

1932:   Looking on the Bright Side (Associated Radio Pictures)

1933:   This Week of Grace (Real Art Production)

1934:   Love, Life and Laughter (Associated Talking Pictures)

1934:   Sing as We Go (Associated Talking Pictures)

1935:   Look Up and Laugh (Associated Talking Pictures)

1935:   Riders to the Sea (Uncredited producer) (Flanagan-Hurst Production)

1936:   Queen of Hearts (Associated Talking Pictures)

1937:   The Show Goes On (Associated Talking Pictures)

1938:   We're Going to be Rich (USA: He Was Her Man) (Twentieth Century Fox)

1938:   Keep Smiling (USA: Smiling Along) (Twentieth Century Fox)

1939:   Shipyard Sally (Twentieth Century Fox)

1943:   Young and Beautiful (Vitaphone production reel #1113A)

1943:   Holy Matrimony (Twentieth Century Fox)

1943:   Stage Door Canteen (Sol Lesser Productions)

1945:   Molly and Me (Twentieth Century Fox)

1945:   Paris Underground (UK: Madame Pimpernel) (Constance Bennett Productions)

Television films:

1956:   The Old Lady Shows Her Medals (The United States Steel Hour), (Armchair Theatre)

1956:   A Murder is Announced (Goodyear Television Playhouse)

1958:   Mrs. Arris Goes to Paris (Studio One in Hollywood)

1958:   A Tale of Two Cities (The DuPont Show of the Month)

Index

Author biography

With Jane McDonald in Capri.

SEBASTIAN FIRST BECAME AWARE of Gracie Fields in 2005, during research for a high school project on the Second World War. After hearing her unusual voice on a compilation CD, he decided to research further into the life of Gracie Fields and discovered the star was born less than twelve miles away from his hometown of Hyde.

With a keen interest and passion to preserve the memory of 'Our Gracie,' Sebastian created 'The Dame Gracie Fields Appreciation Society' in 2009. This expanded over the years and in March 2012 he, and fellow Gracie fan Shaun Hewitt, began work on the first 'official' Gracie Fields website. Found at **www.graciefields.org**, it is ever-growing to become the largest online database of Gracie Fields information.

From 2015, Sebastian spearheaded a campaign with Rochdale Council and Rochdale Rotary Club East to permanently honour Gracie Fields in her hometown, which resulted in the unveiling of eight purple Gracie Fields heritage plaques around the town and a 1.5x life size bronze statue of Gracie Fields outside Rochdale Town Hall.

Sebastian has previously written and spoken about Gracie for: the Manchester Evening News; the Rochdale Observer; Rochdale Council and Link4Life; BBC Manchester; BBC Lancashire; BBC North West Tonight; ITV Granada Reports; Cherry Red Entertainment; the Stockport Plaza; Radio Woodville (New Zealand); Tameside Radio; English Heritage; the British Music Hall Society; English Heritage; LW Theatres and the British Film Institute. Sebastian has also appeared on BBC One's *'The One Show'* and *'Antiques Roadshow,'* BBC Radio 4 *'Great Lives'* and Channel 5's *'Cruising with Jane McDonald.'*

An English Literature graduate from the University of Manchester, and now a high school English teacher, Sebastian regularly gives talks on Gracie's life to enthusiastic groups and travels annually to the Isle of Capri to tend to Gracie's gravesite.

He is always looking to hear from Gracie Fields fans worldwide, and can be contacted at: sebastianlassandro@yahoo.co.uk .

At the London Palladium.

With Chris Webster in Rochdale.

CPSIA information can be obtained
at www.ICGtesting.com
Printed in the USA
LVHW081904140419
614160LV00005B/13/P

9 781629 334202